Renaissance Humanism

An Anthology of Sources

Renaissance Humanism

An Anthology of Sources

Edited and Translated, with an Introduction, by

MARGARET L. KING

Hackett Publishing Company, Inc.
Indianapolis/Cambridge

20 19 18 17   2 3 4 5 6 7

For further information, please address
   Hackett Publishing Company, Inc.
   P.O. Box 44937
   Indianapolis, Indiana 46244-0937

   www.hackettpublishing.com

Interior design by Elizabeth L. Wilson
Composition by Graphic Composition, Inc., Bogart, Georgia

Library of Congress Cataloging-in-Publication Data

Renaissance humanism : an anthology of sources / edited and translated, with an
   introduction, by Margaret L. King.
      pages cm
   Includes bibliographical references and index.
   ISBN 978-1-62466-111-2 (pbk.) — ISBN 978-1-62466-112-9 (cloth)
      1. Humanism—History—Sources. 2. Renaissance—Sources. I. King,
   Margaret L., 1947– editor of compilation.
   B778.R427 2014
   144—dc23   2013030804

CONTENTS

in memory of my father,
Reno C. King, Jr.
the greatest humanist of them all

GENERAL INTRODUCTION

The humanists of Renaissance Europe would have been astonished to learn what is meant by today's "humanism," or "secular humanism," or "Humanism," with an initial capital as some of its proponents insist. Modern humanism, which has been around since at least the 1920s, dispenses with theism and replaces divine providence with the scientific method, social justice, and multiculturalism. Not so the Renaissance antecedents of today's humanism, whose passions and commitments arose from and extended the legacy of the Latin Christian civilization of medieval Europe. Their humanism embraced both Cicero and God.

But what was it? On that question, scholars have not reached full agreement, although there is a consensus on certain essentials. Renaissance humanism was not a philosophy. It entailed no common set of principles (other than those that were the common assumptions of the age) about the natural, social, or political world. It was more like a way of life. It involved a commitment to the world of ideas guided by the classics, which were to be read in the original Latin (more rarely, Greek), mastered, imitated, and to some extent enacted, in communities that gathered in schools and homes and shared public spaces. The process was consistent: humanists read and interacted with the classical tradition. The content, however, varied: over time, from setting to setting, according to circumstances, and among actors of different social classes and occupations.

The classical tradition that the humanists reintroduced to Europe had long roots. It was, of course, the product of a fused Greco-Roman civilization that was the last to emerge in the ancient Mediterranean region. It triumphed with Rome's political ascent, the civilizational adjunct to the Roman conquest of the Mediterranean world. It lingered even after Christianity arose within its bosom, before the Roman Empire dwindled and, in its Western zone, decayed. Christianity had been born in the Levant, far from the capital, and quickly implanted itself in the major Roman centers of Constantinople, Antioch, Alexandria, and Rome. Here Christian thinkers incorporated classical thought into a new set of Christian classics, written in the same prose, both Greek and Latin, of the masters of secular literature. Greek and Latin culture would live on, wrapped in Christian integuments.

Increasingly, the Latin and Greek cultural zones diverged: the Greek-speaking scholars of Constantinople pursued their studies almost without

The never-failing assistance of the Brooklyn College librarians, especially Bridget Nowicki and Sherry Warman, made possible the writing of this book.

interruption into the fifteenth century, while Latin became the language of a western Christendom anchored in Rome. Though Latin never died in the West, it was gravely imperiled by, on the one hand, the invasions of preliterate peoples from the North and East and an expanding Islam from the South, and, on the other, the near-total cessation of long-distance trade and consequent impoverishment of Europe.

But the Latin tradition survived. Ancient books were copied and recopied in the monasteries that were the bastions of early medieval culture. The Frankish dynasties of the ninth and tenth centuries encouraged a renewed attention to classical texts, which circulated vigorously in the twelfth century, along with an infusion of new works translated from the Greek. These three moments earned from modern scholars the titles of the "Carolingian," the "Ottonian," and the "Twelfth-Century Renaissance." By this time, in the ruined shells of the Roman cities of northern Italy, scholars had begun the systematic study of Justinian's Code, containing the whole legacy of Roman law. In these thirteenth-century settings, the very first pioneers of what would come to be called "Renaissance humanism" began to pore over, and imitate, Latin texts, reading them with a new energy and passion.

For the next two centuries, the humanist movement unfolded mainly in Italy, in the highly urbanized region north of Rome where an audience existed for humanist ideas, where burghers and nobles had funds to expend on the education of their promising sons, and where princes and city-states offered employment to gifted wordsmiths.

In the fourteenth century, in their middle age, Petrarch and Boccaccio crossed paths and became fast friends, both dedicated to the revival of the classical past. They read the ancient texts and discovered new ones, developed tools to manage the mass of information they acquired from their study, struggled to learn Greek and tap the rich lode of that other ancient language largely forgotten in western Europe, composed letters and treatises and soul-searching monologues, and compiled biographies of the great men and even the great women of the ancient world. The world of learning inherited by the generation of their followers had been transformed. Humanism, committed to the recovery, imitation, and extension of classical culture, was now the dominant intellectual movement of the era: in Italy primarily, at least for now, but soon in all of Europe.

In the first half of the fifteenth century, a whole generation of elite youth schooled in the classics extended the reach of humanism into every corner of contemporary life. They wrote letters to each other on a variety of topics, recalling the enthusiasms of their school days, when their minds had been awakened by daily contact with learned men of compelling personal qualities. They composed and delivered orations celebrating the arrivals of kings and bishops, the marriages of their peers, the conferring of offices, and the signing of treaties. They wrote treatises and dialogues on the state, on the family, on the human condition, on death, on nobility, on poverty, on education; the histories of Rome, Venice, and Florence, among others; and poetry on every possible topic from the sacred to the erotic. They seized the works of Aristotle from the professors of philosophy—whose Latin versions of the original Greek were meager texts often laden with Arabic terms betraying the route by which they had arrived—and translated them into fluid and accurate Latin, and then acquired, translated, and digested the works of Plato. They collected variant manuscripts of classical Latin texts, purged them of errors, supplied them with annotations, and lectured on them in university settings previously reserved only for the discussion of law, metaphysics, and theology. Miraculously, the printing press arrived soon after the midpoint of the century, and by 1500, nearly the whole of the classical tradition—both Latin and Greek—had been published in small, manageable editions, that flew off the presses and soared over the Alps to other communities of the learned who eagerly awaited them.

Already in the fifteenth century, travelers from the north had come to study in Italy and become imbued with its humanist culture. By the sixteenth century those interactions multiplied, while at the same time numerous Italians traveled abroad, exporting humanism to such distant lands as England and Poland. Humanism was now an international phenomenon. But it was no longer the humanism of the early Italian period: not a separate and autonomous phenomenon. Instead, it was now intermixed with other kinds of intellectual endeavor: with literary, philosophical, and scientific writing; with both the Protestant and Catholic Reformations; and with the investigation of new worlds and the conversion of newly-encountered peoples. The broadcasting of humanism into all areas of culture was facilitated by the adoption of the humanist program as the curriculum of the public schools that were now proliferating in Europe; these were private, in the American sense, because fee-based and selective, but public in that they were not limited to residents of monasteries, cathedrals, or courts, as had previously been the case. Among these schools were the prestigious Jesuit "colleges," or boarding schools, which offered an exceptional humanist preparation.

Most striking of the sixteenth-century manifestations of humanism is the version represented by the Dutch thinker Erasmus. The Christian humanism of which Erasmus is the primary exemplar is completely Christian—in all of his endeavors, Erasmus pleads for a non-dogmatic, practical, and heartfelt Christian commitment—and also completely humanist: he insists on an advanced and error-free study of original Greek and Latin texts, which he himself edits, translates, and explains to people who find their meanings alien. Even in his political writing, Erasmus is Christian, insisting that the state accommodate Christian moral principles. And even in his religious work, Erasmus is a classicist, notably in his translation and edition of the New Testament, where he employs rigorous editorial principles to prepare a text that could help build Christians. The case of Erasmus, like that of his equally important predecessor Petrarch, is a caution to those who wish to equate humanism with secular modernity. Both were deeply Christian.

By the seventeenth century humanism was virtually universal, in that it was shared to some extent by the whole of the intellectual elite. Yet it was also diminishing. Those who preoccupied themselves with classical texts were primarily editors and schoolmasters. Philosophers, scientists, and writers, in contrast—the intellectual giants of the age—effortlessly employed the Latin honed by humanist masters, and easily summoned up apt classical references, without themselves being authors of humanist works of the sort produced by the Italians of the fourteenth and fifteenth centuries. Neither Galileo nor Descartes, nor Cervantes nor Milton, were humanists; but all bore the impress of humanism.

From the fourteenth century to the seventeenth, at the core of humanism was a love of the classics: as a body of literature to be imitated, of ideas to be understood and enacted, of a kind of sociability that culminated in a European-wide network of intellectuals—a *respublica litterarum,* or "republic of letters," as the participants themselves named it. The members of this intellectual elite came from different regions, different social ranks, different genders, different faiths, different professions. They were formed by schools taught by humanist masters, and sent their children to schools offering a humanist curriculum, ensuring that the humanist approach to learning remained dominant even after humanism itself had intersected with and been superseded by the thought of the Enlightenment.

Themes of this volume

Since humanism does not offer a unified set of precepts or principles, it is best approached thematically, as this volume proposes to do in the ten chapters that follow.

Chapter 1 looks at the humanists engaged in the discovery of the classical tradition. It was not literally "discovered," of course, by the authors represented in this chapter. Yet there is evident in their works an emotional intensity as they approach classical texts in a new way. Here Francesco Petrarca (known to English speakers as Petrarch) engages in a genuinely strange exercise: he composes letters to ancient authors, questioning, chiding, imploring them as though they stood before him, yet always conscious of the distance between them as measured by time and cultural context. The reader senses the pain of Petrarch's yearning for a past age, and begins to yield as well to that feeling. Giovanni Boccaccio, in contrast, is all business—serious business. He recognizes that the classical corpus poses an enormous problem to Christian readers: it is saturated with a mythological worldview that is alien, featuring adulterous deities who acknowledge no higher law and fear no final judgment. He must rescue these texts, showing that their mythological content is no barrier to a deep engagement with them, and that it may in some ways be conformable to a Christian framework.

Writing a generation later, the task of Pier Paolo Vergerio is easier, but still tricky. Hired to tutor the son of the prince of Padua, he must make the case to both father and son for an education in liberal studies—that is, the liberal arts, which in the work excerpted here Vergerio redefines to serve as a foundational humanist curriculum. They in turn seek the polish that the new learning confers, but still cherish the notion that a nobleman's education comes down to horsemanship and swordsmanship. The last section in Chapter 1 is a set of paired letters by Poggio Bracciolini and Cencio Romano, two of the participants in a hunt for ancient manuscripts that took place during a lull in the general church council held at Constance in 1415–1418. The monasteries of Europe, and especially those of the Frankish lands, had served during the Middle Ages as laboratories for the preservation of classical texts. Here books were copied and stored—and then often forgotten. The early generations of humanists took on the challenge of locating those texts and fragments, sometimes, as our authors report in this case, in neglected heaps of unread volumes in damp monastery cellars.

All five of the authors represented in this first chapter are Italian, necessarily, since it is in northern, urban Italy where humanists construct the paradigm of a new learning. The works range in date of composition from around the middle of the fourteenth century to the early years of the fifteenth.

In Chapter 2, the humanists look inward, engaging in a process of self-exploration that is for some students of humanism its most compelling feature. The importance of this process is, of course, momentous. The encounter with the classical tradition is seen here to stimulate an inquiry into the nature of the human condition, even as the Christian contours of the understanding of the self are not discarded but reaffirmed. Petrarch makes a second appearance in this volume (the only author to do so) in his letter "To Posterity," in which he reveals himself—selectively, in a nice compote of narcissism and candor—to an audience of future readers that he assumes will be interested in him.

The fifteenth-century Italian humanists Giannozzo Manetti and Giovanni Pico della Mirandola provide more extensive explorations of the self in two of the most important works of the humanist corpus. Refuting a medieval work on the wretchedness of the human condition, Manetti explores the many dimensions of human existence, from the physiological to the eschatological, and strikingly identifies the human ability to reason as the unique characteristic of the species and a source of profound pleasure. Pico—who had set for himself the task of reconciling all inherited intellectual traditions, including not only the Aristotelian and Platonic but also the Arabic, Kabbalistic, and esoteric—searches for the cause of human uniqueness and locates it in the unlimited capacity for freedom implanted at the moment of divine creation. Finally, the French author Michel de Montaigne, writing a century after Pico, characteristically avoids considering anything so large as the cosmos or the end of time, but focuses on his own feelings and circumstances in which he finds the incommensurable uniqueness of his own being.

The works of the authors included in this chapter range over a broad expanse of time, from the mid-fourteenth to the late sixteenth century, befitting a theme that is central to humanism from its early to its later stages. In this focus on the "dignity of man," Renaissance humanism most closely approaches modern secular humanism. The Renaissance vision of the human, however, unlike the modern, is lodged within a Greek cosmological and Christian theological framework.

In the lively city-state environment of northern Italy, replicated in some areas to the north, humanists engaged in the discussion of political and social issues, as exemplified in Chapter 3. The republicanism of city-state governments, always vulnerable to takeover by local strongmen, was a compelling theme. It was especially so in Florence, where its prominence fostered "civic humanism," a variety of humanism driven by the notion of political liberty. Two representatives of this humanist current appear in this chapter: Leonardo Bruni, who discourses on the excellence of the city of Florence, especially as characterized by freedom in its political, social, and even material conditions; and Alamanno Rinuccini, a disappointed liberal after the seizure of power by the Medici family, who laments the city's lost tradition of liberty. So stirring is the ideal of freedom for these and other civic humanists that modern scholars have been tempted to identify Florentine republicanism with that of the American tradition, and the enemies of political liberty in the Renaissance with the despots of the twentieth century.

Broader social issues are addressed by two other spokesmen. The Venetian Francesco Barbaro, a nobleman from a city the success of whose ruling elite depended on the biological and social reproduction of political competence, writes in his treatise on marriage about the importance of the selection of a wife. The Spanish-born Juan Luis Vives, translocated to the Flemish city of Bruges, offers solutions for the endemic poverty experienced by that small city-state as the dispossessed of the countryside thronged to the city to find employment, without success. His recommendations of workhouses for the elderly, disabled, and young, and compulsory labor for the able-bodied, would be realized over the next decades and centuries in many other settings. Limits of space prevent the inclusion of humanist perspectives on other social issues, including wealth and nobility.

Spanning from northern Italy to the Low Countries, the works gathered in this chapter were composed between 1404 to 1526, a long century in which humanism reached its full maturity. Those in the next chapter, all by Italian authors, take us through the century from 1453 to 1555: from the Turkish conquest of Constantinople in the eastern Mediterranean, through shocking conflicts in Florence and Rome, to the turmoil of religious warfare in the German lands.

Chapter 4 looks at humanists in action, when our authors are closely touched by some of the critical events of the age. Humanists here are eye-witnesses, advocates, and victims, in contrast to their usual role as authors of authoritative treatises and well-reasoned dialogues. The Venetian Lauro Quirini from nearby Crete describes the Turkish capture of Constantinople soon after it occurred, based on the first-hand reports of refugees who had experienced the sack. His urgent voice calls for a broad European mobilization against an imminent enemy who threatened not just an outpost of Europe but its core. Angelo Poliziano describes a more intimate crisis: the assassination of the younger of the two Medici brothers who were then the effective strongmen of Florence. Present at the chaotic scenes triggered by the murder, Poliziano vividly portrays the ruthlessness of political struggle in a city that was at this moment the epicenter of the Renaissance.

Luigi Guicciardini's eyewitness account of the sack of Rome, featuring chilling accounts of torture and extortion, is also local; yet the faceoff in Rome between pope and empire, and between Protestant and Catholic, encapsulates the larger politics of the era. Finally, Olympia Fulvia Morata's letters from the German lands, where she had gone as an Italian native in voluntary exile to escape the retributions of the Roman Inquisition, depict the horrors of religious warfare that would overcloud the later sixteenth century. Herself a victim of a brutal siege, she lost her writings—her lifework—in the turmoil, and died at not yet thirty years of age as a result of her vicissitudes.

In Chapter 5, attention narrows to three monumental figures whose intellectual product dominates the first decades of the sixteenth century, at the point when the Italian Renaissance largely cedes to the wider European movement. The diplomat, historian, and political theorist Niccolò Machiavelli sketches in his diminutive work *The Prince* the ground rules of modern politics: they are detached from traditional moral principles and focused solely on the acquisition and exercise of power. While his other works explore the possibilities of republicanism, the mode of government he most admired and the ideal he pursued for much of his career, the necessity imposed by events leads him to a distillation of political experience found in *The Prince*.

A mere three years later, and in the very same year, Desiderius Erasmus and Thomas More also composed their principal political statements, and as Machiavelli, in brief compass. Erasmus' recommendations for the formation of a Christian prince to consider above all the welfare of his subjects could not be more distant from his Italian contemporary's portrait of a ruler whose main concern is to wield power. More's utopian vision—the first of its kind—departs from both the Machiavellian and Erasmian focus on the personality of the ruler. He proposes a republic that can exist "nowhere" (the literal meaning of the Greek title *Utopia*), in which offices rotate, citizens equally engage in necessary labor, private property is abolished, and the family is absorbed by the community. All three of these influential works, by an Italian, a Dutchman, and an Englishman, were written from 1513 to 1516—and those by Machiavelli and More, at least, are still current five centuries later.

Chapters 6, 7, and 8 look at how humanist themes and genres intersect with other major cultural streams: art, religion, and philosophy—the latter including what moderns in this era understand as science. Chapter 6 considers the visual arts, the efflorescence of which, alongside or even more than that of humanism, constitutes the cultural phenomenon of the Renaissance. It opens with a work by a man whose multifaceted abilities seem to characterize the era: Leon Battista Alberti's *On Painting,* in which a humanist master of classical texts on the arts applies his knowledge to his equally substantial understanding of painting, derived from his own experience. The letters that the Mantuan *marchesa* Isabella d'Este exchanged with her agent about her relations with two of the great northern Italian masters, Andrea Mantegna and Giovanni Bellini, inform us about the mechanisms and tensions of the patronage networks in the context of which the products of Renaissance art were accomplished. The letters of the German artist Albrecht Dürer from Italy home to his patron and friend, Willibald Pirckheimer, offer a different image of patronage relations, as well as the distinctive voice of an artist writing by his own hand. Another such personal voice, conveying a range of ambitions, anxieties, and outbursts of bravado, is heard in Benvenuto Cellini's *Autobiography.* Composed between 1435 and 1566, a span of years including the culminating High Renaissance period, these works in sum illuminate the craft of painting, the personalities of the artists, and the patronage system that supported their work.

Chapter 7 considers the relations between humanism and religion, two domains sometimes thought to be antipathetic. Lorenzo Valla conspicuously nurses some antipathy toward the papacy as an institution, as evidenced in his brilliant exposure of the so-called "Donation of Constantine," authorizing the western church's territorial possessions and sovereignty. What is called into question here, however, is not the truth of the Christian religion, which Valla takes pains to affirm, but its right to seize the property of other entities and to claim lordship over those lands.

Valla writes in the first half of the fifteenth century, at a time when papal expansion threatened the interests of some of the Italian city-states. The remaining three authors—one French, and two Italian—write between 1523 and 1540, when Protestant reform threatened the church in a more fundamental way than could the secular Italian powers. Jacques Lefèvre d'Étaples and Bernardino Ochino speak out for evangelical reform, which originated prior to the Lutheran break with the Roman church and continued thereafter during the turbulent era when the various currents of the mighty Protestant Reformation had not yet been sorted out. Both writers advocate the kind of faith that moves the heart, and spend little time on church history or governance. For Lefèvre, that faith will be awakened, immediate and whole, upon the reading of the Gospels in an accessible vernacular version instead of the Latin Vulgate, the only version that the Roman church recognized. For Ochino, faith is aroused by the emotional participation in the life of Christ, which he encourages in his meditative dialogues that probe deep into the Christian experience.

With Gasparo Contarini and his colleagues, appointed to make recommendations for the correction of church abuses, we return nearly to Valla's position of a century before: the problem, implicitly, is seen to lie in the operation of church governance. If pope, cardinals, and bishops simply performed their tasks as they should, these experts suggest, there would be no need for fundamental change in the church. In this recommendation, the formulation of which Contarini participated in and signed, the Venetian cardinal actually departs from his own past, which bore the impress of profound religious experience, an openness to evangelical approaches, and even a recognition of the plausibility of some Lutheran positions. The Roman church would in time institute the kinds of remedies specified in Contarini's report, however, and make no compromise with the Lutherans or any of that ilk.

Chapter 8 looks at some of the intersections between humanism and philosophy or science, taking us from Italy in the fifteenth century to northern Europe in the seventeenth. As in the case of Alberti with regard to the arts, the Florentine Marsilio Ficino, the translator of the complete works of Plato into Latin for their wider dissemination, is a perfect hybrid: a humanist editor and translator of Greek philosophical texts; a humanist who communicates advanced philosophical concepts in informal conversation and its literary equivalent, the dialogue; and a philosopher who seeks to unite the Christian and the Platonic traditions within the context of his own age, distant from late antiquity when the unification of dissonant truths was first attempted.

Greek was also important for Nicholas Copernicus, who had journeyed from his native East Prussia to Italy for advanced studies, and so encountered the Greek texts in Italy that led him to reconceptualize the Ptolemaic cosmological model—itself a Greek paradigm. His years of astronomical observation and analysis supplied the evidence for his heliocentric hypothesis of planetary motion, but his study of Greek scientific thought had provided context for his inquiries.

Two generations later, the Italian Galileo Galilei largely accepted the Copernican hypothesis, which had by this time circulated widely in Europe without changing the prevailing understanding of the cosmos. Galileo would supply the proofs for that hypothesis, grounded in his experimental work in physics and his astronomical observations that were assisted by the telescope, which he had invented. Not only was he able to defend the Copernican view with substantial data, but he proceeded to communicate its importance to a broad European audience, especially in his *Dialogue Concerning the Two Chief World Systems*. Equally important was his defense of empirically-grounded scientific knowledge as independent from religious truth, grounded in the Bible, which he especially developed in his *Letter to the Grand Duchess Christina*. Like Alberti, who was both an artist and a theorist, Galileo is both a scientist and an advocate of the new science being created at that time.

By the generation of the Frenchman René Descartes, the most innovative work of the humanists and the most important scientific and philosophic insights derived from humanism were already in the past. But Descartes, who was trained by the Jesuits, came to philosophy imbued with a humanist outlook. That perspective is wonderfully displayed in the opening sections of his *Discourse on Method*. Here Descartes engages in a process of self-exploration, reminiscent of Petrarch and Montaigne, as prelude to the announcement of a new metaphysical system that, in itself, marks the beginning of modern philosophy.

Chapters 9 and 10 offer examples of humanism reaching out in new directions. Chapter 9 looks at four women humanists, beginning with the three major Italian figures of the fifteenth century. A most thoroughly masculine endeavor, humanism yet appeals to and conditionally even welcomes female participants, who find in their study of the classical tradition an alternative vehicle for self-exploration and advancement than that long offered by the church in the opportunities for mystical experience and administrative action. Isotta Nogarola not only engages in male humanist circles as the writer and recipient of letters and author of orations, but she also grapples, in a singular debate with a male interlocutor, with the biblical text that was the springboard for the longstanding deprecation of women: the Genesis account of Eve's temptation of Adam and their expulsion from Eden. Laura Cereta and Cassandra Fedele, similarly, participate in humanist networks of correspondence: Cereta, additionally, offers spirited responses to both male and female critics of learning in women, and Fedele argues for the benefits of women's access to the liberal arts curriculum. These discussions continue into the sixteenth century, and culminate in the seventeenth century with Marie Le Jars de Gournay, a French professional author—she supported herself by her publications—who brings to a close the discussion that had energized participants from across Europe for over a century. She declares, authoritatively, the equality of men and women: they are absolutely equal in rational capacity and in every other regard except in their procreative roles.

In Chapter 10, men educated in the humanist curriculum engage with non-Western peoples as European states send out explorers, administrators, and missionaries to establish outposts in the Americas, Africa, and Asia. The Italian Amerigo Vespucci opens this story, fittingly, as it is he who identifies the American landmass as a "new world," a recognition that marks, as much as Columbus' discoveries ten years earlier, the opening of the era of exploration and colonialism. A little over a century later, Garcilaso de la Vega, with the title "El Inca," describes the conquest of Peru from the dual vantage point of the defeated natives, from whom the author was descended on his mother's side, and the Spanish victors, from whom he was descended on his father's.

Between the guideposts of 1502/1503 and 1609–1617, when Vespucci and Garcilaso wrote of American ventures, two Portuguese writers convey their visions of the European presence in the Eastern hemisphere. Saint Francis Xavier made lengthy visits to India and the East Indies and died as he waited to enter China, but he appears here as an apostle to Japan, where he evangelized from 1549 to 1552. His letter reveals a man of profoundly Christian identity who nonetheless immerses himself in an alien culture so as to understand and communicate with the people whose lives he wished to change. Finally, Luís Vas de Camões, writing at the very zenith of the Portuguese imperial venture: in a cherished humanist genre, Camões unapologetically celebrates that extension of power to peoples and places unknown to the ancients and only recently encountered. Modeled on Virgil's *Aeneid* and other epics of the European literary tradition, *The Lusiads* lionizes the heroes—Vasco da Gama in particular—who sailed around the Cape of Good Hope and opened India for Portugal—whose skill, determination and courage would reach from Brazil to Madagascar to Java to China, and so encompass the whole of the planet.

The ten chapters of this volume will constitute for the reader, it is hoped, an introduction to Renaissance humanism: one that considers both the principal aims of the movement and its relations to European culture more broadly during an era of dynamic change. The thirty-nine authors included are, of course, but a sampling of the hundreds who participated in the humanist movement and its ancillaries. Some dimensions of humanism could not be fully explored in a reasonable space: its contributions, for instance, to scholarly method, including the editing and translation of texts, and its relations to printing and publishing; or its interactions with the Protestant and Catholic Reformations, many of the leaders of which were trained humanists; or, except for the single example of Vergerio, its consequences for pedagogy. The bibliographical note that follows may provide guidance to those who wish to pursue these aspects of the humanist movement.

From 1350 to 1650, Renaissance humanists reintroduced the Greco-Roman component of European culture—already present during the Middle Ages, but in diminished form—to the predominant Judeo-Christian one. This is the last recombination of these two mighty streams that feed Western civilization, the first having occurred during the late Hellenistic and early Christian centuries. Their fusion holds all through the period of Europe's expansion and into the nineteenth century, when it is overcome by the combined effects of Enlightenment, political revolution, and modernism. Grounded in the conviction that reason was the distinguishing feature of the human condition, a feature in which the human most resembled the divine, Renaissance humanism embraced the whole of the European cultural tradition that is challenged today by the radical skepticism of post-Modernism. Which is the better path?

BIBLIOGRAPHICAL NOTE

Presented here are suggested readings about the humanist movement in general, including both the principal classics and some recent reconsiderations. See Texts and Studies for citations of the original language texts and translations for each of the component works of this volume, along with full citations of works appearing in chapter notes and suggested biographical and critical studies for each author.

Baron, Hans. *The Crisis of the Early Italian Renaissance: Civic Humanism and Republican Liberty in an Age of Classicism and Tyranny.* Rev. 1 vol. ed. Princeton: Princeton University Press, 1966. Major statement of the Baron thesis that "civic humanism," triggered by political threat, was the core principle of humanism.

Cassirer, Ernst, Paul Oskar Kristeller, and John Herman Randall, eds. *The Renaissance Philosophy of Man: Selections in Translation.* Chicago: University of Chicago Press, 1948. The most renowned and still irreplaceable anthology of humanist texts, focusing on those devoted to the subject of the human condition.

Celenza, Christopher S. *The Lost Italian Renaissance: Humanists, Historians, and Latin's Legacy.* Baltimore: Johns Hopkins University Press, 2004. Explores the centrality of Latin to any understanding of the Italian Renaissance.

Garin, Eugenio. *Italian Humanism; Philosophy and Civic Life in the Renaissance.* Trans. Peter Munz. New York: Harper & Row, 1965. Perhaps the most concise and yet comprehensive introduction to Italian humanism of this scholar's many works.

Grendler, Paul. "Humanism." In *Oxford Bibliographies Online: Renaissance and Reformation.* http://www.oxfordbibliographies.com/view/document/obo -9780195399301/obo-9780195399301-0002.xml (accessed February 27, 2013). A masterful and comprehensive overview of the many dimensions of humanism.

Hankins, James, ed. *Renaissance Civic Humanism: Reappraisals and Reflections.* Cambridge: Cambridge University Press, 2000. A series of essays reflecting on the Baron thesis and the continuing study of Renaissance republicanism.

Kerrigan, William, and Gordon Braden. *The Idea of the Renaissance.* Baltimore: Johns Hopkins University Press, 1989. An overview of the grand philosophical themes of international humanism from Nicholas of Cusa to John Milton, with analysis of the views of the Renaissance of Jacob Burckhardt and Ernst Cassirer.

King, Margaret L., and Albert Rabil. *Her Immaculate Hand: Selected Works by and about the Women Humanists of Quattrocento Italy.* Binghamton, NY: Center for Medieval and Early Renaissance Studies, 1983. Still useful after the publication of individual volumes of works by most of the figures represented, it offers a one-volume overview of women humanists and their circle.

Kohl, Benjamin G., and Ronald G. Witt, eds. and trans. *The Earthly Republic: Italian Humanists on Government and Society.* Philadelphia: University of Pennsylvania Press, 1978. Excellent compilation of major humanist texts on social and political themes, with extensive critical introductions.

Kraye, J., and M. W. F. Stone, eds. *Humanism and Early Modern Philosophy.* London: Routledge, 2000. Explores the interactions between humanism and philosophy, with attention to the long currents of Aristotelianism, Platonism, Stoicism, and skepticism.

Kristeller, Paul Oskar. *Renaissance Thought and Its Sources.* Edited by Michael Mooney. New York: Columbia University Press, 1979. One of the several compilations of the essays of Kristeller, the most important twentieth-century scholar of Renaissance humanism, offering a comprehensive representation of his views.

Mazzocco, Angelo, ed. *Interpretations of Renaissance Humanism.* Leiden: Brill, 2006. Collects essays by several of the leading scholars of Renaissance humanism, including Alison Brown, Paul Grendler, James Hankins, Ronald Witt, and Charles Nauert.

Nauert, Charles Garfield. *Humanism and the Culture of Renaissance Europe.* Cambridge; New York: Cambridge University Press, 1995. Perhaps the best concise overview of international humanism.

Parker, Holt N. "Women and Humanism: Nine Factors for the Woman Learning." *Viator* 35 (2004): 581–616. A brilliant analysis of the conditions for the participation of women in the humanist movement.

Rabil, Albert, ed. *Renaissance Humanism: Foundations, Forms, and Legacy.* 3 vols. Philadelphia: University of Pennsylvania Press, 1988. Monumental compilation of more than forty essays introducing aspects of humanism in Italy and in Europe.

Schiffman, Zachary Sayre, ed. *Humanism and the Renaissance.* Boston: Houghton Mifflin, 2002. Collects classic essays constituting the major statements by twenty authors, beginning with Jacob Burckhardt and

Johann Huizinga, and proceeding to luminaries such as Paul Oskar Kristeller, Anthony Grafton, and Donald Kelley.

Trinkaus, Charles Edward. *In Our Image and Likeness: Humanity and Divinity in Italian Humanist Thought.* 2 vols. Chicago: University of Chicago Press, 1970. Connects humanist anthropology—and its understanding of the nature of the human condition—to its religious outlook.

Witt, Ronald G. *In the Footsteps of the Ancients: The Origins of Humanism from Lovato to Bruni.* Leiden: Brill, 2000. Witt traces the origins of humanism to the classicizing experimentation of northern Italian authors as early as the last decades of the thirteenth century.

Witt, Ronald G. "The Origins of Humanism." In *Oxford Bibliographies Online: Renaissance and Reformation.* http://www.oxfordbibliographis.com /view/document/obo-9780195399301/obo-9780195399301-0223.xml (accessed February 27, 2013). Focuses on the early period of humanism's emergence, with attention to the surrounding controversies.

Chapter 1: Antiquity Reborn

Introduction

The nature of the Renaissance and its relation to humanism are matters explored in hundreds of scholarly works since the term was first used. Some of these question if any "rebirth," the literal meaning of "Renaissance," did in fact occur. But on this point there is agreement: if there was such a rebirth, it was classical antiquity that was reborn.

That rebirth took place (for this presentation maintains that there was one) in two parallel efforts. From the early decades of the fifteenth century, painters, sculptors, and architects examined, copied, and imitated the forms of classical art—human, animal, floral, and architectural—and incorporated them into their modern productions, which acquired, in the process, a more naturalistic and rational sense of space. Meanwhile, beginning in the late thirteenth century and accelerating into the middle of the fourteenth with the work of Petrarch and Boccaccio, the humanists read the surviving corpus of Latin texts (Greek came later) with a new attention and responsiveness; at the same time, they launched a hunt for texts known to be missing, some of which were in fact recovered. This rebirth, consisting of the recovery, rereading, and reconceptualization of the classical past, is not the whole story of the Renaissance, or of the centuries some scholars prefer to call "early modern." But it is fundamental to the cultural movements that emerge and flower from the fourteenth to the seventeenth centuries, in the visual and performing arts, literature, historical writing, political thought, science, religion, and philosophy.

In recovering the thought and sensibility of the classical past, the humanists began with the Latin language as written by ancient practitioners. It was closely related to the vernaculars they spoke in their daily lives, which were disparate yet also ancestral to modern Italian. But classical Latin was saturated with a different outlook: it was logical, tough, muscular, laconic; it required decoding, both because of the grammatical complexities of the ancient tongue and because of the numerous references to events and circumstances beyond the ken of fourteenth- and fifteenth-century readers. The learned monks, priests, and prelates of the Middle Ages had ignored these dimensions of Latin as epiphenomenal. They took what they could and wished from the ancient books while crafting their own, more modern Latin, grammatically simpler but capable of expressing large philosophical and theological concepts. The humanists rejected this flexible and often abstract Latin of their

1

predecessors as barbarous and paid little attention to the ideas that it conveyed. Instead, they drank in the linguistic vapors of the classical age until,
thoroughly imbued, they could read it without mediation, imitate it flaw-
lessly, write it fluently, think in it, and even speak it—the humanist Erasmus
famously conversed only in Latin with his cosmopolitan circle of friends, who
indeed had no other common language in which to speak.

In order to understand the Latin of the ancients, the humanists learned
all that could be known about classical civilization: places and events, wars
and festivals, occupations and recreations, laws and customs. Their grasp of
these ancient realities was closer to our own, for we have benefited from centuries of scholarly investigation, than it was to that of their contemporaries
who had not entered into this impassioned pursuit of the classical past. They
approached their mission with determination, even though a millennium had
lapsed and every facet of their culture had been touched by the dissolution of
ancient Rome and the formation of European Christendom.

For Christianity itself was an enormous barrier between the humanists
and ancient times. There is no doubt the humanists were Christians, even
though at times they display more than a hint of anti-clericalism and advocate full participation in a civic, secular life as opposed to the Christian ideal
of retreat from the world. For them, as Christians, the soul was immortal
and would be judged by an omnipotent and righteous God who ruled the
cosmos and entered into every human heart. Not so the ancient authors the
humanists longed to know and to emulate. The ancients worshiped many
gods and revered a host of other spirits; there was neither divine providence
nor judgment (although an angry god could wreak vengeance in particular
instances); above all, there was no theology, no creed, no connection between
the ethical and the religious domains. And every product of ancient thought,
whether literary or historical or legal or philosophical, is saturated with an
essentially polytheistic worldview that is antithetical to the Christian. How
could Christians access those messages? Should they? And if so, at what risk?

This chapter presents four snapshots, ranging from 1345 to 1415, of the
humanists who responded to the allure of the ancient Latin authors and
constructed a rationale by which modern Christians could legitimately and
wholeheartedly embrace the legacy of the classical tradition. It begins with
Francesco Petrarca, known to English speakers as Petrarch (1304–1374),
an assiduous imitator and inspired disciple of Latin models, for whom the
ancient authors are real—more real than contemporaries—as seen in his
letters to long-dead authors. Giovanni Boccaccio (1313–1375), an author
of both poetry and prose like his friend Petrarch, constructed the first and
most widely-read defense of classical literature, defusing the arguments that
it was harmful to one's faith or morals. A scant generation later, Pier Paolo
Vergerio (1370–1444), while employed as tutor to the adolescent heir to the

lordship of the city of Padua, crafted a defense of liberal studies—consisting of the *studia humanitatis,* the disciplines based on the classical corpus that were at the heart of the humanist project—thus initiating a new pedagogical ideal that would endure for the next five centuries. Soon afterwards, some young humanists of the fifteenth century embarked on a mission to rescue "lost" Latin texts, copies of ancient originals executed from the ninth century onwards and sequestered in the libraries of the monasteries where their scribes had once labored. Exemplary reports of their investigations and impassioned responses are given in two letters by Poggio Bracciolini (1380–1459) and Cencio Romano dei Rusticci (1380/1390–1445). These are mere samplings, yet they convey the eagerness of the humanist pioneers who in their forays recovered the ancient past.

Francesco Petrarca (Petrarch)

Between 1345 and 1360, among his many other literary and epistolary activities, Francis Petrarch (1304–1374) wrote ten letters to men who were long dead. All were great exemplars of classical civilization: they were poets, philosophers, rhetoricians, and historians; eight Latin (of which two were Cicero) and one was Greek. By his own direction, they were gathered together and placed in the last book, or section, of the multivolume collection of his *Familiar Letters,* or "letters to his friends."

All of Petrarch's letters are packed with food for thought. But there is something especially haunting about this trove, each of which reveals a man of the fourteenth century poignantly reaching out to touch the soul of a long-dead author. Petrarch questions these dead men, reproves them, seeks to learn from them, lavishly expresses his admiration for them, and says farewell, as though he is burying them a second time after a suspension of the laws of time had permitted him a brief moment of contact. Two of these letters are given here: the first in its entirety, to the Roman statesman and author Marcus Tullius Cicero (106–43 BCE), which was written in 1345; and the last in representative excerpts, to the Greek poet Homer (fl. c. 750 BCE), written in 1360.

Petrarch wrote his first letter to Cicero only months after his discovery of that author's *Letters to Atticus* (with related works) in the library of the cathedral of Verona. It was a discovery of immense importance, setting off a flurry of book-hunting and triggering renewed interest in the classical legacy. The Cicero letters opened to Petrarch and his successors the possibilities of what was to them a new genre, the familiar letter—a letter with no official purpose but only that of engaging with a friend on whatever matter presented itself at the moment. It is this model that Petrarch later followed in grooming his own important collections of *Familiar Letters* and *Letters of Old Age*. And it is this model that he follows in writing to Cicero and Homer.

So it is that Petrarch speaks to Cicero in a familiar tone, as though to a contemporary, with frequent expressions of affection: Petrarch loves Cicero "without limit," and will pour out to him a lament "born of deep love." The main thrust of the letter is not so much to lament, as to rebuke. Cicero had made a decision of grave, indeed fatal significance in the last years of the Roman Republic, a decision that would end with his assassination in 43 BCE. Cicero was a renowned orator, the prolific author of treatises and dialogues on political and philosophical matters, the inventor of the familiar letter, and the translator of major works from the Greek to the Latin. But upon Julius Caesar's rise to power, he joined other senators in opposition to the dictatorship; and after Caesar's death he wielded the full power of his pen and tongue against Caesar's former lieutenant and would-be successor, Mark Antony. Antony was unforgiving: when he joined forces with Octavian, one of the terms of their agreement was the proscription—the assignment to death—of Antony's hated opponent Cicero. Soon afterwards, Cicero was assassinated as he left his beloved country villa for a dash to the sea and safety.

Petrarch takes Cicero to task for ignoring his own good advice to others to stay out of public affairs. He had sacrificed "the leisure suited to your age, your profession, and your destiny" and was in consequence dragged "through senseless turmoil to a death unworthy of a philosopher." Cicero's resistance to tyranny, as he watched the Republic slip away, might strike us as heroic, but to Petrarch it was foolish. For Petrarch was constructing a different form of heroism, of which he was the principal exemplar: that of the man of letters, who avoids the minutiae of civic or religious officialdom to dedicate himself to study and to the exercise of the imagination. His beloved Cicero had chosen a different path.

In closing, Petrarch closes the loop his letter has opened by reframing his relationship with Cicero in time and place. Alive and sitting solidly in Verona, he sends his "eternal farewell" to a friend far away, among the dead below, who had not lived long enough to know the Christian savior born soon after Cicero's death and more than thirteen centuries before Petrarch's own: "From the land of the living, on the right bank of the [river] Adige, in the city of Verona in Italy north of the Po, on the sixteenth of June, in the one thousandth three-hundredth and forty-fifth year since the birth of that God whom you never knew."

A different kind of dialogue transpires between Petrarch and Homer, the Greek author of the monumental epics the *Iliad* and the *Odyssey*, nearly unknown in fourteenth-century Europe. Petrarch's letter to Homer is part of a literary game initiated by another writer but which he puts to his own use: an unknown correspondent had sent Petrarch a letter, in Latin, purporting to have been written on behalf of Homer then in the Underworld, the shadowy realm of the dead described in Greek mythology. Petrarch responds in kind, dealing one by one with the matters "Homer" raised in his missive. But Petrarch diverts the discussion to another end, one of maximal concern to him: the problem of blocked communication. It was hard enough to talk to dead men—but what if they spoke only Greek?

Petrarch raises the issue in the first sentence of the letter, immediately following his salutation of Homer as "prince of Greek poets": "For some time I have been meaning to write you a letter, and I would have done so except that we have no common language." Petrarch had tried but failed to learn Greek, and Homer knew no Latin. But as Petrarch explains with some convolutions, Homer had "spoken" Latin in antiquity because Roman authors, whose knowledge of the Greek language and literary tradition was excellent, had translated his words—something that the authors of Petrarch's own era could not do, because due to their "negligence," knowledge of Greek had been lost. In this assertion, Petrarch sweeps away the whole sequence of cataclysmic historical events that separated antiquity from the fourteenth century, and which caused among its many other effects a distancing of the Latin Christian European world from the ancient Greco-Roman—a distancing Petrarch bridled at, and wished to overcome.

Petrarch knew of Homer's achievement because he had encountered mentions of his epics in the Latin works he carefully and ceaselessly studied. He yearned to encounter Homer's text directly; but there was hardly anyone in contemporary Western Europe who could assist. True, Genoese and Venetian merchants had direct contact with modern Greeks and perhaps had some command of ordinary conversation. But the ability to read ancient Greek books was an altogether different matter. For these reasons Petrarch, together with his friend Giovanni Boccaccio, who was equally eager for direct contact with Greek texts, had commissioned Leonzio Pilato, a Calabrian-born scholar of Greek ethnicity and mediocre ability, to translate Homer for them. The work was slow in coming, and when it was completed, some years after Petrarch's letter to Homer, it was crude. Petrarch repeatedly tells Homer how urgently, and how passionately, he awaits Pilato's translation: "But there is now one man, inhabiting this age in which I live, who will restore you to us in Latin," he assures Homer; he has seen a fragment already, "Greek perfume in a Latin vessel"; he already possesses a copy of Homer's text in Greek, although he cannot read it, and "if that Thessalian Greek [as Petrarch thought Pilato was] of whom I have spoken completes what he has begun," he will soon "have you whole in Latin."

Beyond the discussion of translation and stymied communication, Petrarch also addresses various complaints of Homer's—the complaints of a fellow author, beset by third-rate imitators who steal his work and mar its beauty in their simulacra of the original. Petrarch soothes Homer with platitudes, before returning in the end to his main theme: the distance between him and his correspondent, severed from each other by language and culture, by time and space. "All these words I have spoken to you as though you were standing here with me," but now he realizes "how far away you are" and fears that the Greek will have difficulty reading his letter "in the shadows of the Underworld." Now that their conversation has ceased, Homer will return to his "eternal home," so Petrarch sends greetings to the others who dwell there—the mythological figures Orpheus and Linus and the once-real playwright Euripides—and says "Farewell forever." As with his letter to Cicero, Petrarch concludes this letter with a very specific description of where he is—in Milan, between the Po, Ticino, and Adda rivers. And when he writes, "on the 9th day of October in the one-thousandth three-hundredth and sixtieth year of the final age of mankind," he means the last age of Christian history, soon to culminate in the Apocalypse.

Petrarch, *Letter to Cicero* (16 June 1345)

Hungrily did I read your letters which I had sought for so long and found at last where I least expected them to be.[1] In them, O Marcus Tullius, I heard you speak: discoursing of many things, complaining much, revising your views often. I had always known what kind of mentor you had been to others; now finally I understand how much you were also mentor to yourself. Now it is your turn to listen, wherever you may be: not to the counsel but to the lament of one of your descendants who loves you without limit, a lament born of deep love, poured forth not without tears.

O ever restless and unquiet wretch, or to recall your own words, O rash and disastrous old man,[2] why did you choose to throw yourself into so many quarrels and contests promising no possible useful outcome? By which you sacrificed the leisure suited to your age, your profession, and your destiny? What false glimmer of glory lured you, in your old age, into young men's wars, and dragged you through senseless turmoil to a death unworthy of a philosopher? Alas, disregarding your brother's advice and your own numerous and wholesome principles, it seems that you forged through the dark night holding your lantern high to show others the right path—while you yourself stumbled and fell.

I pass by Dionysius, I pass by your brother and nephew, I even pass by Dolabella, if you please, men whom you alternately praised to the skies and

---

1. Earlier in 1345, Petrarch had made the historic discovery of Cicero's *Letters to Atticus* in the cathedral of Verona. Here he gives his first response to the new voice and spirit he detected in the genre of the familiar letter.

2. Petrarch believed that Cicero used these words in his letter to Octavian, which is now considered apocryphal: Umberto Bosco, *Le familiari*, ed. Vittorio Rossi (Florence: G. C. Sonsoni, 1933–1942), 4, note to 226, lines 11–12.

lashed out at with unexpected fury—these outbreaks were perhaps forgivable.[3] Nor will I comment on your treatment of Julius Caesar, whose unstinting mercy was a refuge even for those who had injured him; nor will I speak of Pompey the Great, with whom, given your friendship with him, you might have been able to get somewhere. But what madness impelled you to take on Antony? Love of the republic, I believe you would say, although you already knew it to be wholly defunct? But if it was pure idealism, your devotion to liberty that drove you, why then were you so cozy with Augustus? How then would you have answered your friend Brutus, who said, "If you can accept Octavius, then you seem not to have hated tyranny, but only to have sought a more amiable tyrant."[4]

You made one last mistake, O unlucky Cicero, and this one was decisive: that very man whom you had so praised you then denounced, although he had really done you no harm, except to accommodate those who wished to harm you. I grieve for your fate, my friend, and am ashamed and sorry for your errors; yet I must now agree with Brutus, who said, "I do not at all esteem those arts, in which I know that you were most accomplished."[5] Seriously, what is the point of teaching others, what profit is there in always preaching grandiloquently about virtue, if you yourself ignore the sermon? Oh, how much better it would have been to have grown old in the tranquil countryside, especially for a philosopher, reflecting on the life that is eternal, as you write somewhere, and not on this present brief one; never to have cherished the trappings of office, never to have dreamed of triumphs, never to have inflamed your soul in the pursuit of Catiline.[6] But all these things are said in vain. An eternal farewell, my Cicero.

> *From the land of the living, on the right bank of the Adige, in the city of Verona in Italy north of the Po, on the sixteenth of June, in the one thousandth three-hundredth and forty-fifth year since the birth of that God whom you never knew.*

---

3. Petrarch names Dionysius, Cicero's slave-secretary; also Cicero's brother Quintus Tullius Cicero, his friend Marcus Junius Brutus, and his son-in-law Publius Cornelius Dolabella. The other figures named in this paragraph—Julius Caesar, Pompey the Great, Mark Antony, and Octavian, known as Augustus—are towering figures of the late Republican era.

4. Cicero, *Ep. ad Brutum*, I.16.7.

5. Cicero, ibid., I.17.5.

6. When Cicero was consul in 63 BCE, he vigorously suppressed the conspiracy of the aristocratic malcontent Lucius Sergius Catilina, a prosecution accompanied by a now-famous series of four speeches known as the *Catilinarian Orations,* and resulting in the death of his target.

Petrarch, *Letter to Homer* (9 October 1360)

For some time I have been meaning to write you a letter, and I would have done so except that we have no common language. For neither have I been happy in my efforts to master the Greek language, nor have you been able to speak to me in Latin, as you once were with the aid of our authors who knew both languages—an ability which, through the negligence of their descendants, has since been lost.[7] Since we have no means of communication, I have said nothing. But there is now one man, inhabiting this age in which I live, who will restore you to us in Latin.[8] Assuredly, the Ulysses you sang of in your *Odyssey* did not await his reunion with Penelope more patiently or passionately than I await your reappearance.[9]

Yet that hope languished; for other than a few opening phrases of your works, in which I could see far in the distance the dim and shimmering image of my longed-for friend, or perhaps of his fleeting shadow, no Latin text has materialized, and I began to doubt that I would ever see you face to face. . . . Still this man I mentioned, if he lives long enough, may yet produce you for us whole. He is already at work, so that we are beginning not only to taste the precious fruit of your lofty thought, but also delight in the charms of your style—of which I have recently received a sample, Greek perfume in a Latin vessel, giving clear evidence of the infinite capacity of your mighty and brilliant mind. . . .

    A discussion of stylistics follows.

About literary style, enough. Now I come to the matter of your letter. You complain about a number of things, when you could properly complain about everything; for where in human existence, I might ask, is there lack of just cause for complaint? Yet such complaints are increasingly useless and soon cease to be justified; for while they do have a cause they lack an effect:

---

7. "Our authors," for Petrarch and the other humanists, are the ancient Roman writers who generally knew Greek, and who in some cases—Cicero is a prime instance—translated Greek works into Latin for contemporary readers. Later Latin authors of the European Middle Ages, belonging to the inglorious "last age" that Petrarch refers to several times in this letter, had (with few exceptions) no Greek.

8. The "one man" of whom Petrarch speaks in this letter was Leonzio Pilato, a native of Calabria of Greek ethnicity who pretended to be a Greek from Thessalonica, or Thessaly, whom Petrarch and Boccaccio had commissioned to translate Homer's work into Latin. As a modern, he was an inhabitant of "this age," referred to twice later in this letter as the "last age" of the world or of human existence, a notion probably derived from the medieval prophetic tradition launched nearly two centuries before by the monk and abbot Joachim of Flora.

9. Ulysses is the Latin form of the name Odysseus, the hero of the *Odyssey,* one of Homer's two great epics.

which would be, while condemning what has happened in the past, to offer counsel in the present moment and prepare for a better future outcome. But since in the meantime they solace the troubled spirit, they are not wholly without value. . . .

Petrarch reviews Homer's account of his life and the loss of his works, before addressing his complaints about literary imitation.

You complain much about your imitators, about those ingrates who filch your ideas and ignoramuses who besmirch your work. Justly do you complain about all these things—if you alone had suffered them, and if it were not common to the human condition that other men annoy us. So you must calm yourself: you are first among men, I recognize—but you are not the only one. Now what can I say about imitation? You should have known, as you soar on the wings of your imagination, that you would have imitators. Rather than complain, you should rejoice that many men wish to be like you, but not many can. And why should you not be pleased that you have imitators, assured as you are of always standing in first place, when even I, the least of men, am pleased, but more, greatly rejoice that I have won such fame that others—if it can really be that there are such—choose to imitate and mimic me? I shall rejoice even more if my imitators surpass me. . . .

After a further discussion of imitation and professional resentments, Petrarch turns to Homer's remaining complaints.

It remains for me to deal with the bits of complaints scattered throughout your letter. You grieve that your imitators have mangled your work. So it must be, since there is no one capable of matching the measure of your genius. You rage that they have clothed themselves in your garments, snatching the fine flowers of your verse to prettify their own. So it happens: if they had not profited shamelessly from your labors, they could not truly be the ingrates that they are. You grieve that the ancient jurists and physicians esteemed you, while their successors despise you, and you do not know why.[10] But these latter would-be experts are inferior to their predecessors; if they were their equals, they would equally revere and delight in you. Let your anger, let your sorrow cease, and take heart. To have displeased evil and ignorant men is the sure sign of virtue and genius. . . .

Petrarch proceeds to assuage Homer's distress that so few people in Italy know who he is or can read his works; though there are few, Petrarch agrees, there are more in Italy than elsewhere! Now he turns to his own concerns.

---

10. Jurists and physicians were the two dominant categories of professionals in Petrarch's Italian world, although not in Homeric antiquity.

But now let this discourse turn to me, as I, the child of this last age of the world, come last in genius.[11] In your predicament, you seek my help. O harsh and bitter fate! Would that I could help in any way! For if I could succor such a man, for this alone, beyond all honors that I have achieved or hope to achieve, I would win perpetual fame! However—as Christ is my witness, that God unknown to you—beyond sincere sympathy and friendly advice, there is no way at all I can help you. For how can he aid another who can do nothing for himself? . . .

As for myself, although I may not be worthy to host such a guest, yet I have you at home in Greek, and I hope soon—if that Thessalian Greek[12] of whom I have spoken completes what he has begun—to have you whole in Latin. Know, too, that to offer you a more private refuge, most lovingly and reverently I have prepared for you a special domicile in the core of my soul. In sum: my love for you is brighter and hotter than the sun, my esteem for you so great that it could not be greater.

I have conveyed to you what thoughts I could, my lord and father. To free you from the mockery of the mob, except when it might lessen the future recognition of your special and unique glory, is not something I or anyone else can do, unless there is someone who can silence the ravings of the ignorant; which might be possible for God to do, although he has not done so yet, and I think he will not do it.

All these words I have spoken to you as though you were standing here with me. But coming down to earth now from the realm of the imagination, I realize how far away you are, and I fear that you may struggle to read my missive in the shadows of the Underworld—except that in those same shadows you were able to compose so long a letter to me. Farewell forever; say hello for me to Orpheus and Linus and Euripides and the others when you have returned to your eternal home.[13]

> *From the land of the living, in the Midland between the brightly sparkling waters of the Po, the Ticino, the Adda, and others, from which Milan, some say, takes its name, on the 9th day of October in the one-thousandth three-hundredth and sixtieth year of the final age of mankind.*[14]

---

11. Once again, Petrarch places himself in time as living during the "last age," a less exalted one than the ancient one in which Homer lived; so he is "least" both in intellect and in temporal position.

12. Leonzio Pilato, that is.

13. Petrarch here is imagining Homer as a resident of the Greek Underworld (not quite the same as the Christian Hell), which was populated by the principal mythological and historical figures of the classical Greek era, including the musician Orpheus, Linus, the inventor of melody and rhythm, and the playwright Euripides.

14. *Mediolanum* is the Latin name of the city called Milano in Italian and Milan in English; it seems to mean "in the middle," or on the body of land adjacent to several rivers, and the

Giovanni Boccaccio

The classical tradition fascinated Boccaccio (1313–1375), as it did Petrarch. But where Petrarch yearns for the classical world—to know it, to immerse himself in it, to bring it back to life—Boccaccio is more of a hoarder. He combs through the books of the ancients for content, which he then arranges for contemporary readers. He does so in a series of encyclopedias. In *On the Fates of Famous Men* (1355/1363), he profiles the downfall of 56 classical figures, complementing his *On Famous Women* (1361/1362), which offers brief biographies of 106 women, all but 6 of them drawn from antiquity. In *On Mountains, Woods, Springs, Lakes, Rivers, Swamps, and on the Names of Seas* (1355/1364), he identifies a vast array of geographical and geological phenomena appearing in classical literary works, facilitating their reading. Finally, his *Genealogy of the Pagan Gods* (1360/1374), of all these the most important and most widely read, catalogs the mythological material in those same classical works, which were in Greek as well as Latin. Although Boccaccio knew little Greek, he accessed a wide array of Greek works by consulting the epitomes and translations made of them by Roman authors, whose own original works also rest on the substratum of the Greek literary corpus.

In the *Genealogy*, however, Boccaccio is much more than a careful cataloguer of what others have written. He grapples with mythology not only to acquaint his audience with the cast of self-willed and insouciant deities, but because he recognizes that mythology lies at the heart of classical literature: the stories about the gods are not decorative adjuncts to the body of classical thought but are its center and substance. The great works of the Greco-Roman tradition were written within a religious and intellectual framework whose literary manifestation was expressed in the language of mythology. To ignore or deny the mythological integument was to be excluded from the core meaning of the works of the ancients.

And so Boccaccio's *Genealogy* is about the gods and their intricate histories and interrelationships, as the title announces. But it is also about classical poetry, which is saturated with mythology and unreadable by anyone unfamiliar with its language. Consequently, the *Genealogy* is about the whole of the classical tradition, to approach which requires an openness to the antics of the Olympians and their companions. To us, for whom mythological fables have largely lost their power and become the playthings of children, it seems odd that Boccaccio must first justify mythology in order to enter into the world of classical antiquity. But it is not so strange—although in a

---

convention of referring to it as the "Midland" is followed here. Once again, Petrarch calls attention to his temporal identity as living during the "last age."

post-Christian age stranger than it once was—when we consider how essential to the medieval consciousness are Christian thought and experience.

Boccaccio's urgent task, then, is not only to catalogue mythical figures (which he does so, enumerating 950 and more in the first thirteen books of the *Genealogy*), but also to justify the reading of classical literature. Why was such justification necessary? Because of the profound and essential asymmetry between the Christian and the pagan worlds. For Boccaccio's contemporaries, the cosmos was ruled by one omnipotent God who presided over a moral order; but the Greeks and Romans, for all their rich cosmological imaginings, shared no consensus on the system of the world and were untroubled by the irrationality and immorality exhibited by their deities. This outlook, readily evident to anyone reading the principal classical authors, appalled the gatekeepers of new ideas: it was frivolous, it was senseless, and it was possibly heretical—a serious matter in the middle of the fourteenth century. To combat such perceptions, Boccaccio wields his wisdom, his humor, and his good sense in books XIV and XV of the *Genealogy*.

The pages that follow (only a few from close to a hundred pages of Boccaccio's sprightly and discursive text) are excerpted from Book XIV, in which the author declares war on the several classes of his critics, and closes with a declaration of victory and an invitation to treat of peace. He begins with a portrait of the critics of poetry, who will gather around his work "more intent on uncovering defects than on discovering anything of value." They are of various minds, but in sum, they charge that poetry is empty and meaningless and, moreover, a danger to Christian faith. Boccaccio will oppose these critics: "Against these fools I declare war, against these I raise my weapons so as to skewer them with arguments more powerful than theirs."

But if the critics are wrong, and poetry is not useless, then Boccaccio needs to say what poetry is—which he does with quite remarkable formulations. Poetry is no idle occupation, but "a venerable branch of knowledge," an art "ripe with promise [*succiplena*, "full of juice"] for those who strive by the mental act of constructing fictions to give external expression to inner thoughts and feelings." It is "a kind of fervor for exquisitely crafting, then conveying in speech or writing, whatever the mind has invented," a fervor that originates from God himself and, having the quality of the miraculous, is possessed by very few. It has "effects that are sublime": "it compels the mind to yearn to express itself; it devises strange and novel constructs of the imagination; it arranges these meditations in a proper order, adorning what it has thus composed with a unique patterning of words and sentences, so clothing the truth in a tissue of lovely fictions." Boccaccio's analysis of poetry is complex and compelling. It stands, in fact, at the beginning of the modern literary tradition, which will also yield the later apologies for poetry of Sir Philip Sidney and William Wordsworth that, directly or through intermediaries, derive from the insights of our fourteenth-century humanist.[15]

---

15. Sidney's *Defence of Poetry* (1579, published posthumously 1595) and Wordsworth's "Preface" to the second edition of the *Lyrical Ballads* (1802).

Poetry, of course, is fiction, in the sense that it is a kind of literature that is produced by the imagination and is not beholden to fact; and classical poetry, in addition, is full of fictions—principally, the stories about the gods that Boccaccio records and classifies, which are the target of his hostile critics. So Boccaccio tangles, as well, with the problem of "fiction." If something is fictional, is it necessarily untrue? Is it, in short, a lie?

Certainly not, for the fictions that comprise a poem, and that are the poem, are a robe or veil woven of words that cover a profound truth: "every reasonably intelligent reader knows that some greater truth lies hidden under the surface of the story." Poetry, therefore, is akin to philosophy and to religion; indeed, the first poets were also prophets, and the verses they sang were celebrations of the divine. Not all readers, of course, will recognize the core truths that poetry contains: "those without learning [will be] amused by the superficial narrative, while the minds of the learned labor to unearth its hidden meanings."

But the enemies of poetry deny that poetry conveys deeper meanings, and insist that it is a ruse perpetrated by poets on an unsuspecting audience that is tricked by an empty display of eloquence into believing dangerous falsehoods. Poets, moreover, are not liars, even though they write fictions that are not, literally, true; but lies are told so as to deceive the listener, whereas the intention of poetic fictions is not to deceive but to edify. As to the charge that the poets believe in many gods, rather than the one omnipotent Christian God, Boccaccio argues, it is wholly untrue: for these "learned men who are the zealous investigators of truth, who have the capacity to look deep into the human soul, know without question that there is only one God. . . ."

Yet the enemies of poetry still thunder their objections and threaten readers with damnation: "renounce these wicked books of poetry, burn them in the flames, and scatter them on the winds," for to allow these books on your bookshelf, to even think about reading them, is a mortal sin, and will "drag you down to Hell." So they bellow and blather, with "unconquerable" rage. Boccaccio has done all he can. If they are unwilling now to put aside their anger, "no words I can write could ever silence [their] insatiable resentment."

Thus does Book XIV of the *Genealogy* directly confront the objections of the keepers of Christian civilization to the reading of ancient literature. Its importance cannot be overstated. It could be said that Boccaccio's work is the essential gateway to humanism and the Renaissance and to the modern literary and intellectual traditions that issue from those movements. For Boccaccio, with Petrarch, stood at a fork in the road: Europe could continue to elaborate upon its inherited cultural legacy indefinitely—for it was a rich and inexhaustible one—or it could fully embrace the ancient Greco-Roman heritage, adding new dimensions and complexities to its mental world. It chose the latter path. Boccaccio deserves a good share of the credit for that courageous and epochal decision by which Western civilization, its energies recharged, entered upon an era of dynamic innovation.

Giovanni Boccaccio, *Genealogy of the Pagan Gods,*
Book XIV (1360/1374)
In which the author, responding to criticisms, addresses
the enemies of poetry

After an introduction addressed to a patron, Boccaccio turns in the second
chapter to confront those ignorant critics who disdain poetry, and with it, the
whole of the classical literary tradition.

CHAPTER 2: SOME THOUGHTS ON THE IGNORANT

As often happens when a new book appears, a mob of incompetents will rush
to judge it. Some learned men will gather, too; and after they have looked
it over, since doubtless some of them may be worthy of respect for their
integrity, intellect, and knowledge, they will praise whatever is commend-
able, and with a scholarly reticence criticize whatever is weak. I bless them,
I thank them, I take my hat off to them, and I celebrate their fine behavior.
But a far more numerous crowd will circle around the volume to scrutinize it
for any hidden faults and flaws, more intent on uncovering defects than on
discovering anything of value. Against these fools I declare war; against these
I raise my weapons so as to skewer them with arguments more powerful than
theirs. Of course, I won't take them on all at once, letting them surround and
quickly dispatch me; but I'll divide them into smaller cohorts, while my arm
becomes accustomed to the battle, and so bit by bit, I'll grind them into the
ground. I'll aim my javelins first at the weakest of them. . . .

In Chapters 3 through 6, Boccaccio identifies four groups of opponents, of
whom the most learned, and on that account the most dangerous, are those
who deny the value of poetry. From these he turns immediately to a discussion
of poetry: its purpose and its positive role in human civilization.

CHAPTER 6: POETRY IS A USEFUL ART

A mere David, I enter into the fray against these hulking Goliaths who pre-
sume to affirm that poetry is either no art at all or a useless one. . . . If this
is so, I ask: Why through all the ages have so many great men sought to be
called poets? Why do we have so many volumes of poetry? If poetry is nothing, why did this word, "poetry," come into use? Surely, if they answer at all,
I believe they will give some vague response; because really there's nothing
they can say that does not contradict their foolish premise. For it is most certain—as will be shown later—that this, like all the other arts, has its origin

in God, the source of all wisdom; and like the others, it has its name from its effect. From the term "poetry" is derived the glorious name of "poet," and from poet, "poem." Given all this, poetry absolutely cannot be dismissed, as they claim, as nothing. . . .

After further charges against his opponents, Boccaccio concludes.

But what more is there to say? Poetry is not merely something, but a venerable branch of knowledge, and as has often been seen already and will be seen again below, it is not a futile art, but one ripe with promise for those who strive by the mental act of constructing fictions to give external expression to inner thoughts and feelings. And so it appears—not to drag this out further—at the first onset of conflict, our opponents have turned and fled, with little effort on our part, and deserted the field of battle. But what poetry is remains to be explained, so that these losers may see how stupid they are to think that the art of poetry is useless.

CHAPTER 7: WHAT POETRY IS, WHERE IT COMES FROM, AND WHAT IT DOES

Poetry then, which the lazy and ignorant despise, is a kind of fervor for exquisitely crafting, then conveying in speech or writing, whatever the mind has invented. This fervor proceeds from the spirit of God and is instilled, I think, in only a few minds; indeed, it is a kind of miracle, such that true poets have always been exceptions in creation. This poetic fervor has effects that are sublime. Consider these: it compels the mind to yearn to express itself; it devises strange and novel constructs of the imagination; it arranges these meditations in a proper order, adorning what it has thus composed with a unique patterning of words and sentences, so clothing the truth in a tissue of lovely fictions. Further, as the invention requires, poetry arms kings and sends them off to war, dispatches fleets of ships, portrays the sky, the earth, and the seas, bedecks fair maidens with garlands and flowers, describes human nature in its various forms, awakes the somnolent, spurs the idle, restrains the bold, punishes the guilty, extols the great with litanies of praise—and many other such are the effects of poetry. . . . And since from this poetic fervor, which sharpens and brightens the forces of the mind, nothing is produced except by artifice, we call poetry an "art" . . . . that is born from the bosom of God, that takes its name from its effect, that addresses many high and important matters of profound concern even to those who deny its existence.

After an eighth chapter inquiring how poetry began and who were the first poets, Boccaccio launches the argument that the fictions poets compose contain a deeper meaning below the surface, and so are of benefit to readers.

CHAPTER 9: IT IS USEFUL, NOT DAMNABLE,
TO COMPOSE STORIES

The self-important enemies of poetry bellow, too, that poets are storytellers—or to repeat the more vile and vulgar term that these raging cattle use,
liars. No doubt the ignorant will find this a particularly hateful objection,
but I think nothing of it. The filthy speech of these nobodies cannot sully the
glorious name of the illustrious. But it sorrows me to see these red-faced buf-
foons let themselves loose on the innocent. But what can be said in response?
I concede that poets are storytellers, or rather, composers of stories. But it
is no more disgraceful, in my estimation, for a poet to tell stories than for a
philosopher to construct a syllogism.[16] . . .

But let's grant these critics a point. To compose stories would be a vain and
senseless thing, I do not deny, if what poets composed were simply stories.
But every reasonably intelligent reader knows that some greater truth lies
hidden under the surface of the story. On which account, many accept this
definition of a story: "A story is a discourse which under the guise of fiction
teaches or demonstrates something true, such that as the reader penetrates
below the surface, the intention of the storyteller is revealed."

*Boccaccio now outlines four levels of allegorical interpretation, by which a
reader comes to fathom the truth that lies within the superficial fiction.[17]*

What more is to be said? Stories are fictions allowing those without learning to be amused by the superficial narrative, while the minds of the learned
labor to unearth its hidden meanings; and so in one reading, each is edified
and delighted. Now may those stiff-necked and wrong-headed critics cease to
vomit their ignorance and ill-will against the poets. . . .

*Boccaccio continues to unfold his theory of allegorical interpretation in
Chapter 10.*

---

16. A paradigm for constructing an argument, consisting of a major premise, a minor premise, and a conclusion that necessarily follows the first two terms—if the syllogism is properly
constructed.

17. From late antiquity, medieval commentators had adopted the fourfold system of allegorical interpretation, wherein the first level is the *literal* reading of a text; the second the *typologi-
cal,* showing the foreshadowing of present events in the past; the third *tropological* or *moral,*
giving the prudential or didactic purpose of the text; and the fourth *anagogical,* relating the
superficial fiction to a profound and universal meaning.

CHAPTER 10: IT IS FOOLISH TO BELIEVE THAT POETS INTENDED NO MEANING BENEATH THE SURFACE OF THEIR STORIES

Some of these critics are so rash, that without any authority, they dismiss as insane the belief that the most famous poets, under the surface of their stories, had hidden something of deeper significance. Rather, they say, the poets composed their fictions in order to showcase the power of their eloquence, by which they tricked the simple into believing the false things they wrote to be true. O the iniquity of men! O ridiculous stupidity! O foolish malice! While they put others down, they think that they are raising themselves up. For who but a fool would say that the poets deliberately composed vain and foolish stories, with only a superficial meaning, so as to demonstrate their eloquence? As though eloquence cannot be engaged in service of the truth! . . .

After some exposition, Boccaccio begins his conclusion.

Let these stupid bleaters keep quiet and these prideful critics hold their tongues, if they can, since it must be recognized that men of great distinction, reared on the milk of the Muses,[18] trained in the precincts of philosophy, and imbued with sacred studies, have always embedded the most profound meanings in their poems.

After exploring in Chapter 11 why poets live solitary lives and, in Chapter 12, defending poetry against the charge of obscurity, Boccaccio returns in Chapter 13 to the theme of the truths hidden in poetry, denying that poets lie when they construct their fictions. As part of this argument, he concedes that poets often speak of a plurality of gods, and affirms that they, like Petrarch's contemporaries, know nonetheless that there is only one, omnipotent God, the author of creation.

CHAPTER 13: POETS ARE NOT LIARS

These malicious critics of poetry also call the poets liars, and they try to bolster that accusation by offering examples of untruths found in the stories poets tell: as when a man is turned into a stone, for instance, which seems to be a total fabrication. They complain as well that the poets lie when they speak of many gods, when it is most certainly the case that there is only one God, who is true and omnipotent. . . .

But I respond . . . that the poets are not liars, as these critics would have them, because a lie, as I see it, is a kind of falsehood that closely resembles

---

18. The nine Muses, all daughters of the god Zeus and the goddess Mnemosyne, were the source of all knowledge, and inspired artists and thinkers in their creative activity.

the truth, but which suppresses the truth and replaces it with an untruth. The theologian Augustine delineates eight types of such lies, none of which, although some are more serious than others, can be knowingly uttered without sin and disgrace.[19] If the enemies of poetry were to consider fairly the meaning of this definition, they would realize that their assertion that poets are liars cannot stand: the stories composed by poets in no way accords with any of the types of lies specified, since it is not their intent, in constructing those fictions, to deceive anyone. Nor do poetic fictions closely resemble the truth, as a lie does, but for the most part do not resemble it at all—in fact, they are at odds with and completely other than our normal reality. . . .

It can't be denied, however, that poets write of many gods, when there is only one God; but this should not be charged to them as a lie, since they do so not as believers or witnesses but in the service of their art. For it is impossible that anyone trained in philosophy could be so demented as to believe in many gods. If we keep our heads, we will recognize that learned men who are the zealous investigators of truth, who have the capacity to look deep into the human soul, know without question that there is only one God. . . .

In the next four chapters, Boccaccio continues to defend poetry's moral soundness and intellectual value, raising and dispatching in Chapter 18 the possibility that reading poetry could be a mortal sin.

CHAPTER 18: IT IS NOT A MORTAL SIN TO READ THE BOOKS OF THE POETS

These arbiters of justice—or of injustice, rather—seeking in their burning rage the destruction of poetry, as if they had not already said more than enough about it, now roar from on high this clamorous denunciation: O excellent citizens, O you who have been redeemed by the sacred blood of Jesus, O you chosen people of God, if there is in you any reverence, any devotion, any love of the Christian religion, any fear of God, renounce these wicked books of poetry, burn them in the flames, and scatter them on the winds. For to keep them on your shelves, to read them, even to want to read them, is a mortal sin.[20] They infect the soul with deadly poison, they drag you down to Hell, and bar you forever from the celestial kingdom. . . .

---

19. The philosopher Saint Augustine categorized the species of lie in his two treatises *On Lying* and *Of Lying*, which he then reviews in his *Retractions*, Book I, final chapter; see Keven Knight, "On Lying (St. Augustine)," at *New Advent*: Kevin Knight, http://www.newadvent .org/fathers/1312.htm (accessed July 26, 2011).

20. In Catholic doctrine, a mortal sin is one that, if not confessed and absolved, condemns a person to hell after death.

Mocking the enemies of the poetic art with this hyperbolic denunciation,
Boccaccio refutes their charges, enlisting as witnesses a series of Christian
authors who defend the value of poetry and the classical tradition which it
embodies. That exposition completed, he concludes.

What do they have left to shriek about now, these mighty bellowers? Will
they keep on howling and assailing the songs of the poets, though refuted by
their own evidence, and debunked and vanquished by the testimony of the
saints? Let them keep on howling, then: their rage is unconquerable. . . . But
God, most just of judges, will punish them in the end for their malice and
their envy, and they shall suffer to the same degree that they brought suffering to others.

Following more discussion of similar themes in Chapters 19 through 21, in
the final chapter of Book XIV, Boccaccio summons the enemies of poetry to
abandon their foolish opposition.

CHAPTER 22: THE AUTHOR REQUESTS THAT THE ENEMIES OF POETRY CHANGE THEIR MINDS

Now therefore, O prudent men, if you are wise, you will put away your anger
and soothe your troubled spirits, for we have contended long enough, indeed
too much. You took the first step in taking up arms against poets, determined
to wipe them from the face of the earth; I in turn opposed you with all of my
faculties, aided by God and the worthiness of my cause, so that the innocent
would not suffer at the hands of their enemies—although if they had come
forth themselves to face you on the field of combat, you would have learned
to your sorrow how much stronger my army was than yours. But now the
war is over; and putting aside both the thrill and the toils of battle, it is time
to put aside the craving for victory and make a just peace. Let us do so then,
and willingly, so that we may rest from our labors. . . . If you agree then that
poetry is not to be spurned, nor rejected, but treasured, as are the poets themselves, then enough has been said; but if you persevere stubbornly in your
hostility, then I am sorry for you: for no words I can write could ever silence
your insatiable resentment.

Pier Paolo Vergerio

"We call those studies liberal," Vergerio (1370–1444) announced in his treatise *On Liberal Studies and the Moral Education of the Free-Born Youth,* "which are suited for a free man [*liber*]." With these words, Vergerio opens up a new phase in the career of humanism, when it comes to inform and animate a new system of education. By this new humanist pedagogy, through the nineteenth century at least, the leaders of modern Europe would be trained.

If Petrarch is the most prominent of the humanists to "discover" antiquity and exploit its legacy, and Boccaccio is the first to offer a systematic justification for the modern appropriation of ancient, secular thought, Vergerio pioneers by defining the set of intellectual disciplines by which humanist teachers will equip young Europeans with the knowledge that only the study of the classics provides. That set of intellectual disciplines constitutes the "liberal arts," a curriculum different from both the ancient and the medieval, although informed by both, and one that endures, if in tatters, even today.

The term "liberal arts" originates in ancient Rome, serving to distinguish between the "arts," or forms of knowledge, befitting free men, and those called "mechanical" or "manual" that were proper to slaves. Those who studied the liberal arts would receive a full preparation for the finest kind of life, enriched by a moral and intellectual understanding refined by reading and conversation. This cultural program was not, theoretically, limited to the elites, although members of the elites predominated among those imbued with the liberal arts. Rather, it was seen, though unrealistically, as an ideal for all humankind, much as the Greeks had earlier envisioned an *enkyklios paideia,* a broad cultural preparation for the elevation of the human being.

Neither classical Greece nor Rome, however, defined a set of intellectual disciplines as Vergerio later would. Instead, history records various groupings of studies. In classical Greece, the two main cultural pursuits were "music," encompassing all of literature, and "gymnastics." By Hellenistic times, a variety of pursuits were added to the intellectual program, notably the advanced studies of rhetoric and philosophy. The Romans adopted the Hellenistic model.

In the last days of antiquity, the African-born Latin writer Martianus Capella codified the liberal arts as consisting of seven intellectual disciplines: namely grammar (the study of the Latin language and its literature); dialectic (logic); rhetoric (the art of composition); astronomy (which included astrology); arithmetic; geometry; and music (closely related to theories of number). In the medieval schools and universities that formed from the twelfth century on, these seven were divided into a set of three, the *trivium*, which was concerned with words (grammar, dialectic, and rhetoric), and a set of four, the *quadrivium,* which was concerned with quantities (astronomy, arithmetic, geometry, and music). These were the liberal arts that were taught widely in Europe when Petrarch, Boccaccio, and Vergerio were born. But they were to be replaced by a different set of pursuits, defined by the humanists.

To organize the corpus of Latin (and later Greek) works whose study the humanists promoted, they identified a set of *studia humanitatis*: literally, the "studies of humanity," which may be understood as the "studies of matters that relate to the human condition," or the "studies that enable human beings to develop to their highest potential." These were codified by the middle of the fifteenth century as including the five disciplines of grammar, rhetoric, poetry, history, and moral philosophy.

The choices are revealing. First, while grammar and rhetoric had constituted two of the medieval curriculum of the trivium, the humanist sequence dropped the third verbal art of dialectic, which was for their taste too closely associated with the systematic intellectual practices of the scholastic philosophers who presided in the universities. Secondly, poetry, whose value had been proclaimed by Boccaccio, and history, essential for the humanist recovery of the culture of antiquity, were promoted to become mainstays of the academic curriculum. Third, philosophy was elevated above theology, which makes no appearance at all; and not all branches of philosophy, but specifically moral philosophy, which was concerned not with metaphysical speculation but with the lived human experience. Finally, the quadrivial arts, which were the basis of university studies in medicine and philosophy, were markedly absent.

Vergerio is a key figure in the establishment of the *studia humanitatis* as the ideal curriculum for the preparation of future political and social leaders. A teacher of the arts, medicine, and law at the universities of Padua, Florence, and Bologna, who held positions in both the church and imperial bureaucracies, he was recruited to teach Ubertino (1390–1407), son of the Carrara ruler of Padua, Francesco Novello. While so employed, he wrote *On Liberal Studies,* and addressed it to the student, then twelve or thirteen years old, who had been entrusted to him.

Francesco Novello had shown foresight in summoning Vergerio to educate his son in this new humanist mode. Heretofore, the sons of the lords of Italian city-states, like the sons of the nobility generally, had been trained as warriors. But the rulers of cities were among the principal patrons of Italy's innovative and resurgent culture. If a new type of education was coming into vogue, their sons must have it—much as they would demand the latest fashion in the matter of doublets or the training of horses.

Writing before the eventual codification of the five disciplines just listed, Vergerio's system is somewhat different: he first names history, philosophy, and eloquence (or rhetoric), in that order. He further names poetry, which leads him to review the verbal arts of the trivium, and so describes grammar, the fifth discipline that would later be included in the canon of the *studia humanitatis*. This new sequence of humanist studies Vergerio marries to the inherited tradition of the liberal arts.

In doing so, he effects the transformation of the liberal arts. The schooling of the elite—for the most part, only the children of the elites received more than a rudimentary education before the eighteenth century—would hereafter be increasingly directed according to humanist curricular principles. The object was distinctly not to produce a university student destined for a professional education but a person formed and animated by the values embedded in classical literature.

Written in the form of a letter addressed to the young Ubertino, *On Liberal Studies* begins with a discussion of the personal and moral characteristics of an ideal student, then proceeds to a discussion of the liberal and military arts. Although Vergerio's main purpose in the treatise is to define and defend the liberal arts, his discussion of the military arts is important and illuminating: for while he acknowledges the utility of the latter, by insisting on the value of the former, he inaugurates the new cultural ideal of the liberally educated gentleman that would be depicted also by the Italian Baldassare Castiglione in his *Courtier* (1528) and advanced by the Englishman Roger Ascham in *The Scholemaster* (1570).

The men of the Carrara clan were warriors, accustomed to the respect owed to those who can successfully exert violence. How anomalous would it seem, in the fourteenth century, that a warrior should also be a master of the classical tradition. Yet this is the bridge that Vergerio builds. From this moment on, the warrior nobleman will be tamed, and turned into a gentleman who can accompany his conversation with a whiff of Latinity. Vergerio's student Ubertino was one of the first of this ilk: for he has with "eagerness and diligence tenaciously embraced both kinds of learning," Vergerio writes, and "not neglecting the military art," has sought to add to his family's "ancient and glorious" renown in war "the new and praiseworthy accomplishment of letters."

But for what reason? What benefit does a member of the nobility, or anyone else, for that matter, derive from the study of the liberal arts? The sections of *On Liberal Studies* excerpted here address that question. These studies begun in childhood are the "consolations" that "may one day delight a worthy old age," Vergerio writes: "those same studies which are tedious to the young will grant the aged a joyous leisure." Even those who are not old but in the prime of life and engaged, especially, in the active life of the citizen and merchant, find that liberal studies are a remedy both for boredom and for anxiety: they "find no other occupation more pleasant, when they are fatigued, than to read good books." And when the turbulence of public life makes it necessary to retire at home, "books come to our aid." For no other form of activity is so pleasurable as the reading of books, "[i]n which pursuit, men living today come to know what happened long ago; the present generation may speak to generations yet unborn; and we make all times our own, both past and future."

Books are the finest companions: they do not complain; they are always at hand; they never disappoint. They "constitute a secure storehouse and universal repository of all that is knowable," and should be carefully preserved and passed on to future generations, as they have been received from generations long gone. Tragically, many of the ancient books were destroyed in the course of time, and with them the memory of many great events, written down in histories that no longer survive.

At this juncture, Vergerio defines the three intellectual disciplines of most benefit to the active citizen: history, moral philosophy, and eloquence (or rhetoric). All of the liberal arts are useful and suited for free men, but philosophy, uniquely, freeing the mind from falsehoods and distractions, makes men free. In all, those who have studied the liberal arts have mastered the art of speaking well, and zealously seek to act well—two virtues which are characteristic of the very greatest men.

The goals of a humanist education are thus defined. Though they were not always realized—perhaps only rarely—these aspirations would govern the educational program for the next several centuries. As generation after generation of the sons and to some extent the daughters of the elite pursued the humanist curriculum, they assured that the thought and sensibility of classical antiquity would be absorbed into the mainstream of the European intellectual tradition.

Pier Paolo Vergerio, *On Liberal Studies and the Moral Education of the Free-Born Youth* (c. 1402/1403)

WHAT LIBERAL STUDIES ARE: A GENERAL DISCUSSION

We call those studies "liberal" [*liberalia*] which are worthy of a free [*liber*] man. They are those studies by which virtue is practiced and wisdom sought so that body and soul may obtain the loftiest goals. . . .

Vergerio proceeds to recommend that liberal studies be pursued by the young, some of whom may be distracted from the pursuit, while others persevere, as has the young man whom the teacher now addresses.

TWO EXCELLENT PURSUITS: THE STUDIES OF ARMS AND OF LETTERS

I see that something of that sort, Ubertino, has also happened to you. For among the different kinds of preparation for life that human beings may pursue, two are especially suited for the cultivation of virtue and the acquisition of glory: the studies of arms and of letters. And although it was your father's inclination that you should pursue military studies only, which is the particular preserve of your family, you have with such eagerness and diligence tenaciously embraced both kinds of learning that you have left your peers far behind, and may compete even with your elders to win praise in both endeavors. You have therefore acted well: not neglecting the military art, in which your ancestors have always excelled, you have sought to add to that ancient and glorious family tradition also the new and praiseworthy accomplishment of letters. . . .

> *Vergerio names Roman emperors who were learned as well as mighty, as well as Ubertino's own ancestor, Giacomo da Carrara, who although not learned himself, generously patronized learned men. Then discussion turns to the need to begin a literary education early in life.*

A man may choose to be learned when he is old, but in fact it is not easy to be so unless, with effort and toil, he has cultivated learning from his earliest youth. In childhood, then, those consolations are to be readied which may one day delight a worthy old age; those same studies which are tedious to the young will grant the aged a joyous leisure. And these same studies are also healing remedies which relieve dull tedium or soothe pressing anxieties. And they are useful in both the two kinds of life that are suitable for free men—the one devoted wholly to leisure and contemplation, the other to action and business[21]—for no one can doubt that the knowledge and practice of letters is essential for the first, and they are also greatly useful for the second, as the following explanation shows.

For those engaged in the active life, whether they serve the state, fight wars abroad, or pursue at home their own business or that of their friends, find no other occupation more pleasant, when they are fatigued, than to read good books—not to mention how much wiser they become from reading the precepts written by learned men, or the examples of great men about whom they write. And when those moments come when it is necessary to retreat from these activities—for we are often excluded from political office,[22] and wars are not always underway, and sometimes there are days or nights when we must stay at home and keep to ourselves—at such times, therefore, when we are not able to amuse ourselves outdoors, books come to our aid. . . .

> *After a discussion of how posterity remembers the virtues and faults of great men, Vergerio returns to describing the benefits of learned studies.*

---

21. Respectively, the *vita activa* and the *vita contemplative*, the active and the contemplative forms of life much discussed by the humanists.

22. A reference to cycles of office-holding, but also to periods of involuntary exile.

But if there were no other benefit to be gained from literary studies—and its benefits are many and great indeed—there is this one of great magnitude, that during the time when we are wrapped in our reading, we are distanced from the many things that we can neither think of without shame nor remember without pain.[23] For if there is anything either in ourselves or in our condition that worries us, for this reason we easily find relief, that once the seed of knowledge is implanted in the soil of a good mind suited for its cultivation, learned studies bring marvelous pleasure to the souls of men and bear in time incomparable fruit. When we are alone, therefore, and free from all our many obligations, what better thing can we do than to summon forth our books, in which are found all things either most pleasant to know or most useful for living a good and worthy life?

For if they are valuable also for many other purposes, the monuments of letters[24] [those written records that have come to us from the past much as have monuments made of stone or bronze] are vitally important for preserving the memory of ancient times. In these are contained the deeds done by great men, unexpected turns of fortune, awesome acts of nature, and, most importantly, the characteristics of each historical era. For the memories men recount and the objects they leave behind are soon forgotten and scarcely survive one human generation, but what has been properly inscribed in books lasts forever. Possibly a painting or carved marble or forged bronze monument[25] may last longer than a book, but these can neither evoke a historical moment, nor adequately describe forces of change; they reveal only an external reality, and are easily destroyed. What is committed to writing, however, not only captures what people have said, but also records their manner of speaking and preserves their thoughts; and if it has been published in many copies, it cannot easily perish, so long as the diction is elegant. For what is written without elegance carries no conviction and cannot long survive.

What mode of existence could be more enjoyable or indeed more profitable than always to be engaged in reading or writing? In which pursuit, men living today come to know what happened long ago; the present generation may speak to generations yet unborn; and we make all times our own, both past and future. How splendid is a household full of books!—as we might say; or as Cicero aptly puts it, "What a delightful family, what amiable companions!"[26] For they do not whine or argue; they are not vicious,

---

23. Perhaps a reference to penitential concerns, a constant feature of lay piety in this age.

24. Another humanist phrase; I have interpolated a discursive equivalent as a gloss, along with the force of the original.

25. These are references to the kinds of objects surviving from ancient times, which were at this point just being explored and discovered.

26. Cicero, *Fam.*, 9.1: Craig W. Kallendorf, ed., *Humanist Educational Treatises* (Cambridge, MA: Harvard University Press, 2001), n87.

voracious, or cantankerous; on command they speak, and on command they are silent; at all times they are ready to obey you absolutely; and they tell you only what you want to hear, and only so much.

Since our memory is not perfect and retains only a little and is shaky on details, books, I believe, should be acquired and kept as a kind of second memory.[27] For literature and books constitute a secure storehouse and universal repository of all that is knowable. On which account, even if we ourselves produce nothing of note, we must take care to transmit those books we have received from our forebears whole and uncorrupted to our posterity; and in so doing we may usefully guide those who will come after us, and we may repay those who preceded us with at least this reward for their labors.

Regarding this matter, we can perhaps justly accuse a certain past age[28] and the ages that came after it: we may rage, though quite uselessly, that they allowed so many splendid works by illustrious authors to perish. Of some of these only the names have come down to us, although they were once widely renowned; of some other works we have snatches and fragments. The glorious reputation of these books and that of their authors makes us long for them. The loss of the rest of these works is all the more grievous because the fragments that have survived are of such worth and excellence—even if these have come to us in a condition so woefully damaged, marred, and mutilated that it almost might have been better if nothing at all had reached us.

But of this catastrophe, which is enormous, not the smallest part is that we have been left ignorant of important events that happened to our Latin-speaking ancestors, here in Italy, knowledge of which perished with the books and monuments that recorded them. What the barbarians did we know; but what our Roman forebears did, because of the destruction of books, we do not.[29] So it has come to this: for our knowledge of Roman civilization we must rely on Greek authors, since the few Latin accounts we have give only a scant report of what happened, or none at all, while much information is found in Greek books; and worse, the Greek language itself, which our ancestors used daily with great ease, largely died with them—and among us it is virtually extinct, except for a few rare souls in our own age who have revived it and may now rescue it from the tomb.[30]

---

27. In the Renaissance, memory was conceived of as a kind of storehouse, a large structure full of rooms.

28. Vergerio alludes here to the era of late antiquity and the early Middle Ages, when much of the ancient literary tradition was destroyed.

29. Like Petrarch before him, Vergerio identifies with the Latin-speaking Italians of Roman antiquity and considers the Germanic newcomers who arrived in Italy from the sixth century on as "barbarians."

30. Vergerio refers to the recent revival of Greek studies in Florence, triggered by the residence there of Byzantine scholar and diplomat Manuel Chrysoloras in 1397–1400, who taught the

But I return to history, whose loss is more serious because it is both more useful and more enjoyable. For the knowledge of history and the study of moral philosophy are especially suited for the educated men who are leaders in politics and society. The rest of the liberal arts are called "liberal" because they are proper for free [*liberos*] men, but philosophy is "liberal" because its study makes men free [*liberos*].[31] Philosophy offers us precepts of moral behavior, while history offers us examples of men who have behaved well. The former details the duties incumbent on all men, and what is fitting for each individual; the latter details what was said and done in each historical era.

To these two, I believe, there should be added a third, which is eloquence, an art pertaining to civil existence. Philosophy teaches us to discern rightly the first principle of any matter; eloquence allows us to speak with authority and elegance, a skill essential for winning over the minds of the multitude; while history helps us to do both. For if we consider old men to be wise on account of their age, and we willingly listen to what they have learned during their long life both from their own experience and from what they have seen or heard other men do, how greatly we should esteem those who have stored in their memory the things worth knowing from many epochs, and who can offer in any circumstance some enlightening example?

These liberal studies accomplish this goal, that whoever has pursued them can speak well, and strives always to act well. These are the distinctions of the greatest men and the most exceptional minds.

Poggio Bracciolini and Cencio Romano, Book Hunters

In the last months of 1416, while assembled at Constance (Konstanz, modern Germany) for a general council of the church, a group of papal secretaries went on an outing to a nearby monastery that housed, they had heard, a horde of old books. It was a treasure trove, in fact: full of fine copies of classical texts, including a few priceless books that had been lost to view. The two letters presented here by Cencio Romano dei Rusticci (1380/1390– 1445) and Poggio Bracciolini (1380–1459) document the find itself, as well as the excitement of the humanist book hunters who won the prize.

---

first generation of Italian Hellenists, among them Leonardo Bruni, Francesco Filelfo, and Guarino Guarini.

31. The word "free" in Latin, the root of our English word "liberty," is embedded in the concept of the liberal arts—a connection that modern educators occasionally forget.

The Council of Constance, the fifteenth ecumenical council of the Roman church, met from 1414 to 1418 on the shores of Lake Constance (German: *Bodensee*) in the shadow of the Swiss Alps to resolve matters of fundamental importance about the future of the papacy, the nature of church governance, and the threat of heresy. During these four years three popes were set aside and a new pope selected with a mandate for reform; and, infamously, Jan Hus, the leader of a Bohemian reform movement deemed heretical, was burned at the stake.

Yet amid these epic events, at least some of the cohort of papal secretaries in attendance—these were lay members of the church bureaucracy needed to record minutes and draft documents—had other things on their minds. Italians steeped in the classical tradition, they longed to hunt for books, which the famous monasteries that peppered this alien land north of the Alps housed in abundance. Those books, crafted over centuries by monastic scribes, are the indispensable link between ancient and modern times. Had they not been copied, as early as the eighth and ninth century, from ancient prototypes, much of the Latin tradition would have been lost—for with the exception of a few papyrus scrolls and fragments and some late-ancient parchment books, nothing from the classical era physically survives. While many of these books had been copied in numbers sufficient so that the early humanists, like their medieval predecessors, had access to them, some existed in unique copies in remote locations—their value often not recognized by the more recent monastic occupants, whose discipline had slackened over time.

This was the situation that our humanists encountered in 1416 on their outing into the Alps to the abbey of Saint Gallen, founded in 719, just twenty miles from Constance. There they had the good fortune to discover new books; and we have the good fortune to have their letters recounting the adventure. The letters of Poggio and Cencio are typical humanist products—both familiar and chatty, on the one hand, and formal on the other, self-consciously presenting the writer and his doings to maximum advantage. Yet they are remarkable for their freshness: rarely do humanist letters narrate in detail the events of daily life, as these do, providing eyewitness accounts of a historic recovery of ancient texts.

The papal secretary Cencio, a humanist of secondary stature, writes to his colleague and mentor Francesco da Fiano, who is known to have had a notable library and to have written, like Boccaccio, in defense of the classical tradition. After a few words of introduction in which he encourages Francesco to write, Cencio comes to the point: "In Germany there are many libraries full of Latin books," he writes, leading him to hope that some "which were thought to be entirely lost" might be found in the abbey of Saint Gallen. So he and his companions Poggio Bracciolini and Bartolomeo da Montepulciano set off on an outing that had splendid results. In the library itself, they found fine exemplars of works by the Latin authors Flaccus, Pedianus, Lactantius, Vitruvius, and Priscian, as well as a rare late-ancient papyrus compilation of miscellaneous literary works. But the real treasure was in the basement of the adjoining tower: "But when we entered the tower standing alongside the church of Saint Gallen, in which were imprisoned as captives a nearly infinite number of books, and examined that library, debased and defiled by dust, worms, dirt, and all other things pertaining to the destruction of books, we broke out in tears, recognizing that this was how the unsurpassed glory and honor of the Latin language had been expunged."

Cencio blames the monks, who should have cared for these precious works, but were "completely illiterate" and a "mob of barbarians." But why should we be surprised at their irresponsibility, he continues, when daily, in Rome, marauders destroy monuments of antiquity—presumably to deter any reverence for the pagan gods associated with them; he goes on to suggest that capital punishment would be warranted for those "who destroy the *studia humanitatis,* who injure the liberal arts, and who indeed deprive humankind of its proper nourishment, without which men can live only a bestial life?" Reminiscent of Boccaccio and Vergerio, who defended the classical tradition and lamented its passing, Cencio calls on his teacher to "write something against these enemies of the splendid monuments of antiquity," and by doing so, "win for yourself immortal honor, and for them, eternal shame."

Poggio Bracciolini, unlike Cencio, belongs to the first rank of humanists, and following his career with the papal curia, he rose to the high position of chancellor of Florence, the principal city of the Italian Renaissance. So too does Guarino Guarini, to whom he writes, one of the first Italians to master the Greek as well as the Latin tradition. Poggio promises Guarino a letter of special import, then seems to wander off with a standard humanist celebration of reason, which distinguishes humans from the beasts, and eloquence, without which the products of the mind cannot be communicated. But this is all preparation for the introduction of Quintilian, the first-century CE Latin author of the *Principles of Oratory,* the most important classical work on the subject. The humanists had known from references in other texts that this work existed, but they had only fragments of it—"so mutilated, so mangled, ravaged, no doubt, in the toils of time"—which did not permit them to reconstruct its full import.

But in the bottom of a derelict tower at Saint Gallen, they found a complete, clean manuscript of Quintilian—one of the major humanist finds during this era. Poggio mentions, as well, the recovery of Flaccus and Pedianus that Cencio had named, and says that he has copied all of these "by my own hand." These copies he had sent off to two others of their circle: Leonardo Bruni, who would become, after Poggio himself, chancellor of Florence; and Niccolò Niccoli, a Florentine collector and connoisseur. Guarino, he knew, would want a copy as well, but Bruni's claim was preeminent: "Leonardo must be satisfied first." Revealing in this coda the existence of a network of humanists who shared intellectual values and circulated works among themselves—what the Venetian Francesco Barbaro would famously name the "republic of letters"—he counsels Guarino to claim his own copy of the recovered Quintilian: "But you know where it is, so that if you wish to have it (as I think you will right away) you can easily obtain it."

For these literati, the ancient authors are alive; they are real, and so are their books. Strikingly, both Cencio and Poggio describe the books they found in the Saint Gallen tower as living, but tormented, human beings. Cencio says that the books there were "imprisoned as captives," and attributes these words to them: "Lovers of the Latin language, do not allow me to be annihilated by this awful neglect; rescue me from this prison, whose darkness even the light of learning cannot illumine." Poggio goes further. In an extended passage, Poggio speaks of Quintilian's book—not Quintilian, the author, as Petrarch would have done, but the book itself, the physical object—as a living creature. Quintilian's work had been so mutilated "that it was impossible to recognize in him"—the book—"his form or his nature." Since the discovery, "our sorrow and grief on account of this man's"—the book's—"mutilation" has turned to rejoicing, for "he"—the book—"has been restored to his original condition and worth, to his ancient form and complete good health." They had "recovered this one and unique star of the Roman firmament . . . not merely from exile, but virtually from annihilation," for if they hadn't come when they did, "he"—the book again—"would have died the next day"; indeed he, the book, looked "[d]ejected, dressed in tatters as though in mourning, with unkempt beard, hair matted with dirt," as though he was about to be marched off to "an unjust execution." But Poggio and his friends came just in time and "found Quintilian"—once again, the book—"still safe and sound but full of mold and mired in filth."

Such a protracted metaphor of book as man, a man who can suffer pain, humiliation, death, and restoration to health, in the hands of a master author like Poggio, is surely intentional. In it, he gives expression to the passion for the classical past that the humanists were engaged in unearthing—sometimes by recovering books from a trash heap, sometimes by reclaiming the meanings that they contained. This moment of humanist fervor is a turning point in the history of the Western intellectual tradition, after which all is changed.

Poggio Bracciolini, *Letter to Guarino Veronese* (Constance, 15 December 1416)

I know well that, on account of your generosity to all and your particular kindness to me, even when you are pressed you always welcome the arrival of my letters. Yet I beg you earnestly to pay special attention when you read this one: not because there is anything special about me that should claim the attention even of a person without pressing business, but because of the worthiness of the matter about which I shall now write, which I assure you, knowing how vastly learned you are, will bring you great pleasure, as it will to other men of learning. For by eternal God, what is there that could be either to you or to others among the literati, more pleasing, more delightful, more welcome, than the knowledge of those things which make us more wise, and what is even more important, more elegant in our power of expression.

> *Poggio celebrates the endowment of the human species with intellect and reason by Nature, and above all for the faculty of speech, and expresses gratitude to those who transmitted to us "the rules and norms of proper speech," allowing us to "greatly surpass the common run of men."*

Many excellent Latin authors were expert in the crafting and adornment of the language, as you know, yet of these one stands out conspicuously: Marcus Fabius Quintilian, who so skillfully and with such absolute mastery established the principles that pertain to the training of the ideal orator, that he may be judged supreme in both the highest learning and exceptional eloquence. From this man alone, even if we did not have Cicero, the father of Roman eloquence, we would have acquired the perfect science of proper oratory. But up until now, here among us in Italy, he had been so mutilated, so mangled, ravaged, no doubt, in the toils of time, that it was impossible to recognize in him his form or his nature. . . .

We should mourn, surely, and weep, that we had caused by the cruel mutilation of so eloquent a man so great a calamity for the art of oratory. But however great then was our sorrow and grief on account of this man's mutilation, more greatly now are we to be congratulated, since by our diligence he has been restored to his original condition and worth, to his ancient form and complete good health. For if Marcus Tullius Cicero rejoiced when Marcus Marcellus returned from exile[32] . . . what now should learned men do, and especially those devoted to eloquence, when we have recovered this one and unique star of the Roman firmament . . . not merely from exile, but virtually from annihilation? For God knows, if we had not brought aid, he would have died the next day. Nor can it be doubted that this splendid man, cultivated, elegant, conscientious, humorous, could not have endured any longer the foulness of that prison, the filth of that hole, the savagery of the guards. Dejected, dressed in tatters as though in mourning, with unkempt beard, hair matted with dirt, he seemed by his face and bearing to declare that he had been sentenced to an unjust execution. He seemed to reach out, to implore the citizens of Rome to protect him from unfair judgment, to rage and complain that he who had once by his support and eloquence defended many, now could find neither patron to take pity on his misfortune nor anyone at

---

32. Cicero, *In Verrem,* 2, book 4.

all to look out for his welfare or save him from being subjected to an unjust punishment.

But . . . [b]y a stroke of good fortune—partly his, but even more ours—while we were at Constance with time on our hands, a longing seized us for seeing that place where he was kept captive: that is, the monastery of Saint Gallen, about twenty miles from Constance. And so several of us set out, both for our amusement, but also to hunt for books, of which it was said there were a great number. There amid a huge pile of books which it would take too long to itemize, we found Quintilian still safe and sound but full of mold and mired in filth. For these books were not in the library, as their worth required, but in a kind of dark and loathsome prison at the base of a tower, where not even criminals condemned to die would be incarcerated. Yet I know for certain, that if others like us rummaged through these barbarian dungeons in which they detain these prisoners, and recognized them to belong to our ancestral heritage, those authors would have experienced a fate similar to that suffered by Quintilian, which we now lament.

Besides Quintilian, we found the first three books and half of the fourth of the *Argonautica* of Gaius Valerius Flaccus, and some a commentary or digest of eight of Cicero's orations by Quintus Asconius Pedianus, a most accomplished author whom Quintilian himself mentions. These I copied by my own hand, and with great haste, so that I might send them on to Leonardo Bruni and Niccolò Niccoli, who when they learned from me about the discovery of this treasure, pressed me urgently in their letters to send them Quintilian as soon as possible.

My dearest Guarino, you now have from me all that a man most devoted to you can offer at the moment. I would have liked also to be able to send you the book, but Leonardo must be satisfied first. But you know where it is, so that if you wish to have it (as I think you will right away) you can easily obtain it. Farewell, and love me, as I do you.

Cencio Romano, *Letter to Francesco da Fiano* (Rome, summer 1416)

Cencio opens by reproaching his friend for not having written of late, and sends this letter as proof of his own continued intention to write to Francesco.

In Germany there are many libraries full of Latin books. That fact aroused my hope that various books of Cicero, Varro, Livy, and other great authors, which were thought to be entirely lost, might come to light, if only a serious investigation were launched. So a few days ago, our zeal kindled by the fame of the library, Poggio Bracciolini, Bartolomeo Montepulciano, and I set out together for the town of Saint Gallen. As soon as we entered the library we found *Jason's Argonautica* by Valerius Flaccus, written in shimmering and powerful verse falling not far short of poetic majesty.[33] There, too, was a book that epitomized the arguments of some of Cicero's orations, making patently clear the legal procedures and principles of ancient times.[34] Also found was a book small in size but prodigious in the quality of its eloquence and wisdom: Lactantius' book on the creation of man,[35] where he plainly refutes the reasoning of those who have declared the human condition to be lower and more wretched than that of the beasts. We also found in this trove Vitruvius' *On Architecture*[36] and the grammarian Priscian's commentary on some of Virgil's poems.[37] In the library, too, was an unusual book whose pages were of papyrus, made from reeds called *libri* in Latin, from which, according to Jerome, the word book, *liber* in Latin, derives its name.[38] This book was over-brimming with odds and ends of things, yet I devoutly embraced it for the sake of its pure and sacred antiquity.

---

33. The version of the Argonaut tale by Gaius Valerius Flaccus written c. 70 CE, based largely on the earlier Greek work of Apollonius of Rhodes.

34. This would be the *Orationvm Ciceronis qvinque enarratio* (commentary on five of Cicero's orations) written between 54 and 57 CE by Quintus Asconius Pedianus (9 BCE–76 CE), of which Poggio's copy, made on the spot, is the earliest surviving exemplar. See the recent edition of Pedianus' *Commentaries on Speeches of Cicero,* ed. and trans. R. G. Lewis, Jill Harries, and Albert C. Clark (Oxford: Oxford University Press, 2006).

35. Cencio writes "Lactantius on the two types of man," but the book he saw must be the *De officio dei vel formatione hominis* by the Latin Christian author Lucius Caecilius Firmianus Lactantius (c. 240—c. 320 CE), sometimes entitled simply *De officio hominis,* discussing God's creation of man, in which the human being is described as perfect in form, gifted with reason, and endowed with an immortal soul. See Ludwig Bertalot, "Cincius Romanus und seine Briefe," in *Studien zum italienischen und deutschen Humanismus* (Rome: Edizioni di storia e letteratura, 1975), 2:145n4; and the recent edition of the Latin text with French translation and commentary by Béatrice Bakhouche and Sabine Luciani (Turnhout: Brepols, 2009).

36. Marcus Vitruvius Pollio (born c. 80–70 BCE, died after c. 15 BCE), author of the most important ancient work on architecture, which enormously influenced Renaissance practitioners.

37. Priscianus Caesariensis (fl. 500 CE), whose work on the principles of grammar became the standard for the subsequent era, also wrote a schoolbook guide to Virgil's *Aeneid* (the *Partitiones xii. versuum Aeneidos principalium),* which Cencio and his friends found at Saint Gallen.

38. Cencio is not familiar with papyrus, which was the universal writing material of late antiquity; it was processed from Egyptian papyrus reeds, few exemplars of which survived into the fifteenth century, whereas book pages were made of parchment at first, and later paper, in the Middle Ages. Cencio refers to the substance as the "bark of trees." Bertalot identifies the manuscript in question, "Cincius Romanus und seine Briefe," in *Studien,* 145n6, and corrects Cencio's attribution of the etymology of *liber* to Isidore of Seville, rather than Jerome, at 145n7.

We have of course made copies of all of these books. But when we entered the tower standing alongside the church of Saint Gallen, in which were imprisoned as captives a nearly infinite number of books, and examined that library, debased and defiled by dust, worms, dirt, and all other things pertaining to the destruction of books, we broke out in tears, recognizing that this was how the unsurpassed glory and honor of the Latin language had been expunged. Surely if this library were able to speak for itself, it would shout: "Lovers of the Latin language, do not allow me to be annihilated by this awful neglect; rescue me from this prison, whose darkness even the light of learning cannot illumine." The abbot and monks who dwelled in that monastery were completely illiterate. What barbarous foes of the Latin language, what a damned sewerful of men!

But why do I assail this mob of barbarians for their neglect of letters, when the Romans themselves, progenitors of the Latin language, have more gravely wounded and more harshly abused the language, supreme above all others, that we have inherited from them? . . .

Cencio laments the destruction of libraries and monuments by the ancients themselves, and by their successors in Rome, especially its Christian rulers and popes.

They should be condemned all the more, because it is their responsibility to oppose all kinds of evil. . . . We should hurl curses at this crude and brutal stupidity. And you, my teacher, who excel as an author of both poetry and prose, write something against these enemies of the splendid monuments of antiquity. If you do so, you will win for yourself immortal honor, and for them, eternal shame.

Chapter 2: Explorations of the Self

Introduction

Modern "humanism," as encountered in polemics in the press and in daily life by adherents to a secular ethical code centered on human nature and possibilities, places the human being front and center, free of any religious framework. Renaissance humanism is, as seen in the previous chapter, a different phenomenon: it is grounded in the study of the Greek and Latin classics, which embody outlooks that were sometimes at odds with, yet ultimately blended with, contemporary Christian ones. Yet Renaissance humanists, like modern ones, were appreciative of human capacity and creativity. And some humanists delved deeply into questions about the human condition. Four of them are featured here: two who reflect in a personal and discursive way on human existence, fascinated by its complexities and idiosyncrasies, and two who grasp the horns of the bull, confronting with the philosophical tools at hand, including those of both ancient and medieval origin, the problem of human nature. What does it mean to be human? What is the value of human life? All four marvel at the human being; all four do so without disposing of God. These four thinkers, writing between 1351 and 1588, are Francis Petrarch (1304–1374), already introduced in Chapter 1; the Florentine patrician and diplomat Giannozzo Manetti (1396–1459); the scion of the princes of the tiny feudal state of Mirandola, Giovanni Pico (1463–1494); and the French nobleman and public official, Michel de Montaigne (1533–1592).

Petrarch and Montaigne, the first and fourth of these figures, offer intimate reflections on their own humanity and on the human condition more broadly. They address their readers directly, as though conversationally. Petrarch addresses a single letter to an unknown audience of future readers—the letter *To Posterity* (written around 1351 and subsequently revised) of which excerpts are given here—inviting them to get to know him better. Montaigne addresses the readers of his three books of *Essays* (published originally in 1580, 1582, and 1587), a literary form of which he was the inventor and the prodigious producer, in a brief prefatory letter, *To the Reader*, and then again, repeatedly, in the essays themselves, which constitute dialogues between Montaigne and his audience: the essay excerpted here, *Of Experience*, typifies that approach. Each author speaks as "I," not interposing a buffer between himself and the reader. And each takes a special interest in the readers' own inclinations and motivations: Petrarch muses that perhaps his reputation has reached them; Montaigne archly suggests that they might more profitably use their time than in reading his essays. These two authors, more than any others before modern times, expect their readers to be curious about their lives and attentive to their eccentricities.

In the body of these texts, both Petrarch and Montaigne give an informal account of their existence, with a stress on the quotidian. Petrarch notes that he needs eyeglasses to read; Montaigne speaks of the deep joy he feels upon walking, all alone, in a garden. Montaigne feels no need to place the events of his life in any order. Petrarch, in contrast, does offer a chronologically-ordered review of his career, but it engages both him and us less than the more colloquial opening section of his letter. Both delve into their own personalities and share the details with their readers, demonstrating a complete embrace of the complexity of human individuality.

Manetti and Pico, two participants in the brilliant Florentine Renaissance of the fifteenth century, pursue philosophical inquiries into the nature of the human condition. Their language, although fluid and readable in the humanist mode, is formal and impersonal: their audience does not consist of friends known or unknown to be admitted into the circle of their intimacy, but of the whole of the world of learning. The project they take on is colossal: it is to demonstrate the *dignitas hominis*, the "dignity" or value of the human being. Each has a particular concern. Manetti's is to counter the prevailing view of the human condition as miserable: prone to sin, weak in body and mind, trapped by mortality. He responds in his extensive treatise *On the Dignity of Man* (1452/1453), utilizing a full array of classical authors and, especially, the Greek philosopher Aristotle, as well as drawing on his knowledge of the Bible. Pico's task is to justify the claim made for the excellence of the human condition: given that Man is the greatest of all creatures, what philosophical explanation can be made to explain his greatness? In responding in his *Oration on the Dignity of Man* (1486), Pico draws on an even broader array of authorities than Manetti had, and authorities of a different sort: Plato and various Neoplatonic and other late ancient thinkers, as well as the Hermetic and Kabbalistic mystical traditions. Both place their visions within a Christian cosmos, although Manetti's understanding of human value is more conventionally Christian than Pico's, who stays within but presses against the boundaries of Christian thought.

The argument for the dignity of man is for many observers the central contribution of humanism, leading to a modern concept of human dynamism and capacity. A famous and still invaluable anthology of humanist texts published in 1948 by three distinguished scholars, long a staple of undergraduate classrooms and still in print and read, marks the high-water point of that assumption.[1] Today, more than sixty years later, scholars of humanism

---

1. Ernst Cassirer, Paul Oskar Kristeller, and John Herman Randall, eds., *The Renaissance Philosophy of Man* (Chicago: University of Chicago Press, 1948).

acknowledge the centrality and, indeed, the monumentality of the humanist discussion of human dignity, but they see it as interwoven with many other themes in a complex tapestry of literary, philological, anthropological, historical, and religious memes, infusing the others but not dominating the whole. Nonetheless, to the extent that the Renaissance is the era when humanist advocates place the human being confidently front and center, the four authors presented here are among the most important figures to voice that new claim.

Petrarch

The previous chapter presented two of Petrarch's ten "letters to classical authors," which he appended to his collection of his *Familiar Letters*. Here we consider another of Petrarch's letters, that he addressed "to posterity," and that he planned to append to the collection of his *Letters of Old Age*. In both cases, we are looking at this most prolific author, who wrote in many genres and is considered equally fundamental in two language traditions, through the single genre of his letters—and rather idiosyncratic letters, at that: the former written to persons long dead, the latter to those not yet born. Passing by his important Latin works on the solitary life, on his quarrel with Aristotelian philosophy, on the lives of famous men, and on his own life, not to mention the large corpus of his Italian vernacular poems, and even the letters he wrote to contemporaries about issues of current moment, we focus on these. We do so because they shine a special light on Petrarch's humanism, and in a brief space identify unique aspects of his thought. The letters to classical authors, as has been seen, illuminate Petrarch's outlook on the ancient world. His letter *To Posterity* illuminates his understanding of himself.

To write a letter about oneself to an audience yet unborn is an act of stupendous originality and, some might think, arrogance; all the more so because Petrarch must have begun the work while still young—before 1351, the date of the last event noted, when he was not yet 40—even if he has reached old age before he sets his pen down. Even in our own day, not all authors permit themselves to assume a readership well into the future. In the fourteenth century, when the notion of a celebrity author had not yet emerged, it is striking that Petrarch does so. His words are modest, but the assumption that precedes them is immodest in the extreme: that his literary works have enduring value, and that his ideas and perceptions will move readers in a different time and place to wonder about their creator. A letter *To Posterity* is an unprecedented construct, a statement of personal import that could never again have the same effect. Any later author who attempted such a communication would be seen as a mere imitator. Petrarch here seizes his place in history.

The letter consists of two parts. In the first few introductory pages, of which nearly the whole is included in the excerpt that follows, the author gives to his readers in future ages an account of who he is: what he looks like, how he thinks, what moves him. In the remainder of the letter, somewhat longer than the introductory section, of which only a few extracts are presented here, he traces his career from his birth in Arezzo until his departure for France in 1351. The first section gives us in a nutshell an autobiography of the inner man; the second, slightly more expansively, gives us a chronicle of the outer one. The boldness of Petrarch's thought is mainly apparent in the first section.

Petrarch approaches his imagined audience courteously and modestly. He is not certain that his "poor and obscure name" will have traveled to his readers through "time and space"—although he would not have penned the letter if he did not think it would have done so! He assumes that they will want to know about his books, if they have heard of these, and, audaciously, something about who he is. He presents himself as ordinary: in social origin, in moral character. But he is not so ordinary, for he has developed over time, through experiences that, as he fully realizes, changed him: "Youth deceived me and manhood corrupted me, but age corrected me." As for physical characteristics, he was not especially strong, but agile; not especially handsome, but with glowing skin and bright eyes. Age has changed him: he now reads with "the aid of a lens," and suffers "the usual array of ills."

Petrarch did not pursue riches, not because he didn't crave wealth, but because he could not tolerate anxiety. He avoided lavish banquets, but greatly enjoyed the company of a small circle of friends. As a young man, he fell terribly in love: "I was troubled by love of the fiercest kind." That experience of love—his enduring love for the elusive Laura, which was at the root of his creative work—he admits was accompanied by lust when he was young, although he has now transcended that vice, while the lady herself has died.

He admits to the passions of pride and anger, but returns again to his enjoyment of friendship, and in his old age, his sadness that so many friends have died. Among those with whom he had a kind of friendship were great men, princes and rulers, who sought him out and showered benefits upon him: "The greatest monarchs of my age loved and honored me."

Describing his intelligence as "balanced" rather than "penetrating," Petrarch describes his love for poetry and moral philosophy, and more recently, the study of the Bible, "finding a hidden sweetness in [it] that I had once despised." Above all, he liked to study ancient times, and wished that he had lived then and not in the present age: "If love of those dear to me had not pulled me in a different direction, I would have preferred to have been born in any other age and to forget this one." Accordingly, he read history, making his way through variant accounts of the past. He admitted he "never aimed at eloquence" in conversation, although a high tone was much valued in his day: "For myself, so long as I lived righteously, I set little store by how I spoke."

With these remarks on eloquence, Petrarch comes to the end of the first part of his letter, launching the second part with the announcement of his birth, to honorable parents, exiled in Arezzo, on July 20, 1304. Quickly reviewing childhood stays in Arezzo, Incisa, and Pisa in Italy, he describes his boyhood in Avignon (modern France), the city to which at that time the papacy had been removed: "I spent a boyhood that was guided by my parents, and then an entire youth that was guided by frivolous pleasures." In Avignon and nearby Carpentras, he "learned what little grammar, dialectic, and rhetoric I could learn at that age, or what can be learned in schools," adding disparagingly: "You can guess how little that means, dearest reader." Then prodded by "the watchful eye of my father," he studied law for several years at universities in Montpellier (France) and Bologna (Italy), giving up that vocation before he began it. For the next two decades, he journeyed through France, Germany, and Italy, at the invitation of wealthy and powerful patrons, stopping in Padua at the warm invitation of Jacopo da Carrara the Younger, its ruler. But Jacopo died—in fact, he was assassinated—and Petrarch soon returned to France, in 1351, where both this narrative and the letter end: "I did not know how to stay still, and was driven less by the desire to see again places I had seen a thousand times than to attempt, as sick people do, to cure my ills by changing location."

Petrarch offers his future readers a charming account, only a few pages long. It touches on his character and quirks, his intellectual makeup, his love for his friends and for one woman in particular, his impatience with institutions and posturing, his restlessness and his openness to what experience and study will bring. It documents well the life of a man who does not boast of greatness, yet embodies it.

Petrarch wrote his letter *To Posterity* over time, and frequently revised it, as was his regular practice with his correspondence. Its final revision came in 1371–1372, as his life was drawing to a close; and given its importance as a statement about his life, the author places it deliberately as the last item, the only letter of the final Book XVIII, of his collected *Letters of Old Age*. Despite its high importance and frequent revision, however, the letter is unfinished: Petrarch stops his account of his life in 1351, when much of his major work was yet to be written. All this is fitting. In the letter, Petrarch allows the reader to glimpse who he is, and who he is, like the letter, is still fluid and in process.

Petrarch, *To Posterity* (1351/1372)[2]

Perhaps you will have heard something about me, although it is uncertain whether my poor and obscure name will travel far through time and space. And then perhaps you will want to know what kind of man I was and what

---

2. From Petrarch, *To Posterity (Ad posteritatem)*, in *The Essential Petrarch*, ed. and trans. Peter Hainsworth (Indianapolis, IN; Cambridge, MA: Hackett Publishing Co., 2010), 237–44.

happened to the books I wrote, especially those whose reputation has reached you, or of which you have heard some vague report. . . .

I was . . . one of your race,[3] a mere mortal man, of neither particularly high nor particularly low origins. . . . In character I was neither vicious nor immodest, except in so far as I was infected by bad behavior in others. Youth deceived me and manhood corrupted me, but age corrected me. Thus I have learned from experience the truth of something that I had read much earlier, that is, that youth and pleasure are vanities. Or rather I was given the lesson by the Creator of all times and ages, who sometimes allows wretched mortals to swell up with baseless pride and to go astray solely in order that they may sooner or later become mindful of their sins and come to know themselves. As a young man, I was not especially strong physically but very agile. I do not boast of being exceptionally good-looking, but in my greener years I had a certain appeal. I had a healthy complexion that was neither too pale nor too dark, and quick eyes. My sight was very sharp for a long time, although it became unexpectedly much weaker in my sixties when I had to resort reluctantly to the aid of a lens. My body was always very sound, until the coming of old age beset me with the usual array of ills.

I was a stern despiser of wealth, not because I did not want riches, but because I hated the efforts and worries that are their inseparable companions. I had neither the means for splendid feasts, nor the bother that comes with them. . . . I always found so-called banquets distasteful, considering them excuses for gluttony and inimical to modesty and decency. I thought it was profitless and wearisome to invite others for such a purpose and also to accept invitations myself. However, I found the company of my friends such a pleasure that I could think of nothing more satisfying than their visits and never willingly took food without company. I disliked luxury particularly, not merely because it is a bad thing in itself and contrary to my humility of spirit, but because it creates difficulties and disturbances. In my youth[4] I was troubled by love of the fiercest kind,[5] although it was a single, honorable love, and I would have been troubled by it for longer if its already cooling fires had not been extinguished by a cruel but beneficent death. I would like to be able to say that I was quite free from physical lust, but I would be lying. I can say with certainty, however, that even when the fervor of youth and my own tem-

---

3. By "race," Petrarch intends "the human race."

4. The word Petrarch uses is *adolescentia*, which denotes the ages fourteen to twenty-seven: see Hainsworth ed., n3.

5. Petrarch is describing his love for Laura, the quasi-fictional woman who is the subject of his vernacular poems, which create the modern genre of lyric poetry centered on (mostly heterosexual) desire.

perament carried me away, in my heart I always deplored lust as something contemptible. Then, as my fortieth year approached, when I was still quite susceptible, and quite vigorous too, not only did I put aside the obscene act itself but also all memory of it; it was as if I had never looked upon a woman. I count this one of my prime sources of happiness, and thank God who freed me, still hale and flourishing, from a servitude I felt to be so vile and loathsome.

But, to turn to other things, I was aware of pride in others but not in myself. Though I was of slight importance, I always judged myself to be of less. My anger hurt me often enough, others never. I can boast fearlessly—for I know I speak the truth—that I was quickly incensed, but forgot offenses just as quickly, while remembering kindnesses done to me. I eagerly sought out honorable friendships and cherished them faithfully. A torment reserved for age, however, is to have to shed tears with increasing frequency for close friends who have died. I was fortunate, even enviably so, in my familiarity with princes and kings and in my friendships with men of noble rank. But in spite of deep attachments I kept away from many of them. So deeply rooted in me was my love of liberty that I strenuously rejected any who found the word itself unpalatable.[6] The greatest monarchs of my age[7] loved and honored me. I do not know why and guess it was up to them. But sometimes it was not a case of my looking for their company as much as they wanting mine. I was not incommoded by their eminence, but rather derived many advantages from it.

I had a balanced rather than a penetrating intelligence, one that was fitted for all forms of virtuous, healthy study, but was especially drawn to moral philosophy and poetry. In the course of time I left the latter alone and took great pleasure in the Holy Scriptures, finding a hidden sweetness in them that I had once despised, and treating poetic writing as purely ornamental. Among my many activities I devoted myself particularly to the study of antiquity, since I always disliked the age in which I lived. If love of those dear to me had not pulled me in a different direction, I would have preferred to have been born in any other age and to forget this one, striving always to penetrate other times at least in spirit. So I took pleasure in the historians. When I was disturbed by disagreements between them, I dealt with the problem by following the version of the facts that seemed most probable, or was put forward by the most authoritative writers. My formal speech, some people said, was clear and forceful, although to me it seemed weak and muddled. But really,

---

6. He is presumably defending himself against those who criticized him for accepting the patronage of the Visconti rulers of Milan: Hainsworth ed., n4.

7. He is probably alluding particularly to Robert of Anjou, king of Naples, and the emperor Charles IV, king of Bohemia: Hainsworth ed., n5.

in ordinary conversation with friends and acquaintances I never aimed at eloquence. . . . However, when the topic, the occasion, or the audience seemed
to require something more, I did try to raise my tone. How effectively I do
not know, and leave judgment to those who were present. For myself, so long
as I lived righteously, I set little store by how I spoke. That glory is mere wind
that seeks renown only through the glitter of words.

> *Here begins, extending to the end of this unfinished letter, a review of*
> *Petrarch's career to 1351.*

My parents were honorable. Originally from Florence, they were middle-
ranking but, to tell the truth, verging on the impoverished. Since they had
been driven from their home city, I was born in exile, in Arezzo in the year of
our Lord 1304, around dawn on Monday, 20 July.

Chance and choice have divided my lifetime so far as follows. I spent not
quite the whole of my first year in Arezzo where nature first thrust me into the
light of day. My mother's exile having been revoked, the next six were spent
at Incisa, about fourteen miles upriver from Florence, on a farm belonging
to my father. My eighth year was spent in Pisa, and the ninth and subsequent years in Transalpine Gaul on the left bank of the Rhône in the city of
Avignon, where the Roman pontiff has long kept the church of Christ in disgraceful exile, although it seemed a few years ago that Urban V had restored
it to its rightful home.[8] . . . So there, on the bank of the windswept river,[9]
I spent a boyhood that was guided by my parents, and then an entire youth
that was guided by frivolous pleasures.

Not that there were not lengthy absences. I lived a full four years of this
time in Carpentras, a small town not far to the east of Avignon. In these two
places I learned what little grammar, dialectic, and rhetoric I could learn at
that age, or what can be learned in schools. You can guess how little that
means, dearest reader.

I then went to study law at Montpellier, where I spent another four years.
From there I went on to Bologna, where I stayed another three, studying the
whole body of civil law.[10] I was a young man who would have gone far, in the
opinion of many, if I had persisted. But I abandoned my legal studies completely as soon as the watchful eye of my father was removed. . . .

---

8. The papal court moved to Avignon in 1309. Pope Urban V moved it back to Rome in
1367, only to return to Avignon in 1370, where he died that December: Hainsworth ed., n8.

9. The Rhône: Hainsworth ed., n9.

10. Petrarch studied in Montpellier from 1316 to 1320 and effectively spent six years, not
three, at Bologna (1320–1326): Hainsworth ed., n10.

Petrarch proceeds to detail his travels and literary pursuits from his early twenties through his forties, during which he spent time in France and Germany, and in Rome, Naples, Parma, and Verona in Italy. In 1348, he settled in Padua (Italy) for two years, under the protection of its signore, Jacopo da Carrara the Younger.

My reputation had long won me the favor of Jacopo da Carrara the Younger,[11] a man of real excellence, who I think, or rather am certain, had no equal among the lords of his time. For years I had been subjected to letters and communications from him, even when I was beyond the Alps and wherever I was in Italy, seeking to establish a friendship with me. Though I hoped for nothing from anyone privileged by fortune, I finally decided to go and see what a great man whom I did not know was so insistent about. . . . My reception by that man who has left such a luminous memory behind him, did not merely show human warmth, but resembled the reception blessed souls must be given in heaven. He was overjoyed and displayed unimaginable affection and concern, so much so that I cannot find adequate words to describe his behavior and will add nothing more. . . . All told, if he had lived longer, it would have meant the end of all my wanderings and journeying. But, alas, there is nothing lasting for mortal men, and any sweetness that befalls has a bitter end. God granted him to me and his city and the world for less than two years, and then took him away. . . . He was succeeded by his son,[12] an outstanding man of great practical wisdom, who followed his father in always holding me dear and honoring me. But I had lost one who was much closer to me, not least in years, and I returned to France.[13] I did not know how to stay still, and was driven less by the desire to see again places I had seen a thousand times than to attempt, as sick people do, to cure my ills by changing location.[14]

Petrarch's letter ends here, bringing us to 1351, when he was forty-seven years old, with much of his literary and intellectual work still ahead of him. Although the letter is an incomplete record of his career, he did revisit the part of it we have in his later years.

---

11. Jacopo was the ruler of Padua from 1345 until his assassination in 1350: Hainsworth ed., n27.

12. Francesco da Carrara, expansionist ruler of Padua from 1355 until his death as a prisoner of the Visconti [rulers of Milan] in 1392: Hainsworth ed., n28.

13. Petrarch arrived back in Vaucluse in the summer of 1351; it was to be his last stay there. He moved definitively to Italy in 1353: Hainsworth ed., n29.

14. The letter is incomplete and undated: Hainsworth ed., n30.

Giannozzo Manetti

If Petrarch was a self-absorbed wanderer, a man who belonged only to himself, Giannozzo Manetti was embedded within the urban environment unique to northern Italy. He was a Florentine, a citizen of one of the leading centers of the burgeoning Renaissance. He was a member of the city's elite, or patriciate: a descendant of a mercantile family who had engaged in the enterprises of banking and textile production that made the city one of the wealthiest corners of Europe. He was in one other significant way a product of the Florentine patriciate: in a pattern that was rare though not unknown elsewhere, he was highly educated—expert not only in Latin but also both Greek and Hebrew—and an enthusiastic participant in the classical studies that were the defining core of humanism. The humanist Manetti authored, among other works, translations of the New Testament and of Aristotle, biographies of Dante, Petrarch, and Boccaccio, and a consolatory dialogue on the death of his son. His most important work, however, is the treatise *On the Dignity and Excellence of Man.*

Thus Manetti was not, as was Petrarch, a professional author and thinker. He was primarily a diplomat, sent out to represent Florentine interests at other Italian cities and courts. It was a diplomatic commission that in 1452 brought him to the court of Alfonso, a prince of the ruling house of Aragon (modern Spain), and, by conquest, king of the southern Italian realm comprising the island of Sicily and the city of Naples, known simply as *il Regno,* "the kingdom." Here at Alfonso's request—who had already received one work on the subject and found it lacking—Manetti wrote a refutation of those who had argued the wretchedness of the human condition. Manetti's *On the Dignity and Excellence of Man,* conceived thus in the context of inter-Italian tensions and scholarly rivalries, rises well above the circumstances in which it was created. It is a pioneering work, a celebration of human existence bolstered by persuasive philosophical and religious arguments.

Manetti's principal opponent is the thirteenth-century pope, Innocent III, who had written on the misery of the human condition. For Pope Innocent, the human being is born in filth, and wails in pain from the outset; he suffers from bodily weakness and spiritual loss; his whole life is a burden until he is rescued by God. These arguments Manetti confronts not only with a humanist's optimism about the potentiality of the human spirit, but a quiver full of arguments from ancient pagan, biblical, and early Christian authors who recognized, in contradiction to Innocent, the joy experienced by human beings from exercising their mental, physical, and spiritual faculties. The differences between Innocent's views and Manetti's are stark; indeed, their positions are polar opposites, to such a degree that readers, falling too quickly into a trap, can easily liken them to the difference between the medieval and Renaissance "outlooks," or between the religious and secular mindsets. But such a reading is simplistic; for Manetti does not reject the past, but revisits it; and he does not repudiate religion, but employs its meanings to new ends.

Manetti's work *On the Dignity and Excellence of Man* consists of four substantial chapters, or "books," totaling 144 pages in a modern edition of the Latin text (cited below). The excerpt here consists of a few passages taken from the fourth, culminating, book: a very small selection from a large and closely-reasoned presentation. In this fourth book, as Manetti explains with sharp clarity, he will review, first, the arguments others have made against the soundness of the human body; then those against the excellence of the human soul; and finally, against the worthiness of the whole person. Having done so, he will refute these arguments in turn, ending with an affirmation of his claim to the preeminence of the human condition. The passages presented here pertain to the first and third issues—the critiques of the human body and of the whole human person—because they articulate Manetti's most stunning and original positions.

With regard to the human body, where his opponents had enumerated the weaknesses, diseases, and discomforts to which it is prey, Manetti argues the body's essential goodness. The human body is inherently both mortal and immortal, he maintains. It is only because Adam sinned that its immortal destiny is set aside until the ultimate moment of resurrection. Bodily weakness, therefore, derives from sin, and not from the body itself, which is the wholly good creation of God. As he sums up this point, "All the wailing and lamenting of both secular and sacred writers about the body's deficiencies . . . must cease and desist, since . . . that condition did not proceed either from God himself or from nature, which he created, but is the product of sin."

All well and good, Manetti imagines his critics respond; but nonetheless, for whatever reason, the body is subject to many deficiencies. To which Manetti counters that the pleasures we experience exceed the problems: "For there is no activity undertaken by man, wondrous to say, . . . from which he does realize at least some small delight." He then enumerates the pleasures derived from the external senses of seeing, hearing, smelling, tasting, and touching. To these he adds also the experiences of the "interior senses": those engaged in the mental activities of conceptualizing, analyzing, measuring, remembering, and understanding, from which are derived "a pleasure that words cannot satisfactorily express or explain."

The high valuation placed on the physical and intellectual functions of the body—the latter, interestingly, assigned to body and not to soul—is a new note: one ultimately derived from ancient philosophy, but as formulated here, quite original and specific to the humanist outlook. In the final section of the fourth book, as Manetti responds to the critics of the whole person of "man"—effectively, those who doubt the worthiness of the human condition—he is equally original, neither so secular nor so materialist as in his defense of the human body.

In this last section, Manetti's opponents are those who point to "the many discomforts and sorrows of human life," which lead some to prefer death in theory, and others, who take their own lives, to do so in practice. But God created all things good, Manetti responds; thus the claims of these critics are self-evidently false. Discomforts there may be, but the human being who senses them does so because of his rational capacity, itself the unique creation of God, and one that destines him for eternal life. The rational soul permits the human being to experience the highest forms of pleasure, so that "during his entire life, from the moment of his birth until his death, at all times and forever, man experiences delight." And it enables him to achieve, at the moment of resurrection of both body and soul, the "Vision of God, the sweetest and most glorious of all sights," which is the *summum bonum* (highest good), the greatest fulfillment that can be experienced by humankind.

In closing the fourth book, and the whole of his work *On the Dignity and Excellence of Man*, Manetti restates his arguments presented in the first few books—"first, how great and how wondrous is the dignity of the human body; second, how lofty and sublime is the human soul; and third, consequently, how excellent is the nature of man that is composed of these two elements"—and underscores the purpose of the fourth, that is, the refutation of his opponents on all these points. He summons his listeners, finally, addressing King Alfonso and all other "kings, princes, [and] emperors" to reject vice, and pursue virtue: "love it, follow it, reach for it, . . . engage it, embrace it, since by continual and determined acts of virtue we are not only made blessed and happy, but we are remade . . . in the image of the immortal God. . . . [and] will with him live in perpetual and eternal blessedness and pure delight, rejoicing evermore, singing songs of exultation and jubilation."

Manetti's culminating argument against those who denigrate the human condition is Christian, and profoundly so. It is grounded in his study of biblical and patristic texts, and integrated with a philosophical outlook that was fed by his study of ancient and unmistakably pagan philosophy. For those who continue to maintain in the face of abundant evidence that Renaissance humanism was secular—a quite different claim than the patently true argument that its proponents were more often lay than clerical—the case of Manetti must be confronted: a politically active layman and paradigmatic humanist from fifteenth-century Florence, virtually the epicenter of the Renaissance. For he is and remains a Christian as he integrates the classical tradition with the more recent European one, utilizing the recombined intellectual synthesis in his consideration of what it means to be human.

Giannozzo Manetti, *On the Dignity and Excellence of Man* (1452/1453)

Up to this point, in the preceding three books, I have reviewed in order and clearly and plainly explained, so far as my small competence allowed me to do, everything important that pertains to or illuminates the unique and special dignity and excellence of man. It seems, then, that the right and fitting time has come to bring this work to an end. And I would do so now, except that it is essential to investigate those things which, as I have read, many ancient and modern authors wrote either to praise death, or to lament the misery of human life, especially since their views contradict the points I have earlier made.

> *Manetti will first discuss the arguments of other authors about the weakness of the human body; then their arguments about the failings of the human soul; and finally their objections about the whole person of man. Having reviewed their charges, here Manetti brings to culmination his own case for the goodness of the human body.*

Desiring greatly to rebut and disprove all the points enumerated above, I shall proceed to their refutation in the same order in which those objections were laid forth. So beginning with the body, I shall boldly respond to complaints about its fragility and other failings. Our Catholic[15] experts attest that the human body, which the omnipotent God crafted from the mud of the earth, was made so that it would be in part mortal, allowing the First Man to sin, as we know that he did; but also in part immortal, as it would become if he had not sinned. Thus the first man was endowed with a body that was somehow both mortal and immortal: which leads to the question whether he possessed both these attributes because of the original condition of his body, or whether rather its immortality derived from the gift and favor of divine grace. In either case, as the experts argue, in his first state, his condition was such that if he had willed it to be so, he could have been, without doubt, immortal. In his second state, however, they maintain, having sinned, he so lapsed from his original condition that, degenerate and debased, he fell subject to the certain and relentless law of death. But in his third state, that of his glorious resurrection, they hold, he shall achieve a state so wrought by grace that he shall no more be destined to die. This state I shall describe at the end of my work, with God as my helper, in greater depth and detail.

Thus the weakness of the human body, beset by all sorts of illnesses and

---

15. At the time Manetti wrote, there were as yet no Protestant churches. The term "Catholic" here refers to writers within the Western Latin Christian tradition, as distinct from both the ancients and contemporary Greek Orthodox, Jewish, or Arabic thinkers.

the medley of other discomforts which I earlier posited, derives not from
nature, but from sin. . . . All the wailing and lamenting of both secular and
sacred writers about the body's deficiencies, therefore, so great that death
would be preferable, must cease and desist, since, as we see, that condition
did not proceed either from God himself or from nature, which he created,
but is the product of sin.

Still someone may yet object: let all that be granted, but the outcome is
the same. Whether the weakness of human bodies proceeds from nature or,
as you assert and attempt to prove, from sin, those bodies, nonetheless, have
become and remain prey to frailty, sickness, and death, and a host of other disabilities. Since these great disabilities burden the human body whatever their
source may be, or from wherever derived, still this burden has existed since
the beginning of the world: for from the moment of its birth and throughout
all time, clearly, the human body has been subject and slave to the law of
death, and other attendant evils.

There is truth in these arguments, I agree, and others like them, yet I
would dare to respond . . . that we experience more pleasures than problems in our ordinary, everyday lives. For there is no activity undertaken by
man, wondrous to say, if we carefully and closely examine its nature, from
which he does realize at least some small delight. Indeed, the exterior senses
of seeing, hearing, smelling, tasting, and touching, regularly produce so
many and such powerful pleasures, that they may at times be felt as excessive and overwhelming. How many are the pleasures that human beings may
experience—sometimes from the vivid sight of beautiful bodies, at other
times from hearing exquisite sounds and complex symphonies, or from smelling the aroma of flowers or other such scents, or from tasting diverse types of
sumptuous delicacies and elegant wines, or, finally, from touching the softest
objects—is difficult to say, or rather, it is impossible.

What shall I say about the other, interior senses? How great is the pleasure
obtained from observing and discerning the attributes of material things provided by the senses which, in their sum, the philosophers call the "common
sense"? What great delight do we take as well in conceiving in our minds
the great diversity of substances and accidents; what delight in judgment?
In memory? In sum, in understanding? When those things which we have
apprehended by one particular sense, we then proceed to conceptualize, ana-
lyze, measure, remember, and understand, experiencing a pleasure that words
cannot satisfactorily express or explain.

Accordingly, if in living their daily lives men experience more delights and
pleasures than they are tormented by pains and trials, they should rejoice and
celebrate rather than wail and lament—especially since nature furnishes us
abundantly and sufficiently with sure remedies for the chills and fevers, pains
and spasms and diseases that we suffer, antidotes for these ills that are not

harsh, bothersome, or bitter, like many of those often found in pharmacies, but rather mild, smooth, sweet, and pleasant. For when we eat and drink these, we delight in the miraculous cessation of hunger and thirst; likewise, when we are feverish, or chilled, or somnolent, in the same way we find relief. . . .

To sum up, then: all those who examine the nature of things with any diligence, and consider it with a modicum of care, will dismiss as frivolous, empty, and fatuous all these complaints and charges about frailty, chills, fevers, pains, hunger, and thirst, things that smell foul or taste bitter, visions and sensations, lassitude, sleeplessness and sloth, food and drink, and other similar inconveniences encountered in human existence.

> *Having disposed of the complaints against the soundness of the human body, and subsequently accusations against the human soul, Manetti now turns to a defense of the complete human being.*

Finally, we come to the charges that are made against the whole human being, considering first which authorities addressed the matter and then the arguments they present. Those authorities include Hegesias, Crantor, Alcidamas, Cicero, Pliny, Herodotus, Euripides, Cleombrotus, Socrates, and Cato[16]— some of whom praised death, while others actually took their own lives in order to escape in death the many discomforts and sorrows of human life.

From the outset, we shall find the ancient opinions of these gentile writers[17] to be entirely untrustworthy, since they are wholly at odds with the Catholic and Christian position. Clearly, all things created by God are good, as Holy Scripture testifies, and as has never been doubted in any age by anyone of sound mind. So if this is the case, then certainly we cannot properly doubt or deny that man, for whose sake all things were certainly made good and, more, as best as they could be, is not only an excellent being but even, if I may say so, more than excellent. The human existence, therefore, that man is said to live, cannot be or become wholly miserable; for then it would follow that that which has been shown to be excellent lives a life of continual and unrelenting misery. But since this is manifestly false, it must be concluded that, indisputably, the allegations made by the poets, orators, and philosophers who have spoken or written on the misery of human life are untrue, empty, and absurd.

The truth of this argument that has been demonstrated above is also

---

16. Manetti names a sequence of distinguished ancient thinkers and authors: the Greek philosophers Hegesias of Cyrene, Crantor, Socrates, and Cleombrotus of Ambracia, a follower of Socrates as portrayed in Plato's *Phaedo*; the Greek rhetorician Alcidamas; the Greek historian Herodotus; the Greek tragedian Euripides; and the Roman authors Cato, Cicero, and Pliny, the Elder or Younger.

17. By "gentile writers" Manetti means the Greek and Roman ancients.

confirmed by the renowned testimony of the blessed Augustine,[18] who wrote these words in the twelfth book of *The City of God*: "Just as it is better to be a creature that feels, even if it is in pain, than a stone, which feels no pain, so a rational being is superior, even when miserable, to one devoid of both reason and sense and which, consequently, cannot be miserable. Since this is so, this being was endowed with such excellence that, although its nature is subject to change, yet by adhering to a good that is changeless—that is, to the *summum bonum [the supreme good]*—it may achieve salvation."[19]

> *Dismissing the cases of figures like Cato, who committed suicide, Manetti argues, in part to pursue a kind of personal immortality, and disputing the negative messages of Christian authorities (Ecclesiastes, Job, Saint Ambrose, and Pope Innocent III), Manetti asserts that human life is characterized more by pleasure than by pain, both here on earth and in an ultimate state of resurrection.*

Wherefore it follows that during his entire life, from the moment of his birth until his death, at all times and forever, man experiences delight. . . .

The same kind of response can be given to the problem raised about the many worries and various anxieties of humankind, lest I linger on such clear and evident matters longer than the nature and complexity of the issue seem to require or demand—especially since all the complaints about human existence posed earlier, as well as any new ones which could still be raised and argued, are easily dismissed and fully and definitively refuted by a consideration of the resurrection of our bodies at the end of time. For when we rise from the dead, then our old bodies will be gloriously transformed into new ones lacking any stain, or corruption, or weakness, or any kind of deformity; they will not only be wholly and entirely free of all the failings, flaws, and all other defects which now torment us so much each and every day, but they will also be radiant with every possible ornament of exquisite beauty. . . .

> *After enumerating seven qualities that will be experienced by our resurrected bodies—health, youth, beauty, freedom from sin and suffering, perfect rest, and endless joy—Manetti reflects on the profound joy felt by the risen saints who experience the Vision of God.*

Anyone who knows even a little bit about sacred things is aware that the joys of the saints are many and great, indeed infinite. Above all, they enjoy the Vision of God, the sweetest and most glorious of all sights . . . [and] behold that splendid presence, in which is contained as in a marvelous mirror all things human and divine. The great magnitude of happiness that will

---

18. Saint Augustine (354–430 CE), prominent Christian theologian.

19. Augustine, *City of God*, XII.i.46–55.

be derived from perceiving that Beatific Vision, as it may be called, cannot be adequately described or imagined. For if the sight of gems, or stars, or of graceful and lovely human bodies delight us immensely, how much more shall we delight in the vision of the omnipotent God! Indeed we shall feel such great delight that we shall rejoice forever and without end, with boundless and infinite joy. This wondrous and incredible happiness that we shall experience from this divine vision will surprise no one who has realized that all created things, wherever they are, are so reflected in the face of God that to all who look upon him they appear brighter, as they say, than the light of day, and more vivid. . . .

What more can be said about this insuperably immense and infinite happiness . . . when our Christian scholars have most emphatically stated in their doctrines that the Vision of God is the full and fitting reward for a holy life? When the blessed come to recognize the superb and admirable conditions of their glorified bodies—lightness, loveliness, sprightliness, painlessness, agility, and agelessness—conferred upon them as matchless gifts and unique privileges, they will rejoice incredibly and beyond all limit. For the bodies of the saints will be so filled with light, that there is nothing in this human world that can be compared to such great and overpowering splendor.

After further discussion of the glorious condition of the blessed in heaven, and the correspondingly horrible fate of the damned, Manetti draws his work to its conclusion.

Wherefore, so that I may put an end to this discussion and bring this work to a close, in which I have expounded at length and completely in the foregoing three chapters, first, how great and how wondrous is the dignity of the human body; second, how lofty and sublime is the human soul; and third, consequently, how excellent is the nature of man that is composed of these two elements. In this fourth chapter, finally, I have taken care sufficiently to debunk and confute those arguments which appeared most to oppose and resist my views. It remains for me to exhort those now living and those yet to come to diligent and careful obedience to the divine commandments in the short space of our human existence, so that we may justly deserve to ascend to an eternal home in paradise. . . .

For which reason I summon and beseech the readers of this work, whoever they may be, to put other things aside and attend diligently to this brief and loving little exhortation, so that they may live and act in the ways that I shall try here briefly to encourage them to do. O men, or rather, O brave and worthy men, and indeed, O kings, princes, emperors, you have been established and commissioned in such great dignity and excellence that all things in the world, whether on earth, or in the seas and rivers, or in the air, the ether, or the heavens, were made to be subject and subordinate to your rule and sway, do not in any way doubt what I have written here, but let virtue be your goal. Suppress and crush vice, but love virtue with all the force of your mind and body; love it, follow it, reach for it, I entreat you, engage it, embrace it, since by continual and determined acts of virtue we are not only made blessed and happy, but we are remade, as it were, in the image of the immortal God . . . [and] will with him live in perpetual and eternal blessedness and pure delight, rejoicing evermore, singing songs of exultation and jubilation.

Giovanni Pico della Mirandola

Giovanni Pico della Mirandola takes the discussion of human nature to a level beyond that entered into by his two Italian humanist predecessors. Petrarch, appropriately for a thinker critical of systematic philosophy, was interested in the foibles and eccentricities of a specific individual: himself. Manetti, while as much a humanist as Petrarch, employed his considerable knowledge of ancient philosophy and Christian theology to construct a rational defense of human excellence, countering a pessimistic strain of medieval thought. Like Manetti, Pico is concerned with the human condition in the abstract, rather than with particular individuals. He also, like Manetti, brings a vast store of knowledge—indeed, a vaster one, for Pico was one of the most erudite men in Europe, a genius of immeasurable intellectual energy—to bear on the question. Where Manetti tilted toward the Aristotelian tradition, however, placing a high estimation on sensory experience, Pico tilted toward the Platonic, the other major and only recently fully explored ancient Greek school, and to other, later, and more mystical streams of thought: Neoplatonic, above all, but also Hermetic, Syriac, Christian, and Kabbalistic. Uniting these variegated ideas into a complex amalgam, Pico turned to the question of the human condition and identified the source of uniqueness: freedom. In Pico's vision, the human being is uniquely free, alone of all cosmic beings, except perhaps for God.

Pico composed the *Oration on the Dignity of Man* under extraordinary circumstances, which had dramatic consequences. It was not intended to stand alone but was conceived as a preface to a set of "questions," or philosophical points, that in 1486 Pico invited the learned of Europe to debate with him, face to face, in Rome, the city of the popes. It was no small set of issues that Pico defined: 900, in fact, the number itself bespeaking a kind of bravado normally foreign to the conventions of scholars. The issues Pico raised emerged from his studies, in multiple languages (Greek, Latin, Hebrew, Arabic, and "Chaldean," the neo-Aramaic language of the Syriac

Orthodox church), of the diverse philosophical traditions described above. Although they were phrased within a Christian framework, the author's philosophical syncretism scandalized some theologians, who complained to papal authorities, who in turn launched an investigation. The papal commission identified 7 of Pico's 900 theses as heretical, and 6 more as problematic. Pico promptly issued a defense of his views, but prudently thought it best to flee Rome—this was a time when charges of heresy were seriously prosecuted. After fleeing first to France, he took refuge in Florence, the vortex of Renaissance artistic and intellectual culture, under the protection of that city's unofficial ruler, Lorenzo de' Medici. He did not return to Rome, but after some years as a follower of the Christian prophet Girolamo Savonarola, he died in 1494 at the youthful age of thirty-one. His *Oration on the Dignity of Man* was never delivered as intended.

The discussion of human freedom in the opening paragraphs of Pico's *Oration*, given here, is closely related to the discussion that follows in a work that reaches more than thirty pages in length in a modern translation. If the human being is free to choose his own destiny, as Pico famously argues, then, should he spurn lesser things, and choose to ascend to the heights of human knowledge, he will need to inquire into philosophy. The arguments for human freedom occupy the opening pages of the *Oration*, accordingly, while its great bulk is devoted to an overview of the major philosophical traditions—and all of this together is prefatory to the 900 questions, or theses, which are the product of the philosophical investigations detailed. The whole project—oration and theses together—are conceived as a unity. Yet modern readers are irresistibly drawn to the initial discussion of human excellence.

The *Oration* begins, as Pico greets the "worthy Fathers" he expected to be assembled as an audience, with a statement of the problem: that no satisfactory explanation has been given for the assumed "greatness of the human condition." The reasons that have been offered—the role humans play as intermediaries between creatures, and the sharpness of human senses, and the power of the human intellect, among others—are inadequate: "For why should we not admire more greatly the angels themselves and the blessed heavenly choirs?"

So Pico pursued the issue, and has found an answer: he has identified what that condition is "to which [man] has been assigned in the universal system, to be the envy not only of brute beasts, but of the stars, and of the minds beyond this world." This is why the human being is uniquely wonderful and worthy of admiration. "But now hear, Fathers," he says, "what is the nature of the human condition, and . . . attend to what I have to say."

God completed his Creation, Pico explains, combining the narrative of that event in the biblical book of Genesis with the assumption of a hierarchically-ordered cosmos inherited from ancient Greek science, having filled each region with appropriate creatures: angels in the heavens and animals in the air, on the earth, and in the sea. All places had been filled;

all tasks were assigned. But God, "the Artisan," was not satisfied. There was no creature in his Creation to admire the universe he had constructed, "and wonder at its magnitude." Since it was impossible to create another creature with an assigned role and purpose, the divine solution was to create a being who belonged to no specific place, with no fixed functions. So finally, "the chief Craftsman determined that since he could give his new offspring nothing proper to himself, he would bestow upon him, as a composite, all the unique qualities that had previously been given to others."

In this way, God created man, an exception in the cosmos, "a creature of indeterminate form." Setting Adam—as Genesis had named the first man—"at the midpoint of the world," God gave him his instructions. He had been given no specific place and no specific function, and so he was free to claim whatever seat, whatever form, whatever abilities he himself preferred. God predetermined the nature of all other creatures, but God made Adam "neither mortal nor immortal," so that "as the maker and molder of [himself]," he may determine his own nature.

These are extraordinary words. They look ahead to the existentialism of modern times as much as to ancient cosmology. They identify the human condition as contingent, multivalent, and indeterminate. It is Adam who will "fashion" himself, and be his own "maker" and "molder"—the words Pico chooses, with all deliberation, just as he names God as the great "Artisan," evoke the explosive creativity of the epoch in which the author lived. God is the creator of the universe, and the creator of man; but he creates man as a being who may create himself. Pico's vision is unprecedented, its era-defining originality as potent as its narration—barely 1000 words—is concise.

Since Adam has all the capacities of God's creation available to him—God having created his nature as a compendium of everything else he had created—he may choose either to descend or ascend the ladder of God's creatures, which is to say, the hierarchy of the cosmos. If he develops his bestial or vegetable capacities, he will be as stupid and violent as the beasts, or as lazy and stagnant as the reeds and grasses. If he cultivates his rational and intellectual nature, he will become like an angel. Or he can reach higher, and become godlike himself, essentially merged with the essence of the divine: "becoming one with the spirit of God, in the solitary darkness of God who is set above all things." He is capable of being all things: the "chameleon" of God's cosmos.

Pico provides this narrative prologue, he explains, so that we should understand the purpose of what is to come. If freedom is the essential quality of human nature, then we should exercise it for the best, choosing to exercise our rational and intellectual capacities, not those also possessed by vegetables and beasts: "May a certain holy ambition invade our mind," unwilling to stand in second place to the angels, "we shall emulate their greatness and glory."

At the end of these ruminations, Pico turns again to his audience, whom he had addressed at the outset. He will not apologize for the great number of his theses; had he stretched his points, as others do, he would have had nearly an infinitude. He had intended to show "not so much that I know many things, as that I know things of which many know nothing." That said, his discourse will no longer delay the disputation he had prepared, but now, "as if at the sound of a trumpet, let the battle begin."

Note should be made of the strong visual impact of the opening sections of Pico's *Oration*, already implied in the comments on the author's allusions to the arts. The cosmos he has inherited from ancient philosophers, and which he fully accepts, is plainly hierarchical: base substances and creatures inhabit its lower reaches, and rational and angelic creatures, culminating in God himself, the upper ones. Superimposed on this framework, almost like an elevator poised before an iron grid, is the figure of the solitary human, "Adam." Adam alone has mobility, desire, and choice. The human being is not only excellent and wondrous, fit to praise God's creation; but the human being alone has the qualities that can possibly lead to meaningful action. If Renaissance humanism had produced no other apprehension, this one would have been sufficient.

Pico's *Oration on the Dignity of Man* is a concise statement of the Renaissance philosophy of man at its height, when humanistic thought had absorbed Aristotelian, Platonic, and other traditions. It is not Pico's only work, by any means. In his last years in Florence, he was especially pro-ductive of philosophical works representative of his project to show that all truths that the philosophers and theologians had uttered were concordant and were one: among these, notably his *On Being and the One* (1491). Indeed, Pico's ambition to demonstrate the One Truth was as bold as his proposal to defend 900 theses in a public arena in Rome.

Giovanni Pico della Mirandola, *Oration on the Dignity of Man* (1486)

I have read in the books of the Arabs, worthy Fathers, that when Abdul the Saracen was asked what in all the spectacle of the world he found most admi-rable, he said that nothing existed more wonderful than man. To his opin-ion, this one of Hermes Trismegistus may be added: "How great a wonder, Asclepius, is man!"[20]

Turning over in my mind what might be the basis of these claims, it seemed that the many explanations that many have proposed for the great-ness of the human condition are insufficient. They have argued that man

---

20. *Asclepius* I.6, in *Hermetica, the Ancient Greek and Latin Writings Which Contain Religious or Philosophic Teachings Ascribed to Hermes Trismegistus*, ed. Walter Scott, 4 vols. (Oxford: Clarendon Press, 1924), 1:294.

is the intermediary among all creatures, a servant to those above him, the superior of those below. Or that his acute senses, his inquisitive mind, and his luminous intellect make him the interpreter of nature. Or that he is the link between changeless eternity and shifting time, and the knot, as the Persians say, that binds the world together—indeed, the marital knot. Or that his rank is just "a little lower," as David testifies, "than the angels." [21]

These are all fine arguments, but they are not the principal arguments, such as could justly merit the prize of the highest admiration. For why should we not admire more greatly the angels themselves and the blessed heavenly choirs?

At last I have realized why man is the most fortunate of all creatures, and so worthy of complete admiration, and what, finally, is the condition to which he has been assigned in the universal system, to be the envy not only of brute beasts, but of the stars, and of the minds beyond this world. It is a wondrous thing, beyond belief. And why should it not be so? For on this account, man is rightly said and deemed to be a great miracle and a creature worthy of admiration.

But now hear, Fathers, what is the nature of the human condition, and with friendly ears, as befits your generosity, attend to what I have to say.

Now God the Father and highest Architect had already built by the laws of his unfathomable wisdom this world that we see, our home, and a most sacred temple of divinity. He had adorned the supercelestial region with minds; he had enlivened the ethereal spheres with eternal souls; he had filled the excrementary and filthy parts of the lower world with creatures of every kind. But when the work was done, the Artisan longed that there might be someone who could comprehend so great a creation, appreciate its beauty, and wonder at its magnitude.

And so, when all else had been accomplished, as the Bible and Plato report, God turned his mind at last to the creation of man. [22] But there were no archetypes left by which to fashion a new creature, and nothing left in the treasury to bestow on a new heir, and no seat anywhere in the universe where this new contemplator might sit. For all things were complete; all things had been distributed to the highest, the middle, and the lowest orders. But it was not in the nature of his paternal potency to fail in this final act of creation; it was not in the nature of his wisdom to waver for lack of inspiration in so necessary a matter; it was not in the nature of his beneficent love, that he who would praise God's generosity shown to others, would curse its absence in regard to himself.

Finally, the chief Craftsman determined that since he could give his new

---

21. Psalm 8:5.
22. Genesis 1:26–27; Plato, *Timaeus*, 41b ff.

offspring nothing proper to himself, he would bestow upon him, as a composite, all the unique qualities that had previously been given to others. So God made man a creature of indeterminate form, and placed him at the midpoint of the world, and addressed him thus:

> Adam, you have been given no fixed place, no form of your own, and no particular function, so that you may have and possess, according to your will and your inclination, whatever place, whatever form, and whatever functions you choose. Divine law assigns to all other creatures a fixed nature. But you, constrained by no laws, by your own free will, in whose hands I have placed you, will determine your own nature. I have placed you at the center of the world, so that you may easily survey all that is in the world. I have made you a creature neither of heaven nor of earth, neither mortal nor immortal, so that exalted and empowered as the maker and molder of yourself, you may fashion yourself in whatever form you choose. You will have the power to degenerate into the lower forms of life, which are bestial. You will have the power, by the judgment of your soul, to be reborn into the higher forms of life, which are divine.

O supreme generosity of God the Father! O supreme and stupendous felicity of man, to whom it has been granted to have whatever he wants and to be whatever he wishes! From their birth, beasts are equipped . . . with all they will ever possess. At creation or a moment after, lofty spirits have already become what they will be perpetually throughout eternity. But on the new creature Man, the Father has conferred the seeds and germs of every living thing and every kind of existence, so that he will himself become the fruit of whichever of these he cultivates. If he cultivates what is vegetative, he will be like a plant; if what is sensual, he will be like a beast; if what is rational, he will become a celestial being; if what is intellectual, he shall be an angel and the son of God. And if he chooses to be no one kind of creature, but withdraws into the center of his own unity, becoming one with the spirit of God, in the solitary darkness of God who is set above all things, he shall exceed them all. Who will not wonder at this chameleon that is man? What else is there anywhere more worthy of wonder?

For it is not the bark that makes a tree, but its unthinking and unfeeling nature; nor the hide that makes the ox, but its bestial and sensual soul; nor do the spheres make the heavens, but their perfect order; nor is an angel an angel because it has no body, but because it has a transcendent mind. For if you see a man ruled by his belly, like a snake slithering in the mud, it is not a man but a plant that you see. If you see someone who has been enslaved by his senses, blinded by the vain tricks and fancies of Calypso[23] and corrupted

---

23. The seductive goddess who imprisoned Odysseus for years: Homer, *Odyssey*, 7:240–69.

by fleshly enticements, it is not a man but a beast that you see. If you see a philosopher who judges all things according to right reason, revere him: for he is a celestial not a terrestrial being. If you see a pure contemplator who knows nothing of his body, but has withdrawn to the innermost places of his mind, he is neither a terrestrial being nor celestial: he is a most sacred spirit clothed in human flesh. . . .

May a certain holy ambition invade our mind, so that not content with lesser things we thirst after higher ones, and—since we can do it if we wish to—we valiantly pursue these with all our strength. Spurning earthly things, disdaining celestial ones, despising all that is of this world, let us soar to that place that is beyond the world and stand in the presence of Almighty God. There, as the sacred mysteries reveal, the Seraphim, Cherubim, and Thrones, hold the first rank; unwilling to yield to them or accept a lesser place, we shall emulate their greatness and glory. If we will it to be so, we shall be no less than they. . . .

After a long discourse on various philosophical schools and views, Pico turns again to his audience, comments on the abundance of his theses, and invites them to the debate.

And still my critics pursue me like barking hounds, saying that I have heaped up a pile of trivial and silly issues just to put on a huge show, as if these were not questions that are vigorously disputed and requiring debate, over which the gladiators of the academy have contended; and as if I had not brought my own original and never-tested theories to the attention of these very men who attack me, and consider themselves princes among philosophers.

Far from needlessly multiplying propositions as I have been accused, I have carefully structured my argument under the fewest possible headings. If I had wished—as others often do—to dice it up and divide it into all its parts, it would have grown indeed to an innumerable number. . . . But this I shall say emphatically—for I shall say it, although immodestly and quite unlike myself, since those who envy me force me to say it, my detractors force me: I wanted to show in this contest of mine not so much that I know many things, as that I know things of which many know nothing.

But so that the plain facts may be laid out before you, worthy Fathers, my protracted oration will delay us no longer—as is your wish, excellent Doctors,[24] who I am delighted to see are ready and armed and eager for the fight, may it be fortunate and favorable. Now, as if at the sound of a trumpet, let the battle begin.

---

24. The "Doctors" are the university-trained philosophical scholars Pico wishes to engage in his disputation, as opposed to the "Fathers," the eminent prelates, who are the audience to which he directs his oration.

Michel de Montaigne

Writing a century after Pico, more than a century after Manetti, and more than two after Petrarch, Montaigne's outlook and approach are strikingly different than those of his Italian predecessors. Like them, he inquires into the human condition and finds it good, at least in part because God made it so. Like Petrarch, he thinks that ordinary people will be interested in the ordinary events of his life. Like Manetti, he relishes the delights conveyed by the senses. Like Pico, he finds the mind to be a spacious place, dwelling in which brings human existence closest to its greatest possibilities. But unlike the Italian humanists—even unlike Petrarch, who has some of the same resistance to order that characterizes the Frenchman—Montaigne rejects system. His message is his method, and his method is wandering, associative, and fluid, as are, in his view, the qualities of the human mind, and the nature of the human heart. In consequence, Montaigne is both an easy read and a difficult one: easy because he demands no long expanses of the reader's attention; difficult, because the route he takes through the wilderness of his thoughts is easily lost.

The distance between Montaigne and earlier humanist writers on the human condition is the product not only of time, but also of space and circumstances. Montaigne was a French nobleman (a status his father acquired, not unusually for the era, by purchase) and a public official. He belonged to the elite of a society long accustomed to hierarchy and was identified with a monarchical regime; in contrast, the northern Italian towns that nurtured the first generations of humanists were complex societies, made up of a diverse range of mercantile, clerical, bureaucratic, and feudal strata, and shared, if nothing else, an aversion to kings. Montaigne lived in a castle, not in a busy alleyway just steps from the piazza that was the center of political and all other public business. He was surrounded by warfare, of the kind that most pained him, driven by religious allegiances, and complicated by persecution and intolerance. No wonder he found in his own mind matter more to his liking that what he observed all around him.

Like the Italian humanists—and we may consider Montaigne a French humanist, although not all his readers would agree—Montaigne was immersed in the classical tradition. The immersion began in early childhood, when Montaigne's father hired a tutor to teach the precocious infant Latin, and commanded that members of the household speak to the boy in no other language. He learned Latin before he learned French, or his local dialect, and by the age of six was dispatched to a boarding school where his conversational Latin would be honed by the ceaseless perusal of the classics. In later life, when he began his great writing project comprised of his *Essays*, a wholly unprecedented genre, he would spike the meanders of his sentences with crisp epigrammatic Latin, always ready at hand in his capacious memory.

Montaigne published his first volume of *Essays* in 1580, and by his death had composed three books of them, which he edited and corrected and assigned an editor to continue the task after his death. Of central importance is that the essay, the prose form Montaigne created, is tailor-made to present what Montaigne had to say; his readers soon recognize that Montaigne probably could not have written in any other way. Through these short prose pieces, he introduces himself to the world, as is his purpose, and introduces the literary world to a new kind of thinking and creating: a means of communication that is less rigorous but more open, free, inventive, and daring than any previously available.

The excerpts presented here illustrate the virtues of the essay as a genre, at the same time admitting us to Montaigne's conception of human nature. The first item (dated 1580), presented in its entirety, is Montaigne's opening message *To the Reader*, whom he inaugurates into his world in a few brief sentences. The remaining paragraphs are drawn from the extended essay *Of Experience*, written in 1587–1588 as the thirteenth essay in the third book of *Essays*, when Montaigne was already well advanced in his project of observing himself and his world.

Addressing his reader in the singular, because Montaigne speaks here as he does generally, from one heart to another, the author promises that the present book is written in "good faith": it admits from the outset that its purpose is purely "personal and private." He does not write it to advance his own interests, or to instruct his audience. From it, his friends will have some tidbits by which to remember him when he is gone—implicitly inviting the reader as well into that domestic circle. He has not dressed up, as for a formal portrait. Indeed, if custom permitted it in his country, he would gladly have presented himself entirely naked, so he might be more fully revealed. For the purpose of the book is to display Montaigne whole—"You see, reader, I am myself the matter of my book"—if there is any reader out there who might for some reason wish to spend his time on a subject so "frivolous and vain."

The essay *Of Experience* is as promised, like most of Montaigne's essays, about the author. It does not begin as such: it opens with the lofty philosophical statement, "No desire is more natural than the desire for knowledge." But quickly, Montaigne turns away from knowledge, so difficult to attain, and settles for experience, a "weaker tool" that may yet lead us to the truth. Indeed, knowledge is problematic, because it quickly fractures into a multitude of statements. Indeed, no two ideas are exactly alike; nor even the same idea held by a man "at different hours of the day."

For the human mind, Montaigne continues, really can't attain to certainty. It sees a distant glimmer that may be the truth, but it is an illusion—an illusion that the perceiver pursues passionately nonetheless: our spirit "struggles onwards and exceeds its strength; it surges forward beyond what is possible;

if it does not advance, charge, resist, strike, it is only half-alive." But it cannot reach what it seeks: "our end is in the other world."

With certain knowledge unattainable, Montaigne turns to himself, because he at least can know something about Montaigne: "I study myself more than any other subject." When he pursues philosophical question, his aim is only his own amusement. There is nothing wrong with being ignorant of grand matters; it is restful: "Ignorance and incuriosity compose a pillow soft and sweet, a sound resting place for a sane head." His own life, indeed, offers plenty of material: he can learn as much about living properly from consulting his own experience as by reading up on the life of Caesar, which "does not offer a better example to us than our own."

With "no other profession than to study [himself]," Montaigne finds within the limits of his own mind an infinity of knowledge—such that his ignorance, in that he does not know what the professors and savants have labeled as knowledge, is all-sufficient. Not only does he not know what the experts do, but he cannot—nor does he wish to—present his ideas systematically, as they do; rather, he presents them "without system, vaguely and tentatively . . . in disconnected parts." But that disconnection, that complexity, actually corresponds to reality, which is a synthesis of diverse elements, just as things both good and bad "are consubstantials of our existence."

Ill-health was one of those bad things in Montaigne's life: he suffered from kidney stones. From that suffering, as from other elements of his experience, he also learned. In this arena, as in others, he prefers to dwell within his own experience than to bow to the experts, in this case the doctors who lord it over him "with their dogmas and magisterial scowls, threatening me now with grave diseases, now with imminent death." But he accepts the disease as the consequence of old age—"It is our common fate, so why would I be spared by some miraculous intervention?"—recognizing that many like him also have it, and that it is not so fearful as it used to be, now that he is its victim. In fact, he enjoys being the hero, like the knights-errant of old. His friends watch him sweat and twist in pain, while he is insouciant: "Meanwhile you chat normally with those in attendance, jest now and then with your friends, join in a lengthy conversation, apologize for your pain and make light of your suffering." So he is ill, and may die; so do we all. It is not the disease that is at fault: "Death finishes you off without the help of illness."

But he does not always suffer, and still partakes of life, as when he strolls alone in a beautiful garden, returning always when his thoughts stray elsewhere "to the promenade, to the orchard, to the sweetness of this solitude, and to myself." We foolishly think that we must always be accomplishing something; it is sufficient to live. "Our grand and glorious masterpiece is to live properly." He loves the life that God has been pleased to grant him. "He is all good, and all that he does is good."

The themes reviewed here, drawn from the selections of *Of Experience* included here, go down many but by no means all of the several pathways

Montaigne roves in this important and characteristic essay. He rates experience over knowledge, diversity over system, friends over experts, and takes pleasure in life and accepts even pain as part of a dialectic between the goods and evils that are "consubstantials of our existence." Above all, he explores the capacity of the human mind and spirit, which are greater than all that the philosophers and the physicians can encompass, and wholly at peace with God and Nature.

Montaigne, *To the Reader* (1580) and *Of Experience* (1587–1588)

TO THE READER:

Here is a book written in good faith, reader. It lets you know from the start that my only purpose is personal and private. I do not plan to offer you any service, nor to win for myself any glory. My capacities are insufficient for such ends. I intend it for the particular use of my friends and relatives, so that when they have lost me (which will happen soon enough) they may be able to find here some traces of my moods and opinions, and so cultivate a more complete and vital understanding of who I was. If I had sought the world's favor, I would have dressed up more, and presented myself in a more formal posture. I want to be seen in my natural aspect, unadorned and ordinary, without artifice or contrivance: because the portrait I paint is of me. My defects will be vividly apparent, and my figure as bare as norms of public decency permit. If only I were a citizen of one of those lands which are said to live still in sweet liberty according to the primal laws of nature, then I assure you I would gladly have shown myself fully, entirely in the nude. You see, reader, I am myself the matter of my book: there is no reason for you to spend your leisure on a subject so frivolous and vain. Farewell then, from Montaigne, on the first of March, 1580.

OF EXPERIENCE

No desire is more natural than the desire for knowledge. We try every means in our power to achieve it. When reason fails us, we employ experience . . . , which is a weaker tool, and less esteemed. But truth is so great a thing, that we must not disdain any device that can lead us to it. Reason has so many dimensions that we do not know where we stand; experience has quite as many. The conclusion we wish logically to draw from the similarities between things is uncertain, because those same things are also at the same time dissimilar. There is no quality so universal among things that appear to be the same as their diversity and variety.

....

I don't know what can be said about [the diversity of opinions], but experience suggests that such a whirlwind of interpretations dissolves and disrupts the truth. Aristotle[25] wrote so that he might be understood; if he didn't succeed, still less will a less able commentator, worth but a fraction of the original author, who drew out his thoughts from his own mind. We open up the bottle, and the substance expands and dissipates; of one subject we make a thousand, which we multiply and subdivide until we land ourselves in the infinity of the atoms of Epicurus.[26] Never have two men reached the same judgment about the same matter, and it is impossible to find two opinions exactly alike held not only by two different men, but even by the same man at different hours of the day.

....

Men do not understand the inborn weakness of their mind: it hunts and seeks, and ceaselessly twists, turns, and thrashes about, as silkworms do in a bucket, and so strangles itself. . . . From a distance, it perceives some kind of illusory vision of light and truth; but in the pursuit, so many difficulties impede the way, so many traps and detours that distract and confuse it. . . . It is this peculiar weakness which leads us to content ourselves with what others, or what we ourselves have already discovered in this hunt for knowledge; a more gifted seeker will not thus content himself. There is always room for a new seeker, and yes, for ourselves, another road. Our seeking will not here reach its end; our end is in the other world. The spirit signals its evanition when it rests content, or its exhaustion. No noble spirit stops of its own accord: it struggles onwards and exceeds its strength; it surges forward beyond what is possible; if it does not advance, charge, resist, strike, it is only half-alive. Its pursuits are without limit and without form. It feeds on admiration, the attempt, and ambiguity.

....

I study myself more than any other subject. That is my metaphysics, that is my physics. . . . Immersed in this university of my own mind, I allow myself stupidly and idly to be ruled by the general law of the world—a law I shall know sufficiently when I feel it. My wisdom will not change its direction; it will not alter its path for me. It is folly to hope it will, and much greater folly to worry about it, because that law is necessarily plain, public, and common.

---

25. The ancient Greek philosopher Aristotle (384–322 BCE), whose ideas underlay much theological and philosophical thought from the twelfth through the seventeenth centuries.

26. A Greek philosopher (341–270 BCE), who followed Democritus (c. 460–c. 370 BCE) in positing that the universe was made up of atoms.

The value of being governed, and its purpose, is that it frees us utterly from the business of government.

Our philosophical ventures and musings have no higher function than to feed our curiosity. Quite rightly, the philosophers send us back to the laws of Nature; but these have nothing to do with their so-sublime knowledge. The philosophers distort those laws, presenting us with a Nature that is too pretty and too precious, from which falsification spring so many and various images of a reality that is unitary. Just as Nature has given us feet for walking, so has she given us prudence to guide our living; not the clever, puffed-up, and pompous Prudence of their invention, but the commonplace, simple, and wholesome prudence which does very well what the other one talks about, in a man who happily knows how to employ himself without pretense and in good order, that is to say, naturally. The more simply we commit ourselves to Nature, the more wisely do we do so. Ignorance and incuriosity compose a pillow soft and sweet, a sound resting place for a sane head.

I would much rather know all about myself than about Cicero.[27] From the experience that I have of myself, I find enough matter to make me wise—if I were a good student. He who summons up in memory the excess of anger he once felt, and how beyond control that fever carried him, sees the ugliness of this passion better than Aristotle did, and hates it more effectively. He who recalls the dangers he has faced, and those that menaced him, and the trivial events that altered him from one state to another, prepares himself through these experiences for future dislocations and for an understanding of his condition. The life of Caesar[28] does not offer a better example to us than our own; whether a man who rules an empire, or a man of the people, it is always his own life that is hammered by the circumstances of human existence. Let us only listen: we tell ourselves exactly what it is we need.

....

I, who make no other profession than to study myself, find there a depth and variety so infinite, that my apprenticeship has no other fruit than to make me realize how much there remains for me to learn. To my weakness, of which I am fully aware, I owe my inclination to modesty, obedience to the beliefs prescribed for me, a steady coolness and moderation in my opinions, and the hatred for the irksome and peevish arrogance of those who trust and rely wholly on themselves, the fatal enemy of discipline and truth. Listen to them

---

27. Marcus Tullius Cicero (106–43 BCE), the Roman statesman, orator, philosopher, and rhetorician.

28. Gaius Julius Caesar (100–44 BCE), great Roman general and author who brought the Republic to an end and laid the way for the establishment of an empire.

dictate: they announce their stupidities with the same weighty style used by the first founders of religion and of law. . . .

....

It is from my experience that I target human ignorance, which is, to my mind, the most impenetrable subject in the school of the world. . . . The savants divide and denote their fantasies with the greatest specificity, and in detail. I, who see nothing beyond what my experience tells me, present mine without system, vaguely and tentatively. As I do here: I pronounce my thoughts in disconnected parts, as though I speak of something that cannot be said at one time and in one block. Coherence and conformity cannot be found in base and common minds like mine. . . . I leave it to artists—and do not know if they can untangle something so confused, so meager, and so accidental—to arrange and frame this infinite diversity of appearances, and to stanch my incoherence and put it in order. Not only do I find myself unable to link my thoughts one to another, while keeping each distinct, but I find myself unable to group them properly according to some guiding category, so are their images doubled and blurred in a cacophony of lights.

....

We must learn to endure what cannot be avoided. Our life is composed, like the harmony of the cosmos, of contrary things, as it is of contrary tones—sweet and harsh, sharp and flat, soft and loud. The musician who likes only some of these has nothing to say. He must learn to make use of all of them in combination. As must we as well with good things and bad, which are consubstantials of our existence. Our being demands this mixture, and neither component is less necessary than the other. . . .

I seldom call in the doctors about the pains I suffer, because these fellows take over when they have you at their mercy. They stuff your ears full of their prognostications. Once, finding me weakened by illness, they patronized me with their dogmas and magisterial scowls, threatening me now with grave diseases, now with imminent death. I did not yield and held my own, but I was mauled and battered; if my judgment was not muddled or disturbed by them, it was certainly challenged. There is always agitation and conflict. . . .

Would you like an example? They tell me that it is for the best that I have the stone;[29] that this aging body will naturally suffer some deterioration—it is time for it to let go and break down. It is our common fate, so why would I be spared by some miraculous intervention? So I pay in this way the price of old age, knowing that I have been given a bargain. There is really no need

---

29. Montaigne was a chronic sufferer from kidney stones, from about the time he began writing his *Essays*.

to console me, as I have happened into the most ordinary complaint suffered by men of my age. I see them all around me, struck by the same disease, and I am pleased to be one of that worthy company, in that the stone tends to afflict men of stature: its essence partakes of nobility and honor. . . .

Fear of this disease, I tell myself, used to torment you, when it was unknown to you. The cries and the despair of those whose lack of courage made it worse aroused your horror. . . . The fear that people have of this disease, and the pity they feel for those who suffer it, cast glory upon you—a quality which, even though you have purged it from your mind and deleted it from your conversation, still your friends find a hint of it in your makeup. It is pleasurable to hear people say about you: "now there is strength, now there is fortitude!" They see you sweat in pain, turn pale, turn red, tremble, vomit blood, suffer strange contractions and convulsions, gush forth huge tears from your eyes, pass urine that is thick, black, and horrid to behold, or to have it obstructed by a stone bristling with spikes which cruelly pokes and tears the neck of your penis. Meanwhile you chat normally with those in attendance, jest now and then with your friends, join in a lengthy conversation, apologize for your pain and make light of your suffering.

Do you remember those knights-errant of old who avidly sought out danger, so as to hone and exercise their virtue? Consider that nature is leading and pushing you to a glorious endeavor of that sort, in which you would never otherwise have willingly entered. If you tell me that it is a dangerous, a mortal malady, which maladies are not? The doctors deceive us when they make exceptions, naming diseases that do not progress directly to death. What is the difference if they do so nonchalantly, gliding and sliding along the road that leads us to that end? But you do not die because of that which makes you ill; you die because you are alive. Death finishes you off without the help of illness. And for some, their malady has postponed death: they lived all the longer while they were busy dying. . . .

....

When I dance, I dance; when I sleep, I sleep; and when I walk alone in a beautiful orchard, even if my thoughts are tied up in other matters part of the time, the rest of the time I return to the promenade, to the orchard, to the sweetness of this solitude, and to myself. With maternal care, Nature has seen to it that the requirements she has placed upon us for our well-being should also be pleasurable, so that we comply not only by the persuasion of reason but also by that of appetite. It is wrong to oppose her laws. . . .

We are great fools. "He has lived his life in idleness," we say; "I have done nothing at all today." What, have you not lived? That is not only the fundamental but the most worthy of your occupations. "If I had been placed in a position to manage great affairs, I would have shown what I could do." Have you known how to guide and manage your life? Then you have performed the greatest task of all. To show herself and her powers, Nature has no need of fortune: she shows herself equally to all viewers, and completely, from all angles. To compose our character is our duty, not to compose books, and to win not battles and provinces but order and tranquility in our behavior. Our grand and glorious masterpiece is to live properly. All other things—to wield power, to hoard wealth, to build monuments—are at most only appendices and addenda.

For me, then, I love life, and cultivate it just as it has pleased God to grant it. . . . I accept wholeheartedly, and gratefully, all that Nature has done for me, and am pleased that I do, and praise myself for doing so. One wrongs this great and all-powerful Giver by refusing his gift, annulling it, and disfiguring it. He is all good, and all that he does is good. "All things that are according to nature are worthy of esteem."[30]

---

30. Cicero, *De finibus*, iii.6.

Chapter 3: The Civic Experience

Introduction

The Italian Renaissance, and the humanist movement that was its dominant intellectual expression, were formed during the fourteenth and fifteenth centuries in the cradle of the cities of northern Italy—about forty of them, ranging in size from a few thousand to as many as 100,000 inhabitants. The dynamism derived from intense levels of commercial enterprise and an exceptional degree of political activity fueled a remarkable burst of intellectual and artistic productivity. Not surprisingly, the civic experience is itself reflected in the products of this creative surge. In the visual arts, it is seen in the proliferation of public buildings, and in the inclusion of miniature cities in the backgrounds and margins of paintings depicting some quite different event. In humanist works, it is seen in the prominence of social and political themes, as distinct from religious, philosophical, or literary content.

So prominent, indeed, is the discussion of social and political issues in some authors and settings, that it has acquired a name in Renaissance scholarship: "civic humanism." Hans Baron, one of several modern Jewish émigré experts on Renaissance culture, is the principal architect of the concept of civic humanism, and a proponent of the hypothesis that humanism was, in essence, civic: civic humanism does not merely constitute one subset of humanist themes, but is in itself the core of the humanist movement.[1] Baron's thesis was preponderant in the decades immediately following World War II, and reached its high-water mark in the late 1970s with the publication of two important anthologies of humanist texts on political and social themes.[2] Since then, civic humanism has receded in importance as scholars have adopted a more complicated and multifaceted view of humanism.[3] Yet, undoubtedly,

---

1. For Baron's hypothesis, see especially *The Crisis of the Early Italian Renaissance: Civic Humanism and Republican Liberty in an Age of Classicism and Tyranny*, rev. ed. (Princeton: Princeton University Press, 1966), and *In Search of Florentine Civic Humanism: Essays on the Transition from Medieval to Modern Thought* (Princeton: Princeton University Press, 1988).

2. Renée Neu Watkins, ed. and trans., *Humanism and Liberty: Writings on Freedom from Fifteenth-Century Florence* (Columbia, SC: University of South Carolina Press, 1978); Benjamin G. Kohl and Ronald G. Witt, eds., *The Earthly Republic: Italian Humanists on Government and Society* (Philadelphia: University of Pennsylvania Press, 1978).

3. Among recent assessments of civic humanism, see especially James Hankins, "The 'Baron Thesis' after Forty Years and Some Recent Studies of Leonardo Bruni," *Journal of the History of Ideas* 56.2 (1995): 309–38; Hankins, ed., *Renaissance Civic Humanism: Reappraisals and*

civic themes are explicit in many humanist works, and are characteristic for some authors.

The four works presented in this chapter, composed from 1403 to 1526, are illustrative of the civic humanist strand of the humanist movement. The authors are the native of Arezzo and future chancellor of Florence Leonardo Bruni (1370–1444); the Venetian nobleman and statesman Francesco Barbaro (1390–1454); the Florentine patrician and statesman Alamanno Rinuccini (1426–1499); and the Spanish-born, self-exiled itinerant intellectual Juan Luis Vives (1492–1540). The first and the third authors, separated by nearly 80 years, reflect from different standpoints on the mission and history of Florence. The second and the third, from markedly different geographical and social origins, reflect on two social issues of pressing importance in the cities in which they lived: marriage and poverty.

Bruni's oration *In Praise of the City of Florence* (1404) finds Florence praiseworthy for its geographical setting, its physical structures, the nature of its citizens, its history, and its public institutions. In all, the city has realized to an exceptional degree the peerless ideals of justice, equity, and liberty. Three generations later, Rinuccini disagrees. Writing in exile his dialogue *On Liberty* (1479), he shows how the city's commitment to the ideals Bruni celebrates—justice, equity, liberty—have been traduced by Lorenzo de' Medici, the third of his family to rule Florence from behind the scenes through the manipulation of its constitutional machinery. Rinuccini's dark vision of a citizen body corrupted by the dictatorship, with a few transformed into flatterers and toadies and the rest cowed into silent immobility, poses a strong contrast to Bruni's optimism.

Rinuccini's outlook, like Bruni's, is overwhelmingly political. Barbaro and Vives, in contrast, address themselves to social institutions. Nonetheless, like the Florentines, they are spokesmen for a civic ideal.

Barbaro's treatise *On Marriage* (1415) probes the ramifications of selecting a wife for the well-being and effectiveness of the social elite. If young men choose wives for their beauty or their wealth, rather than for their moral character and lineage, consequences follow: the children produced by the match will be inferior by nature and inadequately nurtured by mothers of lesser moral quality. Not only will the individual be disappointed in his domestic situation, but he will be responsible for the degradation of his family and, accordingly, his city. Barbaro accepts social class distinctions unabashedly; yet

Reflections (Cambridge: Cambridge University Press, 2000); Mark Jurdjevic, "Hedgehogs and Foxes: The Present and Future of Italian Renaissance Intellectual History," *Past and Present*, no. 195 (2007): 241–68; and Hanan Yoran, "Florentine Civic Humanism and the Emergence of Modern Ideology," *History and Theory* 46.3 (2007): 326–44.

as he does so, he valorizes the woman who as wife and mother is the key to the social survival of the class whose interests he promotes.

Vives offers a different perspective in his treatise *On Assistance to the Poor* (1526). The citizens, and even more the city's governors, must assume responsibility, he argues, for the management of poverty, because it is right to do so, and because the city will be threatened by the ensuing social breakdown if the problem is not addressed. Without labeling the poor as essentially inferior to any other social group, Vives pragmatically details how different subgroups of the poor must be handled: able-bodied natives must be sent to work in trade, foreigners should be expelled, the ill must be cared for in residential institutions, children must be sent to school until they can join the ranks of laborers.

Although modern readers may approve more of Vives' empathy for the poor than Barbaro's concern for the perpetuation of a social elite, they should recognize that both equally are examining the city as a social system, in which actions taken by some groups will impact others and so affect the future of the whole organism. Social institutions and interactions, they implicitly argue, matter as much for the welfare of human society as do the political ones that primarily interest Bruni and Rinuccini.

Leonardo Bruni

In this showpiece oration—a work for paper only that was never delivered—Leonardo Bruni sums up the nexus between style, humanism, and the city that characterizes the Italian civilization of the Renaissance. As he praises Florence in a fluid and practiced Latin, he interrelates its aesthetics, ethics, and politics, the overlapping mental categories that together organize "civic life"—a phrase meaning both living in a city, and living civilly, guided by a high social and intellectual standard.

Born in Arezzo, the son of a notary, Bruni spent his youth in Florence at the dawn of that city's engagement with humanist culture. He became the protégé of the Florentine chancellor, the humanist Coluccio Salutati, and studied Greek with the Byzantine diplomat Manuel Chrysoloras, who taught in Florence from 1397 to 1400. After the interlude during which he worked in the papal Curia (1405–1414), he returned to Florence, rising to the office of chancellor in 1427, a position he held until to his death in 1444. He was a young man not long past thirty when, in 1404, he composed the work of which excerpts are given here. Consciously imitating the oration in praise of Athens by the late-ancient Greek rhetorician Aelius Aristides, Bruni offers a carefully filtered image of the city, focusing on its monuments and its political life—with only a few scattered words about the mercantile activity that sustained Florentine wealth and power.

The first section of *In Praise of the City of Florence* is a description of the physical city. From this rich rhetorical excursus he turns to the people of Florence, especially concerned to demonstrate that Florence was founded during the Republican phase of the Roman domination of Italy, and the citizens were thus descended from the free citizens of that ancient city. Next he profiles the role played by Florence in the political affairs of the northern Italian cities, showing the city to be a peacemaker and a defender of liberty against the pull of tyranny. In the final section, he describes the Florentine government system and the liberal ethos that animates it—an ethos that also supports the psychological energy and cultural attainments of its citizens. The excerpts that appear in this chapter are taken from the first and the last of these major themes in Bruni's oration.

Nestled within the walls of Florence, as Bruni describes it, "every part" of the city "is resplendent and aglow with exceptional beauty." Whereas other cities may possess some marker of excellence—fine buildings, a wholesome site, numerous and busy inhabitants—Florence contains all of these at once. Florence particularly excels in one regard: it is impeccably clean. Whereas in other cities, "the filth produced at night greets the eyes of the citizens in the morning, thrown into the streets to be pounded underfoot—than which nothing more disgusting can be imagined," in Florence, "no foul sight offends the eyes, no rank stench the nose, and no pile of filth the feet." Bruni's emphasis on the sparkling cleanliness and shiny neatness of the city seems to document the arrival of a new cultural ideal, one of refinement and polish.

But above all, Bruni praises the buildings of Florence, applying to them the adjectives *pulcher* and *ornatus*—they are "beautiful" and "ornate"—and the nouns *magnificentia* and *lautitia*—they possess "magnificence" and "elegance." No other city displays a building stock of this quality: they do not have so many fine buildings; or the fineness is only superficial, not extending beyond the façade to the other surfaces or the interior spaces; or their fine buildings are only found in the principal square or street, whereas in Florence, fine buildings densely pack the urban spaces. "For just as blood flows throughout the body, so beauty and delight are diffused throughout the city."

Bruni's celebration of the built environment includes a human or sociological dimension. He notes the importance of "throngs" of people or a "bustling" population: clearly both numbers and level of energy are intended in these appositions. He commends the layout of bridges and streets that permit people to move easily from one part of the city to another, while the riverbanks provide a fine setting for an evening stroll. And he suggests the parallelism between the "sacred" and "secular" buildings—the churches and the private homes—each housing a portion of the city's inhabitants, the latter the living, and the former the dead. A concern with the citizenry will also be displayed in Bruni's discussion, toward the end of his oration, of Florentine governance.

Bruni's description of the councils that constitute the city's government employs some of the same aesthetic descriptors used to describe the built environment: "Never has there been such order, such elegance, and such harmony" as in the interwoven systems of government institutions. Each body has a distinct purpose; each office performs a different role. In the Priorate, the principal executive, nine citizens—two from each of the four designated quarters of the city, plus one, the leader, at large—live together in the public edifice of the *Signoria* for terms of two months, their coresidence and removal from a domestic setting insulating them from any distractions, and the brevity of their office-holding preventing a too-great attachment to power. Other small and large councils are similarly drawn from different segments of the population, and constrained by brief electoral terms—practices consonant with those in other Italian cities, where the fear of concentrated authority was just as great.

Animating this tight network of councils and offices are two sacred principles: justice and liberty. "To these two conjoined principles, as though to a guiding star or safe haven, all the institutions and laws of this republic are directed." The Florentine notion of justice has some features, as Bruni describes them, which seem to strike a modern chord. If a magnate (the term used in Florence for those descended from the nobility, which by Bruni's time was an outlawed social distinction) threatened an ordinary citizen, the Florentine courts would offer protection, and extract a higher fine from the perpetrator than would be demanded from a malefactor of lesser social rank.[4] "The consensus has been reached that it is reasonable that different penalties should be applied to men of different condition, and both prudent and just that whoever is in greater need, to him more aid should be given." In fact, any humble man threatened by a more powerful one was free to respond that "I, too, am a Florentine citizen." In Bruni's figuration, Florence achieves social equality by weighting the scales of justice against the powerful and in favor of the poor.

From this discussion of justice, Bruni turns to another kind of cultural attainment: the high moral ethos of the Florentine people, who are "industrious, generous, magnificent, pleasant, affable, and above all, urbane," and their remarkable excellence in artistic and intellectual endeavors. The liberal arts, especially those studies "which are particularly suited for free men," and "which have always flourished among every great people, flourish vigorously in this one city."

---

4. Here Bruni refers to the exceptional anti-magnate legislation in the Florentine *Ordinances of Justice* of 1293–1295.

Leonardo Bruni, *In Praise of the City of Florence* (1404)

After a flowery opening, Bruni proceeds to a description of the physical city, ideally located neither too high, "on the mountaintops," nor too low, on a spreading plain that would make it vulnerable to impure air and fog; nor is it exposed to extremes of either cold or heat. Next, he considers the built environment, which exceeds all others for the splendor of its architecture and the cleanliness of its streets.

A handsome circuit of walls crowns the city—which itself is so large it encompasses both highlands and valleys—neither so imposing as to intimidate or humiliate by its mass, nor so modest as to seem negligible or deficient. How can I describe the throngs of people, the splendor of the buildings, the magnificence of the churches, the incredible and marvelous elegance of the entire city? By Hercules, every part of it is resplendent and aglow with exceptional beauty.

But its excellence can be told better when it is compared to other cities. That is why only those who have spent some time away fully understand, when they return to Florence, how much this flourishing city greatly exceeds all others. For there is no city in all the earth which does not lack some major component of excellence. One is deficient in the number of its inhabitants, another in the splendor of its buildings, still others, while they do not lack these benefits, are located in an unwholesome site. Some cities, indeed, are so dirty that all the filth produced at night greets the eyes of the citizens in the morning, thrown into the streets to be pounded underfoot—than which nothing more disgusting can be imagined. Even if it had a thousand palaces, and endless wealth, and an infinite number of inhabitants, still I would condemn such a city for its filth and could never esteem it. For just as a body that is deformed in one regard, even if it has other excellent features, cannot be sound, so also cities, if they are filthy, even if they are otherwise worthy, absolutely cannot be considered beautiful. And who does not see that if a city lacks beauty, it lacks the highest and noblest excellence?

In my judgment, Florence is so sparkling clean that no other city can be found that is tidier. Unique indeed is this city, unmatched in all the world, where no foul sight offends the eyes, no rank stench the nose, and no pile of filth the feet. With the greatest diligence, the citizens have planned and provided for the removal of all filth of this sort, so that you may encounter only what can bring joy and pleasure to the senses. Thus Florence exceeds in magnificence all the cities perhaps that now exist, and in elegance, certainly, all those that are now and ever shall be. . . .

Another city may be clean, but lack elegant buildings; or it may have elegant buildings, but lack a wholesome climate; or it may have a wholesome climate, but lack a population that is numerous and active. But from first to last, Florence has all the qualities that make a city ideal. For if you delight in antiquity, you will find an abundance of antique objects both in its public and private buildings. If you love what is modern, nothing is more magnificent or splendid than Florence's new buildings. Whether the river that flows through the center of the city offers more utility or more pleasure it is difficult to say. But four magnificent bridges built of squared stone blocks join the two banks of the river at such convenient intervals that there is no interruption of the movement of traffic through the principal streets, so that you may proceed as easily through the city as if no river traversed it. As you wander through every quarter, you will see splendid piazzas, the decorated porticos of the houses of noble families, and the streets alive with crowds of people. Of the houses built along the river, some face the riverfront, their walls washed by the waves; others are set further back on the other side of an intervening street, where a busy crowd may gather to engage in business or in pleasure. There is no place more pleasant for strolling than here along the river, either at midday in the winter, or at dusk in the summer. . . .

In truth, whenever I compare other cities with this one, I feel sorry for them. For another city might have one or at most two elegant streets, while all the others are so lacking in adornment that they blush mightily when visitors catch sight of them. But in this city of ours, there is no street, nor any quarter, that is not adorned with grand and elegant buildings. . . . Yet among the other fine buildings there stand out with an especially imposing grandeur and magnificence the churches and chapels which abound in great numbers throughout the city . . . than which nothing is more richly decorated, more ornate, or more splendid. For exquisite care has been taken to adorn not only secular buildings but also sacred ones, conferring excellence not only on the habitations of the living but also on those of the dead.

But I return to the homes of private citizens, which have been conceived, designed, and built for pleasure, for comfort, for honor, and above all, for magnificence. What could be more charming or more pleasant than to view the entryways and foyers, courtyards and dining rooms, and the other interior spaces of these homes! To wonder at their spaciousness, capable of hosting a multitude! To admire their exquisitely crafted cornices and arches, crested roofs and paneled ceilings, and, something seen in many homes, separate apartments for summer and winter living! Here are found splendid bedchambers, elegantly furnished, with bedcovers and curtains woven with gold and silver, and precious carpets! . . .

Now clearly, in other cities, a visitor should not stay too long. For if it has anything worth seeing, it is probably on display out in front and on the surface, for all visitors to see as soon as they have entered the town. But if they leave the public places, and seek to examine not the shell but the kernel of the city, if I may put it thus, what they see will not accord with their first impression: for instead of homes they will see hovels, and instead of elegance outside, filth inside. The case is different with Florence, where the full beauty of the city cannot be experienced unless one probes deeply. . . . For there is found no less adornment or magnificence behind the walls of its buildings than on the surface; nor is just this or that street splendid and sparkling, but all of them, in all parts of the city. For just as blood flows throughout the body, so beauty and delight are diffused throughout the city. . . .

> *Bruni turns next to the people of Florence, descended from the ancient Romans who first founded the city, and to the leading role Florence plays in the political world of the Italian city-states, which leads to a discussion of the Florentine government system.*

Just as this city is to be admired for its actions abroad, so too for its governance and institutions at home. Never has there been such order, such elegance, and such harmony. For just as a musical chord provides resolution when, following discord, one tone out of many achieves harmony, than which nothing is more pleasant or sweet to the ear, in the same way this most prudent city so arranges all its parts that it comprises a republic that is in the highest degree concordant, whose concord delights the minds and sight of its citizens. Nothing in it is misplaced, nothing unresolved, nothing irrational, nothing missing. All its components are assigned a particular role, each one clearly defined, but all part of a system: distinct offices, distinct magistracies, distinct tribunals, distinct ranks.

First of all, every provision is taken so that in this city justice is held to be sacred, without which a city cannot even exist; and secondly, that there may be liberty, without which the people of Florence could not live. To these two conjoined principles, as though to a guiding star or safe haven, all the institutions and laws of this republic are directed.

So as to preserve justice, magistracies are constituted with the authority to control malefactors, so that they may assure that no force is stronger in the city than that of law. To these magistracies, then, both worthy citizens and even men of the lower order must all obey and defer, showing respect to the insignia of office. But lest any of these guardians of the law assume absolute power for themselves, working not to protect the citizens but to tyrannize over them, and so, in exercising unjust power, endanger liberty, many safeguards are instituted.

The first of these is the supreme magistracy, which has the highest executive power, yet is constrained by this precaution, that it is held by not one but by nine men equally, and not for the term of a year but of just two months. In this way it manages the republic most excellently, as the diversity of opinions guards against bad decisions, and the brief term of service prevents arrogance of office. From each of the four quarters in which the city is divided, . . . two men are elected to serve in this supreme magistracy, not by lot but by the judgment of the people who deem them competent and worthy of such an honor. Set above these eight citizens designated to govern the republic, a ninth man, excellent in virtue and authority, chosen from one of the four quarters by lot, serves as head of the council, and as a sign of his power over disturbers of the peace, bears the flag of justice. These nine men, then, to whom the governance of the republic is committed, live together for their term of office in an official residence, the *signoria*, so as to always be ready to carry on the business of the republic; nor may they go forth from that place without an escort of lictors, so as to proclaim visibly the dignity of their office.

> *Having introduced the nine-man Priorate, the most important of the Florentine government councils, Bruni surveys the others, small and large, stressing again that the number of officials and councils is protective of liberty: "Thus liberty thrives and justice is devoutly preserved, since the designs of this or that individual cannot prevail against the judgment of so many men" (Laudatio Florentinae urbis 260, ll9–11). Finally, he commends the political ideology that underlies the Florentine government system, and praises the Florentines for their intellectual and moral virtues.*

Under these magistracies, therefore, so diligent and excellent is the governance of this city that no prudent father ever ruled a more disciplined household. Accordingly, no one here can suffer an injury, nor unwillingly suffer loss of his property. For the courts and the magistracies are always available, and the councils and even the highest tribunal always open. . . . Nor is there any place on earth where the law is more equitable to all; for nowhere else does liberty thrive so vigorously, available equally to men of high and low station. Now in this also may be seen the prudence of this city, the greatest I hazard than of all other cities: for when the great magnates, protected by their wealth, menace and injure the less wealthy, the republic itself defends the interests of those who are less able to defend themselves, and extracts from the wealthy due compensation for their losses and bodily harm. The consensus has been reached that it is reasonable that different penalties should be applied to men of different condition, and both prudent and just that whoever is in greater need, to him more aid should be given. And so a kind of equity is achieved among the different ranks of men: their own power protects the great, the state protects the poor, and the fear of punishment restrains both. From these arrangements arises the phrase often hurled against the magnates, to whom when they menace those of lesser rank, the victim retorts, "I, too, am a Florentine citizen." These words attest and clearly warn that no one may disregard him because he is weak, nor threaten to harm him because he is powerless. The condition of all men becomes equal, because the state promises to defend those of lowly station. . . .

But now, who can adequately describe, in the time remaining, the honorable manner of living and high moral standards of the Florentines? Men of great genius are found in this city, and whenever there is a task that needs doing, those who can easily exceed all other men in doing so. Whether they enter the military, or commit themselves to governing the state, or pursue knowledge or business, or any other career or task, they greatly surpass all other mortals, nor do they cede their place to any others. They endure trials in times of danger, seek glory avidly, offer counsel expertly; they are industrious, generous, magnificent, pleasant, affable, and above all, urbane.

Now what can I say about the oratorical skill and verbal elegance of the Florentines, who in these matters undoubtedly reign supreme? For it is agreed that, of all of Italy, in this city alone is found the purest and finest speech. All who wish to speak well and correctly, therefore, follow the pattern of this one city, where there are such experts in the common vernacular tongue that, compared to them, their rivals look like children. The study of letters, moreover—not the vulgar curriculum found in mercantile schools, but the liberal arts which are particularly suited for free men—which have always flourished among every great people, flourish vigorously in this one city.

What ornament, then, does this city lack, and in what way does it fall short of the highest honor and greatness? In the greatness of its ancestors?—who are descended from the Romans! In glory?—when Florence has done and daily does such great deeds, both honorable and excellent, both at home and abroad! In the splendor of its buildings? In its adornment and elegance? In its wealth? In its bustling population? In its healthful and pleasant location? What more is there that any city could desire? Nothing whatever!

What then shall we say now, and what remains to be done? Nothing other than to thank the Creator for his great beneficence and to offer him our praise. You, therefore, omnipotent and immortal God . . . ; and you, most holy mother . . . ; and you, John the Baptist, the patron saint of this city; protect this most beautiful and precious city and guard its people from every danger and every evil.

Francesco Barbaro

In the remarkable treatise that follows, the young Venetian nobleman Francesco Barbaro (1390–1454), who was not yet married himself, addresses to his friend, a young Florentine patrician, on the occasion of the latter's wedding, an extended meditation on marriage. It is remarkable for two reasons. First, it is wholly original, having only one ancient precursor,[5] which it exceeds in scale and depth of argument. Second, it is firmly rooted in the context of Renaissance Italian, and specifically Venetian, society. It presents the spectacle of a conversation between two youths from the uppermost circle of the social elite on an institution of central importance to their class and to their cities.

One of Venice's most important statesmen during its triumphal fifteenth century, Francesco Barbaro was also one of its most important humanists. In 1415, however, when he composed *On Marriage* and dispatched it as a wedding gift to Lorenzo de' Medici,[6] Barbaro had not yet begun his political career. At age twenty-five, rather, he had just completed his education: a thoroughly modern one for that era, requiring an immersion in Latin and Greek literature, and tuition by the finest teachers then to be had.

Thus equipped, Barbaro tackles an issue of current importance that had received no attention in recent times, and little in antiquity. His treatise has two parts: the first concerned with the selection of a wife, and the second with the duties of a wife. His dedicatory letter to Lorenzo is the preface. Of these elements, two have been published in modern English translation: the dedicatory letter, and the second section "On Wifely Duties."[7] Presented here are excerpts from the first section, "On the Selection of a Wife," translated from the original Latin.

A few words about the prefatory letter: it was written in the autumn of 1415, when Lorenzo de' Medici, scion of a family that would soon seize power in Florence, was on the verge of marrying a young woman from an equally distinguished family. Barbaro explains that he will not, as was customary, send a lavish wedding gift. Lorenzo is already wealthy, and requires no such gift. Barbaro will instead send him his book: something "not from my fortune but from your friend Francesco." He hopes that not only Lorenzo, but also others, will find the book useful: for "I am also attempting to teach several others of our age through you."[8] Barbaro is wise beyond his years: for the youth of Italy's urban patriciate, marriage was indeed a matter of consequence.

The patriciates of the Italian cities understood that they must perpetuate themselves through strategic marriages and the cultural preparation of their offspring. The Venetian patriciate was especially conscious of this necessity, as nobility of birth was the prerequisite for participation in government.

---

5. Plutarch's *Precepts on Marriage*, one of that author's *Moral Essays*, is a fundamental source and inspiration. Barbaro also uses the pseudo-Plutarchan *On the Education of Free Children*.

6. This is the elder Lorenzo, son of Giovanni di Bicci, brother of Cosimo the Elder, and great-uncle of Lorenzo de' Medici surnamed "the Magnificent," the unofficial ruler of Florence from 1469 to 1492.

7. In Benjamin G. Kohl and Ronald G. Witt, *The Earthly Republic: Italian Humanists on Government and Society* (Philadelphia: University of Pennsylvania Press, 1978), 177–228.

8. Kohl and Witt, *Earthly Republic,* 190.

Hence marital choice and the conveyance of noble status to offspring were especially keen issues. It is in this context that Barbaro writes his treatise *On Marriage*, and its first book "On the Selection of a Wife."

Barbaro opens with a familiar definition of marriage: it is a "perpetual conjunction of man and wife, lawfully instituted for the procreation of offspring or for the avoidance of fornication." The theme is recurrent: the goal of marriage is the procreation of children. In the animal world, similarly, individuals of different species engage in coition for the sake of procreation and are (and this four centuries before Darwin) considered successful only if they have reproduced. In human society, mere procreation is not sufficient; it must occur within the boundaries of legitimate marriage. The children of legitimate unions ultimately make better citizens: they are the true "walls of the city." And legitimate marriage has its joys of intimacy and amiability. What could be finer than "to be wed to a modest wife who in both good and bad is partner, companion, and friend?"

Barbaro next outlines the five criteria to be considered in the choice of a wife: moral character, age, family origins, beauty, and wealth. Of these, moral character is preeminent. To illustrate its importance Barbaro produces two examples, not from antiquity but from the Venetian patriciate. Each features a wealthy nobleman who chooses for his wife a woman of good birth and exceptional moral character, even though she lacked wealth. In our post-romantic age, these examples seem obvious and perhaps trite. But in Barbaro's day, marriage was a business, governed by the dowry, the wealth that a wife brought to the new household. For the most part, marriage without a dowry—and the largest one that could be obtained—was nearly inconceivable. Barbaro was himself a member of that elite, yet here he confronts and challenges one of its key principles.

Proceeding to the second criterion, that of age, Barbaro recommends youth over maturity. A young wife is more easily molded to a husband's temperament; moreover, the older wife is most likely a remarrying widow, a figure about whom Christian Europe, among other societies, had considerable anxiety: often viewed as loathsome and sexually predatory, and assimilated to the figures of the wicked stepmother, hag, crone, and witch.

The third criterion for the selection of a wife is, like the first, critical: family origin, or more explicitly, nobility of birth. Just as in horticulture the best fruits come from the finest seed grown in the richest soil, so among humans, "worthier offspring" come from "women of greater worth." Barbaro's viewpoint here is distinctly at odds with modern sensibilities: but not surprisingly, as a Venetian of the fifteenth century, he believes that some people are inherently of greater value than others, and that intermarriage only between two persons of that exalted type will be sure to yield progeny of the highest quality. While Barbaro's assumptions about the innate superiority of members of one social group may shock us, we might suspend our outrage a moment to note that he credits the woman, as much as the man, with conferring the ingredient of innate nobility to children: it is a quality "that they acquire not from their father alone, but also from their mother," which they may then "piously and righteously transmit as an inheritance to their own posterity."

The fourth criterion, that of beauty, Barbaro dismisses as minor, although for others it is often an overriding concern. Beauty is only desirable, he writes, if it complements other, more necessary qualities: "if beauty be joined to noble character and other admirable qualities, I would value it highly; but apart from these, I would in no way praise it." Let us by all means marry beautiful women, he says to his audience, "if they possess the other qualities necessary to make marriage pleasant for us, and honorable and beneficial for our offspring."

The fifth and final criterion in the selection of a wife is that of wealth, and here Barbaro is cautious. As a member of an elite whose status derived from its amassment of riches, Barbaro does not discount wealth: it is useful. But young men, he complains, are crazed by the desire for wealth, and seem to demand nothing else of a future bride. They will be disappointed, writes Barbaro: "I urge them, if they can afford to do so, to consider the other factors I have written about here in choosing a wife." He knows his position will be unpopular: "I fear I shall be criticized for saying this; yet I must say what I believe." They should make their marriage choices "with more care and less greed . . . lest for the sake of money, or in the hope of gain, they make themselves the slave of a dowry." Instead, they should choose "wives endowed with virtue, youth, nobility, beauty," and, yes, "wealth."

In *On Marriage*, Barbaro identifies a critical contemporary issue. Urban elites propagate themselves through marriage. If they select wives lacking fine moral character and noble descent, they endanger the future of their families and the city itself. Wealth, beauty, even youth, each considered alone, are not sufficient qualifications for wifehood. Men must think beyond their own immediate advantage or pleasure and consider their progeny. A man of the establishment, Barbaro does not hesitate to challenge, at least on some issues, from his storehouse of humanist and Christian principles, the lesser instincts of his peers.

Francesco Barbaro's treatise *On Marriage* enjoyed great success, attested to by the more than fifty extant Latin manuscripts of the work, composed two generations before the arrival of the printing press, and its numerous Latin editions and translations into Italian, French, German, and English.[9] A tribute to its continued influence as late as 1677 is given by the editor of the first English version: "This Treatise was first written in Italian [sic], and so well liked of that it was translated into Latine, and printed in Holland, where it hath gained an Universal Applause. It is now at last translated for the benefit of the English Reader."[10]

---

9. Kohl, introduction to "On Wifely Duties," in Kohl and Witt, *The Earthly Republic*, 186n15.

10. *Directions for Love and Marriage, in two Books, Written Originally by Franciscus Barbarus, a Venetian Senator, and now Translated into English by a Person of Quality* (London: Printed for John Leigh at the Bell, and Tho. Burrell at the Golden Ball, under St. Dunstan's Church, in

Francesco Barbaro, *On Marriage* (1415)

WHAT MARRIAGE IS

Before I discuss the choice of a wife and her responsibilities, I first wish to define here what marriage is, utilizing the views of learned men, so that we may understand from the start the subject of our future discourse. . . .

Marriage, then, is the perpetual conjunction of man and wife, lawfully instituted for the procreation of offspring or for the avoidance of fornication. About this subject there are many and diverse views; and to investigate and evaluate them all would be tedious. Instead, I shall turn to the most famous pagan and Christian thinkers, who by general consensus are considered authoritative.

Now the Romans, so as to increase the number of legitimately born children, levied a tax on anyone who remained celibate into old age. For they respected the pattern set by nature, which has instilled in every species of animal a desire for coition for the sake of procreation, and a belief that their success consists in having reproduced. For the drive to generate in animals is powerful, as we see with birds, . . . whose instinct to nest provides for both the birthing and the nourishment of their young, which may be likened to marriage among humans. By this means, just as the body is sustained by food, both animal and human species are perpetuated. . . .

Experience has shown that the children born of legitimate marriages are more inclined to honor, are more responsibly reared, and ultimately make better citizens, who will in turn make the city loved by its allies on account of its commitment to justice, and feared by its enemies on account of its courage. For experience, that great teacher, demonstrates that those who were conceived in lust and outside of wedlock are for the most part violent and dishonest and inclined to all that is base. But the splendor of their ancestors demands that those born honorably achieve excellence: they know that the glories of their forefathers will be more of a burden than a blessing unless they by their own merit match the dignity and greatness of their forebears. For they realize that all eyes will be turned on them in expectation that they will in some way reiterate in their own lives the virtue they have inherited from their ancestors. We may call those born thus honorably the walls of the city. . . . For truly, we protect and defend our country, gods, patron saints, altars, houses, parents, wives, and children not with wood or brick, but with virtue. And besides, what is more pleasant than to share our thoughts with

---

Fleet Street, 1677), A3v. The *De re uxoria,* of course, was composed in Latin, and later translated into Italian.

our wives, and so resolve domestic cares? And to be wed to a prudent wife who in both good and bad is partner, companion, and friend? To whom you may confide your innermost thoughts about things that lie within her competence, to whom you may entrust the little children that you bear together? To whom in sweet conversation you may unburden your cares and sorrows? Whom you so love, that your own hope of happiness depends in some measure on her well-being? . . .

But enough has been said about marriage, about which learned men have written at length. But so as to clarify the essential points, I have reviewed them here. Now . . . we shall inquire what kind of woman should be chosen as a wife. . . .

CHAPTER 1: THE MORAL CHARACTER BEFITTING THE WOMAN CHOSEN AS A WIFE

The ancients . . . thought that a prospective wife should be judged for her character, age, descent, beauty, and wealth, and that if any of these is neglected, we will certainly bring dishonor and sorrow to our families, and often grief to ourselves; but if we attend to them diligently, we win honor for our family, and for ourselves, reputation and enduring joy.

We turn first to character, where the preeminent requirement is virtue. It has such great power and worth that, even if other qualities are lacking, yet the marriage should be considered a good one; and if they are present, then the marriage is certain to be most successful. For the domestic matters committed to a wife's care will not be managed well unless the woman in charge guides, governs, and orders them with prudence, diligence, and industry. . . .

After supplying many ancient examples, Barbaro brings up one very close to home.

Our own city is full of examples of this sort, of which it will be sufficient to name a few. Andrea Barbaro, an excellent man and father of our Marco, an eminent citizen of honorable rank, took as his wife Lucia Viara, a woman of such remarkable and conspicuous probity that, having gained the necessary permission, he met and spoke with her at home, and setting aside any consideration of wealth, asked if she would marry him. And so, overlooking the absence of wealth, he took her as his wife for the sake of her virtue and goodness. This most prudent man did not err in making this decision, since she cherished his children with such concern and piety that no greater harmony or peace could be desired than prevailed in their household. Many years later, this Barbaro, my ancestor, served as a pattern for the renowned and excellent citizen Giusto Contarini. For having ascertained the moderation, modesty, and exceptional beauty of Francesca, the daughter of Pantaleone Barbo, he first spoke to the father alone, declaring that he had grown more and more to love his daughter, and though she was poor, if he were willing, he wished most earnestly to make her his wife. Pantaleone, a man of illustrious family and great learning, was delighted by this declaration. He requested time for deliberation, and summoned, as was customary, his friends and advisers. To these he laid the matter out fully, and they approved it wholeheartedly by unanimous consent. Giusto, who was advanced in age, was accepted by the most noble young woman, although she brought a very small dowry, as the family's circumstances dictated. I would call this a splendid marriage, which, having been established on a foundation of virtue, endured inviolate with the greatest faith and trust. . . .

What else is there to say? Let us choose a wife of good character, whose domestic virtues, together with honor, goods, and pleasure, we may cherish, treasure, and love.

CHAPTER 2: WHAT IS THE PROPER AGE FOR A WIFE?

In this brief chapter, Barbaro explains why it is better to marry a young woman than an older one—who would be, necessarily, a remarrying widow, a figure generally mistrusted in Christian Europe as in many other societies. A young woman, he argues, will easily learn the things her husband wishes, and if she has any faults, they will be easily corrected: "For we can easily make impressions in wax when it is soft, while those impressed on surfaces that are hard and unyielding are difficult to erase." This issue dispatched, he moves on to an issue of major importance: whether a wife should come from noble stock.

CHAPTER 3: FROM WHAT FAMILY BACKGROUND SHOULD A WIFE COME?

Barbaro opens this chapter with a message to his friend Lorenzo—fittingly, because both are sons of noble families. He will begin by taking a look at nature.

Let us start in this matter by looking to nature itself. A flourishing pasture, planted and sown, is a strong argument to us that for the sake of the children we wish to have, we should marry women of noble birth. For seeds are better or worse according to their origins; and the best seed bears the finest fruits. And we know that there are many fine berries, nuts, and fruits which, unless they are planted in proper and suitable soil, will not bear fruit; and if they are transplanted to an ignoble field, they lose their noble spirit, and "forgetting the sap they once had, the fruits wither."[11] . . . All this is true also of humans, who can anticipate worthier offspring from women of greater worth. . . .

Maternal nobility greatly affects not only the birthing but also the rearing of children. . . . For though the finest seed is planted in a field, to return to the metaphor used earlier, unless that field is cultivated with skill and diligence, it struggles to produce its despicable fruit. With nobly-born mothers, there can be no doubt, it is more likely that the splendor of the parents will shine forth even more brightly in their offspring. . . . The person born to an honorable rank acquires new honors easily. Who doubts that by universal consent, these will be preferred to those of more humble birth? Who does not understand that, even if their own merits do not make them worthy of honor, yet often much is granted them because of the worthiness of their ancestors? We read that many men chose to die for their country, both so that they might perform their duty, but also so that they might leave the memory of their name as a rich patrimony to their sons. . . .

We must affirm, therefore, the merit of the noble origin of both our parents, and communicate it to our children. While other things are uncertain, shifting, and transitory, this legacy of nobility is fixed with the firmest roots, can withstand any force, and can never be demolished. . . . Therefore we praise those marriages especially by which we acquire honor, and so make our children more glorious and potent. . . .

Therefore let us take noble wives—just as you, Lorenzo, have most wisely done—so that our domestic life may be more pleasant, and having acquired sons made noble both by nature and by nurture, and having prepared them for glory by the example of their forebears, we may abundantly bestow upon them honor and power. For they shall honor the memory of those from whom they have their origin, think about them always, incline their soul to them, so that the merit that they acquire not from their father alone but also from their mother, they may piously and righteously transmit as an inheritance to their own posterity.

CHAPTER 4: HOW IMPORTANT IS BEAUTY IN A WIFE?

In this chapter, about as brief as the earlier discussion of age, Barbaro almost reluctantly discusses the component of beauty in the selection of a wife— although for many, beauty is the first and most important factor to be considered. He sums up his argument:

Although I have written here much about beauty, yet I would wish to state, that if beauty be joined to noble character and other admirable qualities,

---

11. Virgil, *Georgics,* 2.59.

I would value it highly; but apart from these, I would in no way praise it. For just as fire is easily ignited from kindling, and unless sturdier wood is added easily dissipates, so the love between man and woman, if excited by the loveliness of the body, unless a worthy mind, good character, and sanctimony of life nourish it, is soon extinguished. . . .

But why do I extend this discussion further, as if I were discussing some weighty topic? We love beautiful women, if they possess the other qualities necessary to make marriage pleasant for us, and honorable and beneficial for our offspring.

CHAPTER 5: HOW IMPORTANT IS WEALTH IN A WIFE?

Concerning character, age, birth, and beauty, I have spoken sufficiently. Now, as planned, the subject of how much wealth is to be desired in a wife remains to be discussed, about which I shall mention a few things that are useful to bring up. Since therefore we value all things that promote the worthiness and honor of marriage, as well as our own ease, abundance, possessions, and riches, it is prudent to consider the dignity and utility of wealth. . . .

I wish that we lived in that age long ago when young people were taught, and not misled as they are now, that they should not too greatly esteem wealth and possessions in marriage: truly that would have better served the interests of human society. But most young men from their childhood have been so infused and imbued with the love of gain, that they will perform any labor and expend any effort to acquire and achieve it, not neglecting any path by which they may satisfy their avarice. But I do not wish to incite or inflame our youth to acquire wealth through marriage, but rather I urge them, if they can afford to do so, to consider the other factors I have written about here in choosing a wife. I fear I shall be criticized for saying this; yet I must say what I believe. I cannot accuse those enough, who though they be very wealthy themselves, yet zealously seek wives who possess in no way the qualities necessary in a wife. . . .

But unless we first free ourselves from the lure of pleasure and luxury, . . . we shall never deliberate properly and fittingly about a wife. . . . So let our young men collect themselves, and consider marriage with more care and less greed—here they might follow your example—lest for the sake of money, or in the hope of gain, they make themselves the slave of a dowry, and so kindle a domestic fire that cannot easily be put out. If they wish to do what is best for them and their families, as I recommend, they will select wives endowed with virtue, youth, nobility, beauty, and wealth. . . .

Alamanno Rinuccini

In his dialogue *On Liberty* (1479), Alamanno Rinuccini (1426–1499) offers the most important discussion of liberty between Leonardo Bruni, earlier in the fifteenth century, and Niccolò Machiavelli, early in the next. Like Bruni (to Machiavelli we shall return in Chapter 5), Rinuccini sees liberty as the core value of the Florentine people, and as the animating principle behind Florence's rise to greatness. But where Bruni's vision is optimistic and dynamic, Rinuccini's is chastened by experience: his personal experience of the rise to supremacy in Florence of one family, the Medici, who without dismantling constitutional structures, played the levers of power behind the scenes. Rinuccini himself was their victim, at least for a while. His exile from the city, which provides the framework for this most important of his works, affords him the opportunity for a deeper meditation on liberty than Bruni pursued. Drawing on the same cluster of classical authors, Rinuccini provides a philosophically rigorous definition of liberty that unites the political liberty experienced by the people of a state with the existential liberty possessed by the individual. In Rinuccini's *On Liberty*, the loss of the former occasions, and seems to necessitate, the pursuit of the latter.

Rinuccini was well-positioned to witness the shifts of government action and public sentiment in Florence in the most critical century of its history. His lifespan embraces the rise and fall of the first phase of Medicean domination and corresponds to a nearly continuous series of wars with other Italian powers. His own political career began in the 1450s, when he was a supporter of Cosimo de' Medici il Vecchio, the first Medici strongman. Out of favor from 1466 to 1472, Rinuccini soon returned to the fray, holding important offices—including, most appropriately, that of trustee (as one of a board of five) of the Florentine university, a position he held from 1473 to 1477 and again from 1480 to 1484. He was a spectator and silent approver of the 1478 Pazzi conspiracy to unseat the Medici. The following year—a year in which his only son died of plague—he wrote *On Liberty*, a work which notes his strong opposition to Lorenzo de' Medici and suggests that he had reached the end of his political career. But he had not: he received more political appointments from 1480 until his death in 1499.

Although Rinuccini is not among the leading humanists as measured by frequency of notice or circulation of works, he was prolific. Most of his works—letters, orations, translations—date from the early years of his career, from around 1455 to 1475. *On Liberty* might be seen as his last major work, although written twenty years before his death—his political career having outlasted his literary one. Indeed, it is difficult to see the author of *On Liberty* as the kind of pragmatist who could have returned to the Medici patronage mill. For Rinuccini the author, if not Rinuccini the actor, is uncompromising in his indictment of the Medici regime.

On Liberty is a dialogue with three interlocutors, given abstract and fictive names: Eleutherius, meaning "lover of liberty," is Rinuccini himself, an identification made within the pages of the work where Rinuccini's ancestors are named; Alitheus, meaning "truthful," and Microtoxus, meaning perhaps "short arrow," are unidentified characters, perhaps composites of some of Rinuccini's friends from his informal academy of learned Florentines.[12] These invented names add a tone of unreality to what is already an idealized setting: a villa, such as the one in which Cicero sets his own dialogue On the Republic, for instance. These notes of unreality lead the reader to expect lofty themes to be discussed, as they will be; not so much, the vitriol that thrills in the language of at least two of the speakers, Alitheus and Eleutherius, who in their different ways will be the advocates of liberty in, respectively, the first and second books of the work.

The first book celebrates political liberty. The "truth-teller" Alitheus, portrayed as an active member of the Florentine elite, offers a definition of liberty, and traces the deterioration of the Florentine state from its original dedication to the ideal of freedom. The excerpts that follow are drawn from this part of On Liberty, because of its clear political focus. The second book is, however, also highly interesting. Here Eleutherius explains why he is not living in Florence, but in retreat in his modest country villa. He has been disgusted by the Medicean takeover, and has sought solitude in the country so that he may pursue a different kind of liberty than the one his fellow citizens had suffered to be extinguished in Florence. That liberty is scholarly and philosophical—existential, one might say. With his books and his thoughts as his companions, Eleutherius, the "lover of liberty," may live in perfect liberty, one no longer available in the political maelstrom of Florence. His sublimation, however, does not inhibit him from periodically addressing the political betrayal, as he sees it, that he has left behind: the Florentines, he grieves, pressed by their servitude, "have been despoiled of their former zeal for honor, faith in life, spiritual strength and love of liberty."[13]

To return to the first book and Alitheus' presentation it, too, has two parts. In the first, he presents his definition of liberty; in the second, his narration of the history of Florence, which traces the decline from an earlier dedication to liberty to the present autocracy. Liberty, for Alitheus, is the power to act: not merely to live a vegetative existence, but to make choices and achieve goals. It is a freedom that those intimidated by tyrants no longer possess—a point that brings us to the second part of the presentation.

---

12. The first two names are given as translated by Watkins, *Humanism and Liberty,* 194; the third, which resists translation, is my own translation.

13. Alamanno Rinuccini, *Dialogus de libertate,* ed. Francesco Adorno, *Atti e memorie dell'Accademia Toscana di scienze e lettere La Colombaria,* 22 (1957), 297.

Here, Microtoxus invites Alitheus to "please now explain how we at present have begun to lose what you have defined as liberty," a situation which, Alitheus responds, is "not merely very sad to talk about, but also most burdensome to think about, which I can never recall without tears." He grieves to see the people who had made Florence great not subject to the "whim of this one youth"—by whom he means Lorenzo de' Medici[14]—and to see so many worthy Florentines "oppressed by the yoke of servitude, yet scarcely recognizing that they in their blindness brought this servitude upon themselves." The foundation of liberty is the equality of the citizens: "It requires this first of all, that the wealthy not oppress the poor, or equally that the poor not assault the rich, but that each may preserve what is his safe from the aggression of others." But this fundamental principle has been violated: "What must absolutely be preserved uncorrupted in a free city has been so perverted that even to think about it defiles us." Free speech has been abolished in the councils, and public officials, instead of being chosen by lot (which was the common practice in Italian cities, valued as a means of preventing manipulation of the vote), are selected to be "the mignons of powerful citizens or servitors of their lusts and pleasures." Above all, there is the waste of money, extracted from taxpayers and lavished on unnecessary building projects or diverted "to feed endless bevies of horses, dogs, birds, actors, flatterers, and parasites."

It was not always so: the Florentines in the past had vigorously defended their liberty, a point Alitheus defends with a long narration of the many wars the city had fought for that purpose. The story is told, he concludes, so that all might "see how great was our ancestors' concern always to preserve and protect liberty, which they defended with their blood, . . . and . . . with boundless sums of money." He closes by apologizing for his prolixity, but if his listeners have derived any benefit from his words, "you may give thanks to liberty itself, just to hear the name of which is lovely."

Rinuccini is not utterly frank in his celebration of the Florentine devotion to liberty prior to the Medicean takeover. Here, as in most premodern states, elites held sway, and did not always administer the state, or deal with their subordinates, justly and fairly. But his outrage at the corruption of justice, the stifling of free expression, the appropriation of citizens' wealth for the private purposes of the ruler, are palpable. Most striking is his understanding of the psychology of oppression: those in servitude become demoralized, losing their will to live according to their own principles—which is to say, their liberty.

---

14. This is Lorenzo "the Magnificent," grandson of Cosimo il Vecchio, and great-nephew of the Lorenzo de' Medici to whom Francesco Barbaro dedicates *De re uxoria (On Marriage)*.

Alamanno Rinuccini, *On Liberty* (1479)

MICROTOXUS: This little villa of yours, with the fields around it, so exquisitely cultivated, yet really rather small, it seems to me, clearly delight you greatly, Eleutherius—and yet they make me laugh, or perhaps marvel. For up to now, when you frequently absented yourself from the city, I thought you were drawn away to supervise work on your fields or your buildings, and could easily accept that you were fleeing, as though from a prison, the burdensome restraints of your urban existence to seek freedom in the country—which makes sense, since your name "Eleutherius" connotes your love and zeal for liberty. But now, when I see that your fields are perfectly cared for and your little villa much smaller than your city home, I do not really understand why you remain so long in the country. Nor can I believe that passivity or lack of ambition has caused your avoidance of the city, as happens with many, since you are endowed with those skills by which you may not only keep busy in the city but also win honor. And I believe Alitheus thinks so too.

ALITHEUS: In fact, Microtoxus, I do not marvel at Eleutherius' country life so much as I admire it, and praise the frugality and modesty of his field and villa, which are the size that usefulness and necessity, not luxury, require. And so considering his character and the life he has led—and especially, as you have said, his name—I would say that he has made the right decision, one arrived at not by accident but in accord with the established pattern of his life. For if indeed what he wants is the freedom to live a good life, that is found in purer form in this solitude than in the city.

MICROTOXUS: You are telling fairy tales, Alitheus, if you believe that he alone, among so many thousands of men, cannot find liberty in this city—especially since it is that one which more than all the other cities in Italy is a champion of liberty, and which has defended the cause of liberty not only for itself and for its citizens but for many of the cities of Italy, sparing no expense or difficulty. I could easily defend this claim with the evidence of history, except that it would be a superfluous labor since I am speaking to you, who already know these things well, both from the words of our ancestors and those written in books, with which both of you are thoroughly familiar.

ALITHEUS: What you say is true indeed, Microtoxus. For there is no other city in all Italy, I would say, which has defended liberty so strenuously and for so long, or where such a complete and pure liberty has flourished. For if you trace its history from the beginning until the present age, you will find that no foreign state or tyrant has ever suppressed the liberty of this people. . . .

After further discussion, Microtoxus tasks Alitheus to do two things: to define liberty, and to show in what way the Florentines have lost the liberty they once had. Alitheus begins with a definition.

ALITHEUS: We have said that liberty is the "power to live," where "to live" means specifically to be able to act. For I do not accept the definition Aristotle intends, when he said that in living things, "life" is "to exist." Life defined in this way belongs to plants as much as to animals, and to grass and to anything that has a vegetative soul. But the life of which I speak consists in action, and so is assigned to animals only, and among these especially to humans. . . .

For no one would call a man "free" who, in the senate or in the council-chamber or in any kind of court, was inhibited by fear or greed or any other cause from daring openly to say or do what he believed. Liberty accordingly . . . may be seen as related to fortitude, since both the free man and the strong man display their virtue in action. But where the strong man wins praise for rationally confronting great danger, the free man does so by speaking and persuading. Yet each performs his duty with a noble and lofty spirit, for neither flags in the face of danger nor pales before threats. These qualities are most useful to free cities, where citizens can speak unrestrainedly in advising what they think is best for the state. Wherefore I believe that I was correct to define "liberty" as the "power to live," unless you strongly object. . . .

Microtoxus inquires what kind of limits there may be on liberty, and Alitheus responds.

ALITHEUS: I would not think a man deprived of liberty because he was forced to obey the laws of his city, since it is rather the highest form of liberty to obey the laws, as Cicero says, since it is on the basis of the laws that we are made free.[15] Indeed, there are many things in life which are forbidden, yet that prohibition does not take away our liberty. For no one, as I see it, would ever be called unfree because he was not allowed to strike another citizen with impunity, or to seize his goods by force, or to rape his wife. All of these things the laws of well-ordered cities prohibit, and are punished with the most severe penalties. Nor, in my judgment, does the prohibition against many other deeds not forbidden by law, but barred by civic norms and customs—things only a madman would do—limit the perpetrator's liberty. . . . Or do you think otherwise?

MICROTOXUS: Not at all. You have presented these matters so persuasively that nothing more convincing could be said. But since you have

---

15. Cicero, *Paradoxa*, V.I.34.

explained the first matter we agreed to discuss, and have given a definition of liberty in all its particulars, I am eager to move on to the second. . . . So please now explain how we at present have begun to lose what you have defined as liberty—for I doubt if you will be able to prove it.

ALITHEUS: Friends, you press me to revisit a matter that is not merely very sad to talk about, but also most burdensome to think about, which I can never recall without tears. It shames me, indeed, who was born in this city and in this age, to see the people who once dominated most of Tuscany as well as regions nearby led about in circles by the whim of this one youth;[16] and so many men of lofty mind and illustrious for their wisdom and prudence oppressed by the yoke of servitude, yet scarcely recognizing that they in their blindness brought this servitude upon themselves, nor daring to free themselves from it—but rather, which is worse yet, they are forced against their will to oppose his enemies. Without a doubt, the spirit of our age has degenerated so greatly from the virtues of our ancestors that if they came back to life, they would deny that they had given us birth. For they founded, protected, and increased this republic, providing it with excellent customs, sacred laws, and institutions supporting a well-regulated life. . . .

For so long as our city lived in accord with those laws, it grew greater in wealth, dignity, and power, exceeding the other cities of Tuscany, to which it served as a conspicuous example not only of power, but also of moral principle. But now I see that those very laws have been so despised by all and degraded, that now the city is ruled instead by the desires of a few corrupt citizens. Think about this: who does not recognize that the firm foundation of liberty is the equality of the citizens? It requires this first of all, that the wealthy not oppress the poor, or equally that the poor not assault the rich, but that each may preserve what is his safe from the aggression of others. Now judge for yourselves how well we have obeyed these principles. What shall I say about the administration of justice? What must absolutely be preserved uncorrupted in a free city has been so perverted that even to think about it defiles us. I certainly cannot record this without great sorrow, that no one by word or vote dares to challenge those judgments based on the pile of false denunciations contrived by a party of powerful men. In these circumstances, I would consider it to be among the gifts of fortune, and not among the least of them, if a person could avoid by some honest excuse the necessity of sitting in judgment. . . .

How shall I compare the freedom of speech once exercised both in the senate and the public assemblies with the silence that prevails today? Where there sparkled the sharpness of mind, the eloquence of speech, and the great love

---

16. Alitheus speaks of Lorenzo de' Medici, at this time the unofficial ruler of Florence.

of country of the most gifted citizens? Where serious men so freely discussed the pros and cons of the proposals for action made, that the strengths of each were easily discerned. On which account a poor decision was rarely made, and once a decree was issued, it was not immediately reversed by second-guessers. . . .

But now, the arrogance of a few, and the cowardice of many other citizens, have allowed a party of ambitious men to usurp for themselves what should be common to all, whose blind lust for power has reordered all things, so that virtually nothing remains of the authority of the councils or of the people. . . .

And shall we look at the way magistrates are chosen? In free cities, as we all know, these are chosen by a lottery system, which is considered to be consonant with liberty and justice, for by it all those who individually support the state by the payment of taxes are made participants in its benefits and rewards. Now, however, for the first time we see that all the offices which offer some kind of dignity or benefit are filled not by lot but by appointment. The result is that those chosen are not good men, conspicuous for their prudence or merit, but the mignons of powerful citizens or servitors of their lusts and pleasures, who mindlessly serve their masters as abjectly as they can. . . .

Yet I cannot pass by in silence this outrage, the most scandalous of all, which all our citizens should seek at all costs to overcome. What could be more shameful than what has happened in recent years when, though all of Italy was at peace, the wealth of our citizens, except for a very few, has been exhausted by extraordinary tax levies? And this money supposedly required for the unnecessary purchase of grain or some other fantastical purpose has been diverted to gratify the appetite of one man. So no one should wonder now from whence comes the wealth to erect all at once so many buildings in both city and country, or to feed endless bevies of horses, dogs, birds, actors, flatterers, and parasites. . . .

These happenings and others of this sort, Microtoxus, have powerfully undermined liberty, or rather, I would say, have now destroyed and extinguished liberty altogether. In themselves wicked and nefarious, and to be avoided at any cost by men of sane mind, yet these things are felt to be so much more bitter and intolerable when we recall, spurred partly by what our elders have told us, partly from the reading of history, how much our ancestors struggled to preserve liberty, and how great their zeal to preserve equality among the citizens. . . .

At that time, there resided in the people a great love of liberty, when they themselves, as is proper, took charge of all things and guided the helm of state. But now they are in an almost desperate state, bending to an alien will and bowing to alien powers. Nor did this happen by accident or neglect, but coerced by the threat of force, they do not dare to assert their rights. Yet formerly, they defended their liberty against aggressive states or tyrants both with their own blood and with the expenditure, in addition, of huge sums of money. . . .

> *Alitheus proceeds to an account of all the "tyrants and princes" the Florentine people have warded off, rather than lose their liberty. Of these many events, notice may be taken of one famous one: the prolonged struggle with the Milanese strongman Giangaleazzo Visconti that gravely imperiled Florence until, in 1402, he fortuitously died while encamped outside the city.*

ALITHEUS: . . . Not long afterwards they waged a prolonged and dangerous war with Giangaleazzo Visconti, the tyrant of Milan, funded by a nearly inconceivable amount of wealth. And yet after the Florentines had waged this war for many years, unable to settle a peace treaty agreeable to the Duke, he violated the truce and launched intrigues and maneuvers against Florence. In response, the Florentines called Robert, Duke of Bavaria, to their aid, with the promise of 40,000 florins, collecting one half of that huge sum in a single night, the citizens themselves carting the money off to the officials: so great was the hatred of tyrants, so great was the love of liberty and of country.

> *Alitheus comes down to the present conflict (1478–1479) with the pope and the king of Naples.*

But I do not really know what to say about the war in which Florence is now engaged with Pope Sixtus IV and King Ferdinand of Naples. Both of them, in words spoken and written, have declared that they are waging war not to take away but to restore the liberty of the Florentine people; nor have they taken up arms against Florence, but against Lorenzo de Medici. And everywhere they call him a tyrant not a citizen, the term used in all the ecclesiastical censures hurled against him. So really, I don't know whether those who oppose these men can be said to fight for liberty or for servitude.

I wanted to review all these conflicts briefly and concisely, so that you could see how great was our ancestors' concern always to preserve and protect liberty, which they defended with their blood, so long as it was possible for them to prevail on the battlefield, and later, when they waged war with professional soldiers, with boundless sums of money. . . .

Here you have, good friends, what I have to say about liberty, and I hope you do not find that I have spoken too long; but, by Hercules, despite myself, the subject itself prolonged my presentation longer than I had planned. If my prolixity has been tedious, I beg your pardon; but if it has brought you any joy or pleasure, you may give thanks to liberty itself, just to hear the name of which is lovely.

Juan Luis Vives

In 1526, more than a century after Francesco Barbaro discoursed on the proper management of marriage to the elites of the Italian cities, Juan Luis Vives (1492–1540), scion of a distinguished family of Spanish New Christians or *conversos*, identified the delivery of assistance to the poor as an urgent need for the city of Bruges (in modern Belgium). In this revolutionary work, he proposes nothing less than the creation of a secular welfare system to be managed by city officials. It was composed in response to the wave of immigrants, the dispossessed poor of the countryside, who flooded into the rich cities of the Low Countries (the lowlying regions of Europe on the North Sea, now constituted as the nations of Belgium, Luxembourg, and the Netherlands). The recommendations Vives sets forth would actually guide the poor relief systems adopted by several other municipalities (although not in Bruges itself, ironically), and in a broader sense may be said to underlie modern poverty relief efforts.

This was no small contribution from a man with a complex past and an unrelenting commitment to truth. Born in Valencia (in modern Spain), Vives studied at the University of Paris, the center of scholastic philosophy that was then under attack from humanists who advocated an alternate mode of learning rooted in classical texts. Like his mentor Erasmus, who had earlier endured some years at Paris, Vives was repelled by the systematic and highly abstract reasoning of the scholastic model, and turned to the humanist alternative—fully armed, however, with the training in philosophical ideas and logical method that the university provided. During the 1520s, as a young man, he moved back and forth between the Low Countries, where a populous community of Spanish (and *converso*) merchants could be found, and England, where he enjoyed the patronage of Spanish-born Catherine of Aragon, the queen of (and later notoriously set aside by) the English king Henry VIII. The latter career track was blocked as a result of Henry's repudiation of Catherine; Vives was no longer welcome in England. Nor did Vives ever return to Spain, where, in 1522, the Inquisition culminated its investigation of Vives' family by burning his father and other kinsmen at the stake and confiscating their possessions. The shadow of the Inquisition hovered over Vives: his anxiety about his Jewish origins (if not his continued Jewish identification) surfaces here and there in elaborate reiterations of Christological principles and in critiques of what was then alleged to be excessive Jewish legalism.

By this time, Vives was engaged in writing a series of works, which include a critique of scholastic method (1519), a treatise on the genealogy of the intellectual disciplines (1531), and a treatise on the education of women (1524); among these, as well, his treatise on poor relief (1526).

On Assistance to the Poor is a substantial treatise containing two sections, or books, mirroring the equivocation Vives often expresses. The first gives voice to his emphatic (and as has been seen, anxious) identification with Christian orthodoxy, speaking of the individual's duty to help the poor. The second gives voice to his humanitarian concerns, offering a pragmatic proposal for the rectification of a great wrong: it is, write C. Matheeussen and Charles Fantazzi, "an astonishingly modern practical program on how to deal with the needs of the poor."[17] Both discussions are delivered in a humanist Latin that for Vives is a supple and contemporary language, almost devoid of rhetorical flourish. Fittingly, it is addressed not to some prince or potentate, as are so many of the works of this age, but to the burgomasters of Bruges, whom he called upon to put his plan into action.

The excerpts given here are from the first four chapters (out of ten) of Book Two. The first chapter argues that it is the responsibility of the governors of the city to care for the poor. They should "neglect no part of the community for which [they have] responsibility," for "the neglect of the weak endangers the strong." The poor will turn to theft and violence; or riddled with diseases, they will infect the solid citizens even as they walk into their churches. The second chapter details how the poor should be identified and classified, so that they can be properly placed—some to work outside, some inside the general-purpose "hospital," as Vives (and others of his day) understands that term: an institution that cared for the elderly, the indigent, orphaned and abandoned children, and women without protectors, as well as the sick. Two senators with a scribe will register the poor residing in hospitals; another team of two senators will visit the poor in their homes; and homeless but able-bodied beggars will "declare to the whole senate their names and the circumstances that reduced them to beggary, but in some open place or square, lest their filth infect the senate house."

The third chapter describes how the poor, once placed in appropriate situations, are to be assisted. All of them must work, even the blind, with some small adjustments made for health and old age; foreign-born paupers should be sent back home, but not into a war zone, for "then we must treat them as our countrymen." Vives notes the many trades in which workers may be employed, noting that the wool and silk workshops suffered a labor shortage. The mentally ill are given extended consideration: most can be treated gently and respectfully, and though "some require coercion and chains," these must be used judiciously. When all those who can work but do not—the malingerers, or as Vives terms them, "bloodsuckers"—have been removed, sick paupers may be distributed to the hospitals, with care being taken that "the food allotment is sufficient to fully satisfy their hunger:

---

17. Introduction to Juan Luis Vives, *De subventione pauperum sive de humanis necessitatibus,* ed. and trans. C. Matheeussen and Charles Fantazzi, with J. de Landtsheer (Leiden, Boston: Brill, 2002), xv.

for above all, provision must be made for those sick in body or soul, whose illness worsens if they are not fed."

The fourth chapter discusses the special case of children. Wet nurses must be provided for abandoned children, as was the standard procedure—their own mothers, if possible. At age six, the boys go on to elementary school, where they are to be taught by teachers of refinement and good character; Vives displays here the empathy often expressed by humanists toward those like themselves who are entrusted with the instruction of children. Aside from a few talented boys who may go on to become schoolmasters themselves, or perhaps priests, the children leave as soon as they have acquired some rudiments to work at a trade.

Girls, too, should be sent to school, a notion that is, of course, novel. The first girls' schools date from this period, and Vives is a pioneer of this movement. He had already published, in 1524, his *Education of a Christian Woman*, the first full-scale proposal for the education of girls.[18] He summarizes its main themes here: girls should be taught the rudiments of letters, "and if any girl is keen and apt, she should be able to pursue those studies further." She should be taught to be a good Christian, "and also to spin, sew, weave, embroider, cook, and keep house; to be modest, sober, proper, and polite, and above all, to preserve her chastity, knowing that this is woman's chief asset."

Vives is progressive, but not perfectly so. His empathy for the poor is profound, perhaps nowhere more striking than in the many places where he insists that they have adequate food. Yet he accepts social stratification, not only acknowledging the right of the wealthy to govern, but also commending the civility and manners of the schoolmaster while consigning the great majority of his charges to a life of unrelieved labor. His demand that all work without surcease—even the old, the infirm, and the blind—is a depressing reminder of the harshness of life in past times.

Nonetheless, Vives charts a new course here, siding neither with Catholic ideologues for whom the poor exist as an opportunity for charity—as a prop, as it were, for the salvation of the rich; nor the Protestant ideologues whose dogma of personal responsibility forestalled any notion of the responsibiity of the community to the disadvantaged. Instead, Vives wants the poor to be cared for and poverty simply eliminated. It is a clarion call.

---

18. First published 1524; available in English translation as *The Education of a Christian Woman: A Sixteenth-Century Manual*, ed. and trans. Charles Fantazzi (Chicago: University of Chicago Press, 2000); also in the edition of the sixteenth-century translation of Richard Hyrd, *The Instruction of the Christian Woman*, ed. Virginia Walcott Beauchamp, Elizabeth H. Hageman, and Margaret Mikesell (Urbana: University of Illinois Press, 2002).

Juan Luis Vives, *On Assistance to the Poor* (1526)

BOOK TWO

Chapter I: How the city magistrate should care for the poor

1. Previously I spoke about the individual's responsibility to the poor; now I turn to that of the whole city and of its governor, who . . . may neglect no part of the community for which he has responsibility. For those who care only about the rich and disdain the poor are like a doctor who thinks he may ignore his patient's hands or feet, since they are distant from his heart, and so does great harm to the whole body; in the same way, in a republic, the neglect of the weak endangers the strong. For the poor, pressed by necessity, often turn to theft. . . . They envy the rich, enraged and resentful that the wealthy have enough to feed their fools, dogs, whores, mules, horses, and elephants, while the poor cannot feed their little starving children; that in their arrogance and insolence, the rich waste the wealth which they have stolen from poor men like themselves. . . .

After Vives reflects on historical instances of tensions between rich and poor, he turns to the issue of public health.

3. To social unrest may be added the danger of contagion to the general welfare. How often do we see that a single individual infects the city with some grave and savage disease from which many others die . . . ? Or consider how on major holy days, one must make one's entrance to the church between two columns of diseased wretches with their vomit and ulcers and other obscenities disgusting even to mention—a path down which little boys and girls, the pregnant and the elderly must go? Do you think them all to be made of iron, so that they are not moved at the sight of a wasted body? Especially since all this blood and gore assaults not only their eyes, but also their nose and mouth, and they are almost touched by the hands and bodies of those passing by: so great is the impudence of the beggars. . . .

4. These things must not be neglected by the city magistrates, who must see that the ill are cared for, and that the disease does not spread further. Beyond this, a wise magistrate concerned for the public good should not allow so great a part of the population to be not only idle, but also dangerous both to themselves and to others. When assistance is lacking and there is nothing to eat, some of necessity commit robberies in the city and on the highways, while others steal under cover of darkness; young women, their modesty abandoned, cannot preserve their chastity but sell themselves for nothing to

all comers, nor can they be rescued from this terrible vice; old women take up pandering and its partner, a trade in magic potions; depravity is the only lesson taught the young children of the poor, who with their wretched offspring loiter around the churches to beg but never go inside, nor attend a service, nor does anyone know by what sacred law they live, or what creed or code they follow. . . .

Chapter II: Counting and categorizing the poor

1. Someone may ask: "How then do you propose to assist such a multitude?" If charity burned brightly in us, it would itself be a law to us, since he who loves is free from the law;[19] and it would call on us to hold all things in common, nor would anyone regard another's need as less important than his own.[20] But as we live now, there is no one whose generosity extends beyond his house, nor even beyond his room, nor even beyond himself, so that many feel nothing for their parents nor their children nor their brothers nor their wives. Therefore human remedies must be sought, since divine ones, evidently, are not working. This is how, as I see it.

2. Some of the poor live in what we call hospitals . . . ; others live on the streets and beg; others try to sustain themselves as best they can at home. I would call those institutions hospitals where the sick are fed and nursed; where some portion of the poor are supported; where boys and girls are taught, and abandoned infants nourished; where the insane are confined, and the blind housed.[21] The magistrates of a city should understand that they are responsible for all of these functions.

3. No one may challenge the statutes set by the founders of these institutions; they shall remain inviolate.[22] . . . Yet there is nothing in the city that is so free that it is not subject to the supervision of the city's magistrates, for even liberty entails acknowledging and obeying the public magistrates. . . . Nor can anyone exempt his personal property from the care and authority of the city, unless he wholly removes himself from the city . . . , especially since each

---

19. Vives alludes here to Paul's discussions of freedom from the law through grace, elaborated, among other places, in his epistle to the *Romans*, especially chapters 6 and 7.

20. Cf. Acts 2:44–45.

21. Vives here gives an accurate list of the functions of the premodern hospital, not yet restricted to medical purposes.

22. Hospitals and other benevolent institutions were often set up with endowments, which enumerated functions to be performed and amounts to be expended. Vives here reassures his audience that in his program these will be observed as before.

citizen has acquired his possessions as a kind of gift from a benevolent city, and by its aid preserves and retains them.

4. Therefore two senators together with a scribe should visit and examine each of these hospitals, record their revenues and the numbers and names of those who are housed there, as well as how each one arrived. All this information should be brought before the consuls and senate in the town hall.

5. Those poor persons who remain in their homes should be visited in their parishes by two senators who will register them and their children, noting what their needs are, how they had lived formerly, and what were the circumstances that reduced them to poverty. . . .

6. Vagrant beggars without set domicile but in good health must declare to the whole senate their names and the circumstances that reduced them to beggary, but in some open place or square, lest their filth infect the senate house. . . .

7. Those whom the senate has assigned to examine and execute these things should be given the power to compel and coerce these persons, even so far as placing them in custody; and they should identify to the senate those who do not obey.

Chapter III: How all of these may be fed

1. Before all else it must be understood that the Lord laid on humankind as a punishment for sin that each will eat the bread earned by his own labor.[23] When I say "to eat" or "to be nourished" or "to be sustained," I intend not only the provision of food, but also of clothing, shelter, firewood, candles— that is, all those things which are required for the sustenance of the body.

2. Let none of the poor who can work be without occupation, taking into account his age and health. As the apostle Paul writes to the Thessalonians: "For even when we were with you, we gave you this rule: 'The one who is unwilling to work shall not eat.'"[24] . . . Hence no one should live in the city who is without occupation, just as in a well-regulated household, each person is assigned certain responsibilities. . . .

---

23. Cf. Genesis 3:19.
24. 2 Thessalonians 3:10 (New International Version, or NIV).

3. Allowances should be made for poor health and old age; yet so that the paupers do not evade work by pretending to be sick or infirm, as happens rather often, a doctor's opinion should be sought, and the malingerers punished. Any able-bodied beggars who are foreign should be sent back to their native cities . . . , supplied with food for the journey; for it would be cruel to send a hungry man off without victuals, and whoever does so is simply inviting him to steal. . . . But if any of them are from a city or town caught up in war, then we must treat them as our countrymen, for what Paul teaches must be honored: those baptized in the blood of Christ are no longer Greek or barbarian nor Frenchman nor Flemish, but a new creation.[25]

4. The native-born paupers should be asked whether they have any skills. If they have none, and are the right age, they should be taught whatever skill they themselves prefer, if that is possible, or something similar. . . . Those who squandered their wealth in base and shameful pursuits like gambling, whoring, dissipation, and gluttony, while they should be fed—for no one should be allowed to die of starvation—they should be given the most toilsome tasks and the least food. In this way, they may be an example to others and to themselves and so repent of their former lives, nor easily backslide, restrained by the insufficiency of food and the harshness of their labor. . . .

5. Many kinds of manufacturing jobs are available for the paupers. Those who manufacture wool in Armentières and elsewhere complain of labor shortages, and the silk-makers of Bruges would hire any number of boys to turn their wheels, to whom they would pay a stuyver daily, more or less, in addition to their board, yet cannot find any who will work—for their parents say the children can bring more home by begging![26]

Vives offers more advice about putting the paupers to work, and preventing the able-bodied from loitering in the hospitals.

10. I would not allow the blind to be idle and to sit or wander about. There are many tasks to occupy them. . . . Some may mill grain, some press grapes, others work the bellows for the blacksmith. They may make small boxes or chests, baskets and cages; they may spin thread and wind it on spools. . . . Light tasks appropriate to their age and condition should also be assigned to

---

25. Cf. Colossians 3:10–11; 1 Corinthians 12:13; Galatians 3:27–28; 6:15; Romans 10:12.

26. The textile manufacturing workshops were a major source of the wealth of the Low Countries, as they were also in Italy. Notable here is the reference to child labor in this proto-industrial setting, which would become a marked and much lamented feature of factory labor in the Industrial Revolution. The *stuyver* was a coin introduced in the fourteenth century; 120 stuyvers were the equivalent of the *livre*, the main unit of the French money of account.

the infirm or elderly. For there is no one so lacking in strength that he can do nothing at all. . . .

11. When the hospitals have been purged of these malingerers who drain its treasuries, then the current assets may be calculated, based on a review of expenses and annual revenues, and the resources available to each hospital established. . . . Then there may be sent to each of the hospitals an appropriate number of sick beggars such that the food allotment is sufficient to fully satisfy their hunger: for above all, provision must be made for those sick in body or soul, whose illness worsens if they are not fed. But let there be no delicacies, which foster bad habits.

12. On the subject of the mentally ill—since there is nothing in the world more excellent than man, nor in man than his mind—special care must be taken for the health of the mind; and it must be considered a service of the highest magnitude either to restore a person's mental health, or to preserve another's sanity and stability. When a disturbed person is brought to the hospital, therefore, the first task is to determine whether his insanity is congenital, or whether it has been caused by adverse circumstances; whether there is hope of recovery, or whether the case is completely desperate. Most grievous it is that such a tragedy afflicts the loftiest part of the human soul. . . . To each individual the appropriate remedy should be supplied: for some, warm compresses and a sensible diet are indicated; for others, kind and gentle training, as for wild animals who gradually are tamed; others will respond to teaching; some require coercion and chains, but these should be employed so as not to arouse anger; in general, as far as possible, tranquility must be brought to their souls, permitting the return of reason and sanity.

Chapter IV: The care of children

1. Abandoned infants should be placed in a hospital to be nourished.[27] If their mothers are known, they may stay in the hospital to care for the children up to age six, after which the children are transferred to a public school where they learn letters and morals and are fed. Men should be chosen to head these schools who have been themselves, as much as possible, urbanely and nobly educated,[28] whose virtues will transform a plain and simple school. For there

---

27. Literally nourished—the main function of the foundling homes that began to spread in Europe from the fifteenth century was to find wet nurses who could feed the infants, for there was as yet no adequate substitute for breast milk provided by a woman who had recently given birth. As Vives goes on to say, often the infants' mothers could be enlisted to serve as wet nurse.

28. That is, provided with the kind of upbringing appropriate to an urban patriciate or a nobleman, usually not urban-based.

is no greater danger to the children of the poor than a vile and sordid and uncivil education. In recruiting such teachers, the magistrates should spare no expense; at little cost, they will bestow a great benefit on their city.

2. The children should learn to live soberly, purely, and cleanly, and to be content with little. They should be kept away from all luxuries, so that they do not become choosy or greedy or given to gluttony—such children, when they cannot get something they want, shamelessly beg for it, as some of them will when they are made to go without mustard, or some other delicacy. They should learn not only how to read and write, but first of all, Christian piety and sound principles.

3. The same holds, as I see it, for schools for girls, in which they should learn the first rudiments of letters; and, if any girl is keen and apt, she should be able to pursue those studies further, so long as they lead to her moral betterment. Let her be taught good principles and piety; and also to spin, sew, weave, embroider, cook, and keep house; to be modest, sober, proper, and polite, and above all, to preserve her chastity, knowing that this is woman's chief asset.[29]

4. After this elementary training, the boys most gifted in letters should continue in school, to become teachers themselves or perhaps attend the seminary to become priests. The others may enter whatever trade to which their soul is most inclined.

---

29. These guidelines are elaborated at much greater length in Vives' 1524 work *The Education of a Christian Woman;* see note 18 above.

Chapter 4: A World in Crisis

Introduction

Humanists, on the whole, did not seek out adventure: they preferred symposia, civil conversation, salons, and coteries. But life went on around them, and catastrophes came near and seized their attention. This chapter presents four cases where the most destructive events of the age found the humanists sitting in their studies, or engaged in their ordinary business, and made them take notice. They were not necessarily the best witnesses—we have other eloquent reports of equally disturbing events from non-humanists. But they illustrate the intersection between the world of humanist study and the world that never goes away, of raw events that swirl about bringing danger and change.

The works presented in this chapter, composed from 1453 to 1555, are by four authors from three different cities, of different occupations, ages, and genders—for included here is a sampling of the work of a woman humanist, the first to be considered in this volume, with others to follow in Chapter 9. The first is by the Venetian nobleman and entrepreneur Lauro Quirini (1420– c. 1479), who had recently located to Crete when in 1453 the Ottoman Turks, who had been pressing toward their target for some years, seized Constantinople, capital of the Byzantine Empire. This was by any reckoning a catastrophic event: it changed the relations between the Western world and Islamic states decisively, and closed trade in the eastern Mediterranean to Western merchants with important consequences for European expansion in the Atlantic region. These long-term consequences were not entirely apparent to Quirini, however, in the first weeks after the conquest. The issues that distressed him, instead, were the threat to the unity and supremacy of the Christian religion; the assault on the material and intellectual remains of ancient Greek and Roman civilization embodied in Constantinople; and the threat to Venetian economic and political interests in the Mediterranean. Of these, the first was foremost in his mind when he sent a letter to Pope Nicholas V, urging him immediately to launch a crusade against the Turks.

The second text is by the Florentine scholar and poet Angelo Poliziano (1454–1494), a servitor of the Medici, the ruling family of Florence. In 1478, an attempted coup d'état by members of rival clans resulted in the assassination of Giuliano de' Medici, younger brother of Lorenzo, who then reigned alone until his death in 1492. This was a pivotal event in Florentine history: not because it was the first instance of civic disorder, for there had been a myriad of them in Florence as elsewhere in Italy in recent centuries, but because it set the seal on Medici primacy, which would survive a long interregnum from the 1490s to early 1510s to reign into the eighteenth century. Poliziano was an eager reporter of these events, which permitted him to celebrate the ascendancy of his patron and to document the Pazzi conspiracy in fine classical style and with more than a whiff of partisanship.

The third text is by Luigi Guicciardini (1478–1551), a Florentine statesman who, at the time of the composition of his history of the 1527 sack of Rome, held the supreme executive office of *gonfaloniere della giustizia* ("standard-bearer of justice"). An experienced veteran of political and military affairs—like his more-famous brother, Francesco, likewise a historian and statesman—Guicciardini offers a ruthlessly explicit account of the massacre of Roman citizens by the Spanish and German soldiers of the imperial army. Interwoven with the narrative is the author's palpable disgust at the incompetence of the defenders, the irresponsibility of the pope, Clement VII, and the bloodthirstiness of the invaders.

The fourth textual element of this chapter constitutes a selection of the letters of Olympia Morata (1526/1527–1555), a Ferrarese by birth but destined to become, by marriage and conversion, a German Protestant. In their sparse urgency, quite unlike the ornamented humanist products of her precocious early work, the letters (dated 1551–1555) tell a compelling story of the suppression of Protestantism in Italy, the appeal of the works of Luther and Calvin to a new convert, and the brutal conditions suffered by those living through the wars of religion in Germany. Above all, they speak of Morata's love of her family and friends, her profound convictions, and her determination in a time of troubles.

War, politics, and religion—these powerful forces intervene in the lives of our humanists, demand their attention, and elicit these various and affecting witnesses to events that streamed about them, well beyond their control.

Lauro Quirini

In his palace on the island of Crete, the Venetian patrician and humanist Lauro Quirini (1420–c. 1479) received from the exiled Paduan jurist Paolo de' Dotti a letter dated 11 June 1453, giving an eyewitness report of the fall of Constantinople barely two weeks after it occurred. Some two weeks thereafter, Quirini heard another eyewitness report, in person, from the

Russian-born cardinal Isidore of Kiev,[1] who had fled to Crete from devastated Greece. On 15 July, some six weeks after the fall of the last bastion of ancient Rome, Quirini wrote to the pope in Rome to tell the story he had heard, and to urge the pontiff to take swift action against a threat to all of Christendom.

Quirini's was not the only account of Constantinople's fall—and subsequently, he himself would write three more in its aftermath, as will be seen below. Naval commanders, officials, and merchants wrote other reports immediately following the incident, as did two other humanists, both Venetian state secretaries. But Quirini's has special significance, because it is the account of a man who was at once positioned on Crete, the midpoint of the Venetian maritime empire, and a major actor in the Venetian humanist scene. It is also a fresh and largely accurate narrative, delivered in lucid and pointed Latin prose.

For Lauro Quirini was a man of broad and deep culture. In his youth, he studied at the University of Padua, obtaining degrees in Arts (1440) and Civil and Canon Law (1448). During this period, he wrote three treatises on the then-controversial topic of nobility, defending the notion, as had Francesco Barbaro, of the inherent superiority of privileged groups. In addition he wrote a treatise *On the Republic*, a letter prescribing a curriculum of advanced study to the woman humanist Isotta Nogarola, and various orations and letters to other humanists. He was expert in both Greek and Latin, and a sophisticated reader of philosophy who promoted the study of Aristotle in the original language.

But in 1452, renouncing his first public office, he departed with his new bride for Crete, a prosperous island in the eastern Mediterranean where his family had extensive business interests. Quirini possessed land, traded in wine, textiles, and alum, and purchased and read books, serving for a number of years as the agent of the Greek-born Cardinal Bessarion in procuring and transmitting important manuscripts. He had been in Crete scarcely more than a year when Constantinople fell, the refugees arrived, and he picked up his pen for the salvation, as he saw it, of Christendom.

Quirini's letter to Pope Nicholas has three parts. In the first, he announces the catastrophe that befell Constantinople. In the second, he assesses the Turkish position and intentions. In the third, he beseeches the pope to take the lead in a new crusade effort against the Turkish invader.

---

1. One of those who, following the councils held to advance the reunion of Eastern and Western Christianity, adhered to the Latin "uniate," or unified church. Isidore of Kiev (1385–1463) was made a cardinal and sent as papal legate to Constantinople to lead "the little band of soldiers the Pope sent to help the Emperor": Alexander H. Hore, *Eighteen Centuries of the Orthodox Greek Church* (Piscataway, NJ: Gorgias Press, 2003; facs. rpnt of orig. London: James Parker, 1899), 218.

"The most lamentable fall, then, of this lamentable city happened in this way, as I have learned from reliable men who were themselves participants in the events." So Quirini opens his narrative of events that takes us through a mere eight weeks, from 4 April 1453, when the Turkish army of some 240,000 men took its position before the city, through the following 29 May, when the city fell and the three-day sack began. The fleet of some 250 vessels arrived eight days later in the city's storied harbor. On 15 May bombardment began, which damaged but did not destroy the city walls. At the same time, the Turks rolled out their war machines: ladders, catapults, and siege devices of all kinds. Then there arrived a giant cannon equipped with an immense stone cannonball weighing 1300 pounds. This bomb tore gaping holes in the splendid walls of Constantinople, through which the invaders could now advance.

On 28 May, the attack began. The next morning, the Turkish sultan Mehmed II with his chosen band paraded around the battlefront and shot a golden arrow into the city—in ancient Roman times, a signal of the avowed destruction of the enemy. This act energized his soldiers further, who shot so many arrows and flung so many stones at the defenders atop the remaining battlements that the walls dissolved into fragments that soared through the air, like birds in flight. The city was given over to sack, desecration, and rape: "Wherever you went you heard nothing but groans and wails. . . . Never, . . . I think, has there ever been a more horrific spectacle."

How accurate is Quirini's account? It differs in a few details from the consensus of eyewitness accounts of the fall of Constantinople. Quirini does seem to put Mehmed's extravaganza on the morning after the hostilities began, rather than, as is more likely, the night before a pre-dawn battle was launched; and the golden arrow, plucked out of ancient Roman histories with which Mehmed and his advisers were unfamiliar, is likely an invention, although not necessarily Quirini's.

The facts established, Quirini laments the loss of this last outpost of the Roman empire. Most striking, perhaps, is Quirini's lament for the civilization of Greece itself—he does not distinguish here between ancient Greece with its classical works of philosophy and literature and modern Byzantium with its mostly religious culture:

> Add to this that the raging barbarians who did all these heinous deeds not only captured a royal city, destroyed its churches and defiled their sacred ornaments, but accomplished the ruin of an entire nation, obliterating the civilization that was Greece: more than 120,000 volumes, as I have learned from Cardinal Isidore of Kiev, destroyed. And so, the Greek language, and the literature of the Greeks created, extended, and perfected by so great an expenditure of time, so much labor, so much skill—annihilated, extinguished!

Thus speaks the humanist. But the man of affairs returns quickly, as Quirini assesses the nature of the enemy, not mistakenly alluding to the absence among the Ottoman Turks of a literary or legal tradition—and their allegiance to an alien faith: "A savage people, a crude people, living by no set principles, no laws, but shapeless, shiftless, purposeless, swollen with trickery and perfidy, shamefully and despicably grind all Christendom under their heel."

This last is the principal issue as Quirini pivots from the eastern Mediterranean and turns to the pope in Rome: the great danger posed by the Turks to the Christian faith, and the whole of Christian civilization. A young man swollen with pride, Mehmed II nurtures fearsome ambitions: "What is at stake is whether the name of Christ shall be worshiped in all the earth, or Mohammed's. . . . Come, then, you must see . . . that this is a fierce enemy of Christianity, powerful, proud, and angry, whose nightly dream . . . is to destroy the Christian faith."

When in 1187, the sultan Saladin captured Jerusalem, the popes prodded the rulers of Europe to launch a Third Crusade against the Islamic enemy. The present pope in Rome must do no less. "On you," Quirini instructs Pope Nicholas V, "rests the burden of defense": "all Christian eyes are turned on you, to you they look for hope of rescue and safety." You must "defend the name of Christ, lest it perish entirely," and be willing to die for Christ. The papacy profited from the recent Jubilee celebration in Rome by some one million ducats; you must spend that money in this righteous cause, or else, "what will Christians say about you?" Indeed, the pope is obligated to act, because he received the papacy as a gift from the emperor Constantine—such was the theory embraced by the popes until it was debunked by humanist Lorenzo Valla (of which more later)—and must pass it on intact to his successor. The pope must lead this Crusade, and if he does so, all Christians will follow, with the same spirit and willingness to sacrifice themselves that Quirini sees in his fellow citizens of Crete.

Nicholas was not uninterested in a Crusade, but neither he nor his successor was able to get one together. No other power in Western Europe acted forcefully to address the Turkish threat, although Hungary and Albania, which faced it frontally, were necessarily engaged. Venice struggled with the choice between compromise and offense. It tried offense unsuccessfully in the Long War of 1463 to 1479, and lost ignominiously—after which, it sued for peace. By that date, Quirini had died, having written three times more (in 1458, 1464, and 1470) to bestir the West against the Turk. He feared for Crete; yet Crete, ironically, survived the Ottoman threat the longest of Venice's territories, falling only in 1669.

Modern students schooled in the dangers of Orientalism—the construction of non-European cultures, seen by some scholars as characteristic of the western outlook, as inherently alien and inferior—and the need for multicultural tolerance will shudder a bit at Quirini's laments for Constantinople, his triumphalist celebrations of Christianity and the West, and his unenlightened attacks on the Turkish nation and its goals. But moderns must recognize that from where he sat, on the island of Crete in the center of the maelstrom that was the Turkish advance in the eastern Mediterranean, the peril was great, and his allegiance to his own faith and culture perhaps allowable.

Lauro Quirini, *Letter to Pope Nicholas V, on the Fall of Constantinople* (Candia, Crete, 15 July 1453)

To the most blessed Pope Nicholas V, Lauro Quirini sends wishes for good health in the name of the Lord who is the true health of all:

Although my intellect may not be equal to the material, and though I may be consumed to such an extent with grief, bitterness, and sorrow that I am, as the Greek proverb says, sweating blood, yet I shall try, most blessed father, to describe the grievous calamity that has befallen the most unfortunate city of Constantinople,[2] and to delineate how great is the danger that now threatens Christendom; and lastly to exhort, pray, beg, and finally, to summon your blessedness in the name of all Christendom to take up arms in defense of the Christian faith against the most impious and cruel enemy of Christianity.

The most lamentable fall, then, of this lamentable city happened in this way, as I have learned from reliable men who were themselves participants in the events. On 4 April 1453, as they relate, the Turks with an army of about 240,000 men set up fortifications some 2000 paces from the city, and stationed some light troops. Then on 12 April, a fleet arrived with 14 triremes, and 236 larger and smaller biremes;[3] and since they could not enter the harbor, which is protected by its own natural topographical and geological features, as well as fortified by the military engineers, and defended by a multitude of our ships, 60 biremes were hauled overland for 2000 paces across hill, valley, and plain, and lowered into the water. Then on 20 April, three Genoese ships appeared, plus one command ship. The whole Turkish fleet went out to meet them, with the exception of the biremes that had been dragged to the harbor, and a tough four-hour battle ensued, without effect. . . .

Then on 15 May, a huge bombardment of cannonfire issued from Pera,[4] damaging not only our ships, but also the walls of the city, and so heavy was the bombardment each day thereafter, that the gunpowder alone, it is estimated, cost 1000 ducats. Meanwhile, the Turks set up a fabulous display of machinery—scaling ladders, ballistas,[5] catapults, testudos,[6] and thirteen cages[7]—it is said they had in their employ expert metallurgists, includ-

---

2. Modern Istanbul, Turkey.

3. Triremes (activated by three tiers of oars on each side) and biremes (activated by two) were the standard design of warships prior to the age of sail.

4. Modern Beyoğlu, Turkey; a quarter of Constantinople in which many Europeans lived, north of the Golden Horn.

5. The ballista is a premodern siege machine that hurled heavy projectiles large distances.

6. The testudo ("turtle") is a premodern siege device, a movable screen that shields attackers approaching a target. Those in action at Constantinople may have taken the form of small movable wooden castles.

7. These may possibly have held dogs or other animals that had military functions.

ing Serbian silversmiths and Turkish bronzesmiths, but neither did these mechanical devices do any harm to the city. But there was one cannonball that they shot of an extraordinary magnitude, such as no age has ever seen before—made of stone, easily thrown, weighing 1300 pounds. It had been crafted in Adrianople[8] and, it is said, transported with great difficulty by 500 men hauling 20 carts; and the shot of this cannonball, according to witnesses, caused the land and the sea for 4000 paces around to shake long afterward. This bomb quickly shattered the walls of the city, crafted with such art, and razed them to the ground.

After this, on 25 May, the public criers instructed the people to remove the bodies and to prepare arms. . . . With all things thus arranged, on 28 May, at the first hour of the night,[9] the battle began on land with the soldiers massed on the frontlines, and raged the whole night. But then when the day at last dawned, that terrible pestilence, the Turk, riding in a golden chariot, approached the walls . . . and let loose a golden arrow at the city, condemning it to destruction.[10] When his troops saw this, and heard the great clamor that followed, their souls were aroused with such alacrity and ardor that they fired numberless missiles and arrows so fiercely that the walls collapsed, their fragments soaring through the air, onlookers said, as though they were birds in flight.

In this way in our wretched age this ancient, noble, wealthy city, once the seat of the Roman empire, the mistress of the whole Orient, captured by raging barbarians, was sacked for three days and reduced to wretched servitude, which is the worst of all evils. O how miserable is the human condition! O how fragile and fleeting is fortune! Constantinople, the imperious city, once the bulwark of the Roman empire, the victor and captor of provinces— ah! it is now a vanquished captive, cruelly and basely destroyed; its citizens, descendants of the Romans, brutally slaughtered before their fathers' gates, noble virgins, innocent boys, worthy matrons, venerable nuns, seized, slain, raped; its churches, wondrous for their size and splendor, torn to pieces, the holy objects, the sacred ornaments foully desecrated.

What more is there to say? Wherever you went you heard nothing but groans and wails. O the shameful barbarity, O the inhuman cruelty, O the

---

8. Modern Edirne, Turkey; the ancient city of Hadrianople, later Anglicized as Adrianople, was the Turkish base on the European mainland before the conquest of Constantinople.

9. According to Agostino Pertusi, *Le epistole storiche di Lauro Quirini sulla caduta di Constantinopoli e la potenza dei turchi*, in Konrad Krautter et al., *Lauro Quirini umanista: Studi e testi*, ed. Vittore Branca (Florence: Leo S. Olschki, 1977), 180, the battle began three hours before dawn on May 29.

10. According to Pertusi, *Epistole storiche*, 180–81, this "*passeggiata*," or promenade of Sultan Mehmed II, took place the night before the battle, on 28 May; and the sultan is unlikely to have shot a golden arrow, a ritual once performed by the fetial priests of Rome on the eve of battle, as he is unlikely to have been aware of that classical precedent—although certainly the fifteenth-century humanists were.

intolerable viciousness and savagery of the perpetrators! For who can bear I won't say the sight, but even the report of such slaughter, such destruction, such bloodshed, such pillagery? Never, most blessed father, I think, has there ever been a more horrific spectacle. . . .

Add to this that the raging barbarians who did all these heinous deeds not only captured a royal city, destroyed its churches, and defiled their sacred ornaments, but accomplished the ruin of an entire nation, obliterating the civilization that was Greece: more than 120,000 volumes, as I have learned from Cardinal Isidore of Kiev, destroyed. And so, the Greek language, and the literature of the Greeks created, extended, and perfected by so great an expenditure of time, so much labor, so much skill—annihilated, extinguished! Is there anyone either so ignorant or so heartless that he can hold back his tears? That literary tradition has perished which illuminated the whole world, bestowing righteous laws, sacred philosophy, and all the other liberal arts which refine human existence. And shall we not mourn, shall we not grieve over this most horrible disaster, this most unlucky catastrophe, this unbearable calamity? Ah, what sorrow! A savage people, a crude people, living by no set principles, no laws, but shapeless, shiftless, purposeless, swollen with trickery and perfidy, shamefully and despicably grind all Christendom under their heel.

> *Quirini recalls the prompt and stern response of the successive Popes Urban III (1185–1187), Gregory VIII (1187), and Clement III (1187–1191), who, following Saladin's reconquest of Jerusalem in 1187, supported the launch of the Third Crusade (1189–1192) against enemies of the same faith, but not the same ethnic origin, as the Turks who captured Constantinople in 1453.*

But this is not the time for stories or tears. For what is at stake, most blessed father, what is at stake is the well-being of all of Christendom. . . . What is at stake is whether the name of Christ shall be worshiped in all the earth, or Mohammed's. For this fearsome monster aims to eradicate the Christian religion not merely by words, but by deeds. . . . Come, then, you must see, most blessed father, that this is a fierce enemy of Christianity, powerful, proud, and angry, whose nightly dream . . . is to destroy the Christian faith. . . .

Truly, consider how great is the Turk's power: he has many subjects, and many flourishing provinces from Cilicia and the Taurus mountains[11] as far as the Danube River and lower Pannonia,[12] which comprise a vast and most fertile part of the habitable earth. . . . Moreover, at this moment by his stunning

---

11. Quirini names an ancient province in southeastern Anatolia, and a nearby mountain range, both located in modern Turkey.

12. Pannonia is the ancient Roman province roughly corresponding to modern Hungary.

victory over Byzantium the Turk has acquired the many prosperous cities of the Black Sea, . . . which, moreover, are Christian. As a result, fortune's favor has so inflated his pride that this stripling with an outrageously swollen chest now menaces the whole globe. For now he possesses—alas, he possesses Constantinople, the imperial capital, from which . . . he may easily gain dominion over the whole earth. . . .

As soon as word arrived, then, of the fall of Constantinople, the entire Orient became convulsed with fear; the islands, terrified, pitifully tremble; all the coastal cities shiver in dread. For they see that all of Christendom stands as though on a precipice, in the greatest possible danger. For things have come, most blessed father, to the extreme edge of peril and the boundary of doom; so terror and dread prevail, and melancholy has seized all men's souls, and desperation is seen in each man's face. It shames me, yes, shames me, most blessed father, to convey this news of Christendom's imperilment; yet what has been seen must be told. . . .

O the miserable, O the calamitous, O the lamentable condition of Christianity! My sorrow is just, most holy Nicholas V, I cannot assuage it, it drains me of life that our generation has fallen into such dolorous, such miserable times. But what is needed is a cure, not complaints. Therefore, most blessed father, note that all Christian eyes are turned on you, to you they look for hope of rescue and safety. Above all, note that our universal welfare depends on your holiness. On you rests by virtue of your office, both as the Father of Christendom and as a puissant prince, the burden of defense. . . .

Therefore, you must and can defend the name of Christ, lest it perish entirely; and more, if it is necessary, for Christ willingly to die. . . . Act therefore, most blessed father, for the peace of Italy and of all Christianity, arouse, inspire Christian power to the defense of the Christian faith against this most fearsome enemy of Christianity. And could there be a more just or glorious or magnificent cause to take up arms? Or if I may speak plainly, more necessary? For if we do not attack, the Turk will surely do so. For he is mobilizing the whole Orient, on land and sea. . . .

Hasten therefore, summon up all your courage, and arouse the glorious and conquering Roman and Italian forces as quickly as can be done: for the matter demands speed. . . . And if I may freely and openly raise this to you, the word has spread everywhere, most blessed father, that you collected one million ducats from the Jubilee year celebration:[13] but if you do not defend Christendom when it stands in such danger, what will Christians say about you? Will they call you a beneficent father, or rather an avaricious tax farmer? . . .

---

13. Pope Nicholas V had declared a Jubilee in 1450, the first since 1423, a time of pilgrimage and celebration which brought an influx of funds to Rome and to the Church.

Therefore when you see that Christianity stands in ultimate danger, save it, most blessed father; for you have the power to save. . . . You are obligated to do so by both natural and civil law; for since you accepted dominion over the Roman Church, the gift of Constantine,[14] you must hold it, most blessed father, and restore it on the same terms and in its original condition to his successors—and all the more so now that the issue is not only dominion over the Church, but the obliteration of the Christian faith, the destruction of all of Christendom.

What then remains to be said? Let the Highest Pope lead the way, then, with the redemptive banner of the Holy Cross raised high; let the most Christian Emperor follow, then all the kings and princes of Christendom. For I believe that the rest of the Christian people . . . will display the same courage that I see in the citizens of Crete, whose one desire is to die gloriously in defense of the faith.

Angelo Poliziano

The sophisticated humanist Angelo Poliziano (1454–1494)—a scholar's scholar, a teacher of humanists at the Florentine university, the epicenter of Renaissance learning—offers in *Account of the Pazzi Conspiracy* (1478) a vivid, compelling, and highly partisan account of the conspiracy against the brothers Lorenzo and Giuliano de' Medici, resulting in the latter's death and sealing the former's triumph.

Poliziano was a courtier humanist, poet, and scholar. As a young man desperately in need of patronage, he found it in the Medici family, the greatest patrons of the fifteenth century. In 1475, he was entrusted with the education of Lorenzo's son Pietro. At around the same time, he undertook a verse series in celebration of Giuliano de' Medici, victor of a tournament held in the Piazza della Signoria, the center of Florentine civic life: the *Stanze per la giostra*, a brilliant achievement, though cut short by Giuliano's death in the conspiracy Poliziano would document. In 1478, he was in the Medici entourage, a familiar member of the inner circle that gathered at the family palace in the aftermath of the assassination.

In later years, while Lorenzo continued as the sole if unofficial ruler of the city, Poliziano was appointed (in 1480) as the chair of Latin and Greek at the

---

14. Quirini finds it useful to appeal to the Donation of Constantine, the ninth-century forgery exposed as such by Lorenzo Valla some thirteen years before, as the Venetian most certainly was aware.

University of Florence, a position that gave him the opportunity, through the students he influenced, to shape the humanistic culture of the last decades of the fifteenth century. He survived Lorenzo by two years, living long enough to witness the unraveling, for the moment, of the Medici supremacy.

The Medici had come to power by a velvet coup d'état in 1434, when Lorenzo's grandfather Cosimo il Vecchio seized power. Working behind the scenes, manipulating rather than dismantling the already well-oiled machinery of Florentine oligarchy, Cosimo held secure control over the city until his death in 1464, when his less-able son Piero succeeded. But Piero's reign lasted only five years, and in 1469, Lorenzo and his younger brother Giuliano took charge. Giuliano's murder in 1478 left Lorenzo securely in power, unhampered by any ties or obligations, and surrounded with an entourage of courtiers, assistants, and humanists—Poliziano among them.

Poliziano's account of the conspiracy is a refined work of art. He portrays the conspirators as wholly evil members of two wholly evil families, and the Medici youths as brave, pious, courteous, and prudent—possessors of all the virtues. These good and bad actors clash, with the two noble brothers outrageously outnumbered by their assassins. The story unfolds in three locations, like stage sets. The murder of Giuliano and Lorenzo's heroic self-defense take place in the cathedral, "between the altar and the Eucharist," precisely during the sacrifice of the Mass—blasphemy added to crime. Retribution against the Pazzi and Salviati malefactors takes place principally in the Palazzo Vecchio (the "old palace"), which was the seat of government, or Signoria; from its windows two of the guilty would be hanged. The gathering of the "people," a seething mob of angry Florentines loyal to Lorenzo, intent on vengeance, takes place mainly outside the Medici palace, to which Lorenzo returns triumphantly after his courageous escape.

This is opera more than history: dramatic tableaux, villains and heroes, a chorus of collective, depersonalized, popular feeling. Its effect is to raise these events out of the stream of history, to lock them in time, as an emblem of a political moment, when Justice triumphed in the person of a Medici ruler.

Poliziano opens by stating his intention to tell the story of the conspiracy "because it was by far the most infamous crime to occur in my day, and it very nearly caused the complete downfall of the Florentine republic." The first third of the work consists of profiles of the conspirators: men of the Pazzi and Salviati families, and a few others, including clerics and practiced killers. They are blasphemous and impious, misers and wastrels, gamblers and scoundrels. The two Medici brothers, in contrast, the targets of the assassination, are "excellent," "pious," "worthy," and "noble."

In a second section, constituting again about one-third of the whole, Poliziano details the assault and its outcome. It takes place in the cathedral of Florence, during the celebration of the Mass. While a few of the conspirators took control of the Palazzo Vecchio, the seat of government, the others attack the Medici brothers. One group encircles Giuliano, who is killed in a single blow by one veteran swordsman—who then repeatedly stabs the dead body with his dagger. A less capable fighter nicks Lorenzo, who swiftly draws his own sword and holds off his assailants. Lorenzo and his companions then take refuge in the sacristy, bolting the large bronze doors against their enemy. Supporters arrive, the assailants flee, and Lorenzo is escorted home by a route that tactfully avoids the mangled body of Giuliano on the cathedral floor. Crowds gather at the Medici palace, shouting their support, while armed men and supplies pour in.

In a third section, Poliziano describes the chaos in the streets, the heaps of bloodied bodies lying about in the open, and especially, the retribution visited upon the malefactors, most of whom are hunted down and killed. The Mediceans take charge of the Palazzo Vecchio once more, and Lorenzo himself, while grieving for his brother—and ignoring his own injuries—attends to everything. Again and again, the crowd roars its support for the Medici, whom they see as "the bastion of public well-being," and for Lorenzo, "in whom alone the whole Florentine republic placed its trust, in whom the hope and welfare of the people rested."

Coming to a close, Poliziano describes in just a few brief sentences the mammoth funeral for Giuliano: it is performed in the cathedral with all due rites; the young people wear mourning; he was stabbed nineteen times, not quite as many as the number of years—twenty-five—that he had lived. Giuliano was beloved; but now the welfare of Florence rested in the hands of Lorenzo.

Poliziano's operatic account has echoes of two other works previously considered in Chapter 3: Bruni's laudation of the city of Florence, and Rinuccini's dialogue in defense of liberty. The Brunian theme is heard especially in the description of the Medici palace as it was readied to receive the cardinal, one of the peripheral characters in the drama: the lush textiles, the rich gems, the works of art, the exquisite architectural setting all recall Bruni's praise of the buildings of Florence. So, too, the enthusiastic and loyal citizenry recalls Bruni's characterization of the Florentine populace, loyal to the city where everyone may expect justice.

Rinuccini, of course, is another matter, for he had exiled himself from the city, for fear of retribution, after the Pazzi conspiracy and the reestablishment of Lorenzo's supremacy. But Rinuccini's portrayal of the elite as in some cases corrupt, or for the rest, intimidated into silence, although it is bitterly realistic where Poliziano is propagandistic, nonetheless describes the same faction-ridden city as does the courtier Poliziano. The existence of faction, violence, and revenge is a given in the history of Florence as, indeed, for most of the cities of the Italian Renaissance, which along with their exceptional vitality, their claim of self-determination, and their elaborate governmental systems to protect against manipulation by clan and faction, never succeeded in quelling the struggle for supremacy among the cities' elites.

Poliziano's account of the Pazzi conspiracy may also be compared with Quirini's of the fall of Constantinople. Both works are highly rhetorical: Poliziano's descriptions of the bloodied corpses in the piazza or the enthusiastic cries of the people may be likened to Quirini's description of the people of the Mediterranean, gripped by fear as the Turks advanced. Both are partisan and far from even-handed: in Poliziano's Manichaean vision, the Pazzi and Salviati are all bad, the Medici all good, while for Quirini, a wholly innocent Christendom lay at the mercy of a wholly evil Turkish nemesis. Quirini is more sincere; his anguish at the fate of Constantinople as the last redoubt of Greek civilization is convincing, whereas Poliziano's celebration of the Medici youths has the odor of opportunism and sycophancy. But in all these regards, both works precisely capture the values of the age in which they were conceived.

Angelo Poliziano, *Account of the Pazzi Conspiracy* (1478)

I here set out briefly the course of the Pazzi conspiracy, because it was by far the most infamous crime to occur in my day, and it very nearly caused the complete downfall of the Florentine republic.

When the situation in the city, then, was this, that all worthy men supported the brothers Lorenzo and Giuliano and the rest of the Medici family, the Pazzi clan alone, with a few of the Salviati, began to oppose them— secretly at first, but soon quite openly. They envied the Medici family for its great authority in public affairs and for the splendor of its domestic establishment, and so did everything they could to thwart them.

The citizens and the people alike detested the Pazzi not only for their insatiable greed, but also for their arrogant and insolent posturing. . . .

With this sweeping brushstroke characterizing the Pazzi family, Poliziano introduces the main actors complicit in the conspiracy: Jacopo Pazzi, the head of the clan, at whose country villa the conspiracy was devised, a blasphemous gambler, both miserly and spendthrift; Francesco Salviati, archbishop of Pisa, impious, immoral, and stupid, who with his supporters joined the Pazzi machinations; Francesco Pazzi, the elder Jacopo's nephew, consumed by resentment and vanity; Jacopo Salviati, the archbishop's cousin, a shrewd charmer; Jacopo, son of the humanist Poggio Bracciolini, (see Chapter 1) chronically irresponsible and available to the highest bidder; a fourth Jacopo, also Salviati, the archbishop's brother, a person of no worth; and Bernardo Bandini, another Florentine down on his fortunes, mercenary, ruthless, and eager to get ahead. These seven were the principal conspirators joined by a handful of others, including the Giovanni Battista Montesecco, a professional general, who was assigned the key task of killing Lorenzo de' Medici, but withdrew before the event.

The time has now come to explain how the conspiracy happened.

The Medici family, while always splendid and magnificent in all things, was especially so in the hospitality shown to important guests. For no illustrious visitor ever came to Florence or its countryside to whom the family did not give a magnificent reception. When cardinal Rafaello,[15] then, the son of count Girolamo Riario's sister, stopped for a while at Jacopo Pazzi's villa outside the city, the place where the conspiracy had been hatched, the conspirators found an opportunity to put their plan in action. They sent notice to the two Medici brothers in the cardinal's name that he wished to be received at their country villa in Fiesole. There I went with Lorenzo and with Pietro, Lorenzo's son; Giuliano, who was ill, stayed at home—which circumstance caused the whole event to be postponed. . . .

Then once more, the conspirators wrote affably to say that the cardinal wished to be hosted at a banquet in Florence, in order to view the ornaments of the city palace: the tapestries, the hangings, the gems and silver, the whole precious collection. The fine young men suspected no harm. They prepared the house, put out the ornaments, arranged the tapestries, displayed the silver, paintings, and sculptures, and brought out the gems in their cases. A splendid banquet was made ready.

But then a small group of the conspirators arrived early, and asked, "Where is Lorenzo? And where Giuliano?" Both were at the church of Santa Reparata,[16] they were told, and there the conspirators pursued them. While the Cardinal, as is customary, took his place on a platform in the choir, and while the Mass was celebrated, the archbishop with Jacopo Poggio, the two Jacopo Salviatis, and some other companions went off to the Palazzo Vecchio where, so as to oust the would-be lords of Florence from their perch, they occupied the government offices.[17] The rest of the conspirators remained in the church to carry out the crime. Giovanni Battista,[18] who had been chosen to kill Lorenzo, had withdrawn from the deal, so Antonio and Stefano Volaterrano took his place. The others would take care of Giuliano.

Then as soon as the priest had taken communion, the agreed-upon signal, Bernardo Bandini, Francesco Pazzi, and the other conspirators formed a ring around Giuliano. Bandini, the leader, drove a sword through the young man's chest. Dying, Giuliano backed off a few steps, pursued by his assailants. As his life left him, he fell to the floor. Francesco stabbed at the prostrate

---

15. Raffaello Riario Sansoni, nephew of papal courtier Girolamo Riario, also a cardinal. Cardinal Raffaello played no active role in the conspiracy but suffered the consequences nonetheless.

16. The cathedral of Florence.

17. The Palazzo Vecchio, or the Signoria, was the public building where the principal offices of government were located.

18. Montesecco, a skilled swordsman.

body with repeated blows of his dagger. Thus they slew the worthy youth. Giuliano's servant, terrified, shamefully ran off.

Meanwhile the assassins assigned to Lorenzo attacked him. Antonio took the lead, laying a hand on Lorenzo's left shoulder and aiming a thrust at his throat. Fearlessly, Lorenzo ripped off the torn garment and wrapped it around his left arm, at the same time drawing his sword from its scabbard; but as he reached for his weapon, he was struck by a blow that wounded him in the neck. Then swiftly, sword in hand, this bold and quick-witted man turned on his assassins, eyeing them warily. Panicked, they took flight. . . .

Back in the church, Bandini pressed his attack, while Lorenzo and his supporters took refuge in the sacristy, the author Poliziano soon joining them.

Then I fled to the same place of sanctuary, and along with some others shut the bronze doors, thus holding off Bandini. While we guarded the entry, others were anxious about Lorenzo's wound; Antonio Rodolfo, son of Jacopo, an excellent youth, sucked it out.[19] Lorenzo cared nothing about his own welfare, but asked constantly how Giuliano was, raging all the time at having been threatened by men who with such unfair advantage had sought to take his life. Meanwhile a growing pack of armed young men loyal to the Medici house crowded outside the entrance to the sacristy. With one voice, they declared that they were friends and kinsmen; Lorenzo must come out, come out, they said, before the enemy came back with reinforcements! Inside, we were uncertain whether they were friends or enemies, but asked in any case whether Giuliano was safe. To that question they gave no answer.

Then Sismondo Stupha, a worthy young man who had been bound to Lorenzo since childhood by ties of loyalty and love, climbed a ladder to the organ gallery, urgently seeking an opening from which he could look down into the church; there he saw the prostrate body of Giuliano, and knew at once the crime that had been done. He saw, as well, that the crowd of young men waiting outside were friends, and ordered that the doors be opened. The youths then took Lorenzo into their midst, forming an armed escort to lead him home, while keeping him away from the sight of Giuliano's body.

I headed straight for the Medici palace and, passing through the church, saw Giuliano covered with many wounds, fouled with much blood, wretchedly laid low. Staggering, and gravely disturbed in spirit by the magnitude of my sorrow, I was assisted by some friends and taken to the palace.

The whole place was full of armed men, resounding with the cries of supporters of the Medici, the roof itself reverberating with the roar of the voices. You could see men young and old, clergy and laymen, taking up arms to defend the Medici house as though it were the bastion of public well-being.

---

19. In case it had been poisoned.

At the Palazzo Vecchio, Archbishop Salviati and Jacopo Pazzi attempt to follow through on their plans, but learning that these had been foiled, take refuge.

Meanwhile Lorenzo's men reclaimed the helm of government at the Palazzo Vecchio. They killed all the Perugian [supporters of archbishop Salviati], who had torn down the door [to the room where they had hidden, accidentally locking themselves in.] Then for the others, savagery. They hanged Jacopo di Poggio from the windows of the palace. A detachment of armed men captured the cardinal and brought him back to the palace, with difficulty protecting him from the rage of the mob—which succeeded, however, in killing most of his followers, who were ripped to pieces, their corpses brutally slashed. The trophies were mounted in front of Lorenzo's door: now a head stuck on a pike, now a fragment of shoulder. Nothing could be heard anywhere but the voices of the people crying *Palle! Palle!*—the emblem of the Medici family.[20] . . .

At the Medici palace, meanwhile, the crowd gathered to show its enthusiastic loyalty and support, dragging traitors to their punishment, sparing no threats or abuse as they drove the malefactors to meet their end. The house of Jacopo Pazzi was barely saved from pillage; naked and bleeding and only half-alive, Francesco Pazzi was rushed to the noose by Pietro Corsini's band:[21] for the fury of the mob was not easy or possible to resist. Then from the same window where Francesco Pazzi had hung, the archbishop of Pisa was hanged over the other's lifeless body. . . .

I then recall going to the piazza (for at the Medici palace things were now quiet) where I saw many mangled and bloodied corpses scattered about, which the people loudly cursed and mocked. . . . All were outraged by the murder of Giuliano, lamenting this horrible crime against an excellent young man, the prize of Florentine youth, who least of all deserved to be killed by this heinous, twisted, and treacherous deed, a deed perpetrated by a wayward and sacrilegious family, hostile to God and men. The recent memory of his qualities also riled up the crowd: for a few years earlier Giuliano had vanquished all competitors at a jousting tournament[22] and brought home the crown and the spoils—a thing that enormously impresses the masses. And then there was the shamefulness of the deed: for no crime could be recalled or told that equalled this crime in atrocity. All wailed that this pious and innocent youth,

---

20. On the Medici coat of arms was a circle of five red balls, or *palle,* on a gold field.

21. Corsini was a politically-active Florentine, at this time a Medici supporter.

22. Poliziano had begun a poetic celebration of the tournament and Giuliano's victory, but ceased to work on it after the murder of the hero.

in the church, was cruelly butchered between the altar and the Eucharist:[23] hospitality violated, what was sacred desecrated, the church polluted with human blood. And they had tried to kill Lorenzo, that very Lorenzo in whom alone the whole Florentine republic placed its trust, in whom the hope and welfare of the people rested: this aroused all their outrage.

Then from all the nearby towns a great flood of armed men gathered in the piazza, in the streets, and especially at the Medici palace, to show their support. Groups of citizens with their family and clients pledged their aid, their strength, and their wealth; all said that their welfare, both public and private, depended on Lorenzo alone. For days on end you could see cartloads of weapons brought to Lorenzo's palace, as well as supplies of meat and bread and other necessary provisions. As for Lorenzo, neither his wound, nor fear, nor the grief which he felt exceedingly for the death of his brother prevented him from attending to his affairs. He greeted all the citizens, thanking some individually, saying that he was indebted to them all for his safety, and showing himself from the window to reassure the people anxious for his safety. Seeing him, the crowd all called out, raising their arms to heaven, giving thanks for his safety, joyously exulting. Lorenzo himself was intent on what had to be done, failing neither in spirit or wisdom. . . .

> *In the aftermath of the foiled coup, Florentine and allied forces fend off*
> *attempted invasions and restore order to the city. All the remaining conspira-*
> *tors were hunted down and killed, imprisoned, or exiled.*

Giuliano's funeral was magnificently celebrated, in accord with the sacred rites, in the church of San Lorenzo. Most of the young wore mourning. He had been pierced with nineteen wounds. He had lived twenty-five years. . . .

> *A mob digs up Jacopo Pazzi's body, saying it should not rest in sacred ground,*
> *and reburied it outside the city walls. From there, the body is exhumed once*
> *more by a crowd of boys, who drag it around the town and fling it into the*
> *Arno river, its final destination.*

I was reminded again by all this turbulence of the instability of human fortune, and marveled at the incredible sadness felt by all at Giuliano's burial. About his bodily form, his bearing and his character, I shall say but a little. He was tall, broad-shouldered, with a great and prominent chest, well-muscled arms, strong limbs, a taut belly, powerful thighs, his calves rather full, sparkling eyes and sharp eyesight, a rather dark complexion, with thick black hair brushed back from the forehead to the crown. An expert at horsemanship and throwing the javelin, skilled in jumping and gymnastics, he delighted greatly

---

23. That is, near the altar, at the climactic moment of the Mass.

in hunting. Magnanimous and loyal, attentive to religion and good morals, he loved painting, music, and every kind of refinement. He was a fine poet; he wrote poems in the Tuscan dialect,[24] wonderfully rich and full of insight; he read love poems gladly. He was eloquent and prudent, yet quick; he loved wit, and was himself witty. He hated liars and those who hold grudges. He took no excessive care of his appearance, yet was perfectly elegant and proper. He was respectful and kind, and showed great devotion to his brother; he was great in strength and courage. These things and others won him the love of the people, and the love of his family, while he lived; these same things make sad and sorrowful our remembrance of this excellent young man. We pray to Almighty God that, as Virgil puts it, at least he not prevent "this young prince [Lorenzo] from succouring a world in ruins!"[25]

Luigi Guicciardini

The sack of Rome of 1527 was a pivotal event in the history of the Church and of the European nations. It was one episode in a protracted series of wars, extending sixty-five years from 1494, when a French army suddenly invaded the Italian states, until 1559, when the peace treaty of Cateau-Cambrésis temporarily settled relations between France and Habsburg Spain. In the interval, the balance of power shifted from the Italian states, many of which became Spanish subordinates, to the emerging nation-states beyond the Alps. The events of May 1527 forecast the destiny that awaited Italy, when imperial armies consisting mostly of Spanish and German soldiers (from two of the European regions then subject to the Habsburg dynasty, which also held the imperial title) entered and pillaged Rome, forcing the pope and his curia to flee from the Vatican to the protection of the nearby Castel of Sant'Angelo.

Of these events, Luigi Guicciardini (1478–1551) provides a vivid chronicle, based on his access to reports by persons present at the scene, and undoubtedly much information provided by his younger brother, the even-

---

24. That is, in the vernacular, not Latin.

25. Virgil, *Georgics*, 1:500: "Gods of my country, . . . at least do not prevent this young prince from succouring a world in ruins!" Trans. H. R. Fairclough, Loeb Classical Library (Cambridge, MA: Harvard University Press, 1916), at *Theoi Classical E-Texts*: http://www.theoi.com/Text /VirgilGeorgics1.html (accessed September 17, 2012). Giuliano has died, Poliziano concludes in citing this verse; we must turn to Lorenzo now, hoping that he may save this troubled age.

more-famous historian Francesco Guicciardini (1483–1540). Both brothers were servants of the Medici family, which ruled both Florence and, in the person of Pope Clement VII (1523–1534), the Church. At the time of the sack, Francesco was the commander of the papal armies, while Luigi held the position of *gonfaloniere di giustizia* of Florence, its chief elective position. Both were well-positioned to receive comprehensive and precise accounts of events of such critical importance to the papacy and to Florence.

Both brothers, as noted, were historians; and although neither was, strictly speaking, a humanist, they were imbued with the classicism of their father, a businessman and amateur humanist fully immersed in humanist culture. Indeed, like their contemporary, compatriot, and friend Niccolò Machiavelli, whose work will be considered in the following chapter, they might be denied the title of humanist for two reasons only: that they did not write their major literary works in Latin, and that however classically grounded their training, they were too immersed in contemporary politics to be considered classical scholars. There is no doubt, however, that all three of these authors were full participants in the intensely humanistic culture of Florence, and that their literary contributions would be unimaginable absent that context.

Guicciardini's *The Sack of Rome* contains a thorough account of the events of 1526–1527 preliminary to the Sack, occupying all of the First Book and part of the Second. The excerpts given here begin with a sampling of Guicciardini's introduction to the latter book, in which he laments the disaster that has befallen Italy. Consonant with the views of Francesco Guicciardini and Niccolò Machiavelli, he points to the need to be ready and fully armed when catastrophe strikes, not relying on others; and to the inevitability of shifting circumstances, the cycling between good and evil controlled only by the whim of Fortune. When Fortune's wheel turns to the downside, the only safety lies in one's own strength and determination; and where people are beset by "sloth, pusillanimity, and discord," the result will be catastrophe. Such was the case with Italy in May 1527, when a handful of imperial troops, 1200 Spaniards and Germans (whom Guicciardini refers to as "ultramontanes," because they came from the far side of the Alps), captured, pillaged, and humiliated the city of Rome.

The remaining excerpts deal minutely with the events of May 6, 1527 and subsequent days, when the Spanish and German forces controlled the city. They arrived through an opening in the city wall, which they widened when no one was looking, and quickly dispersed the witless and disorganized defenders. As they marched through the streets, the terrified people fled before them. Meanwhile, the pope, thirteen cardinals, other members of the curia (the papal court), and a mob of others seeking refuge, had rushed to the fortified Castel Sant'Angelo.

The invaders anticipated a rich lode of booty in a city whose leaders for centuries had been hoarding wealth extorted by taxes and fees from all over Europe, and who in Renaissance fashion had amassed in their houses and in their churches a bounty of precious paintings, statues, and bejeweled objects fashioned of noble metals. At first the Spanish, soon joined by the Germans, took prisoners with the explicit aim of extracting information about the location of this wealth. They did so in multiple safehouses they had requisitioned for the purpose of torturing their victims. For Guicciardini, the systematic and relentlessly brutal torture of prisoners is the principal story of the sack. With the hidden loot pinpointed, the invaders hauled it away in huge sacks and cartloads—or, in the case of sacred objects and images in the churches, when these fell into the hands of the German lancers, or *Landsknechte*, many of whom were followers of Martin Luther, they were smashed and desecrated amid curses and blasphemies.

Book Two closes with a glance at the shivering occupants of the Castel Sant'Angelo, who heard the screams of the tortured amid the din of gunfire outside their walls and awaited their own imminent capture, brutalization, and death. Guicciardini imagines the condition of Pope Clement VII, once the greatest and mightiest man in Christendom and now the most abject, who trembled in fear, aware that the ruination of Rome, the Church, and Italy itself was entirely his fault.

Where does Guicciardini stand with regard to the events he describes? Clearly, he sees the imperial soldiers as barbarians, but equally, he views the defenders of Rome as incompetent, cowardly fools. He criticizes the clergy for its greed, the courtiers for their stupidity and self-indulgence, and the church for its "false ceremonies"—a bit of a Lutheran note here! The pope, as has been seen, receives his full share of the blame. Even the gatekeepers at the Castel Sant'Angelo are given a tongue-lashing for not having kept the portcullis clean of rust and smoothly functioning—as though it might one day be, as it would have been that day, of some use. There is no one in this tale of whom the author approves. But for the victims of the torturers, he has compassion; he seems to hear their howls and screams and can barely force himself to write about it, yet he describes the torments in fastidious detail.

Guicciardini composed *The Sack of Rome* soon after the events it chronicles, but only dedicated it ten years later to a Medici prince. That prince was Cosimo I, a scion of the younger branch of the Medici clan, the first to hold the title of Grand Duke of Tuscany as his descendants would for two centuries to come, and the son of one of the few generals in the Italian wars who was generally acknowledged to have done his job well. Apparently, the implicit criticism of the Medici family that was entailed by Guicciardini's portrayal of the pope was not something that put him at risk when he offered this work to Cosimo: perhaps because Clement was dead and the papacy was no longer a Medici affair; perhaps because the inaugurator of a new Medici dynasty would not be displeased by criticisms of one of the last potentates of the old.

Like Quirini's description of the fall of Constantinople, Guicciardini's account of the sack of Rome is not the only one we have—several are collected in the edition by Carlo Milanesi of 1867 (*Il sacco di Roma del MDXXVII: Narrazioni di contemporanei* [Florence: G. Barbèra]), but it is the most important. It reappeared in editions of 1664 (Paris) and 1758 (Cologne), when the event still loomed large in political memory; and then in 1809 (Paris), 1830 (Florence), and 1867 (Florence)—after which it lay largely ignored until it was edited and translated into English by James H. McGregor in 1993 (New York: Italica Press, 1993). Yet as a profile of political disarray and incompetence, it is very current indeed.

Luigi Guicciardini, *The Sack of Rome* (1527)

From the introduction to Book Two:

A great many multiform and unbearable events have unfolded since 1494[26] until this present day, leading to the shameful ruination of all of Italy. In consequence, not only the sage governors of principalities and republics, but even the ignorant multitude must see at last that no planning, and no preparations, are as reliable or as certain as to remain within your own fortified walls defended by the arms of your own soldiers. . . .

> *Guicciardini laments the takeover of Italy by foreigners, who have pillaged and brutalized, at the time of his writing, for thirty-three years; then sums up before launching into his narrative.*

With every new occurrence, everything shifts and slides to its nadir, so that the human race finds itself continually cycling between going up and falling down, from good to evil, and evil to good. But the more we defend our valor and unity by the strength of our own arms, the more we may retain what good fortune and greatness we have acquired. And the more we dally in sloth, pusillanimity, and discord, the sooner we come to total annihilation. Precisely these three ills beset Italy at this moment, more than ever in times past. . . . And so it is no wonder that in our day a mere 12,000 ultramontanes[27] have so easily, at lightening speed, crushed and plundered it. And that they will soon reduce it to complete ruination, anyone reading to the end of the second book of this history will readily acknowledge.

> *We skip now to the moment when, on 6 May 1527, the first imperial troops arrive in the city of Rome.*

---

26. The year in which the Italian wars began with the unexpected invasion of the French royal army.

27. The Spanish and Germans who descended on Italy from the other side of the mountains, that is, the Alps—in Italy's history, the usual path of invasion.

At 10 o'clock, unseen by the rest of the army, a small Spanish detachment showed up in Rome—entering either through the cannon-ports of the walls which they widened with crowbars and picks, or jumping in through the aforementioned cellar window. . . . The first person to notice the Spanish troops within the walls, as many affirm, was Signor Renzo,[28] because he called out suddenly in a raised voice: "The enemy is within; save yourselves, take shelter somewhere strong and secure." Words—if indeed he spoke them—unsuitable to a captain of his stature. . . . But no sooner had he uttered these frightful and pusillanimous words (as those who were there with him have told me), he took himself off like a shot toward Ponte Sisto,[29] followed by everyone else who had stood there with him, with the fracas and tumult that always accompanies such a complete breakdown of order.

There he arrived with a throng of soldiers, where the Roman people, who had not missed the significance of Renzo's flight, had already rushed off to refuge, terrified by the enemy's constant screaming at the top of their voices "Spain, Spain! Kill, kill!"; and having with great difficulty crossed the Tiber, they mixed in with another panicked mob. But those who were unable to cross the Tiber, or who had been paralyzed by fear, or who had been trapped by the great multitude of people running confusedly here or there, took off for the Castello.[30] There not long before His Holiness had arrived in a frenzy, and found it lacking in victuals and other things useful to have while fending off the enemy and essential for sustenance, which long before he had asked to be stocked. Everything that could possibly be had amid such chaos was immediately brought in from the nearby houses and shops.

Now while the terrified denizens of the Castello made these arrangements, at its main entrance there had already gathered a crowd of prelates, nobles, courtiers, women, and soldiers, squashed and squeezed together so that it was not possible to lock the gate. But finally, they dropped the portcullis, which descended and closed with difficulty, since nobody considered ahead of time that a rusty gate would endanger all those who would be left outside, who if they wished to save themselves needed to find some other place of refuge. Nonetheless, more than 3000 persons were already inside.

Later that day, a detachment of Spanish soldiers take the Ponte Sisto, a bridge over the Tiber river, en route to the papal enclave.

---

28. Renzo di Ceri, the officer in charge of some 8000 militiamen defending the walls.

29. A bridge across the Tiber leading from Rome to then-suburban Trastevere, beyond which lay the papal residence.

30. The "castle" or Castel Sant'Angelo, a fortified structure to which the pope fled through a private tunnel from the Vatican, but which also housed numerous other refugees.

And so with a great din from the trumpets and drums, along with other military noise terrifying to those not accustomed to it, at 6 o'clock in the evening they marched briskly toward the gatehouse of the Ponte Sisto. Earlier, a squad of about 1000 arquebusiers[31] had approached it in total silence, so as to overtake unseen those whom they reasonably expected to be on duty to defend it. But finding it abandoned, with only a handful of defenders, and these confused and useless, they took it without difficulty. Immediately then, with no time lost, the rest of the army having arrived, they headed toward Ponte Sisto, which they crossed in fine order and show of force, although they met with little impediment. But then, suddenly divided and scattered by the web of streets, cruelly killing anyone in their path, they committed a wholesale and horrible massacre. But there being no one who resisted their fury, they became in no time the lords of that city so ancient and so noble, full of every sort of wealth that any greedy and ravenous army could desire.

With everyone in their path taking flight, seeing that they were masters of the city, the Spanish began to loot houses here and prisons there, seizing everything inside of them; and as for those who, fleeing in confusion down the streets, happened to join them—these they captured but did not kill. Whereupon the Germans, seeing that the Spanish bands did not observe, as they did, the laws of war, which called for cutting to pieces anyone you could get your hands on—which is absolutely necessary to secure a victory—began to suspect them of treachery. But they were quickly persuaded by the Spanish captains, who explained that since the city was theirs, having been abandoned by anyone who possibly could have defended it; and since they knew that vast wealth was hidden there, it was a great mistake not to keep alive those who could show them where it was—and, beyond that, to give them the names of people outside of Rome who would pay to ransom the captives. Then the *Landsknechte*,[32] too, instructed by the Spaniards, began to rob anyone they encountered, and to loot the most beautiful houses they saw. . . .

How many courtiers, how many refined and well-bred gentlemen, how many elegant prelates, how many devout nuns, how many virgins and chaste matrons with their infants and children, fell prey to these cruel foreigners! How many chalices and crucifixes, figurines and vessels of silver and gold, were snatched from the altars, sacristies, and other holy places where they had reposed! How many rare and venerable relics, covered with gold and silver, were seized by bloody and murderous hands, and scornfully and blasphemously thrown to the ground! The heads of Saint Peter, Saint Paul, Saint Andrew, and of many other saints; the wood of the Cross, the thorns of

---

31. Infantrymen whose weapon was the arquebus, or harquebus, a recently invented matchlock gun.

32. The German pikemen of the imperial army.

Christ's crown, the holy oil, and the consecretated Host, all these were amid this madness shamefully trampled underfoot.[33]

Out on the streets you saw nothing but rogues and marauders carrying great loads of the richest vestments and ecclesiastical ornaments, or huge sacks full of every kind of gold and silver vessel—proofs more of the immense wealth and vain pomp of the Roman court than of the humble poverty and true devotion that should be hallmarks of the Christian religion. Immense numbers of prisoners of every social rank could be seen, howling and scream-ing, being rushed along by the Spanish and German ultramontanes to the torture chambers they had requistioned. The streets were full of corpses; many nobles could be seen, cut to pieces, covered in mud and in their own blood, and many half-dead men stretched out wretchedly on the ground. At times, amid the mayhem, girls, boys, and grown men could be seen to jump, by force or by choice, out of this window and that one, so as not to be left as the living prey of these murderers, and so cruelly, on the streets, they put an end to their own lives.

> *Guicciardini digresses from his narrative to describe the effects of news of the sack on Florence, his own city, and the city from which Pope Clement VII, a member of the ruling Medici family, also came. He then returns to describe the horrible tortures inflicted by the victors on the people of Rome.*

When the Spanish and German soldiers had sufficiently rested and refreshed themselves from the immeasurable effort they had expended in their cease-less raiding and looting to and fro, to return to the point made earlier, they began to torture and brutalize their prisoners to extract from them the loca-tion of their hidden wealth, and to ascertain how much money they would pay for their liberation. Accordingly, since their inquisitors were remorseless and merciless, many of the prisoners, their bodies torn like wild wounded beasts, revealed the hiding places, and many proposed ransom fees so high, in order to escape their present torments, that it was not possible for them ever to pay them. Those who resisted this inquisition and stood firm, bravely refusing to offer the enemy the stated sum—it is not possible to imagine the intolerable pains that they underwent, and worse, the inexpressible fear of the certain end that loomed. For indeed, this side of death, they suffered every possible torment. And even as the tortured prisoners cried out constantly for death, the avaricious and cruel Spanish artfully kept them alive; although they would surely have escaped much pain if their souls had been permitted to escape from their bodies.

---

33. The destruction of sacred objects was mainly accomplished by the German soldiers in the imperial army, many of whom, as early as 1527, had renounced Catholicism for the Lutheran faith. The Spanish were themselves Catholics.

Anyone who walked through the streets of Rome, by day or by night, would have heard constantly from every house and every corner, not sighs and sorrowful laments, but the wretched cries and howls of the unfortunate prisoners. . . . And the grander, the richer, the more refined were the prelates, courtiers, merchants, and citizens in their hands, the more cruelly and scornfully they tortured them, and set higher demands for ransom; so that the more they hoped to become rich, the more brutally did they torture. Some victims were suspended by their arms for many hours of the day, while others had their testicles bound and pulled. Many were hung by one foot above the street, or over the waters, with the threat that the cord by which they hung would be cut. Many were villainously beaten and battered. Some were burned with a red-hot iron all over their bodies; others, denied water, suffered thirst, others the deprivation of sleep. Extracting the back teeth of some prisoners was a cruel and effective torture. Some were made to eat their own ears, or nose, or testicles, roasted. Still others suffered strange and inconceivable martyrdoms, which disturb me too much to think about, let alone to write about, for continually one heard of or saw many cruel and piteous cases. . . .

Guicciardini describes a number of these, then returns to the looting by the Spanish and German troops of the valuable and beautiful things that abounded in Rome.

By torturing the prisoners, which often led them to troves of hidden and buried treasure, they became in just a few days so very rich, that they not only began to despise the domestic furnishings, paintings, sculptures, and ornaments they acquired, although these were precious and valuable, but they also deemed the silver vessels, figurines, and innumerable other objects to have little worth. For they especially esteemed fine gems and pure gold, because such objects were easily transportable, and their worth would be immediately recognized. . . .

The immense riches of the noble barons of Rome, preserved in their families over many centuries, were lost in an hour! The incredible wealth, acquired by churchmen unjustly and dishonestly over many years of usury, theft, simony, and by other cruel and scandalous means, then increased by the investments of courtiers and merchants, in one instant came into the possession of these inhuman Spaniards and Germans! But why should I trouble myself to note this heap or that hoard of wealth which fell so easily and quickly into the hands of these bestial ultramontanes? Since everyone knows that from all of Europe and other parts of the world, there flowed every hour into this unlucky city money, goods, and luxuries, to satisfy the limitless appetites and illicit lusts of these insatiable prelates and courtiers—which wealth, since none of these potentates ever considered that they might lose what they had taken, was discovered, sacked, and seized with incredible force and fury. . . .

The sumptuous palaces of the cardinals, the proud habitations of the popes, the holy churches of saints Peter and Paul, the exquisite papal chapel, the Holy of Holies, and the other sacred places, once the repositories of plenary indulgences and revered relics, now made stables for the horses and brothels for the whores of the German and Spanish invaders. And instead of false ceremonies and lascivious musicales, you could now hear in these places the snorting and neighing of horses, and the continual blaspheming and cursing of God and his saints, while on the altars and in other sacred places there are repeatedly committed lustful and disgusting acts in denigration of the established religion. Many holy paintings and sculptures which had once been reverenced in false ceremonies, now are broken and burned by iron and fire, and many crucifixes shattered by arquebuses and shamefully hurled to the ground, where, scattered and mixed with horse dung and the feces of the ultramontanes, there lay the relics and skullbones of the saints. . . .

I shall not speak at present of the trials and chaos that transpired in the Castello, there being within, along with the pope, thirteen cardinals and numerous prelates, lords, noble ladies, merchants, courtiers and soldiers, all terrified and desperate. . . . How afflicted and tormented in spirit the pope must have been at this moment, hearing and seeing continually the imminent danger that faced him and all of Rome, greatly fearing, as did the other inmates, he might soon fall into the power of such cruel enemies, so thirsty for his blood. And though in the past he had enjoyed dizzying honors and delightful pleasures, now he must pay for them with abject disgrace and bitter misery. And if he then arrived at so great a summit, to be hailed as a wise and glorious prince, now he must confess himself to be the most unfortunate and wretched pope who ever lived. Whereupon we may readily conclude, since he is the cause of the extreme peril in which the Church, the fatherland, and Italy now find themselves, he must look often with tearful eyes toward heaven, and with deep and bitter sighs say with Job: "Why did you bring me forth from the womb? Would that I had died before any eye had seen me."[34]

---

34. Job 10:18; NRSV.

Olympia Fulvia Morata

The historian and theologian Caelio Secondo Curione,[35] an Italian evangelical in exile in Basel, aptly described the epistolary style of Olympia Fulvia Morata (1526/1527–1555), the daughter of his old friend, in his letter to her of 28 August 1555: when the members of his literary circle have heard her letters read aloud and examined, he wrote, "they will see you breathing and speaking: your hand, your elegance, the force in your letters." For they are remarkable letters indeed, written in a fluid and effortless Latin studded with tags of Greek, possessing the directness of Petrarch and the intimacy of Montaigne. She learned Latin and Greek from her father Pellegrino Morato, a humanist at the court of Ferrara. The concision and energy of her prose are the effects of the unusual circumstances of her life.

Raised in humanist circles at an Italian court that was a vortex of Renaissance culture, Morata became expert in classical languages by the age of twelve, about which time she was herself employed by the duchess Renata (Renée de France) as companion to the latter's daughter Anna d'Este. The times were complex: the 1530s were not only a high point of the Renaissance, but the high tide of Italian evangelicism, a reform movement within the Catholic church that appealed to many in the social and cultural elite. The evangelical impulse was especially strong in Ferrara, where Protestant books were available, and reformers from the Swiss and German centers of the revolutionary new faith freely circulated. Morata's father had become a Protestant convert before his death in 1548, and the duchess Renata herself leaned to the new faith and corresponded with the reformer John Calvin.

In 1542, meanwhile, the papacy had launched the Roman Inquisition to silence the evangelicals and pursue any Protestant adherents—or "heretics," as they were called. The evangelical leaders who did not flee to the north were persecuted; Renata was placed under house arrest; and Morata, having married the German Protestant Andreas Grunthler, a student of medicine and philosophy at the university in Ferrara, fled with him to Germany. By age twenty-three, she had acquired an advanced humanist education, embraced a dangerous religion, witnessed its persecution, and chosen exile in a strange land, which as well was already a war zone. Such experiences have an impact on intellectual expression. Thus we find in Morata little of the artful posturing or the stylized classical allusions—although her erudition is

---

35. Curio is the Latin, Curione the Italian. I use the Italian form for the introduction, but the Latin form is retained in the text, since that is how it appears in the original.

amply displayed—of the Italian Renaissance humanists; instead, we find a humanism that has the tempo and urgency suited to a world on fire.

The events of Morata's career are traced in her surviving works (many more, as she describes in her letter to Curione of 25 July 1554, perished in the wars): dialogues, lectures, poems, and psalm translations, and fifty-two letters written between 1540 and 1555.[36] Five are given here, written during Morata's years in Germany, from 1551 to 1555. They include one to her old friend from the Ferrarese court Lavinia della Rovere; one to a traveling German scholar to whom she entrusted letters to be delivered in Italy; and three to Caelio Secondo Curione. A letter from Curione to Morata is also included here, bringing the total to six. A comment on the salient points is given at the head of each letter.

Curione's letter to Morata of 28 August 1555, and Morata's to him sometime before 25 October 1555, refer to his role as her literary executor. In the former, he indicates that he is showing off her letters to his literary friends, and asks her to send him any of her works that are "polished." In the latter, she reminds him that all her works (rather, all of her own copies of her works, since Curione already had gathered copies of some) had perished in the siege of Schweinfurt, but adds that she had recovered some poems from memory and was sending them to him. All of these extant works of Morata's—those of which Curione had retained copies, and those that she sent to him—he compiled in his 1558 *editio princeps,* or first edition of her works (Basel: Petrum Pernam) which went into revised second and third editions in 1562 and 1570 (the year after Curione's death). In so doing, Curione achieved the memorialization of his old friend's daughter, her husband's "Minerva," the "Italian heretic,"[37] Olympia Fulvia Morata.

Olympia Fulvia Morata, *Letters* (1551–1555)[38]

Letter 27: Schweinfurt, 1 October [1551]: to Caelius Secundus Curio, friend of Morata's father who had known her since childhood, an evangelical and scholar, and the eventual editor of Morata's works

Morata thanks Curio for his invitation to her and her husband to stay with his family in Italy. Such a visit is unlikely, she writes, because it is "dangerous . . . to profess oneself a Christian there where the Antichrist," that is, the

---

36. The seventy-one published by Holt Parker, her modern editor and translator, in *The Complete Writings of an Italian Heretic* (Chicago: University of Chicago Press, 2003), include some to Morata from various correspondents.

37. As she is styled in the title of Parker's collection of her works, cited in the previous note.

38. From the letters of Olympia Morata in *The Complete Writings,* ed. Parker, 114–17, 130, 139–41, 174–77.

pope, "has so much power." She mentions the persecution and execution in
1551 of Fanio Camillo Fanini, a reformer deemed to be a heretic.

. . . You ask that if ever we return to Italy we make the trip there to you. I cannot swear that we will never go there, but we are not now planning to return
to Italy. It has not escaped your notice how dangerous it is to profess oneself a
Christian there where the Antichrist has so much power. . . . Last year (I don't
know if you heard), he ordered a certain Fanini,[39] a pious man of the most
constant faith, after he had been in prison for two years (for he was never
willing to abandon the truth, not from fear of death, not from love of his wife
and children), to be strangled and his body cremated. Not content with this,
he then ordered his bones to be thrown into the Po. So although I am held
by the deepest desire for my family, I would rather go to the ends of the earth
than return to where that man has such power to be cruel. But if we have to
leave here, there is nowhere else I'd rather go than to you. For I'd seem to be
among my family, if it should happen that I spend my life with you. So if it's
possible for my husband to follow his profession, either by curing the sick or
by giving lectures, he would willingly accept a post for my sake. If this could
happen, nothing would be more wonderful as far as I'm concerned. I'd be
nearer Italy, and so I could send and receive letters more often from my mothers and sisters, who are always before my eyes night and day. It's extremely
difficult here, but I did get one this month after a long interval. . . .

Letter 28: Schweinfurt [winter 1551/1552]: to Lavinia della Rovere Orsini, Morata's childhood friend from early days in Ferrara

*Morata writes of her longing for news of her home and of her family. Letters
arrive infrequently, dependent on the journeys of couriers, which were often
interrupted in wartime. In this letter Morata also speaks of the benefit of living in Germany, where she may freely read what religious books she wishes,
and urges upon Lavinia the study of the works of reformer Martin Luther, in
the hope that God will "enlighten you with true religion."*

I sent you a rather long letter this summer . . . [but] I don't know whether
you got it. Letters are very rarely delivered in these turbulent times, in which
everything seems to rage with war. We are parted by the greatest distance of
space, as I wrote you before. So my dear Lavinia, if you get my letters less
often (and I've only received one from you after we got here), please don't
think it's happening because of my neglect or forgetfulness of you. If I had
anyone to give them to, I wouldn't let anyone get past. I'd write to my mother
also every day if I could. I always worry about her. I am so far from forgetting

---

39. Fanio Camillo Fanini, an evangelical and Protestant executed in 1550.

you that my anxiety about you increases every day. Indeed, if Germany did not give me the comfort of being allowed to have books of theology that we could not have there, I would not be able to bear my longing for my friends. . . . I'm also sending you some writings by Dr. Martin Luther, which I enjoyed reading. They may be able to move and restore you, too. Work hard at these studies, for God's sake, ask that He enlighten you with true religion. You will not lose. You don't think think that God lies, do you? Why would He have made so many promises, unless He wished to keep them? He invites and summons all the wretched to him. He turns away no one. . . . Goodbye.

Letter 34: Schweinfurt [c. January 1553]: to Laurenz Schleenried, a German Protestant then studying in Italy, to whom Morata entrusted letters for delivery there

Morata thanks Schleenried for having sent on their books from Italy, and asks for news of Ferrara—she has not heard from any of her friends and relatives there for more than a year. She is especially concerned about her mother, whom she left behind along with her sisters when she fled Italy with her husband Grunthler, taking her brother along so that she could see to his education.

We have finally received our books. Enormous thanks for having taken care of this so devotedly and diligently. The book of Avicenna[40] was not in the trunk. If there's anything still owed you, let us know and we'll see to the money for you. We are still staying here in our home town, and there's been no possibility of leaving because of the wars. I'm sure that you've been told that the duke of Saxony has been set free and obtained his former titles. . . .

One thing above all I want to ask of you: to write to us, as soon as you have time, about events in Italy, especially about my ungrateful city of Ferrara. This is now the fourteenth month since I've heard anything about my mother. And although I've often written at length to her and to all my relatives and friends, no one writes me back. So I've decided to send you the letter, which (as you can see) I've appended to this one for you, so that you can take care of sending them on to my mother, and look around if there's any way for me to find out what they're doing. You couldn't do anything more pleasing to me. I beg you over and over again to do this and call on your piety. Goodbye.

Letter 42: Heidelberg, 25 July 1554: to Caelius Secundus Curio, in Jesus Christ

Morata writes Curio a long letter about the siege of Schweinfurt, her husband's bout with the plague, and their narrow escape and eventual safe

---

40. The eleventh-century Arabic philosopher who was still studied in Italian universities.

landing in Heidelberg. She thanks him, too, for the books he had sent: "They were most pleasing, but they perished with my other books, as did everything we owned."

I think, dear Caelius, that I have no need to make use of any excuse to you for not having responded to the letters you gave me so long ago. The war lets me completely off. We've been under attack for fourteen months but have suffered no loss of life from it. As soon as Margrave Albrecht[41] quartered his army at Schweinfurt because of its strategic location, his enemies, who were many, laid siege to the town. They began to assault it and to pound the walls on all sides day and night with siege engines. At the same time, inside the walls we were afflicted with many injuries at the hands of the Margrave's troops, and no one was safe in his own house. Besides, since the money they were owed was not being disbursed, they kept threatening that they would take everthing from the citizens, as if we had invited or brought them here! The city was already completely exhausted from feeding so many soldiers, and then from close contact with them a dire plague invaded nearly all the citizens, so severe that most were deranged from the pain. Death from the disease was the result for half the city. My most loving husband was affected by the disease, so that there seemed to be no hope for his life, but God, having pity on me in my utmost affliction, cured him without any medical intervention (there were no medicines in the town).

. . . Once the plague had been driven back by God, immediately we were besieged by an even bigger enemy army, which kept hurling fire into the city day and night. Often at night you would have thought the whole town was about to go up in flames, and at that time we were often forced to hide out in a wine cellar. At last, when we were hoping for a happy outcome to this war due to the Margrave's departure (he was going to march his army away on the following night), we fell in the greatest misery. For scarcely had he left the city with his army than on the next day the soldiers of the two bishops and of the men of Nuremberg invaded the city, and after pillaging it, had it burned. Truly God snatched us from the midst of the flames, when it was burning in every quarter, because it was about to be burned to the ground. We obeyed him and left, stripped and denuded of everything—we were not allowed to take even a penny. In fact, our clothes were ripped off us in the middle of the town square and I was left with nothing to cover my body except a linen tunic. Then when we had escaped from the city, my husband was captured by the enemy. I was unable to ransom him even at the lowest price, and when I saw him being led away from my sight, I

---

41. Albrecht II Alcibiades, Margrave of Brandenburg-Kulmbach, the commander of the siege forces at Schweinfurt.

prayed with tears and "unutterable" groans to God,[42] Who immediately set him free and returned him to me.

But once we had left the city, we did not know where to turn. At last we made our way towards Hammelburg. I was barely able to crawl there. The village is three German miles from Schweinfurt, and the citizens of the town received us unwillingly, since they had been forbidden to offer shelter to any of us. Among the refugees I looked like the queen of the beggars. I entered the town with bare feet, unkempt hair, torn clothes (which weren't even mine but had been loaned me by some woman). I was so exhausted from the journey that I developed a fever, which I could not get rid of in all my wanderings. For since the citizens of Hammelburg were afraid for themselves, it was not possible for us to remain with them for long, but we had to leave within four days, even though I was sick. Then we were forced to pass through one of the bishop's towns again, and my husband was captured by the bishop's mayor, who said that he had been ordered by his most merciful lord to kill all the refugees who came there from Schweinfurt. We were captives, trapped between hope and fear, until we were let go by a letter from the bishop. Then at last God began to notice us. First someone led us to the most noble Count of Rieneck, then to the renowned Count of Erbach, who had often endangered his life and fortune for the sake of the Christian religion.[43] Both of them received us graciously and loaded us with many gifts. We stayed with them for many days until I was a little better and my husband was admitted to the college of the University of Heidelberg, where he will lecture on medicine.

You have an epitome of our sufferings; more later. Thanks so much for the books. They were most pleasing, but they perished with my other books, as did everything we owned. Greetings to your wife and children.

Letter 43: [Heidelberg, July 1554]: to Caelius Secundus Curio

Morata follows up the previous long narrative letter with a brief one, asking for the gift of one of reformer John Calvin's books, showing her continued interest in theological scholarship at a high level even amid her adversities.

A few days ago I sent you a rather lengthy letter, in which I informed you about our calamities. So now I'm being laconic and just asking as an additional request that you add the *Commentaries on the Lamentations of Jeremiah* by a certain learned man of our time[44] to the books which we want shipped to us here. You'll be doing me a great favor. Goodbye.

---

42. Rom. 8:26, quoted in Greek: see Parker's edition of Morata's *Complete Writings*, 140n325.

43. Philip Graf von Reineck; Georg II, Graf von Erbach.

44. John Calvin, whom Morata avoids naming explicitly.

Letter 69: Basel, 28 August 1555: Caelius Secundus Curio greets Olympia F. Morata

Curio responds to two letters of Morata's, promising to share them with his literary circle in Basel, where they are sure to be impressed by their "elegance" and "force." He expresses concern for her health, sends on some books, and urges her to send on to him any of her works.

I have received from you, my dearest Olympia, who are like a daughter to me, two letters written and sent at various times.[45] What you asked me for in the first, namely that I give your thanks to our printers here for their kindness to you, I will see to most diligently. Or rather, you will do it personally most effectively, for when your letters have been read out loud and viewed, they will see you breathing and speaking: your hand, your elegance, the force in your letters. . . .

Curio expresses sympathy for her illness, and reports on his own recent sickness and his daughter's ill-health.

You will be receiving from the Frankfurt fair certain little books of mine. Once you've read them (if there's time in your illness to read my lucubrations), write me what you think of them. Your husband, Doctor Andreas, whom especially I love for his erudition and piety, will do the same. . . .

Curio inquires about Olympia's brother, and sends greetings.

Farewell, dearest Olympia. Look after your health carefully so that you may continue to adorn our age. We quite envy that town of yours. Send any polished works you have so that we can publish them here, especially your poems. And when you write me back, send me a copy of this letter (get someone to copy it), because I didn't have time to make a copy and I want to keep a copy for some reason. . . .

HER FINAL LETTER

Letter 71: [Heidelberg, shortly before 26 October 1555]: Olympia Fulvia Morata greets Caelius Secundus Curio

Only a few months after Curio's letter to her of 28 August 1555, Morata writes him a last letter—the last she wrote to anyone—informing him that she is in the final stages of a fatal illness. As he requested, she is sending to him copies of any poems she "was able to remember"—she relied on memory, since the originals had been destroyed at Schweinfurt—and reminds him

---

45. Letters 54 and 66 in Parker's edition, not included here.

that "All my other writings were lost." She asks him to collect and edit all the
works of hers in his possession: "I ask that you please be my Aristarchus[46] and
publish them." He did so, in a collection published in 1558, and in two sub-
sequent editions.

You may guess, my Caelius, my sweetest father, what a tender spirit they
have, those who are joined together by true (that is, Christian) friendship, by
the fact that I was unable to keep from tears when I read your letter. When
I heard that you had been called back from death's door, I wept for very joy.
I pray God to watch over you, so that you may long be able to serve your
church by your kind deeds and usefulness. . . .

As for me, my Caelius, you must know that I have lost any hope for a
longer life. As far as it lies in the power of medicines (and I have used many),
there is nothing that can help. They expect that in a few days or hours I will
depart from here. In fact, I don't know whether this may not be the last letter you will get from me. My bodily strength is gone. I have no appetite for
food. Congestion tries to suffocate me day and night. The fever is high and
constant. There are pains throughout my body that keep me from sleeping.
Nothing remains but to pour out my breath. But there is still a spirit in my
body that remembers all my friends and the kindness they have done. So to
you and to those kind men who have blessed me with so many lovely gifts,
I wanted to give great thanks if the fates had allowed. I think I am going to
depart soon. I commend the church to you, that whatever you do be of use to
her. Be well, my dearest Caelius, and don't grieve when my death is reported
to you, for I know that then at last I shall live, and I desire to be dissolved and
to be with Christ. . . .

The poems which I was able to remember after the destruction of
Schweinfurt I am sending to you as you ask. All my other writings were lost.
I ask that you please be my Aristarchus and publish them.

Again, goodbye.

---

46. The ancient Greek critic (c. 217–c. 145 BCE), responsible for the Hellenistic-era edition
of Homer.

Chapter 5: Machiavelli, Erasmus, and More: Visions of the State

Introduction

At the pivotal moment of the High Renaissance, in the space of only three years (1513–1516), three preeminent European thinkers offered distinct and powerful visions of the state—at a time when the nature of the state was itself rapidly coalescing. Based on the nation-state, a successor to the earlier forms of tribal rule, empire, and city-state, the modern state system of Europe crystallized from medieval kingdoms, principalities, and autonomous cities in the sixteenth and subsequent centuries. On the threshold of these developments, the Italian Niccolò Machiavelli (1469–1527), the Dutch-born Desiderius Erasmus (c. 1469–1536), and the Englishman Thomas More (1478–1535)—the latter two were close friends—proposed pathways forward that have not yet outlived their vibrancy or utility.

Machiavelli's *The Prince*, begun in 1513, views the state in chillingly abstract terms: it is a republic or a principality, newly acquired or joined to existing states, won by chance or by the genius of the prince. The prince is a generic ruler: Machiavelli could equally be describing an ancient Roman general, a contemporary king, or an Italian *condottiere* who wins himself a state—and indeed he uses all of these figures and others to exemplify his points. He detaches, as will be seen, the set of qualities required in a successful prince from the inherited complex of moral and pious virtues that had heretofore been the recipe for sovereignty. His exposition, though packed with historical examples, lacks texture: while the "people" make an appearance now and then as a self-interested lot who will support a capable prince who does not touch their property, they are faceless.

Erasmus' *Education of a Christian Prince*, first published in 1516, sees the state as dependent on the personal qualities of the prince, as Machiavelli does, but presents a quite different set of expectations for that ruler. Whereas Machiavelli said nothing about the prince's intellectual or cultural preparation for rule, Erasmus' prince is to be humanistically educated, with the usual Erasmian hope that immersion in classical studies would pay off in moral rectitude. Beyond that, a prince is to ban flatterers from his court, avoid frivolous amusements and debaucheries, work hard, spend little so as to tax his subjects less, repair the infrastructure, and avoid war. If the prince, for Erasmus, is something of a humanist saint, the people are quite real, as they are not for Machiavelli. They work hard, love their families, and suffer much, and from nothing more than the bad policies of the prince—from taxation, lax enforcement of the laws, crumbling roads and undisciplined waterways, and above all, from war.

More's *Utopia,* first published in 1516, is as aware as Machiavelli is of how the real world works, and as concerned as Erasmus for the welfare of the people, the playthings of princes. But his work seeks solutions in another world, not this one: an invented state, appropriate for an age that has just discovered a New World full of wholly new and diverse societies. More describes the government machinery of his fictive state with something of Machiavelli's abstractness, but also more than a dash of humorous detachment; and *contra* Machiavelli, the prince he invents is elected and virtually powerless. But for the most part, More's work is a dialogue with the failed political and social institutions of contemporary Europe, sketching in response a world where people live free of the tyranny of kings and nobles, hold property in common, work skillfully but not very much, love their families though unburdened by family obligations, enjoy fellowship and books, worship however they wish, and leave war, for the most part, to others.

The works of these three authors of different temperaments, writing in markedly different situations, still have noticeable affinities. All three sense the looming importance of princes—or rather, of the kings of nations who will soon gather increased force and dominate Europe as never before. All three are obsessed with war: for Machiavelli, it is a tool; for Erasmus and More, it is always perilous. All three are skeptical of the church, whose powers were all around them: for Machiavelli, the church is a rival to the prince he wishes to groom; for Erasmus, an institution overgrown with luxury, arrogance, and false ceremony; for More, at least in *Utopia,* utterly dispensable. All three are desperate and strive mightily with their pens to ward off the impending catastrophe of corrupt, illicit, and ineffective rule.

Niccolò Machiavelli

Niccolò Machiavelli (1469–1527), Florentine politician, historian, and playwright, dedicated his manual on how to be a prince to one of the Medici princes of his city—one of the ruling family, that is, which had in 1512 retaken Florence after eighteen years of republican rule, and imprisoned and tortured the author. From several perspectives it is a very odd book, and at the same time, one of the greatest works of the Western political tradition. It is odd because its purpose is unclear (just which prince did he have in mind, and where were his dominions?); its relationship to Machiavelli's well-attested republicanism puzzling; its language biting and provocative here, passionate and mystical there. But since Machiavelli belongs to the first rank of both political thinkers and wordsmiths, we must accept this ambiguity as intentional, relish his prose, and discover his meanings.

Machiavelli did and did not belong to the Florentine elite; the ambiguity begins here. The Machiavelli family was poor and without influence. But the author's own father Bernardo, a lawyer and a humanist with a library stocked with classical works, took care that Niccolò received a proper humanist education. His literary product attests that the son devoured his father's books, yet he did not become a humanist—if that title is reserved for those who write works primarily in Latin in a range of humanist genres—however much his thought is saturated with classical literature and history.

When Machiavelli makes his first appearance in Italian affairs, he is already a politician. In 1498, a month after the execution of the fiery prophet Savonarola who had dominated Florence during the four years after the Medici expulsion in 1494, Machiavelli was made second chancellor of the Republic, and was appointed soon after to serve on the Ten of War, a critical council during an era—the same that Luigi Guicciardini described (see Chapter 4)—of constant invasion, shifting alliances, and warfare. Over the period 1498 to 1512, he was sent on important diplomatic missions to France and the papal court, among other destinations, advised on military organization and recruitment, and guided the Florentine reconquest of Pisa. But when Spanish troops overran Florentine territory in 1512, the Medici returned. Machiavelli lost his position in November 1512, and in February 1513, charged with conspiracy, imprisoned, tortured, and released, he retreated to his country villa not far from the city he had so long served. There, he wrote most of his many works, including *The Prince* and the *Discourses on Livy*, his two great contributions to political thought.

These two works, the product of his enforced retirement, are quite unlike each other, yet fundamentally related. *The Prince* is brief, the *Discourses* vast and discursive. *The Prince* seems to advocate autocracy, the *Discourses* most certainly is a roadmap of republicanism. Yet both recur ceaselessly to ancient examples, both display the same kind of epigrammatic judgments on political behavior, both seek a recipe for political success that is, for Machiavelli, the only thing that matters, since the failure to achieve it means political extinction. They were likely written at about the same time, both having roots in 1513, during the first phase of the author's self-imposed exile. But when they were circulated, revised, and completed is unclear. Neither was published until after the author's death in 1527: the *Discourses* in 1531 and *The Prince* in 1532.

The Prince is more widely read, in part because of its brevity. There are other reasons as well, of which two may be noted. First, by its focus on a single ruler, one man with an army, it seems to anticipate the coming age of consolidated monarchies at the head of the large nation-states of Europe beyond the Alps. Second, its repudiation of morality, Christian and humanist alike, as an absolute requirement in the ruler is utterly novel and thoroughly shocking. Up until this time, and afterwards, even very bad men advised princes to be pious, generous, compassionate, and so on. Machiavelli, perhaps a good man, and certainly one wholeheartedly committed to the welfare of Florence and, if secondarily, of Italy, advises the prince to *seem* but not to *be* virtuous; to oppress, slaughter, lie, break faith, and commit a host of sins—sins indeed, whether these are defined as such by the church or by the broader human community.

This new morality is introduced around the midpoint of *The Prince*, although there are hints of what is coming in earlier sections. An overview of the book's twenty-six chapters will be helpful. In the first fourteen chapters, Machiavelli describes in clipped, potent phrases how the prince is to handle various eventualities: whether the principality he is acquiring is used to hereditary rule, or whether the citizens will be allowed to maintain their own laws, or how he is to go about organizing his army. In Chapters Fifteen through Nineteen—the central chapters in terms of length, and the pivotal ones in terms of theme—he outlines his new moral program. In Chapters Twenty to Twenty-Three, he gives advice on fortifications and advisers; in Chapter Twenty-Four, he argues starkly that it is by their own indolence and incompetence that the Italian rulers have lost their states. The last two chapters are grandiose in theme and passionate in tone—a coda; in Chapter Twenty-Five, he evokes the goddess Fortune as the driver of Italy's misfortunes, and calls for a man powerful enough to subdue her, not shirking from implications of rape and assault; in Chapter Twenty-Six, he exhorts the Medici to free Italy, "so long enslaved," and awaiting "her redeemer," to expel the barbarians who have brought about her ruination.

If the prince is to maintain power, Machiavelli argues in the pivotal Chapters Fifteen through Nineteen, he must ignore dictates that constrain all other persons. In Chapter Fifteen, he announces the inversion of the moral universe that is proposed. Others have written on the qualities a prince should possess, but he is dissatisfied with their advice: "But my hope is to write a book that will be useful, . . . and so I thought it sensible to go straight to a discussion of how things are in real life and not waste time with a discussion of an imaginary world." A ruler equipped with good qualities would be a fine thing, but since "we do not live in an ideal world," that requirement must be abandoned. In Chapter Sixteen, Machiavelli discusses the perils of generosity, a virtue that had always been seen as admirable in princes. But the generous prince runs out of money, so must tax and oppress his subjects; whereas a parsimonious prince builds up his stores and, by making himself self-sufficient, wins the gratitude of his subjects.

In Chapter Seventeen, Machiavelli similarly subverts the usual assumptions about cruelty and compassion. The prince who shows compassion may endanger his state, whereas the prince who acts cruelly may ironically benefit his subjects. "So a ruler ought not to mind the disgrace of being called cruel," he writes, "if he keeps his subjects peaceful and law-abiding, for it is more compassionate to impose harsh punishments on a few than, out of excessive compassion, to allow disorder to spread, which leads to murders or looting." Accordingly, although the prince should avoid being hated, it is useful if he is feared: "fear restrains men because they are afraid of punishment, and this fear never leaves them." In Chapter Eighteen, Machiavelli recommends another inversion of accepted morality: it is admirable, in general, to keep one's word, but a prince may need to break his. In the present disturbed times, "those rulers who have not thought it important to keep their word have achieved great things," and "have been able to overcome those who have placed store in integrity." In short, the prince must be able to act at times like a fox, who avoids traps, and at other times like a lion, to chase away wolves. In Chapter Nineteen, finally, Machiavelli urges the prince at all costs to avoid the hatred and contempt of his subjects, but rather "to ensure your actions suggest greatness and endurance, strength of character and of purpose." To do so, he must stay away from "the possessions and the women of your subjects." This is not a counsel of virtue, as it is generally understood, so much as a counsel of strength. The strong prince, who does not arouse the resentment of his subjects, will hold onto power.

The blunt amoralism of Machiavelli's instructions to the prince in Chapters Fifteen through Nineteen pose a striking contrast to his passionate call, in Chapter Twenty-Six, for a redeemer to free enslaved Italy from its destroyers.

Niccolò Machiavelli, *The Prince* (1513)[1]

CHAPTER FIFTEEN: ABOUT THOSE FACTORS THAT CAUSE MEN, AND ESPECIALLY RULERS, TO BE PRAISED OR CENSURED

Our next task is to consider the policies and principles a ruler ought to follow in dealing with his subjects or with his friends. Since I know many people have written on this subject, I am concerned it may be thought presumptuous for me to write on it as well, especially since what I have to say, as regards this question in particular, will differ greatly from the recommendations of others. But my hope is to write a book that will be useful, at least to those who read it intelligently, and so I thought it sensible to go straight to a discussion of how things are in real life and not waste time with a discussion of an imaginary world. For many authors have constructed imaginary republics

---

1. From Machiavelli, *The Prince*, trans. David Wooton (Indianapolis, IN: Hackett Publishing Co., 1995), 47–55.

and principalities that have never existed in practice and never could; for the gap between how people actually behave and how they ought to behave is so great that anyone who ignores everyday reality in order to live up to an ideal will soon discover he has been taught how to destroy himself, not how to preserve himself. For anyone who wants to act the part of a good man in all circumstances will bring about his own ruin, for those he has to deal with will not all be good. So it is necessary for a ruler, if he wants to hold on to power, to learn how not to be good, and to know when it is and when it is not necessary to use this knowledge.

Let us leave to one side, then, all discussion of imaginary rulers and talk about practical realities. I maintain that all men, when people talk about them, and especially rulers, because they hold positions of authority, are described in terms of qualities that are inextricably linked to censure or to praise. So one man is described as generous, another as a miser . . . ; one is called open-handed, another tightfisted; one man is cruel, another gentle; one untrustworthy, another reliable; one effeminate and cowardly, another bold and violent; one sympathetic, another self-important; one promiscuous, another monogamous; one straightforward, another duplicitous; one tough, another easy-going; one serious, another cheerful; one religious, another atheistical; and so on.

Now I know everyone will agree that if a ruler could have all the good qualities I listed and none of the bad ones, then this would be an excellent state of affairs. But one cannot have all the good qualities, nor always act in a praiseworthy fashion, for we do not live in an ideal world. You have to be astute enough to avoid being thought to have those evil qualities that would make it impossible for you to retain power; as for those that are compatible with holding on to power, you should avoid them if you can; but if you cannot, then you should not worry too much if people say you have them. Above all, do not be upset if you are supposed to have those vices a ruler needs if he is going to stay securely in power, for . . . there are some ways of behaving that are supposed to be virtuous, but would lead to your downfall, and others that are supposed to be wicked, but will lead to your welfare and peace of mind.

CHAPTER SIXTEEN: ON GENEROSITY AND PARSIMONY

Let me begin, then, with the qualities I mentioned first. I argue it would be good to be thought generous; nevertheless, if you act in the way that will get you a reputation for generosity, you will do yourself damage. For generosity used skillfully and practiced as it ought to be, is hidden from sight, and being truly generous will not protect you from acquiring a reputation for parsimony. So, if you want to have a reputation for generosity, you must throw yourself into lavish and ostentatious expenditure. Consequently, a ruler who pursues a reputation for generosity will always end up wasting all his resources; and he will be obliged in the end, if he wants to preserve his reputation, to impose crushing taxes upon the people, to pursue every possible source of income, and to be preoccupied with maximizing his revenues. This will begin to make him hateful to his subjects, and will ensure no one thinks well of him, for no one admires poverty. The result is his supposed generosity will have caused him to offend the vast majority and to have won favor with few. Anything that goes wrong will destabilize him, and the slightest danger will imperil him. Recognizing the problem, and trying to economize, he will quickly find he has acquired a reputation as a miser.

So we see a ruler cannot seek to benefit from a reputation as generous without harming himself. Recognizing this, he ought, if he is wise, not to mind being called miserly. For, as time goes by, he will be thought of as growing ever more generous, for people will recognize that as a result of his parsimony he is able to live on his income, maintain an adequate army, and undertake new initiatives without imposing new taxes. The result is he will be thought to be generous towards all those whose income he does not tax, which is almost everybody, and stingy towards those who miss out on handouts, who are only a few. . . . *[A contemporary example follows.]*

So a ruler should not care about being thought miserly, for it means he will be able to avoid robbing his subjects; he will be able to defend himself; he will not become poor and despicable, and he will not be forced to become rapacious. This is one of those vices that makes successful government possible. . . . *[Classical examples follow.]*

There is nothing so self-defeating as generosity, for the more generous you are, the less you are able to be generous. Generosity leads to poverty and disgrace, or, if you try to escape that, to rapacity and hostility. Among all the things a ruler should try to avoid, he must avoid above all being hated and despised. Generosity leads to your being both. So it is wiser to accept a reputation as miserly, which people despise but do not hate, than to aspire to a reputation as generous, and as a consequence, be obliged to face criticism for rapacity, which people both despise and hate.

CHAPTER SEVENTEEN: ABOUT CRUELTY AND COMPASSION; AND ABOUT WHETHER IT IS BETTER TO BE LOVED THAN FEARED, OR THE REVERSE

Going further down our list of qualities, I recognize every ruler should want to be thought of as compassionate and not cruel. Nevertheless, I have to warn you to be careful about being compassionate. Cesare Borgia was thought of as cruel; but this supposed cruelty of his restored order to the Romagna, united it, rendered it peaceful and law-abiding.[2] If you think about it, you

---

2. Cesare Borgia (1475–1507) was the natural son of Pope Alexander VI, and Romagna one of the papal lands, which Borgia pacified and ruled.

will realize he was, in fact, much more compassionate than the people of Florence, who, in order to avoid being thought cruel, allowed Pistoia to tear itself apart.[3] So a ruler ought not to mind the disgrace of being called cruel, if he keeps his subjects peaceful and law-abiding, for it is more compassionate to impose harsh punishments on a few than, out of excessive compassion, to allow disorder to spread, which leads to murders or looting. The whole community suffers if there are riots, while to maintain order the ruler only has to execute one or two individuals. . . .

This leads us to a question that is in dispute: Is it better to be loved than feared, or vice versa? My reply is one ought to be both loved and feared; but, since it is difficult to accomplish both at the same time, I maintain it is much safer to be feared than loved, if you have to do without one of the two. For of men one can, in general, say this: They are ungrateful, fickle, deceptive and deceiving, avoiders of danger, eager to gain. As long as you serve their interests, they are devoted to you. They promise you their blood, their possessions, their lives, and their children, as I said before, so long as you seem to have no need of them. But as soon as you need help, they turn against you. Any ruler who relies simply on their promises and makes no other preparations, will be destroyed. For you will find that those whose support you buy, who do not rally to you because they admire your strength of character and nobility of soul, these are people you pay for, but they are never yours, and in the end you cannot get the benefit of your investment. Men are less nervous of offending someone who makes himself lovable, than someone who makes himself frightening. For love attaches men by ties of obligation, which, since men are wicked, they break whenever their interests are at stake. But fear restrains men because they are afraid of punishment, and this fear never leaves them. Still, a ruler should make himself feared in such a way that, if he does not inspire love, at least he does not provoke hatred. For it is perfectly possible to be feared and not hated. You will only be hated if you seize the property or the women of your subjects and citizens. Whenever you have to kill someone, make sure you have a suitable excuse and an obvious reason; but, above all else, keep your hands off other people's property; for men are quicker to forget the death of their father than the loss of their inheritance. . . .

Providing ancient examples, Machiavelli shows how having a reputation for cruelty is important when one is in command of an army.

I conclude, then, that, as far as being feared and loved is concerned, since men decide for themselves whom they love, and rulers decide whom they fear, a wise rulers should rely on the emotion he can control, not on the one he cannot. But he must take care to avoid being hated, as I have said.

---

3. In 1501.

CHAPTER EIGHTEEN: HOW FAR RULERS ARE TO KEEP THEIR WORD

Everybody recognizes how praiseworthy it is for a ruler to keep his word and to live a life of integrity, without relying on craftiness. Nevertheless, we see that in practice, in these days, those rulers who have not thought it important to keep their word have achieved great things, and have known how to employ cunning to confuse and disorientate other men. In the end, they have been able to overcome those who have placed store in integrity.

You should therefore know there are two ways to fight: one while respecting the rules, the other with no holds barred. Men alone fight in the first fashion, and animals fight in the second. But because you cannot always win if you respect the rules, you must be prepared to break them. A ruler, in particular, needs to know how to be both an animal and a man. . . . *[Classical examples follow.]*

Since a ruler, then needs to know how to make good use of beastly qualities, he should take as his models among the animals both the fox and the lion, for the lion does not know how to avoid traps, and the fox is easily overpowered by wolves. So you must be a fox when it comes to suspecting a trap, and a lion when it comes to making the wolves turn tail. Those who simply act like a lion all the time do not understand their business. So you see a wise ruler cannot, and should not, keep his word when doing so is to his disadvantage, and when the reasons that led him to promise to do so no longer apply. Of course, if all men were good, this advice would be bad; but since men are wicked and will not keep faith with you, you need not keep faith with them.

Nor is a ruler ever short of legitimate reasons to justify breaking his word. I could give an infinite number of contemporary examples to support my argument and to show how treaties and promises have been rendered null and void by the dishonesty of rulers; and he who has known best how to act the fox has come out of it the best. But it is essential to know how to conceal how crafty one is, to know how to be a clever counterfeit and hypocrite. You will find people are so simple-minded and so preoccupied with their immediate concerns, that if you set out to deceive them, you will always find plenty of them who will let themselves be deceived. . . . *[A contemporary example follows.]*

So a ruler need not have all the positive qualities I listed earlier,[4] but he must seem to have them. Indeed, I would go so far as to say that if you have them and never make any exceptions, then you will suffer for it; while if you merely appear to have them, they will benefit you. So you should seem to be compassionate, trustworthy, sympathetic, honest, religious, and, indeed, be

---

4. Loosely, in Chapter Fifteen, but they are codified a few lines hence: "So you should seem to be compassionate, trustworthy, sympathetic, honest, religious, and, indeed, be all these things."

all these things; but at the same time you should be constantly prepared, so that, if these become liabilities, you are trained and ready to become their opposites. You need to understand this: A ruler, and particularly a ruler who is new to power, cannot conform to all those rules that men who are thought good are expected to respect, for he is often obliged, in order to hold on to power, to break his word, to be uncharitable, inhumane, and irreligious. So he must be mentally prepared to act as circumstances and changes in fortune require. As I have said, he should do what is right if he can, but he must be prepared to do wrong if necessary.

A ruler must, therefore, take great care that he never carelessly says anything that is not imbued with the five qualities I listed above.[5] He must seem, to those who listen to him and watch him, entirely pious, truthful, reliable, sympathetic, and religious. There is no quality that it is more important he should seem to have than this last one. . . .

CHAPTER NINETEEN: HOW ONE SHOULD AVOID HATRED AND CONTEMPT

Because I have spoken of the more important of the qualities I mentioned earlier, I want now to discuss the rest of them briefly under this general heading, that a ruler must take care . . . to avoid those things that will make him an object of hatred or contempt. As long as he avoids these he will have done what is required of him, and will find having a reputation for any of the other vices will do him no harm at all. You become hateful, above all . . . if you prey on the possessions and the women of your subjects. You should leave both alone. The vast majority of men, so long as their goods and their honor are not taken from them, will live contentedly, so you will only have to contend with the small minority who are ambitious, and there are lots of straightforward ways of keeping them under control. You become contemptible if you are thought to be erratic, capricious, effeminate, pusillanimous, irresolute. You should avoid acquiring such a reputation as a pilot steers clear of the rocks. Make every effort to ensure your actions suggest greatness and endurance, strength of character and of purpose. When it comes to the private business of your subjects, you should aim to ensure you never have to change your decisions once they have been taken, and that you acquire a reputation that will discourage people from even considering tricking or deceiving you.

A ruler who is thought of in these terms has the sort of reputation he needs; and it is difficult to conspire against someone who is respected in this way, difficult to attack him, because people realize he is on top of his job and has the loyalty of his employees. For rulers ought to be afraid of two things:

---

5. That is, "compassionate, trustworthy, sympathetic, honest, religious."

Within the state, they should fear their subjects; abroad, they should fear other rulers. Against foreign powers, a good army and reliable allies are the only defense; and, if you have a good army, you will always find your allies reliable. And you will find it easy to maintain order at home if you are secure from external threats, provided, that is, conspiracies against you have not undermined your authority. . . . The best protection against these is to ensure that you are not hated or despised, and the people are satisfied with your rule. It is essential to accomplish this. . . .

So we can sum up as follows: The conspirators face nothing but fear, mutual distrust, and the prospect of punishment, so they lose heart; while the ruler is supported by the authority of his office and by the laws, and protected both by his supporters and by the forces of government. So, if you add to this inbuilt advantage the goodwill of the populace, then it is impossible to find anyone who is so foolhardy as to conspire against you. . . . *[Ancient examples follow.]*

Desiderius Erasmus

Only three years after the Florentine Machiavelli drafted *The Prince* and began his *Discourses*, Erasmus of Rotterdam (1469–1536)—or, as he preferred to think of himself, Erasmus of Christendom—dedicated *On the Education of a Christian Prince* to the young man who would soon reign as Holy Roman Emperor Charles V. Erasmus requires of the ideal prince all the virtues that Machiavelli denigrated, and more. Where Machiavelli urged that the prince seem but not be virtuous, Erasmus wished him to embody Christian virtues to an extent found mostly in saints, rarely in ordinary humans, and scarcely known in rulers. He poses an impossible ideal, and believes in it profoundly.

Erasmus is not, however, unaware of how things are done in the real world. His satirical works, especially his *Praise of Folly* (1509), deconstruct the hypocrisy, pomposity, and willful malignity of an array of power-wielding elites in both church and lay society. He urgently summons the prince to resist these patterns of behavior, especially when they are urged upon him by courtiers and sycophants. The well-being of human society depends, for Erasmus, on the integrity of the prince, the embodiment and agent of the "philosophy of Christ"—something rather different than the doctrine of the Church—that it was Erasmus' lifelong mission to promote.

Erasmus' call for virtue in the prince is not new, although his program is more comprehensive than that found in the medieval "mirrors for princes" tradition. What is new—wholly new, and virtually absent in Machiavelli—is the idea suffusing the whole of the work that the prince is responsible for the welfare of ordinary people, whose daily lives of work, family, and action are intrinsically worthy and admirable. They should not be overtaxed—for any purpose, but surely not to support the debaucheries of a royal court. The magistrates and officials set above them should be persons of integrity, like the prince himself. Their agricultural and commercial pursuits are essential functions deserving of protection. Their cities, bridges, roads, waterways, and fortifications should be properly maintained. Above all, their young men should not be sacrificed in wars—any wars at all, for none can be just; and certainly not the meaningless ones that were everywhere in progress. Wars are the very antithesis of a just and Christian society: they make of communities of productive citizens, a wilderness of widows and orphans, raped daughters, maimed and beggared sons. Erasmus may be an idealist but he is also a revolutionary, proposing a social order resembling the one still dreamed of by reformers today.

If the Italian-born Petrarch, also something of a cosmopolitan, can be seen as one bookend of the first phase of European humanism, the Dutch-born Desiderius Erasmus (1469–1536) may be seen as the other. Just as there were humanists active before Petrarch, who nonetheless crystallized their classicizing culture into the intellectual movement that would character-ize the Renaissance, there would be humanists after Erasmus—Montaigne, for instance—whose humanism moves in new directions, as an element in broader cultural shifts. But both Petrarch and Erasmus are mammoth figures, archhumanists, perhaps, the range of whose thought and activity is unequalled by the others, however significant their work may be. Both write in a wide range of genres, and although their predilections vary—Petrarch tends to poetry, Erasmus to theology—they share an interest in education and politics and engage in the profound exploration of the self. Both integrate a Christian vision with their profound classical allegiances. Both seek and receive the patronage of princes, but rise above them. Both recognize the critical impor-tance of the Greek, along with the Latin tradition—although here Erasmus, working nearly two centuries later, had the advantage of the achievement of the Renaissance Hellenists, and himself sets a new standard for the mastery of the Greek language and thought that prevails into modern times.

On the Education of a Christian Prince opens, as its title promises, with a discussion of education pure and simple, in the sense of pedagogy. The prince must be kept away from bad influences, provided with the best possible tutor, and instructed in the humanist mode—a subject on which Erasmus will dilate further in his 1529 work *On Education for Children*. But the education of the prince that Erasmus intends is not limited to instruc-tion in the liberal arts, but to the whole formation of the ruler's character, on which so much and so many will depend. The next topic of discussion, therefore, is on flatterers: a species of sycophantic courtiers, also repellent to Machiavelli, who flourished in every court. The prince will not develop the depth of character that Erasmus envisions if he is exposed to the blandish-ments of flatterers, so they are to be removed from his circle.

Discussion then turns, about halfway through the work, to the way that the Christian prince will govern his realm. It is from this section of the *Education of a Christian Prince* that the excerpts given here are taken, focusing on taxation; princely beneficences; legislation; the prince's peacetime occupations; and the dangers of war.

The prince should tax his subjects as little as possible, tilting the burden to the wealthy and away from the poor, and avoiding any exactions on food and clothing, necessary for subsistence. Instead, he should eliminate any extravagances of his court and dismiss unnecessary and slothful officials. He will show beneficence to his subjects in other ways as well, assisting some personally, or supporting endeavors that are useful to the community: "And in his soul he will feel that the day is lost to him on which he has not bestowed some benefit on someone." Laws, as well, should be crafted for the benefit of the citizens: they should "have no other end than to promote the common good." As with taxation, they should tilt in favor of the poor, and certainly not privilege the wealthy: "they should punish more severely an assault on a poor man than a wealthy one, a corrupt magistrate than an ordinary thief, a criminous burgher than a commoner." There should be as few laws as possible, and these plainly written and communicated openly to the populace.

In peacetime, the prince should not waste his time in the frivolities and luxuries of the court, but engage in a program of public works. He will travel through his realm, strengthening fortifications, building public buildings, improving agricultural productivity, repairing roads and bridges, redirecting rivers, building dykes, or dredging channels. Further, he will promote "the integrity of the magistrates and officials, the holiness of the priests, the selection of capable teachers, the fairness of the laws, and all pursuits conducive to virtue." Just as the celestial bodies keep order in the cosmos, and imperil it if they go astray, the prince keeps order in the state, and must not deviate from the right path.

The prince should not go to war, which always brings great harm especially to the common people; and if war is unavoidable, he should see that as little bloodshed as possible results, and that it be brought to a swift conclusion. "War gives rise to more war: from a small one is born a great one, from a single one its twin, from one that is foolish, one cruel and deadly; and wherever the pestilence of war arises it infects those nearby first, but soon spreads also abroad to those far, far away." The prince should not "insist on learning from experience that war is an abomination," for that wisdom is "purchased at too high a price." He can learn from books, and from others who have survived them, how terrible war is. Not even war against the Turks is justified, although the Ottoman Turks even as Erasmus writes were advancing aggressively northward from the Balkans. When the peoples of Europe become themselves true followers of Christ, then, perhaps, they can rise against his enemies.

The young Charles to whom Erasmus writes would soon become one of the most powerful of European rulers. He was a devout man, who resisted the

Protestant reformers he saw as heretics, and who himself retired to a monastery in his later years. But he was not the "Christian prince" that Erasmus awaited: above all, too much blood was on his hands. Erasmus could advise, but he could not make his listeners follow. In the years to come, the princes of Europe would prove to be disciples more of Machiavelli than of Erasmus.

Desiderius Erasmus, *On the Education of a Christian Prince* (1516)

ON TRIBUTES AND TAXES

If we search the annals of past times, we find that many revolts originate from excessive taxation. So a good prince will take care to stir up popular feeling on such matters as little as possible. If he can, he should reign without exacting taxes. A prince should not concern himself with mercantile affairs that are beneath the dignity of his office. If he is a good prince, then all that his loving subjects possess, he, too, possesses. . . .

There are those who serve the prince who, so as to constantly increase his reputation, wring the people dry, and who believe that they are properly pursuing his interests when they turn his subjects into enemies. But if he follows their advice, he should know that he falls far short of what befits a prince.

Instead, he should diligently seek and devise ways so that as small a burden as possible is laid on the people. It would be an excellent plan for raising revenues if the prince cut back on unnecessary expenses, if he eliminated useless agencies, if he avoided wars and other foreign ventures, if he restrained the greed of his officials and if he exerted himself more for the proper management of his dominions than their increase. . . .

Erasmus expands on the twin recommendations of taxing the people less, and cutting expenditures.

The good prince will tax the least, then, those things which are commonly used, including by the poorest folk, such as grain, bread, beer, wine, clothes, and other such things without which human life cannot subsist. For these are now heavily burdened, and in several ways: first by the heavy taxes which the tax-farmers extort . . . ; then by import duties, which have their own set of collectors; and finally by the monopolies which drive prices higher, with the result that very little profit redounds to the prince compared to the great sum extracted from the poor.[6]

---

6. The first two of these forms of taxation correspond to our categories of direct and indirect taxation; the third describes monopolies, which were often granted by rulers to merchants or companies in exchange for favors, as a kind of hidden tax, since they drive up the cost of goods.

The best way, then, as has been said, of increasing the prince's revenues is by cutting expenditures—as the saying goes, from thrift comes wealth. Yet if it is impossible to avoid any kind of exaction, and if it is for the good of the people, then those foreign and exotic items should be taxed—such as cottons and silks and richly-dyed textiles, pepper and spices, ointments and gems, and any other things of this kind[7]—which are not needed so much for subsistence as for luxury and delight and whose use is limited to the rich. For in this way the pain will be felt by those whose fortunes can best bear it, and who will not be reduced to poverty by this blow, but perhaps be made more frugal, so that the loss to their purse may be repaired by the improvement of their morals. . . .

Erasmus closes this section with a warning against the debasement of the currency.

ON PRINCELY BENEFICENCE

Since generosity and beneficence are the qualities that bring honor to good princes, how do they dare call themselves "prince," the sum of whose policy is to promote their own interests to the disadvantage of others? The wise and vigilant prince will find the way to be of service to all, not necessarily by bestowing gifts. Some he will assist by his generosity, and others he will aid with a favor; some he will free from the hand of unjust authority, while to others he will offer sound advice. And in his soul he will feel that the day is lost to him on which he has not bestowed some benefit on someone. . . .

The prince must use his beneficence wisely, however, bestowing good on those who deserve it and causing no harm to anyone else.

It is no digression to recall that in ancient myths the gods are shown never to go anywhere without conferring a great gift on those who welcomed them. But if in our day, when the prince approaches, the citizens put away their best possessions, lock up their lovely daughters, send away their young sons, hide their wealth, and say to themselves, as if their actions did not already reveal it, what opinion they have of him, when they do the things they would do at the approach of an enemy or a predator? When the prince's arrival causes them to fear an ambush or an assault, from which it is his duty to protect them? They fear treachery from the others of his retinue, but from him, too, they fear violence. For when one man complains that he was beaten up, another that his daughter was abducted, another that his wife was raped, another that he was

---

7. Erasmus here lists the principal luxury commodities of the day, mostly acquired through long-distance and, as such, international trade. Cotton was not yet the easily available and inexpensive textile it would become during the industrial revolution, and dyestuffs, before the advent of modern chemical dyes, were expensive as well.

cheated of his wages, please! How unlike the arrival of the gods is the advent of this prince! When the wealthiest of cities so distrusts the prince, when at the advent of the prince all the ruffians rush out to greet him, while the best and most reliable men are wary and silent—clearly they announce by their actions what opinion they have of the prince. . . .

Erasmus closes this section with reminders that the prince should show generosity not only to his own subjects, but also to foreigners and visitors.

ON MAKING AND EMENDING LAWS

That city or kingdom is most fortunate that has the best laws under the best prince; and their condition is happiest when all obey the prince, and the prince himself obeys the laws—provided that the laws meet the standard of justice and honor, and have no other end than to promote the common good.

A good, wise, and righteous prince is in himself a living law. He should labor, therefore, not to create many laws, but to create the best laws, those most salutary for the republic. For if the city is well-ordered under a good prince and with worthy magistrates, a very few laws will suffice. And if these conditions are not present, no multitude of laws will be enough. For the sick patient will not recover no matter how many drugs an incompetent doctor piles on a mountain of drugs already prescribed.

In creating laws, however, it is necessary above all to beware lest they smell of lucre diverted to the state treasury, or favoritism to the nobility, but that they are in line with the requirements of honor and the public utility—that utility to be defined not according to the general consensus, but to the norm that wise men establish, which should be a requirement in all the councils of princes. In other words, as the ancients also hold, there will be no law unless it is just, and fair, and in accord with the public interest. Nor is a law a law because it pleases the prince, but because it pleases a wise and good prince, who finds nothing pleasing unless it is honorable and appropriate for the republic. . . .

Erasmus explores how the laws differentially impact persons of different social ranks.

This, though, should be the universal goal of all laws: that no one should suffer injury, neither the poor man nor the rich, the nobleman nor the commoner, the serf nor the free man, the public official nor the private citizen. But the laws should incline more to assisting the weak, since the condition of the more humble folk is more vulnerable to harm, and to the degree that they lack the benefits of fortune, then humanity demands that the laws compensate. Consequently, they should punish more severely an assault on a poor

man than a wealthy one, a corrupt magistrate than an ordinary thief, a criminous burgher than a commoner. . . .

> *Erasmus urges the prince to bestow rewards and honors on the law-abiding,*
> *and to discourage those given to idleness: beggars, but also others who are*
> *employed mainly for ostentation or who, like soldiers, are between obligations.*

To review, then, let there be as few laws as possible, and principally those
that are fair and conducive to the public welfare; and they should be clearly
communicated to the people—to which end the Ancients displayed them
inscribed on tables or tablets in public places so that everyone could see them.
For some public officials shamefully use the laws as a kind of trap, trying
evidently to ensnare as many victims as possible, not so much pursuing the
interest of the state as stalking their prey. Finally, the laws should be written
in plain words without convolutions, so that there will be no need to consult
those crafty operators who call themselves jurists and advocates—which profession indeed, when it was the preserve of honorable men, had great dignity,
although it yielded little profit, the thirst for which now corrupts it as it does
everything else. . . .

> *Omitted here are sections on magistrates, treaties, and princely marriage alli-*
> *ances.*

WHAT PRINCES SHOULD DO IN PEACETIME

The prince, then, instructed in Christ's decrees and the precepts of wisdom,
will cherish nothing more—nor indeed will he cherish anything else—than
the happiness of the people, whom he should both love and nurture as his one
body with himself. And to this one end he will direct all his thoughts, all his
efforts, and all his strength, so that he may discharge his duty in such a way
that, at the last day, he will render his account to Christ as judge, and among
mortals leave a remembrance as himself as honorable in all things. . . .

It better suits the prince to carry on his public duties, than to hide away in
solitude. . . . Yet there are some today, who think that princes should only be
concerned with princely things, and not involve themselves in public functions which are beneath them. . . . But the cause of this avoidance of public
affairs is the perverse education of princes. . . . What other course lies ahead
for him who spent his first years among flatterers and females, corrupted by
depravities and pleasures, amid gambling, dancing, and hunting? How will he
then take joy in carrying on those duties which require serious thought? . . .

There are bad morals to be remedied with good laws, perverse laws to be
improved, evils to be corrected; honest magistrates to be identified, and corrupt ones to be punished or restrained. Ways must be sought by which to

lighten the load of the humble folk, to free the realm from thievery and plunder with the least expenditure of blood, to foster and promote lasting concord among his subjects. There are other lesser tasks which are yet not unworthy of a great prince: he may tour his cities, but with the intention of making them all better: he may strengthen their weak fortifications, adorn them with public buildings, tend to bridges, porticoes, churches, embankments, and aqueducts; clear places that are a source of plague either by rebuilding or draining swamps. He may divert rivers that flow in the wrong direction, build dams or open channels on the waterfront as required. He may promote the cultivation of fallow fields so as to increase the grain supply, and improve productivity, as for instance by removing vineyards where grapes do not grow well so that more wheat can be grown. There are six thousand things of this kind which would be a splendid undertaking for a prince, and enjoyable even for a good prince, so that there would never be need because of lack of occupation to go to war or spend the night gambling. . . .

It follows, then, as has been shown, that if the prince concerns himself especially with the things that strengthen and improve the state, he will control and expel those, in contrast, which diminish it. For by his example of his wisdom and diligence, the good prince promotes the integrity of the magistrates and officials, the holiness of the priests, the selection of capable teachers, the fairness of the laws, and all pursuits conducive to virtue. By advancing these goods, those things that are harmful to the state may be easily eliminated, since they will be rooted out from the start before they have had a chance to take over. To be skillful and diligent in these matters is the philosophy of the Christian prince. To engage in these projects for the good of all, to lend them all possible support, this, in sum, befits the Christian prince.

Just as the celestial bodies, if they are disturbed even a little or stray from their proper course, have grave effects on humankind, as happens with solar and lunar eclipses, so too if the greatest princes deviate even a little from the right path, or if they give in to sins of ambition, anger, or ignorance, they immediately imperil the whole of this vast world. . . .[8]

ON GOING TO WAR

While the prince should never act precipitously, he must be especially careful and circumspect—more than in all other matters—in going to war. For although other actions have other consequences, from war uniquely comes the destruction of all good things; it is an ocean overflowing with everything evil, nor is any other evil more tenacious. War gives rise to more war: from a

---

8. Astronomers at this time, who were also astrologers, believed that the motions of the heavenly bodies directly impacted events on earth.

small one is born a great one, from a single one its twin, from one that is foolish, one cruel and deadly; and wherever the pestilence of war arises it infects those nearby first, but soon spreads also abroad to those far, far away.

The good prince will hardly ever go to war, unless after all other remedies have been tried, it can in no way be avoided. If we had observed this principle, people would scarcely ever have gone to war. For if so malignant a thing cannot be avoided, then it must be the first concern of the prince that as little as possible be spent of the blood and treasure of his subjects—I would prefer to say a minimum of blood and expense of any Christian people—and that it be swiftly brought to an end.

First, the truly Christian prince should weigh how great is the distinction between man, an animal born for peace and kindliness, and wild beasts, born to hunt and fight. Then he should consider how great is the distinction between man and a Christian man. Thereafter he should consider how desirable, how honorable, how salutary a thing is peace; and in contrast, how calamitous and depraved a thing is war, and what a parade of evils follows in its train, even if it is a truly just war—if any war can ever be called just.[9] Finally, all feelings put aside, let him apply a little reason to the issue: does he really imagine he can know what will be the outcome of war? And whether its costs are justified, even if victory—which doesn't always fall to the better cause—is certain? . . .

Wisdom in princes will be purchased at too high a price if they insist on learning from experience that war is an abomination—so that at last they may say in their old age: "I did not believe that war was so deadly." But God Almighty! you should have learned that lesson from the innumerable evils that war has inflicted on the world! Eventually the prince will understand that it was useless to extend the boundaries of his kingdom, and what seemed at first to offer promise, later brought disaster—by which time, many thousands of men had been killed or injured. These things are better learned from books, from the recollections of the old, and from the bitter experience of neighboring states—otherwise, for years on end, this prince or that one struggles over this or that dominion, causing themselves more loss than gain. . . .

Erasmus reflects at some length on the futility and costs of war.

The good prince should strive for the kind of glory which sheds no blood and harms no one. In war, the best that can happen is that one side is victorious, while the other side is vanquished. But often, even the victor grieves a victory purchased at too great a cost.

If piety does not move us, or the calamity war inflicts on the world, certainly we should be moved by the harm done to the reputation of the

---

9. The definition of a "just" war had long been a subject of philosophical discussion.

Christian religion. What do we think the Turks and Saracens are saying about us, when they see that after so many centuries the Christian princes have been unable to reach any agreement? Or achieve peace, despite all the treaties? With no end to the spilling of blood? When they suffer fewer conflicts between nations than do we who, according to the doctrine of Christ, preach perfect peace? . . .

Preachers used to try to purge the feelings that lead to hostility from the souls of the common people. Now the Englishman hates the Frenchman for no other reason than that he is French; and the Scot the Englishman, just because he is Scots; the Italian hates the German, and the Swabian the Swiss, and so with the others: each region detests another, each city another city. Why do these meaningless names tear us apart, while the name of Christ, common to us all, cannot bind us together?

Erasmus criticizes the clergy who support today's wars, when the ancient Hebrews acknowledged the sinfulness of even necessary warfare.

Nor do I think that war against the Turks should be hastily undertaken considering above all that Christ's realm was created, spread, and established by very different means. It is perhaps not right that it should be defended in a way other than that it was begun and increased. And we see that wars of this kind have been a pretext by which the Christian people are fleeced—and then nothing comes of it.[10] Now if this fundraising concerns the faith, that is to be increased and glorified by the suffering of martyrs, not companies of soldiers; but if the battle is for dominion, or wealth, or possessions, then we must recognize clearly that it has little to do with Christianity. Indeed, given the kind of people who now fight this kind of war, it is more likely that we will become Turks, than that we can turn them into Christians. First let us establish that we ourselves are truly Christians—and thereafter, if need be, we can rise up against the Turks.

But I have written much elsewhere concerning the evils of war, which I will not repeat here. But this much I will do: I will urge the princes of Christendom to put aside their empty claims and false pretexts and take action seriously and whole-heartedly to put an end to the madness of war between Christians, so protracted and so pernicious, so that among those who have so much in common, peace and concord may reign. To this end they should apply their mind, exert their strength, offer their counsel, and expend all their energy. Those who strive to be great, will also prove their greatness. Anyone who does this will have achieved a victory far more splendid than if he had by his might conquered all of Africa. . . .

---

10. Fleeced, literally; Erasmus means that they are drained by taxes to support a war that then does not eventuate.

Erasmus closes with a farewell to the "most illustrious prince" for whom his work is written, calling on him to be a prince of peace, as Christ was, and to liberate his people from these "insane wars."

Thomas More

The *Utopia* of Thomas More (1478–1535) is a completely novel construction of an imaginary state. The name of the remote island, after which the book is named, means "no-place": its very essence is that it does not exist. And what a state it is! It is a republic that avoids foreign wars, but fights them as much as possible with mercenaries. It is a communist society where the workday is short and no one owns property, but all live in comfort and security. It values the family, but the individual's rights are limited—except in matters of religion, where perfect tolerance reigns, but too much zeal is discouraged. To support matrimony, it invites future spouses to examine each other in the nude prior to a final commitment, and to ease the process of dying, it encourages the terminally ill to commit suicide. It has no coinage nor any use for gold and silver, but it does have slaves, who free the citizens of unpleasant labor. It is the first of future Utopias that will join others on a select bookshelf as the Western tradition evolves.[11] Further, its identification of private property as the source of human misery is squarely in line with socialist principles. Hailed as a Communist hero by Karl Marx, Friedrich Engels, and Karl Kautsky, More's contribution to "the liberation of humankind" is commemorated, at Lenin's suggestion, on a monument erected in 1918 in Aleksndrovsky Garden near the Kremlin.[12]

Of the visions of the state presented in this chapter, More's is the most visionary, yet in some uncanny ways the most modern. For the republic he sketches is closer to our notion of a republic than the one envisioned by Machiavelli, perpetually subject to factional struggles and takeovers, or by Erasmus, effectively a monarchy. And although each Utopian city is ruled by a "prince," this dignitary is elected, whereas Machiavelli's prince, even if he does not seize power, holds it by force, and Erasmus' prince, deserving or not, is born to his throne. Beyond these differences is one more striking: Machiavelli's world is driven by violence and deception, Erasmus' by pretension, hypocrisy, and selfishness, but in More's *Utopia*, where any small

---

11. Passing by, for the moment, ancient Greek contributions to the genre, with which More would have been familiar.

12. J. A. Guy, *Thomas More* (London, New York: Oxford University Press, 2000), 95–96.

instances of wrongdoing are swiftly punished, the citizens breathe freely the balmy atmosphere of communal well-being.

Odd, because More himself did not live in such a world, least of all at the moment of his death. A lawyer by training and a public official most of his life, he rose in 1529 to the position of chancellor to King Henry VIII. That position he vacated three years later, opposing Henry's moves to subordinate the clergy to the king's will. In 1534, he refused to take an oath required by the Succession Act passed in that year that repudiated the pope as head of the church, and established Henry's children by Anne Boleyn, for whom he had set aside his first wife, as successors. Persisting in his refusal, he was imprisoned, tried, and executed on 1536. This advocate of religious latitudinarianism in his *Utopia* of 1516 died a Catholic and a martyr.[13]

How does one understand the irreconcilable elements of More's outlook? How could he be both the inventor of Utopia and a witness to the death for his religious convictions? An examination of his works, filling fifteen volumes of a modern edition,[14] reveals his many dimensions of mind and spirit but does not solve the riddle. He wrote history and biography, theological polemics and devotional works, poems, prayers, and letters—including his heartrending last letters to his daughter Margaret from the Tower of London, the last on the day before his death.

Utopia is a work of his earlier years, written during the period of his closest association with Erasmus and, in the Erasmian mode, is humorous and satirical at the same time that it is idealistic and quite serious. The first book, as the work is often divided, presents a frame story, in which More and his associates discuss possible political forms with the fictional Raphael Hythloday, a man recently returned from his travels to remote places (this scene takes place not even a generation after Columbus opened up Atlantic navigation), who had spent five years in Utopia, to whose excellences he makes frequent reference. The others prevail on him to describe Utopia at length, which he agrees to do. That discussion is the substance of the second book.

Hythloday first describes the geographical position and topographical features of Utopia, and its republican system based on fifty-four largely autonomous cities. He then reports on Utopian economy and society—trades and occupations, social relationships, pattern of mobility, and the institutions of slavery and marriage—before turning to war and foreign policy, and, finally, religious belief and practice. The excerpts here are taken from four sections: on Utopian government; on trades and employments; on society; and on religion.

The government of Utopia, largely republican, is based on the unit of the city. Each of fifty-four cities has 200 groups of thirty households, and each of those groups of thirty elects a Wiseacre. The Wiseacres in turn are responsible to a senate of Timeservers, of whom there is one for every ten Wiseacres. The Timeservers elect a Prince from names proposed by the

---

13. Not quite 400 years later, he was canonized as a saint of the Catholic Church in 1935.

14. *The Complete Works of Thomas More*, 15 vols. (New Haven: Yale University Press, 1963–1986).

households of the four quarters of the city. The Wiseacres, in rotation, witness the deliberation of the Timeservers in the Senate. The Prince serves for life, if he makes no grab for sole power, and the Timeservers are generally reelected repeatedly. All other officials serve one-year terms.

Farming is the backbone of the Utopian economy. All the citizens are farmers, although most also learn a particular trade, generally from their fathers. Women as well as men are trained for fitting occupations, generally those requiring less muscular strength. Utopians perform their work diligently, but not to excess: their workday is limited to six hours per day, and can be shortened under certain circumstances.

Their work is sufficient, however, to supply Utopia with abundant foodstuffs and other commodities. These goods are stored in central storehouses located in each quarter of each city. From here, goods are requested for such purposes as feeding the sick in the hospitals, but then by the purveyors of the halls located at equal distances from each other in each of the 200 districts of the city, each serving thirty households. The citizens take their meals in these halls, being thus freed from the labor and anxiety of preparing food in their homes. They are seated at several large tables arrayed around a large open room, with a high table at one end where the Wiseacres and Priests (if there are any in the district) preside with their wives. Young children stay in the adjacent nurseries, with their nurses, who are generally their mothers. All other children stand, and are grateful for portions of food handed to them by those who are seated; the older children wait upon their parents.

Religious observance in Utopia is largely unregulated—unlike in Europe, as More knew all too well. Citizens are permitted to pursue any number of religious alternatives, so long as they do not become engaged in controversies. But there is a general consensus for the worship of one Supreme Being, and for the beliefs in the immortality of the soul and the direction of the cosmos by divine Providence.

Hythloday concludes his narrative by commending the Utopian form of government and society, which affords to all citizens the possibility of a life without fear of penury or unnecessary toil.

Thomas More, *Utopia* (1516)

ON GOVERNMENT

Each year, every thirty households elect a magistrate, who is called the Wiseacre in their ancient language, but has more recently been known as the Tribal Chief.[15] Over every ten Wiseacres, together with the households that

---

15. "Syphogrant" is a made-up name, with an unclear etymology, but it seems to have some component of the Greek word *sophos*, meaning "wise." I have chosen "Wiseacre" as closer to More's meaning than "Wise Man" or "Elder." There is also a provocative aural resemblance

elected them, are in turn grouped under the authority of a Timeserver, in the old language, now known as the Head Tribal Chief.[16] All the Wiseacres in each city, of whom there are 200,[17] having sworn to choose the best qualified person from the four names the people present to the Senate[18] (one from each quarter of the city), by secret ballot elect the Prince. The Prince holds his office for life, unless he is removed on suspicion of plotting to make himself a tyrant.[19] The Timeservers are elected each year, but are generally reelected. All other magistracies have a term of a single year.

The Timeservers meet in council with the Prince every third day, and more often if necessary. They discuss matters concerning the republic, and speedily dispose of disputes between private parties (if there are any, as these are very rare). Each day two Wiseacres are assigned in rotation to witness Senate deliberations, which must take place for at least three days before any matter of state business can be decided. On pain of capital punishment, it is forbidden to discuss state matters outside of the Senate or other public councils. All these guidelines were instituted to prevent a conspiracy of the Prince and the Timeservers to subject the people to a tyrant, and alter the constitution of the republic. For the same reason, any matter of great importance is first put before the council of Wiseacres, who having discussed it with their constituent households deliberate among themselves and submit their recommendation to the Senate. Sometimes a matter is sent to the council of the whole island. . . . [20]

ON TRADES AND EMPLOYMENTS

Agricultural work is common to all, men and women equally, and in it no one is more expert than another. All learn how to do this work from childhood, partly in school where its principles are explained, and partly in fields

---

to "sycophant," another genuine word of Greek derivation. *Phylarch*, unlike *syphogrant*, is a genuine word used in ancient Greece to designate the head of a tribe. Why More introduces two terms for the same office, with these puzzling relations, cannot be known for sure. I follow Paul Turner, translator of the Penguin Classics edition of *Utopia* (1965), in devising modern equivalents for More's fictional offices.

16. Similarly, "tranibor" here is a made-up word, with a component that suggests "devouring." I have used the translation "Timeserver" as a plausible descriptor of a public official. But *protophylarchus*, for an official superior to the phylarch, is unambiguous.

17. The government system More is describing here is based on the unit of the city, each of which contains 6000 households electing 200 Wiseacres under 20 Timeservers.

18. The assembly of Timeservers.

19. The risk of a legitimate ruler making himself a tyrant is a major theme of Greek political history, to which More here alludes.

20. That is, to the general council of Utopia—which apparently does not have an executive or other magistracies or councils, the work of government being accomplished mainly at the local level.

near the city to which they are taken as though for sports, where they do not merely observe, but using the opportunity of exercising their bodies, engage in labor themselves.

Beyond farming (which is, as was said, the common task of all), everyone also learns a particular craft of his own, such as wool- or linen-manufacture, masonry, metal-work or carpentry. No other craft is practiced by any number of them worth noting, since clothing is made at home: for there is only one kind of garment worn throughout the whole island, pleasing in design, accommodated to all physical activity, equally suited for hot and cold weather, the same for all ages of life, and varying only to distinguish male from female, and married and unmarried.

But of those other trades already mentioned, everyone learns one, women as well as men. But women being weaker engage in the less strenuous tasks of making wool or linen. To men are consigned the other, more laborious trades. For the most part, the child is trained to his father's trade, to which they are most inclined by nature. But if someone aspires to another occupation, he is transferred, by adoption, to a household which practices that trade. Not only his own father, but also the magistrates take care that he is assigned to a responsible and honest householder. And if someone who has mastered one trade desires also to master another, in the same way, it is permitted in the same way. Having mastered both, he may pursue whichever trade he pleases, unless his city requires one more than the other.

The Wiseacre's principal and, really, responsibility is to supervise and ascertain that no one succumbs to laziness, but diligently performs his particular craft—not that he is required to wear himself out like a beast of burden with remorseless toil from sunrise to sunset. For just about everywhere else, such a toilsome life, worse than slavery, is the lot of every laborer—but not for Utopians. Of the twenty-four equal hours into which they divide day and night, they assign only six to work: three before noon, when they go to dinner, after which they enjoy a two-hour period for rest, followed by three more hours of labor until suppertime. . . . At eight they go to bed, and eight hours are given to sleep. Whatever time is left after the hours for working, sleeping, and eating, each person may use as he wishes. . . . For the most part, they devote these intervals to literary study. . . .

Some go to lectures in their free time, and others return to their trade. There is plenty of time left over for recreation, too, as Utopian houses—not ostentatious and always kept in good repair—do not require renovations, and Utopian clothing, as has been seen, makes few demands on the fabricators.

Accordingly, since there is available a great abundance of everything, with everyone working at useful trades which require no great toll of labor, from time to time a great number of workers are summoned to repair the public roads (if there are any in disrepair). But when there is no need for this kind of work, a public announcement is made shortening the workday. For the magistrates do not compel the citizens to perform unnecessary labor, since the constitution of this republic obeys this preeminent principle: that for all citizens, to the extent that common utility permits, as much time as possible should be spared from the service of the body and devoted to the freedom and cultivation of the soul. For in such pursuits, they believe, human happiness lies.

ON SOCIETY

Now we shall consider what kinds of social relations exist among the citizens, and how they manage the distribution of goods.

The city, then, is made up of households, and the households of many persons related by blood. On reaching maturity, the women relocate to the households of their husbands. Male children and grandsons, however, remain in their household of birth, and are obedient to the eldest male, unless because of his great age he is no longer mentally competent; then the next elder becomes householder.[21]

Since each city is made up of 6000 households (not counting those of the outlying villages), to make sure that the city neither diminishes nor increases too much in population, no family is permitted to have fewer than ten or greater than sixteen adults; for no limit can be placed on the number of children. The limitation of household size is easily managed by transferring those who have been reared in larger households to those with fewer members. . . .[22]

If nonetheless a city grows too large, a contingent of citizens is sent abroad to form a Utopian colony, integrating the native population into their transplanted social system. If on the other hand, as happens very rarely, the cities become too small, citizens can be brought back from the colonies.

But to return to the social arrangements of the Utopian citizens. The eldest male, as was said, is the head of the household. Wives are subordinate to their husbands, children to their parents, and the younger children to the elder. Every city is divided in four equal quarters, in the middle of each of which is a general marketplace. The goods produced by each family are brought here and stored in storehouses, each different commodity in its own separate

---

21. Notably, More does not here describe the essentially conjugal family system that prevailed in western Europe and especially in England, but an extended household system (including multiple generations, as well as adult siblings and marital kin) more characteristic of other cultures.

22. More does not admit the possibility of birth control for the limitation of household size, but is untroubled by compelled transfer of members between households, regardless of blood ties.

area. From these same storehouses each householder asks for whatever goods he requires for himself or family members, and without payment of money or any kind of pledge of recompense, whatever he asks for is provided. Why should his request be refused? Since there is both an abundant sufficiency for all, and no fear that anyone will demand more than he requires? For why would it be supposed that anyone would demand a superfluity of goods, when he knows for certain that he will never suffer a lack of them in the future? Certainly the fear of future deprivation makes every living creature covetous and rapacious; and in man, additionally, ambition for glory drives him to outshine others by superfluous and ostentatious consumption. But this kind of vice has no place in Utopia. . . .

> *The narrator Hythloday describes the food markets, which operate on the same principle. Notably, Utopian citizens do not slaughter animals for food, which would offend their sense of compassion. That deed is performed by slaves outside the city precincts. Now Hythloday will describe the common dining experience in Utopia.*

Each district of the city has, in addition, its own large halls, equally distant from each other, each known by its own name. . . . To each of these halls thirty families are assigned to take their meals, fifteen from each half of the district.[23] The purveyors for each hall gather in the marketplace at a pre-scribed hour, and request the foodstuffs needed for the number of persons for whom they are responsible.

> *Before foodstuffs are distributed to the purveyors of each neighborhood hall, all the hospitals are supplied; and after the halls have received their allot-ment, individuals may take food to eat in their own homes—but few do.*

Although no one is prohibited from requesting food from the marketplace to take home, once the halls have been given theirs, yet hardly anyone does so: for even if it is not forbidden to eat at home, yet no one considers it proper, and it would be foolish as well to take on the labor of preparing a lesser meal at home when a splendid and sumptuous one is readily available in the hall nearby.

In the hall, the dirty and laborious chores are assigned to slaves. The other tasks of planning the meals and preparing and cooking the food are assigned to the women alone, those of each family doing so in rotation. The diners sit at three or more tables, depending on their numbers.[24] Men sit along the wall, women on the outside of each table, so that if they are suddenly taken ill,

---

23. These thirty families are here described as a unit of social interaction and food-sharing. They are also a political unit, electing the Wiseacres, the first level of public officials.

24. More envisions long tables placed parallel to the walls of the dining hall.

which occasionally happens to the pregnant women, they may rise and seek the assistance of the nurses without disturbing the dinner.

The nurses, together with their charges, the nursing infants, take their dinner in a separate room equipped with a warm fire, clean water, and cradles where they can lay the babies down near the fire and, when they wish, free them from their swaddling clothes for playtime.[25] Each woman nurses her own child unless death or sickness prevents her. . . .[26]

All children up until the age of five stay in the nursery. The other minors, in which group are included all those of either sex not yet of marriageable age, either wait at table, or if they are not yet old enough, stand nearby without saying a word. Both sets of children are fed what the adults at the table offer them, nor is any other time for dining set for them.[27]

In the place of honor at the middle of the high table—the one placed on a raised platform at one end of the hall at right angles to the others, so that everyone in the assembly can view it—sits the Wiseacre with his wife.[28] Two of the eldest householders and their wives sit next to them, for seating is always in groups of four. But if there is a church in that district, then the priest and his wife sit with the Wiseacre, so that they may preside together. To the left and right of them sit younger people, and then their elders once again, and so on in this way throughout the hall, alternating groups of young and old, so that peers may sit together and yet be intermixed with those of diverse ages. This custom was instituted, they say, so that the dignity and authority of the old—since nothing could be said or done at table that would escape their view, since they were present everywhere—would deter the younger folk from improper speech or unsuitable gestures. . . .

Food is passed to the elder participants first, then shared to the others. Meals are accompanied by reading on a serious topic, by music, and by the pleasant aromas of incense and sweet-smelling herbs.

---

25. Infants were normally swaddled in traditional society. In a warm and safe setting, the nurses may release them from the swaddling bonds so the babies can crawl about and play.

26. The humanists, and most other men of learning, were determined advocates of maternal nursing, although many women especially of the elites were instead relieved of this task by wet nurses. In Utopia, the nurses who care for infants, then, are the babies' own mothers.

27. Odd as this sounds to moderns, for whom even a separate children's table is a dim memory, it was common in traditional society for children to wait on adults and accept, having no plate or utensils of their own, pieces of food from their elders' meal.

28. The Wiseacre is the public official representing the thirty families, by whom he is elected, assigned to a particular hall. The hierarchical seating plan that More describes, sorted by rank and age, is typical for this period, and still exists in certain traditional institutions, such as the older English universities.

ON RELIGIONS

Religions vary not only across the island of Utopia, but even within the cities. Some people worship the sun as divine, others the moon, others one or another of the planets. Others consider some man who excelled long ago for his virtue or his valor to be not only a god, but the supreme god.[29] But by far the greatest number, and clearly the most sensible, have no faith in these gods but recognize a spirit, whom they call Father: unknowable, eternal, immense, inexplicable, beyond the comprehension of the human mind, a force, not a substance, diffused throughout the universe. To him alone they attribute the origin and increase of things, all natural processes, changes, and outcomes; only this one spirit do they consider divine. . . .

> *Thus, although there is no religious conformity, a general belief in a Supreme Being prevails in Utopia. European visitors brought Christianity to the island, which interested the citizens greatly, but did not supplant native religious beliefs.*

Even before his takeover of Utopia, its founder Utopus had heard that the inhabitants quarreled constantly among themselves about religion, and saw that their dissent caused disunity, with different sects each fighting separately for the homeland, making it easier for him to conquer them all. Once victory was won, he ordained immediately that everyone was free to follow whatever religion he preferred, and even convert others to his beliefs so long as he did so by peacefully and modestly presenting reasons—not by attacking other religions if persuasion doesn't work, nor by descending to violence and insult. Anyone persisting in religious conflict would be punished with exile or slavery.

Utopus established these rules not only to keep the peace, which he knew to be undermined by ceaseless conflict and relentless hatred, but because he believed they actually served the interest of religion—the precepts of which he was unwilling to define, since he was uncertain whether God himself didn't inspire his followers to a variety of multiple forms of worship. . . . And so the whole issue of religion was left open for discussion, and each person was permitted freely to decide what he wanted to believe in; except that it was solemnly and strictly prohibited that anyone so betray the dignity of human nature as to believe that the soul dies with the body, or that the world is ruled not by providence, but blind force. . . .

---

29. This statement, in More's day, could be read as a description of Jesus Christ: a historical figure now worshipped as the supreme God. More's description of a supreme being in the next sentences is closer to the Christian, or any monotheistic, understanding of God.

The narrator Hythloday reviews various religious practices of the Utopians, and describes the functions of their priests—quite unlike those familiar to Europeans.

CONCLUSION

I have described to you as faithfully as I can the nature of that republic which I am convinced is not only the best but indeed the only one to which the term "republic" can rightly be applied. Elsewhere, those invoking the public good nonetheless pursue their own private interests; but here, where there is nothing private, the pursuit of the public good is genuine. Both are right to do what they do. For everywhere else, everyone knows that unless he looks out for himself, however much the republic may flourish, he may still die of hunger—which fear urges him to provide for himself, and not for other people, that is to say, the public. But here, where all things belong to everyone, all know that so long as the public storehouses are full, no individual will ever lack a sufficiency. For the distribution of goods is fair, there is no poverty, there are no beggars, and though no one possesses anything, yet all are wealthy.

For who could be wealthier than the person who, relieved of all disquietude, lives with a joyous and tranquil heart? Not concerned about his next meal, untroubled by a nagging wife, not fearing that his son will live in poverty, not anxious about a dowry for his daughter, but secure in the knowledge that all of his family—wife, sons, grandsons, great-grandsons, great-great-grandsons, as long a series of descendants as elsewhere only the privileged assume will succeed them—will have the means of subsistence and of happiness?

Hythloday concludes by comparing Utopian society with European—to the latter's disadvantage.

Chapter 6: Humanism and the Arts

Introduction

For the many travelers who know the Renaissance primarily through visual experience, art is fundamental to the Renaissance phenomenon, whose literature, politics, and culture more generally seems to emanate from the explosion in the visual arts. Given this primacy of the arts in the perception of the Renaissance era, it is important to establish the connections between art and humanism. For these are the two principal currents of the cultural explosion of the Renaissance, and they are closely related.

The legacy of antiquity fueled the Renaissance both of the arts and of humanism, but artists and humanists utilized that legacy in different ways. Humanists, as has been seen in Chapter 1, recovered the written legacy of antiquity, by reading ancient works in a historically informed and newly critical framework, by editing Latin texts and translating Greek ones, and by incorporating into the Western literary tradition texts that had been lost, mangled, or neglected. Artists recovered the visual legacy of antiquity by examining and replicating material objects—some that had always been accessible but were now viewed with a critical eye, some that were literally unearthed, buried remains of the classical past. Both engaged in an orgy of imitation: for through the imitation of classical texts, humanists developed new standards of prose and poetic diction; and through the imitation of ancient forms, artists acquired a new mastery of the human form and its situation in space, along with a new vocabulary of figures, motifs, and decorative elements that could be incorporated in their works of art.

By these parallel routes, artists and humanists plumbed the resources provided by the ancient legacy that, in Italy, was all around them. They also collaborated. Humanists could supply to the artists narratives of the myths—the same myths that Boccaccio had so usefully collected and catalogued in his *Genealogy of the Pagan Gods* (see Chapter 1)—that explained the play of human figures in ancient reliefs and sculptures. Equally, they provided historical accounts that made sense of the events depicted on ancient monuments. Patrons like Isabella d'Este engaged humanists to create scripts, drawing on ancient mythology and history, for the visual sequences with which they decorated their *studioli* (private places of retreat), courtyards, and great halls. And at the level of theory, humanist scholars who had familiarized themselves with ancient mathematical and scientific works, generally from the Greek tradition, could explain to artists, as Leon Battista Alberti did, how such knowledge could assist the representation of space on two-dimensional surfaces, the mastery of which characterizes Renaissance artistic style.

As the Renaissance era opens, artists were enmeshed in the workshop system managed by guilds, in which the young were trained by apprenticeship to an older master who employed several such assistants in producing a commissioned work. Thus they possessed artisan status, in contrast to the humanists, who were generally of middling or elevated social origin—for only those of a certain rank had access to the advanced education essential for a humanist career. Through their interaction with elites, however—both the humanists who advised them and the patrons who employed them—artists began to rise in social status over the two or three centuries of the era. They weaned themselves from the workshop system, and as independent actors increasingly insisted on authority over the matter and style of their work.

These interactions of artists and humanists within the context of Renaissance society are illustrated in the four texts presented in this chapter, written between 1435 and 1566. The first is by Leon Battista Alberti (1404–1472), a figure who bridges the two cultural currents of art and humanism, as well as the social categories of elite and non-elite. The illegitimate son of a patrician Florentine family, he was both an architect of note, who conspicuously incorporated classical form and sensibility into the buildings he designed, and a noted humanist who wrote literary works and two treatises on the family as well as works of art theory, including *On Painting* (1435), of which excerpts follow. In this work, Alberti instructs artisan-rank painters in geometry, optics, and physics, so that they might understand how forms in two dimensions are received by the eye. This knowledge is the essential underpinning to the technique of perspective, which allows representation of three-dimensional space, the hallmark, together with classicizing imagery and ornament, of Renaissance style.

The second group of excerpts are taken from letters exchanged between the aristocrat Isabella d'Este (1474–1539) and her agent in procuring art objects, Lorenzo da Pavia (d. 1517). The daughter of the ruler of Ferrara and wife of the ruler of Mantua, the marchesa Isabella was a woman of the highest rank in Italian Renaissance society and one of the leading patrons of the age, highly educated in the classical tradition that was represented in the fine works that she collected. Yet she was dependent on artists, and on the agents who recruited them, to collect and produce the splendid objects with which she filled her two *camerini*, or "little rooms," within the larger complex of her husband's palace. Here she is seen obtaining necessary materials for one artist, Andrea Mantegna, at work on her premises, and prodding another, Giovanni Bellini, at work in his own remote studio, to complete a commissioned painting. The two figures are among the foremost painters of the northern Italian school at the height of the Renaissance.

The third group of texts is also drawn from an epistolary exchange, in this case between the young and already successful German artist Albrecht Dürer (1471–1528), then resident in Venice, and his friend and patron Willibald Pirckheimer, scion of the most important patrician family in Dürer's native city of Nuremberg. In his two extended visits to Italy—this set of letters illuminates the second—Dürer masters the elements of Italian Renaissance style, which he then transfers to the north. Little of significance about that transmission of cultural style is seen in the letters, however, which are remarkably vernacular in language, in feeling, and in content. Their value lies, rather, in the portrait that the artist creates of himself in his words, and the depiction of relations between patron and client that are on the one hand genuinely amicable, and on the other, inevitably marked by huge differences in wealth and status.

The fourth text is an excerpt from the most important autobiography produced during the Renaissance, written by the Florentine artist, among his other occupations, Benvenuto Cellini (1500–1571). Possessing also, like Dürer's letter, a vernacular quality, the autobiography records the author's vaunting ambitions and fierce self-confidence, as well as the shocking but entertaining incidents of his disorderly personal life. The excerpts here show Cellini in his workshop, engaged in massive efforts to wield wood, fire, and metal to produce a statue characterized by grace and refinement, a masterpiece of Renaissance sculpture, that is at the same time a visual justification of the autocratic rule of the prince, his patron.

All the authors represented in this section write in Italian, not Latin, although Alberti would later translate his own work into Latin for circulation among a scholarly audience. Yet all are written in genres of humanism, and are informed by the literary culture that humanism has created. Uniting the four authors, as well, is their insistence on quality, their immersion in material reality, and an optimism that recalls the humanistic vision of the dignity of man.

Leon Battista Alberti

Leon Battista Alberti (1404–1472) is one of the most astonishing figures of the Italian Renaissance, as appears from his memorable profile by Jacob Burckhardt, author of the classic *Civilization of the Renaissance in Italy* (1860). He was a "many-sided" man who "tower[ed] above the rest": a gymnast who could jump over a man's head, and a skilled rider who could tame the wildest horses; a self-taught musician and composer who won prizes; a painter and an architect who wrote theoretical works on art; an author of prose works and poetry, in Latin and in the vernacular. But most notable of all, for Burckhardt, was "the sympathetic intensity with which he entered into the whole life around him."[1] It is precisely Alberti's versatility, his many-sidedness, that comes to the fore in his 1435 treatise *On Painting*, one of the key literary works associated with Renaissance artistic style.

An illegitimate son of a member of the prominent Florentine Alberti family, who acknowledged and supported him though he was, necessarily, barred from an inheritance, Alberti demonstrated the independence and determination of a man who must define himself in a society that demanded excellence. As a humanist, he was famed especially for his satirical dialogue *Momus* and two important treatises on the family. As an architect, he designed churches and palaces in Florence, Mantua, and Rimini, among others, that are hall-marks of classicizing Renaissance style. As a commentator on the arts, he wrote on sculpture (*On the Statue*), architecture (*On Architecture*), and paint-ing (*On Painting*), the last two of which circulated in Europe into the eigh-teenth century. The latter work, of which excerpts are given here, famously introduced the science of perspective, which enabled Renaissance artists to create realistic representations of human figures in space.

Alberti's *On Painting* is many-sided, like its author. It mediates between the world of humanism and the world of art, which is to say, between classi-cally trained elites and artisans who used their hands. The Renaissance was the period in which the social status of the artist rose, so that he joined the circles of the literati and their aristocratic patrons. But that transformation, while it had begun in Alberti's day, had not yet been realized. So Alberti, who in his own person straddled both worlds, assigned to himself the task of instructing the artisan in the skills and insights proper to an intellectual familiar with mathematics, geometry, and optics. For without these skills, he maintained, however talented he might be, the artist could not attain great-ness.

Written in the vernacular most likely for its wider diffusion, as Rocco Sinisgalli has recently argued,[2] and subsequently translated by the author into Latin for a learned audience, *On Painting* consists of three books. The first introduces the geometrical and optical rudiments that allow the artist to compose his paintings. The second speaks of drawing, composition, and light, or color, the essentials for an artist constructing a painting. The third speaks of the world of learning that furnishes subjects for the painter, and offers useful pointers for inventing *istoria*—the narrative that connects the

---

1. Jacob Burckhardt, *The Civilization of the Renaissance in Italy,* trans. S. G. C. Middlemore, ed. Benjamin Nelson and Charles Trinkaus, 2 vols. (New York: Harper and Row, 1958), 148–50.

2. In his 2011 translation and critical analysis of the *Della pittura* (Cambridge: Cambridge University Press), 3–14, challenging the previous consensus that the Latin preceded the Italian.

figures and objects in the painting—for those who are not able to access that recondite world.

The sections of the first book of *On Painting* given here show Alberti defining for the artisan-artist the geometrical essentials of point, line, and plane, and explaining how, according to the science of the day, the eye perceived the plane in all of its transformations. These were the rudiments of composition, by which the artist arranged objects on a surface to produce a finished painting.

First, Alberti defines point, line, and plane. A sequence of points, without breadth or depth, will form a line, which has length but not breadth, and can be straight or curved. Many lines woven together like threads in woven cloth—we are reminded by Alberti's image that Italy was a world center of textile production—will form a plane. The outer edge of the plane, its contour, can consist of a single curved line or three or more straight ones, joined at angles to form a triangle or some larger polygon.

After describing other features of the plane, Alberti then turns to the matter of perception: by what human mechanism is the plane and its effects perceived? Here he introduces the visual triangle and, more complex, the visual pyramid. Both are created by rays that issue from a single point within the eye and radiate to the contour, the surface, and the central point of the plane: rays denoted as, respectively, the extrinsic, median, and centric. A visual triangle is created by the extrinsic rays extended to two different points on the contour of the plane, between which is a line forming the base, which can be measured by the eye, which forms the apex of the triangle. A visual pyramid consists of all the rays extending from the eye to the plane, which supply to the eye information about all the quantities and qualities of the plane—its dimensions, its colors, and the variable effects of light.

All of this information is vital for the artist. He must understand that his role is to depict on a flat surface a composition of objects made up of points, lines, and planes, which are qualified by size, position, color, and light, and these in sum will produce the painting that his audience will perceive. At the end of the first book, Alberti emphasizes the importance of the difficult material he has explicated: for "only he will become a great artist who has learned the contours of the plane and all its qualities. On the contrary: he will never become a good artist who is not diligent in learning all that has been said here. For these are necessary things, these intersections and planes." He has made an heroic attempt, as he sees it, to present in plain language the rudiments of geometry, mathematics, and optics, to instill comprehension in a group of readers who possess talent but require theory.

Leon Battista Alberti, *On Painting* (1435)

As I write these brief notes on painting, so that what I say is thoroughly clear, I shall take from the mathematicians those concepts which most relate to our subject. When this much is understood, I shall to the best of my ability explain the art of painting from its first principles, which are rooted in nature.

But throughout this conversation, I beg you above all to think of me, as I write of these things, not as a mathematician but as a painter. Using the mind alone, apart from the material world, mathematicians measure the forms of things. But painters want to apprehend things that can be seen, for which approach I shall use the phrase *più grassa Minerva*[3]—that is to say, a "fat wisdom," a knowledge that is not purely theoretical, but grounded in matter. And I shall be very grateful if, to some extent, those who read this admittedly difficult explanation, never before undertaken so far as I know, will understand it. Accordingly, I beg that what is said here be interpreted as the words merely of a painter.

To begin, it is necessary to know that a point is a mark representing something that cannot be divided into parts. I call a mark here anything that rests on a surface in such a way that the eye can see it. As for the things that we cannot see, no one will deny that these have nothing whatever to do with the painter. The painter only examines what he sees with his eyes, and then portrays it.

Now points, if they are joined to each other in succession one after the other, will form a line; and for our purpose, a line can be defined as a mark whose length can be divided, but whose width is so fine that it cannot.

Some lines are straight, and others curved. A straight line is formed when a long mark is made directly from one point to another. A curved line is formed when a mark is made from one point to another which is not straight but bent like a drawn bow. Many lines, when they are arranged alongside each other like threads in woven cloth, make a plane; and a plane is that extreme edge of any body which has no depth at all, but possesses only length and width, in addition to some other qualities. Those qualities are of two sorts: some are inherent in the plane, or permanent, which cannot be removed from the plane without causing its alteration; others lie atop the plane in such a way that, while the plane itself is unaltered, it seems to the onlooker to have been changed.

There are two kinds of permanent qualities. One of these is defined by the outermost edge of the plane—an edge which can be closed by one curved or by several straight lines, which constitute its contour. The curved line will enclose a circle. A plane is circular when a single line winds around, like a wreath, such that if a point is imagined in the middle, any straight line from

---

3. A term used by Cicero to mean a popularized knowledge, but which Alberti adapts here to mean a kind of knowledge that is grounded in matter; see Spencer's introduction to *On Painting* (ed. and trans. John R. Spencer; New Haven: Yale University Press, 1966), 18–19. My translation expands a bit on the text here to clarify the meaning of the term, which might otherwise be quite distracting.

that point to a point on the wreath will be equal to any other; and that point in the middle is called the center. Any straight line which crosses through the central point and intersects the circle at two points the mathematicians call a diameter. I prefer to call it a centric line. . . .

Now let us turn to the plane. Here we see that if the direction of the contour changes, the plane changes both in appearance and name, so that this one is called a triangle, and that one a quadrangle, and so on depending on the number of sides. The contour changes as the lines become longer or shorter, or the angles more acute or obtuse—terms which prompt us now to speak about angles.

An angle is one of the extremities of a plane formed by two lines which intersect each other. There are three kinds of angles: right, obtuse, and acute. A right angle will be one of four made by two straight lines, which intersect each other in such a way that each one of the angles formed is equal to the others. As a result, all right angles are equal. An obtuse angle is one that is greater than a right angle, and an acute angle one that is lesser.

Let us return once again to the plane. Be assured of this: so long as the lines and angles of the contour do not change, the same plane is always before us. Here is illustrated a quality that is permanent, for it never departs from the plane. But now we must speak of the other sort of quality, which is like a skin stretched over the whole expanse of the plane. There are three resulting forms: first, a completely level plane; second, one that is hollowed out, or concave; third, one that is spherical, and swells outward. To these, a fourth may be added, which is a composite of two of the others.

A flat plane is one such that a rigid ruler placed on it will touch it at every point; it is very similar to the surface of still water. A spherical plane is really part of the surface of a sphere—a sphere being defined as a round body, whose surface is nowhere level, from whose center every point on the surface of the body is equidistant. The hollowed plane can be thought of as the inner surface of a spherical plane, like the inside of an eggshell. A composite plane will be one that is flat in one section but hollowed or spherical in another, such as the surfaces found on the interiors of cannons or the exteriors of columns.

To sum up, the nature of the contour (circular or linear) and the surface (flat, concave, or spherical) distinguish the different kinds of planes. But there are two qualities by which the plane can seem to be altered, even though it has not changed at all, which are the effects of changes of position and light.

Let us speak first of change of position, and then of change of light, and so inquire in what way, through these changes, the qualities of the plane appear to be altered. This alteration has to do with the operation of sight, since as the observer shifts position, things appear to be larger in size, or different in shape or color, all of which appearances are registered by our sight. We shall explain why this happens, beginning with the view of the philosophers, who posit that planes are perceived by certain rays, which act as agents of vision, and are called on that account visual rays, which carry the form of things seen to the sense of sight. We can imagine these rays, as thin as the finest hairs growing from a head, to be tied in a dense knot inside the eye, the seat of the visual sense. From this node, like branches from a tree trunk, very straight and fine tendrils shoot forth to the opposite plane.

Now among these rays there are differences in nature and function that must be understood. Some of the rays, upon reaching the contour of the plane, measure its dimensions. Because they make contact with the extreme outer contour of the plane, they are called "extreme" or, if you prefer, "extrinsic." Other rays reach the eye from every point on the surface of the plane, and so are called "median" rays. These have the function of filling the interior of the visual pyramid, of which more is said below, with all the shades of color and light that shine forth from the plane. And there is one other kind of visual ray, called "centric," similar to the centric line discussed earlier. When it touches the plane, the centric ray creates around itself an infinity of equal right angles. And so we have introduced the three different kinds of rays: extreme, median, and centric.

Now we shall explore how each ray serves the visual sense, beginning with the extreme rays, then the median, and finally the centric.

The extreme rays measure quantity. "Quantity" denotes every space on the plane from any one point on the contour to another. The eye measures these quantities with the visual rays as we would with a pair of compasses. On every plane, there are as many quantities as there are spaces between two points: among which are height, from the lowest to the highest; and width, from the right hand to the left; and depth, from near to far; and any other dimension or measurement performed by these extreme visual rays. Thus it may be said that the act of seeing forms a triangle, the base of which is the quantity perceived, while the sides are the visual rays which extend to the eye at the apex from the two points determining the quantity. Without this visual triangle, evidently, it is impossible for any quantity to be seen. Two of the angles of this visual triangle are formed at the two points defining the quantity; the third, opposite the base, is within the eye. . . .

Alberti explains that where more rays are used in seeing, the object appears larger, and conversely, when there are fewer, it appears smaller.

So these extrinsic rays, circling the plane in such a way that each one touches another, enclose the whole plane like the reeds of a cage,[4] constructing what is called the "visual pyramid." So now it is necessary to explain what the pyramid is, and how it is constructed by these visual rays. . . .

---

4. Alberti here is describing a basketlike cage, woven of reeds.

The pyramid is a solid form from whose base all lines drawn upwards culminate in a single point. The base of the visual pyramid will be the plane that is seen; the sides are the extrinsic rays; and the cusp, or apex, are inside the eye, identical to the apex of the visual triangle that measures the quantity of the plane at the pyramid's base.

Up to this point we have spoken of the extrinsic rays from which the pyramid is constructed, have shown how they distinguish the extent of the distance, some a little greater or smaller than others, between the eye and what it sees. Next we must speak of the multitude of median rays, which sit within the extrinsic rays which form the sides of the pyramid. These act, so to speak, like a chameleon, an animal which takes its color from whatever is closest to it: for from whatever point they touch the plane, these rays convey upward to the eye whatever color and brightness is found at that point on the plane, such that, wherever they are broken, you will find that they are distinctively colored and illuminated. And you will find, likewise, that as the distance from the plane increases, both coloration and illumination grow weaker, since, as I believe happens, the rays, laden with light and color, must pass through air that is thickened by humidity, and so become fatigued. Accordingly, we may deduce this rule: the further the plane is from the eye, the dimmer it will appear.

It remains to speak of the centric ray, a single ray which so intersects the surface of the plane that every angle created by that intersection—necessarily a right angle—is equal to every other. This one ray, more bold and vigorous than all the others, when it strikes any quantity, causes it to appear at its maximum size. Much more could be said about this ray but this one will suffice: packed tight among the other rays, it is the last to abandon the object that is perceived, and so merits its name, the "prince of rays."

I believe that I have sufficiently demonstrated that as soon as its distance from the eye is changed, and likewise the position of the centric ray, the plane appears altered. Therefore both distance and the position of the centric ray contribute powerfully to the certainty of perception. . . .

In the long discussion that continues from here to the closing paragraphs, given below, Alberti speaks of the effect of color and light on the appearance of the plane; the varieties of plane; and the proportionality between planes. Then applying all that he has presented to this point, he explains how a painting is composed. He then sums up his first book.

Up to this point I have explained things that are useful but brief and, in my judgment, not wholly obscure. While what I've said will win me no praise for my eloquence, I do consider that they will be readily understood on a first attempt—or else will not be understood even with a great expenditure of effort. For to those who have sharp minds and some talent for painting these things I have written will be easily understood and, however they have been stated, beautiful; while to those who are unskilled and unendowed by nature for this most noble art, what I have written, even if it had been most eloquently expressed, will be of no use. My friends, perhaps, since I have written without eloquence, will read this book with distaste. But I beg you to forgive me if, since I wanted above all to be understood, I have tried to be clear rather than elegant. What follows, I believe, will be less tedious to the reader. . . .

Let's agree on this: only he will become a great artist who has learned the contours of the plane and all its qualities. On the contrary: he will never become a good artist who is not diligent in learning all that has been said here. For these are necessary things, these intersections and planes. Next we will discuss how the painter can execute with his hand what his intellect has grasped.

Isabella d'Este

Just as Alberti, in his *On Painting*, spans the worlds of humanism and of art, so too does Isabella d'Este (1474–1539)—and joins to these worlds a third, that of the princely court. The daughter of the duke of Ferrara and wife of the marquis of Mantua, she inhabited two of the major courts of northern Italy, where the modern court system was invented. She was a learned woman, following in that role the pattern of her cultivated mother, Eleonora of Aragon. In her mother's palace, she received a humanist education from Battista Guarini, one of the leading pedagogues of northern Italy, a preparation that enabled her to supervise the education of her three sons, all destined for major careers. At a time when Italy was the European vortex of artistic production, she was a connoisseur of the arts who wielded both her knowledge and authority to commission artists, including such greats as Leonardo da Vinci, Raphael, and Michelangelo, and to collect art objects, including jewelry, musical instruments, clocks, and antiquities; these she displayed in her own reserved spaces—her two *camerini*, "little rooms," the *studiolo* and *grotto*—within a Renaissance palace complex. As surrogate ruler during her husband's long absences, and as regent for his successor, her son Federico, she showed herself to be a skilled and determined political actor. A figure of multiple dimensions, Isabella d'Este has long been considered the *prima donna* ("first lady") of the Renaissance, if not, as her kinsman extolled her, the *prima donna* of the world.[5] Until recent years,

---

5. Deanna Shemek, "In Continuous Expectations: Isabella d'Este's Epistolary Desire," in Dennis Looney and Deanna Shemek, eds., *Phaethon's Children: The Este Court and its Culture*

when feminist scholarship greatly expanded the roster of remarkable women contributors to Renaissance civilization, she was virtually the only woman recognized by scholars as a major player in the events of the age.

All of these activities she pursued through the medium of the letter. Letter-writing was a principal form of literary composition, ranging between the humanist creations of a Petrarch to the mundane communications in the vernacular by which merchants and statesmen carried on their business. It was also a genre favored by women, who were the principal writers of letters, in which they tracked family members, guided children, confessed their passions, and acquired the things they needed. D'Este stands out as a letter-writer, a craft she undertook as early as the age of nine and pursued throughout her life, leaving a legacy of about 12,000 letters to kings and popes, poor widows in need of assistance, artists and literati, and the many agents she employed to procure for her the luxurious and beautiful things she craved.[6]

Among those agents was Lorenzo da Pavia (d. 1517), a builder of fine musical instruments, who executed many commissions that she entrusted to him. Their relations are documented by 182 letters exchanged between them during the period 1496 to 1515, recording Isabella's efforts to acquire for her rooms at Mantua not only fine works of art, but also harpsichords, porcelains, and exotic civet cats (whose glandular secretions were used as a perfume fixative). From this correspondence are taken the letters excerpted here, which concern her relations with two important artists and illumine the dealings behind the scenes of the production of great Renaissance art.

The two artists are Andrea Mantegna and Giovanni Bellini, two of the leading masters of northern Italy,[7] whom Isabella recruited to assist with the adornment of her *studiolo*, or private study, in Mantua. Between 1497 and 1505, Mantegna painted a sequence of works for the *studiolo*. In 1502, resisting Isabella's prescription of an allegorical program for his painting, Bellini agreed to a Nativity scene according to his own invention.[8]

In the four letters excerpted here regarding Mantegna, the first three, all written in June 1497, concern Mantegna's need for varnish to finish a painting, which request d'Este asks Lorenzo to fulfill, while the fourth reports Lorenzo's comments of 12 October 1506 on Mantegna's recent death. The six concerning Bellini, which extend from April to July 1504, reflect the struggle of wills between d'Este as patron and her servitor, as she would expect, the Venetian painter—who does not, however, bend to her will. In

---

in *Early Modern Ferrara* (Tempe, AZ: Arizona Center for Medieval and Renaissance Studies, 2005), 269–300, at 275.

6. In addition to these 12,000 that she wrote, there exist some 28,000 written to her; Shemek, "In Continuous Expectations," 277.

7. The two were brothers-in-law, Mantegna having married the daughter of Giovanni's father Jacopo, also a major artist.

8. Julia Cartwright Ady narrates the long story of the negotiations between Isabella and Bellini in *Isabella d'Este, Marchioness of Mantua, 1474–1539: A Study of the Renaissance*, 2 vols. (London: E. P. Dutton, 1903), 1:343–53.

an earlier encounter, he had resisted her dictation of a painting's composition. Here, we see a case of procrastination, in which Lorenzo repeatedly intervenes to spur the artist to complete his commission. He is successful in the end, and dispatches the completed painting to his employer.

These exchanges between Isabella and Lorenzo are intense in their emotional expression. On the one hand, Lorenzo abases himself before the powerful patron, repeatedly professing his obedience to her, and swiftly and meticulously responding to her demands. On the other, the two are peers as connoisseurs, almost intimates: both value the fineness of a piece of glass, or the quality of a perfume. Lorenzo feels free to comment on Mantegna as artist—he is a master of composition without peer. So, too, on Bellini, who, Lorenzo is certain, will produce the painting, and genuinely wishes to do so, in Lorenzo's estimation; and when he has finished, Lorenzo comments that it "lacks nothing" and is "truly . . . a beautiful thing," although the figures could be larger, but the artist is certainly "an excellent master of color."

What is striking here is the sense of quality and urgency, shared equally by patron and agent, which so seems to erase, at least at moments, the social distance between them: his standards of taste are aligned with hers. In the quest for beauty that drove the patronage system of the Italian Renaissance, there are engaged discerning minds and passionate commitments.

Isabella d'Este, *Letters on Painters and Painting* (1497–1506)

ON ANDREA MANTEGNA

In June 1497, Isabella d'Este wrote three letters to her procuring agent Lorenzo da Pavia mentioning the artist Andrea Mantegna, who is in need of varnish to finish the work that he is doing for her. Passages from two follow.

Isabella d'Este to Lorenzo da Pavia, 6 June 1497

. . . I have received together with your letter the bone handle that you sent, which is most pleasing to me . . . I remind you to send me some varnish to varnish the painting by *messer* Andrea Mantegna, as you promised to him and to me you would do,[9] using diligence to assure that it is of good quality and let me know the cost so that I can reimburse you. For all that you have written in your letter, I thank you kindly.

---

9. He did so when he met with Mantegna in December 1496: Brown, *Isabella d'Este*, 149.

Isabella d'Este to Lorenzo da Pavia, 14 June 1497

Master Lorenzo, *messer* Andrea Mantegna received the varnish that you sent him, which pleases him greatly except that it is not sufficient, so please send two times as much as that and the faster the better, because he has already begun to varnish the painting.

Five years later, Mantegna is once again in need of varnish, and Isabella d'Este writes Lorenzo da Pavia to obtain it.

Isabella d'Este to Lorenzo da Pavia, 13 June 1502

Lorenzo, send me enough varnish to varnish Mantegna's painting, as much as the other you sent for the other painting, and let it be of as good quality as the other.

In 1506, Lorenzo da Pavia writes Isabella d'Este about several fine objects that he has sent or is procuring for her, then grieves the recent death of Andrea Mantegna.

Lorenzo da Pavia to Isabella d'Este, 12 October 1506

Illustrious Lady, I have seen how pleased Your Ladyship was by the crystal mirror, which delighted me greatly: although I knew it could not be otherwise because Your Ladyship is a good and perfect judge. . . . I have never seen finer crystal. . . . Concerning the payment, God does not wish that I should request anything from you beyond that which I have already done, which pleases him, and to make it my gift to you, but since I must earn my bread, I am forced to be a lout . . . I was very saddened by the death of our *messer* Andrea Mantegna, in whom truly was lost a most excellent man and another Apelles;[10] I believe the Lord God will use him to make some other wondrous work. For my part, I do not hope ever again to see a better designer and inventor. . . .

ON GIOVANNI BELLINI

Between 10 April and 16 July 1504, Isabella d'Este and Lorenzo da Pavia were in frequent communication about the failure of Venetian painter Giovanni Bellini, who had been paid in part, to finish a painting of the Nativity that she had commissioned from him, after he had refused to execute one based on an allegorical program she suggested. After much persuasion, and with much patience, Lorenzo at last is able to report that the job is done.

---

10. A legendary artist of ancient Greece.

Isabella d'Este to Lorenzo da Pavia, 10 April 1504

Lorenzo, since I can bear no longer the great discourtesy that Giovanni Bellini has shown me concerning the painting or panel of the Nativity that he has not completed, I have decided to ask to have my money back from him until the work is completed, which I don't believe will happen. On this account, I have written to his Magnificence Alvise Marcello, my kinsman, to ask for the money, and if he does not willingly restore it, to take the matter to the authority and decision of his Serenity the Doge of Venice. Meanwhile, you must go to his Magnificence and press him to perform this office so that we may escape from the hands of this most ungrateful man. . . .

Lorenzo da Pavia to Isabella d'Este, 21 April 1504

Most illustrious and excellent Lady, I received your letter and on that account saw what needed to be done concerning the painting of Giovanni Bellini. And your letter is right: God knows how many times I asked him, not asked really but importuned, and always he responded with "it will be done," which he delivered in a torrent of words. Finally he told me that it was nearly done. I shall diligently seek the return of the money, together with his Magnificence Alvise Marcello, whom I shall press to perform the responsibility you assign him. So it will be done. For my part, I commend myself to you as your faithful servant. In these recent days I have been very ill with a terrible fever such that I thought I would die, which brought me all the more anguish to think that I would be deprived of Your Excellency's presence, which saddened me extremely. Now by the grace of God I am well enough. . . .

Lorenzo da Pavia to Isabella d'Este, 4 May 1504

Illustrious Lady, I have met with Giovanni Bellini and conveyed to him how often your Ladyship writes me about his commission, and with many other words impressed upon him how great has been his incivility. . . . He offered in response a string of excuses about the many important projects that he has on his hands, and especially those that he must do for the Doge. I explained to him that your Ladyship wants him to return the 25 ducats, which he didn't want to do, but prays your Ladyship to wait another month, by which time he will certainly have finished the painting, since in fact he has already completed, of the four parts, a little more than three. And I am quite certain that he will finish it, because he was greatly saddened by the request for the money because of his great poverty. Concerning his Magnificence Alvise Marcello, he has not yet recovered, but concerning the Doge, he will not be able to do anything, as I have learned from a good source. The error was made when the money was paid to Bellini, and according to Venetian law, when the set time of completion was reached, it was necessary to report it, at which point the office would give him one or two months as it saw fit, and if in that period of time he had not completed the painting, then he would be obliged to return the deposit. None of this was done, and all the time that has passed since the deadline doesn't count. As it is, we cannot extract the money from his hands; we should have had the officials give him notice of a deadline, and then if he had not finished by that date, then he would be obliged to give me the money. I have received a complete explanation of this, although it seems to me to be an abominable law; but I am certain that he will finish the painting, and soon, and he says that he wants to produce a very fine piece: and may God cause this to happen. But I have not seen a painter who could claim with such sincerity that he was ready and eager to do what would please my dear Illustrious Lady, to whom I now commend myself. . . .

Lorenzo da Pavia to Isabella d'Este, 6 July 1504

Illustrious and Excellent Lady, I have spoken several times with his Magnificence Alvise Marcello about Giovanni Bellini's painting, urging him to do and say what is necessary to recover the money, without seeing any result since really he can do nothing. And this morning I spoke with Giovanni Bellini at great length, and found that he had finished the painting, so that it lacks nothing; and truly it is a beautiful thing, really better than I would have believed. I know that it will please your Excellency. And he really put himself into this painting for the sake of honor, and especially out of respect for the excellent Andrea Mantegna. So I pray you are willing to accept the painting for his sake, and also for the quality of the work. . . .

Isabella d'Este to Lorenzo da Pavia, 9 July 1504

Lorenzo, after Giovanni Bellini has finished the painting and it is as beautiful as you say, I am content to receive it and so I send my secretary Baptista Scalona with the 25 ducats that constitute the final payment. Let him know how he should arrange things so that this transfer can most easily and safely be made. I am pleased that you had the maces[11] made and sent, with which we are well satisfied. Purchase an ounce of the best perfume, sending it along with Scalona and let me know how much it costs and I will immediately send you the money. . . .

Lorenzo da Pavia to Isabella d'Este, 16 July 1504

Illustrious Lady, I have received from Scalona the 25 ducats for the final payment for the painting, and so have immediately discharged that office. It seems that Giovanni Bellini is still owed a ducat, which Vianello did not give

---

11. Ornamental staffs.

him originally with the other 24 ducats, and so I have asked him for it. . . . *[Vianello had spent the ducat on another painting.]* And so I had to give Bellini that ducat and more, to cover the cost of packaging the painting. . . . I am eager to know whether your Ladyship is pleased with the painting. Truly, it is a beautiful thing. But if I had commissioned it, I would have wanted the figures to be larger. As I wrote in an earlier letter, no one can match Andrea Mantegna in composition, as he is truly the first and the best, but Giovanni Bellini is an excellent master of color, and of all those who have seen this painting, everyone has commended it as a marvelous work. . . .

Albrecht Dürer

Often ranked with the great Italian masters of the High Renaissance—Leonardo da Vinci, Michelangelo, Raphael—the German native Albrecht Dürer (1471–1528) stood at the node of the crosscurrents of his age: Italian style and northern naturalism, humanist and artisan production, Renaissance and Reformation. Not a humanist, like his patrician friend and patron Willibald Pirckheimer, he was a literate artist, an early representative of that new breed, and avid follower of intellectual and religious trends, especially the Erasmian and Lutheran reform movements.

Although when he died in 1528, two years after his own city of Nuremberg adopted Lutheran worship, those controversies of the early modern age still raged, Dürer had been born in a previous era, trained by his goldsmith father, an artisan, apprenticed to a local painter, and reared in the Gothic atmosphere of the late-medieval German city. His craft heritage endured in his later work, evidenced in the thousands of drawings, woodcuts, and engravings that for some are his most endearing work. These circulated not to a handful of viewers, the normal audience of a painting mounted in a local, and often a private space, but to the thousands throughout Europe who eagerly purchased this product of the printing press, the engine that concomitantly powered the Reformation.

But Dürer stepped out of the craftsman's workshop when, his apprenticeship completed, he undertook his travels abroad, and encountered the civilization of the Italian Renaissance. He first traveled over the Alps in 1494, where he absorbed the influence especially of the northern Italian masters Andrea Mantegna and Giovanni Bellini—the very two, as seen earlier, to whom Isabella d'Este was patron. Returning to Nuremberg, he brought the art of the Italian Renaissance into the northern zone, where independently, a Netherlandish Renaissance had introduced novel humanist elements. Here he flourished as the quintessential German artist of the era, except for occasional forays abroad: notably to Italy again in 1505 to 1507, and to the Netherlands in 1520 to 1521. His production was varied and distinctive: a few large-scale paintings, like the Venetian *Feast of the Rose Garlands* mentioned in the excerpts given here and *The Four Apostles*, his last work, for the city of Nuremberg; close studies drawn, engraved, or in watercolor, featuring a hare, a pine tree, or a mountain pond, perfectly "timeless" *aperçus*, belonging to no era;[12] and portraits in all media, with their expressive tresses of hair and stubbly beard, such as those of his father (1490) or of the Emperor Maximilian (1518) or simply of "a man" (1521); or his own haunting self-portraits.

With its naturalist passages and draughtsmanly bent, Dürer's art is radically distant from the world of Alberti, obsessed with the exact relations of points, lines, and planes, or Isabella d'Este, a voracious consumer of beauty and imperious manager of its makers. So too are his writings. In the German vernacular—he lacked a classical education, yet was literate in Latin, and made good use of his friend Pirckheimer's excellent library—Dürer wrote occasional pieces, journals, and letters, of which a good sampling survives. Presented here are four letters from a group of ten written from Venice in 1506, when at age thirty-five Dürer was already an artist of some renown, to Willibald Pirckheimer, scion of the leading family of Nuremberg, his friend and patron. Full of life, they are all about people, and sometimes about artists, less often about art.

The principal topic of Dürer's letters is his relationship to Pirckheimer, who is his "master" or "lord," while he is his superior's "willing" servant. Pirckheimer has funded the journey to Italy, and Dürer never tires of promising to repay him "honorably"—when he has the wherewithal. For cash is scarce, and the funds from the one big commission he bags are all needed for daily expenses; yet the artist is confident he will pick up other work and be able to repay the loan and more. Meanwhile, Dürer implores his patron not to be angry with him.

Pirckheimer has also commissioned Dürer to buy things—a sapphire, an emerald, a ruby, and a diamond ring, along with some books—and presses him to fulfill the charge. Dürer sporadically but energetically tries to chase down the items Pirckheimer has requested, enlisting unnamed Venetian comrades who are expert judges of fine stone and know how to bargain. Dürer recounts in detail the bargaining, the price he paid, the estimated real worth of these items. One by one, he dispatches to Nuremberg sapphire, ruby, diamond, and emerald rings by the hand of a German craftsman or merchant who voyages north and south over the Alpine passes.

Despite his self-identification as social subordinate, complicated by these mercenary and material concerns, Dürer feels free to tease Pirckheimer about his love affairs, a thought prompted by the latter's obsession with jeweled rings. He is also comfortable asking Pirckheimer to do things for

---

12. The insight of Michael Levey, *Dürer* (New York: W.W. Norton, 1964), 25.

him—especially those that have to do with his family. The artist is especially concerned about his widowed mother, whom he has left with some cash but not enough to make the rent, and so he also expects her to obtain funds by selling his drawings and engravings. He asks Pirckheimer to look out for her, and also for his youngest brother, who is somewhat lazy and needs to get a job, and will respond to the prompting of the important gentleman. Dürer's mother, meanwhile, who is not only an art dealer but literate as well, writes to scold the artist for not writing Pirckheimer regularly. Dürer is less concerned about his wife, whom he has also dispatched to sell artworks, and tells Pirckheimer that if she runs low on funds, she must ask her brother—another wealthy Nuremberger—for assistance.

Clearly this is a different relationship than that between Isabella d'Este and Lorenzo da Pavia. Pirckheimer's social eminence is not in question. But Dürer and his patron are both Nuremberg citizens, and bound by ties of neighborly comity that are absent from the relations between the Italian marchesa and her agent. Nonetheless, Pirckheimer and d'Este have something in common: both are collectors, although on different scales, and work through the people they know to acquire the splendid objects that adorn and enhance their lives.

As for art and artists in one of the artistic capitals of Italy, Dürer has surprisingly little to say. He thinks very highly of Giovanni Bellini, the leading painter of the previous generation, but says nothing about Giorgione, the new champion. He disparages the work of Jacopo de' Barbari, a second-rank artist who lived at this point in Germany. He blasts his local rivals for stealing his ideas, copying his works when they find them in the local churches, and complains that they have reported him to officials and forced him to pay dues to the painter's guild. Of the great works of art that already filled the churches and palaces of the lagoon city, or of the glorious buildings in which they stand, he makes no mention.

These are revealing letters, nonetheless, if not about Dürer's perceptions of Venetian art at its highpoint, certainly about the artist's role in the stratum between patricians and craftsmen, high art and low, north and south, at the crossroads of Renaissance culture.

Albrecht Dürer, *Letters to Willibald Pirckheimer* (January–April 1506)

The four letters given here open with a salutation similar to that in the first: "To the honorable and wise Willibald Pirckheimer, burgher of Nuremberg, my gracious lord."

To Willibald Pirckheimer, Venice, 6 January 1506

First, I wish you and all your family many very happy New Years! And assure you of my willing service, dear master Pirckheimer. I am in good health, and hope yours is even better, God willing. Now as you have instructed me to buy genuine pearls and gems, I must inform you that I can get nothing good that is worth your money; it has already been bought by the Germans.[13] They go to the Riva,[14] they always want to get four times the value for the sum they spend, and they are the trickiest folks who ever lived. You can't expect to get any kind of honest deal with them. Others have told me to steer clear of them, they cheat man and beast; and you can buy better merchandise for less money in Frankfurt than in Venice. And the books you wanted me to order for you, Imhoff has already taken care of that.[15]

But if there is anything else you need, let me know, and I shall take care of it promptly and diligently. And if God wills that I may do you some great service, I would undertake it with great joy; for I know well how much you do for me. And I beg you to be merciful about the money I owe you, since I think about it more often than you do. As soon as God lets me return home, I shall honorably repay you all, with huge thanks. For I have been asked to do a painting for the Germans,[16] for which they have given me 110 Rhenish guilders, of which I shall have to spend for materials not more than 5. I shall be done with the priming and planing of the surface within eight days, after which I will get to work painting right away, since God willing, it must be mounted on the altar by a month after Easter.

With God's help, I hope to save all of this money, and with it, I will pay you back. For I don't think that I need to send any money either to my mother or my wife. I gave my mother 10 guilders when I left home. In the meantime, she has gotten some 8 or 10 guilders by selling some works of art, while Drahtzieher[17] has paid her 12, and I have sent her 9 guilders by Sebastian Imhoff's hand, from which she must pay 7 in rent to Pfintzing and Gattner.[18] I gave my wife 12 guilders and she got 13 more from Frankfurt,

---

13. Dürer probably refers here to the merchants of the Fondaco dei Tedeschi, the residence and warehouse of German merchants in Venice.

14. The Riva degli Schiavoni, a major marketplace.

15. One of the Imhoff family of print engravers, probably the Sebastian referred to later in the letter.

16. A reference to the altarpiece of the *Rosenkranzfest*, or *Feast of the Rose Garlands*, in oil, for the church of San Bartolomeo attached to the community of German merchants of the Fondaco, which Dürer executed during his stay in Venice, and for which he was well paid. It is now in the National Gallery, Prague.

17. One of the brothers Konrad or Franz Schmid, according to Max Steck, ed., *Dürer's Schriften, Tagebücher, Briefe* (Stuttgart: W. Kohlhammer, 1961), n186.

18. Nuremberg citizens, known to the Dürer family; see Steck ed., n188.

which make 25. I think she will not be in need. And if there is anything she lacks, her brother will have to help until I return, when I will honorably repay him. . . .

To Willibald Pirckheimer, Venice, 7 February 1506

I am your dutiful servant, dutiful Master. When things go well for you, then I promise you with my whole heart, they go well for me. I wrote you recently; assure me that you have received it. In the meantime, my mother has written me and scolds me for not writing you; she tells me that you are angry with me for not writing, and says I must excuse myself to you right away; and she is very anxious, as is her habit. Now I don't really see that I have anything to apologize for, except that I am lazy about writing, and that in any case you have been away from home. But as soon as I learned that you had gotten home or would soon be there, then I wrote you right away, and also especially charged Castel[19] to assure you I am your willing servant. So I beg you to be indulgent, and forgive me, for I have no other friend on earth but you. Nor do I believe that you are really angry with me, since I look upon you as nothing less than a father.

I wish you were here in Venice, where there are so many delightful fellows who seek out my company more each day, which pleases me greatly: they are witty and smart, good musicians on the lute or the pipes, astute judges of art, with good hearts and sound principles, and courteous and friendly to me. At the same time, you will also find here the worst tricksters, liars, thieves, and scoundrels as ever lived, I think, on the face of the earth; but if you didn't know better, you would think they were the most pleasant companions to be had. I have to laugh to myself when they talk with me: they know that I know they are rogues, but they just don't care.

I have several good Italian friends who warn me that I shouldn't eat and drink with their artists. In fact, they are my enemies, who copy my works in the churches when they find them—and later insult them, saying that since it is not in the antique style, it is no good. But Giovanni Bellini[20] has praised me to several noblemen. He wanted greatly to have something of mine and came himself to me to ask me to paint something for him, for which he would pay well. And everyone tells me that he is such a really good man, that I have been very friendly with him. He is very old, and is still the best painter here.

---

19. Castullus Fugger, the representative in Nuremberg of the Fugger family firm of Augsburg bankers; see Steck ed., n192.

20. One of the foremost Venetian painters at the time, previously seen in this chapter working on a painting commissioned by Isabella d'Este.

Now that painting that pleased me so much when I was here eleven years ago,[21] I don't like any more. And if I didn't know myself that I once liked it, I wouldn't have believed anyone who told me so. Also let me inform you that there are far better painters here than that foreigner Master Jacob,[22] although Anton Kolb[23] would take an oath that there is no better painter anywhere than Jacob. But others mock him, saying that if he were any good, he would stay here in Venice.

Today I first began to sketch out my altarpiece. But my hands had become so scurfy that I couldn't work; but I have now taken care of that. So now be gentle with me and not so quick to scold, but be even-tempered, as I am—I don't know why you won't learn from me. My dear friend, I want very much to know whether you have killed off any of your girlfriends—that one who lived by the river, or any of the others, so that you could get yourself another one in her place.

To Willibald Pirckheimer, Venice, 8 March 1506

I am your dutiful servant, dear Master Pirckheimer. I am sending a ring with a saphire stone, which you asked me so urgently to do. I could not have sent it any earlier, since for two days now I have been running around with a good friend, whom I have pressed into service, to all the goldsmiths in Venice, German and Italian, and have found none to compare to this one, at least for this price. So after some hard bargaining I bought it at 18 ducats 4 marcelli from a man who wore it on his own finger, and who gave it to me as a favor, since I let him think that I wanted it for myself. And no sooner had I bought it than a German goldsmith wanted to give me 3 ducats more for it than what I had paid. And so I hope that you will be pleased with it. Everyone says that it is a real prize, a stone that would be worth 50 guilders in Germany. You will know whether that is true or not; I really can't judge. I had first bought an amethyst for 12 ducats from someone I thought was my good friend, but he tricked me, for it was not worth 7. But the matter has been straightened out by friends: I should return the stone and make him a gift of some fish—which I was glad to do, and so got my money back.

As my friend reckons the value of the saphire ring, the stone is not worth more than 19 Rhenish guilders, and the gold setting about 5, so I have not gone over your limit, which you stated to be "from 15 to about 20 guilders."

---

21. Dürer made a first trip to Italy in 1494, when he first acquired a knowledge of Italian Renaissance style.

22. Jacobo de' Barbari, a Venetian painter and engraver who lived for some years in Germany; see Steck ed., n194.

23. A Nuremberg merchant resident in Venice who had arranged for the printing in Germany of Jacobo de' Barbari's famous map of Venice; see Steck ed., n195.

But the other stone I have not yet been able to buy, since it is scarcely possible to find two such deals. But I shall keep trying with all diligence. They say that in Germany you can easily find such silly fripperies cheaper than in Italy—especially now at the Frankfurt fair—since the Italians send this stuff abroad. They laugh at me, too, about the jacinth cross, especially when I said I wanted it for 2 ducats. So write to me quickly about what I should do about that. I have learned of a place that might have a good diamond ring, but do not know yet how much it will cost. I'll buy that for you when you have sent me further instructions—for even emeralds are so expensive, I've never seen anything like it in all my days, and you can only get an amethyst if you are ready to spend 20 or 25 ducats.

All this makes me think you have taken a mistress—just watch out, that you haven't acquired a master. But you are prudent enough, when you need to be. . . .

Please, don't be angry with me if I don't send you all the stones at this time, since I haven't been able to get ahold of them. My friends tell me, too, that you should have the saphire placed in a new gold setting, so that the stone will stand out better, since the ring is old and the setting worn. And please, would you ask my mother to write to me, and to take care of herself.

To Willibald Pirckheimer, Venice, 2 April 1506

I am your dutiful servant, dear Master. I received a letter from you on the Thursday before Palm Sunday along with the emerald ring, and took it immediately to the man I had gotten it from. He will return the money I paid for it, although he does not do so willingly. But he said he would, so he must hold to that. And let me warn you that the jewelers buy emeralds abroad, and sell them here at a profit. But my friends tell me that the other two rings are well worth 6 ducats each,[24] for they are clear and sound and have no impurities, and say that you should not take them to an assayer, but ask to see similar rings, which they will be glad to show you, and then you will be able to tell whether they are of equal worth. . . . In the meantime, I sent you a saphire ring by the hand of Hans Imhoff,[25] which should have reached you by now. I think this was a very good buy, since right away they wanted to buy it from me at a higher price. I'll wait for you to tell me, since I understand these things not at all, but rely on what my friends tell me.

Let me tell you that the painters here have it in for me. They have brought me before the Venetian council three times, and I must give 4 guilders to their guild. You should know, too, that I could have made a lot of money if I hadn't

---

24. Ruby and diamond rings that Dürer had previously sent.

25. The elder of the two Imhoff brothers, resident in Nuremberg, while the younger was in Venice.

taken on the German altarpiece, for it is a huge amount of work, and I cannot really finish it before Pentecost.[26] And they are not giving me more than 85 ducats, which as you can imagine will all go for room and board. And then I have bought a few things, and sent some money home, so I don't have much on hand. But understand my meaning: I won't leave here until, with God's help, I can pay you back with thanks and have 100 guilders left over besides. I'd be able to make that much easily, if I didn't have the German altarpiece to paint, since aside from the painters, everyone here wishes me well.

As for my brother,[27] tell my mother to speak with Wolgemut[28] about giving him work until I come back, or finding someone else to do so, so that he can manage. I would have liked to have brought him here to Venice with me, which would have been good for both of us, and he would have learned the language. But his mother was afraid that the sky would fall on him, etc. So I beg you to keep an eye on him; he is lost with only women to look after him. Talk to the boy, as you can do so well, and tell him to tend to his studies and behave himself until I return, and not be a burden to his mother. For there is little I can do from here, although I will do my best. I could manage fine if it were only me, but with so many depending on me, it is tough; for no one is giving money away.

And so I commend myself to you; and please tell my mother that she must go to the yearly fair in Nuremberg to sell artworks.[29] My wife should be coming home, and I have written her as well about all of this. I won't do anything about the diamond ring until I get your next letter.

My guess is that I will not be able to come home before autumn. For the altarpiece, which was supposed to be done by Pentecost, will go entirely for food, rent, and expenses. But after that, whatever I earn, I hope I will be able to hold on to. But if it is all right with you, say nothing about this. For I would like to put this off from one day to another, and to tell them each time I write that I am coming soon. For I am uncertain, and don't know myself what I will do. Write me again soon.

---

26. It was eventually finished in September.

27. Dürer had two younger brothers, whom he helped raise; here he speaks of the youngest, Hans. Both became painters, like the eldest. The three brothers were the only children to survive of the eighteen to whom the artist's mother gave birth.

28. Michael Wolgemut, the Nuremberg painter with whom Dürer was apprenticed from 1486 to 1489.

29. See for the artist's mother's contribution to his enterprise, Steck, ed., n205.

Benvenuto Cellini

Benvenuto Cellini (1500–1571) wrote the most famous autobiography of the Renaissance. As Montaigne (see Chapter 2) announced in the preface to his *Essays*, Cellini is himself the subject of his book. How appropriate that such a work was written by an artist, one of those formidably inventive minds who crafted memorable works for some of the leading figures of the age. He was not only an artist, as his autobiography reveals, but also a musician, a soldier, a murderer, and a sodomite.[30] The patterns of his career are as multiplex and boundless as the passions he describes, befitting the dynamism of the era in which he lived.

Born to a Florentine couple advanced in years, the son of a musician, Cellini was apprenticed to a goldsmith, in which highly-skilled trade he might have found a permanent home had that been his bent. But he burst out of the framework of the artisan caste and workshop culture to become, at some of the major courts of Europe, the supplier of exquisitely beautiful objects—salt-cellars and candlesticks, ornamental objects, medals—wrought in precious materials: gold above all, but also silver, ivory, and gems. In that role he served two popes (Clement VII and Paul III), Francis I, the king of France, and the princes of several Italian cities, including, for the longest stretch, his own (the Medici dukes Alessandro I and Cosimo I). In the latter's service, as seen in the excerpts given here, he also attempted and brilliantly succeeded in producing a sculpture of monumental scale, cast in bronze, in imitation of the ancients.

Thus far, Cellini reminds us of Albrecht Dürer, a goldsmith's son who became a painter of first rank, and the protégé of a great German magnate. But where Dürer's impassioned self-examination was an internal affair that remains to us inscrutable, the contents of Cellini's consciousness were plainly and boisterously expressed. In consequence, his words open a window through which we may observe the creative process at work in an age of extraordinary creativity.

The excerpts from Cellini's *Autobiography* given here describe his work on the statue of *Perseus and Medusa*, his masterpiece, which he intended to stand, as it now does, in the great piazza at the geographical and political center of Florence, the Piazza della Signoria, in front of the Palazzo Vecchio, the seat of Florentine government.[31] That open space, bounded on all sides by the tight-packed stone buildings, already contained some notable statues.

---

30. Sodomy, a capital crime in many Renaissance jurisdictions, was the standard term for and understanding of homosexuality in this era.

31. It stands in the protected space of the Loggia dei Lanzi, the open colonnade that borders the piazza.

Foremost among them were those by two other Florentine sculptors, Cellini's predecessors, who set the highest conceivable standard: these were *Judith and Holofernes* (1460) by Donatello (c. 1386–1466), the leading sculptor of the previous century; and the *David* (1504) by Michelangelo (1475–1564), Cellini's elder contemporary.[32] Both works are celebrations of freedom: the first, constructed at a time when Florence was still a republic, and its Medici patrons aligned themselves with the values of republican liberty; the second, constructed when Florence was once again a republic, having regained her independence with the collapse of Medici dominance in 1494. Cellini's *Perseus and Medusa* (1545) would join these, among others, in a kind of sculptural ballet in the public space of the Signoria. It was not, however, a celebration of Florentine freedom, but rather of the renewed and expanded power of the Medici, identified with the heroic Perseus, as the hereditary rulers of that former republic. Why would it not? The reigning Medici duke, Cosimo I, had suggested the project to Cellini; and if Cellini himself, a dependent of princes, had any political ideals, he said little about them.

Cellini's account of the casting of "his Perseus," as he referred to it, occupies sixteen chapters of his *Autobiography*—some 6000 words, a not insignificant part of his narrative. The two poles of this story within a story, like the two poles of his life, are the workshop and the palace. Cellini works ferociously in the workshop, then takes himself to the palace, where he must struggle to avert the calumnies of rivals and retain the favor of the prince. The prince himself visits the workshop frequently, intensely interested in the progress of his minion's work, and dependent on the artist's skill and perseverance as much as the artist depends on the prince's patronage. And when relations falter, Cellini retreats to his workshop, to toil feverishly on his project, which is for him in a social milieu of false relations a source of pride and meaning.

There, in the workshop, Cellini is a manipulator of things, whereas in the palace, he is the puppet of other people. He tests out the different kinds of clay available in Florence, to test their suitability for making a clay model: the clay, he found, was "good enough," although his predecessor Donatello "had not understood it well." Cellini builds his own furnace in the workshop provided by the duke, and in it he does a first test casting of the Medusa figure, and declares it to be "of the highest grade." Then to cast the main figure of the Perseus, he sends for pine wood from the forests of Seristori, near the outlying town of Montelupo. Around the wax model he makes a mold of clay, reinforced with iron straps, then melts the wax over a slow fire until it drains through the apertures he has readied; in its place, the molten bronze will fill up the mold to produce the statue.

Cellini now suspends the hardened mold over his furnace, and prepares the copper and tin which will fuse to make bronze. The metals liquefy—but

---

32. The originals are now removed for interior display, but a copy of the Donatello is still in the Piazza della Signoria, and one of the Michelangelo in the space named in his honor Piazzale Michelangelo.

then, a catastrophe! He is taken ill, and leaves the supervision of the work to his assistants. The metal resets, until it forms a kind of "baked pudding." A worker comes to his bedroom to tell Cellini that the statue is ruined, and the desperately ill artist rushes back to take charge in the workshop. Now oakwood is acquired and applied to the fire, a fuel that produces a much more ferocious flame; and more tin, which promotes liquefaction, is added to the furnace. The metal melts again; Cellini, in his own words, has "achieved a resurrection," bringing the bronze, and the statue, back to life. Then the furnace explodes, blowing off its cap. This disaster, as well, Cellini averts, plugging two holes and adding more tin. The mold fills with bronze, and the statue is made. After it cools for two days, the artist uncovers his handiwork, and finds that it is perfect: it was "truly . . . a miracle, guided and directed by the mind of God." And he trotted off to Pisa, at this time a territory of Florence, to inform the duke: "Now that my work had been fully accomplished, I departed right away for Pisa to find the Duke, who received me with the most cordial welcome that could be imagined; and so likewise did the Duchess. . . ."

The artists of the Renaissance emerged from the workshop to engage in the highest circles of that civilization not as artisans but as inspired and valued participants. But with few exceptions, every one of them, like Cellini, was circumscribed by the network of favors and rejections that was the patronage system, before there emerged a public market in works of art—one beset by its own vicissitudes. In the world, they were servitors of the great. In the workshops like Plato's Demiurge who fashioned the world from chaos, they were wielders of clay, wood, copper, tin, ropes, and fire, in the service of a new creation.

Benvenuto Cellini, *Autobiography*, Book II (1558/1566)

LXIII. The first piece that I cast in bronze was that large bust, a portrait of His Excellency, which I had first made of clay in the goldsmith's shop in the Palazzo Vecchio[33] while I had pains in my back. This work pleased everyone, although I had done it for no other reason than to test the clays for smelting the bronze. I knew well that the genius Donatello, when he made his works of bronze, had cast them with Florentine clay, but it seemed to me that he had encountered enormous difficulties. Thinking that if these came because of the nature of the clay, I wanted to test it out first before beginning to cast my Perseus.[34] I found that the clay was good enough, although the genius

---

33. The main government building in Florence.

34. The sculptural group of Perseus with the head of Medusa, which when completed joined other such groups by major Florentine artists in the Piazza della Signoria, the main Florentine piazza immediately outside the ducal palace.

Donatello[35] had not understood it well, which led to the enormous difficulties he had in executing his works. And so, as I have previously explained, I conditioned the clay using my special methods, and it worked splendidly, and I used it to cast the bust, using the furnace of Zanobi di Pagno, the bell-founder, since I had not yet built my own.

When I saw that the bust had come out clean, I set out immediately to build a small furnace in the workshop that the Duke had made available to me, according to my own instructions and design, in the very house that he had given me. As soon as the furnace was built, working as carefully as I could, I got everything in order to cast the statue of Medusa, which was to be a contorted female form under Perseus's feet. And since this would be a difficult piece to cast, I did not wish to overlook any of the skills that I had learned, or to make any kind of error. As a result, the first casting that I made in my little furnace proved to be of the highest grade, and so clean that my friends said that it was not necessary for me to do anything further to retouch it. They say that some German and French bronze-casters boast that they have clever secrets which permit them to cast bronze without retouching. But this is complete madness: for bronze, once it is cast, needs to be retouched with hammers and with chisels, as it was done brilliantly in antiquity, and how it is still done in modern times—at least by those moderns who have mastered the art of working with bronze.

This piece greatly pleased his illustrious Excellency, who several times came right to my house to see it, which greatly fueled my desire to succeed. But Bandinello[36] envied me so rabidly that he poured into his illustrious Excellency's ears such forebodings as to make him think that even if I made one or two fine statues, I would never produce a group of them, because my skills were new and untested; and so his Excellency should not waste his money on me. These words had such an impact on those glorious ears, that my budget for assistants was slashed, requiring me to defend myself boldly to his Excellency. Whereupon one morning, having waited for his arrival in the via de' Servi, I spoke to him: "My Lord, I sense that your Excellency has no confidence in me, and so I tell you again that I have the skill to produce work three times better than this one, which was the prototype, just as I promised."

In Chapters LXIV to LLXXII, Cellini describes at considerable length his rivalry with Bandinelli (Bandinello), which disheartens Cellini, and erodes the Duke's support for his work. The Duke does, however, encourage Cellini undertaking a project in marble, while Cellini, though pleased, wishes to

---

35. The foremost Florentine sculptor of an earlier generation (c. 1386–1466), whose *Judith and Holofernes* (1460) stood in the Piazza della Signoria during Cellini's lifetime.
36. Bartolommeo (or Baccio) Bandinelli (1493–1560), Florentine painter and sculptor.

return to work on the statue of Perseus with the head of Medusa, to be added
to the series of sculptures already on display in the Piazza della Signoria.

LXXIII. Having had such good fortune casting the Medusa, I had high hopes
of bringing my Perseus to completion; for I had prepared the wax model, and
it looked as though it would take form in bronze as successfully as had the
Medusa. And since it looked quite complete and beautiful in wax, when the
Duke saw it he was impressed. But whether because others had convinced
him that it could not be produced in bronze, or whether the duke himself
had so conjectured, he came more often to my house than usual, and on one
such occasion, he said to me: "Benvenuto, you will not be able to produce
this figure in bronze, because the art of casting is not capable of it."

I bristled greatly at these words of his Excellency, and said: "My lord,
I know that your illustrious Excellency has very little faith in me; and this
happens, I believe, because your illustrious Excellency too readily believes
those who defame me—or perhaps it is truly because you do not understand
the art of bronze-casting." He did not even let me finish speaking before
he said: "I have made myself an expert, and understand it perfectly well." I
answered immediately: "Yes, as a patron, and not as an artist; because if your
illustrious Excellency understood this art as well as you think you do, you
would believe me on account of the work I have done: first, the beautiful
bronze portrait I made of your illustrious Excellency, colossal in size, which
was sent to Elba; second, my restoration for you of the marble Ganymede—a
task of extraordinary difficulty, requiring more exertion than if I had made
an entirely new one; and finally, my Medusa, which you see right here before
you—a very difficult casting, in which I achieved what no other man before
me had done before in this most mysterious art. Look at this, my lord: I made
for this project a completely new kind of furnace. Besides the other diverse
and effective devices that are utilized, I have made two exits for the bronze,
because given the unusual contortions of the figure it would not otherwise
be possible for it to be molded; and only because of my innovations has it
been successful, which none of the other practitioners of this art would have
believed. . . . Now, my lord, believe me, and support me with the resources
I need, so that I can create a work that will satisfy you. But if your illustrious
Excellency denigrates me and does not provide me with the resources I need,
it will be impossible for me, as it would be for any other man on earth, to
produce anything of worth."

The Duke is skeptical about Cellini's strategy for the casting of the group of
Perseus and Medusa, and Cellini feels bereft of support. Nonetheless, he rallies
his courage and applies himself once more to the Perseus project.

LXXV. . . . So with renewed vigor, and with all the strength of my body and
my purse, committing all of the little money I still had, I began by acquir-

ing several loads of pine wood from the forests of Seristori, near Montelupo. While waiting for them, I clothed my Perseus with the various clays I had gotten ready months before, so that they might be properly seasoned. And having made a robe of clay, as is done in bronze-casting, and reinforcing and tying it properly with iron bonds, I set it over a slow fire to soften the wax, which then drained through the many vents I had constructed, the more of which there are, the better the mold is filled. And once I had drained the wax, I constructed a furnace in the shape of a funnel all around my Perseus, made of bricks laid one over the other, while leaving many spaces through which the fire could be exhaled. Then I gradually added wood to the fire, which burned continually for two days and two nights, so that, all the wax having drained and the mold itself was well cooked, I right away set to digging the pit in which to bury the mold, using all the best techniques that this splendid art of casting dictates. When I had dug the pit, I raised the mold to a perpendicular position, using strong ropes and winches, suspended an armslength over the surface of my furnace, exactly in the middle of the pit; then I lowered it down to the bottom of the furnace, securing it with all possible diligence and care.

Having managed this difficult task, I used the same clay that had been removed to support the mold in position, raising the clay around it while incorporating vents, which were little tubes of terracotta such as those commonly used to carry water and such like. When I saw that it was firmly in place, solidly supported by the clay with all the air-vents properly in place, and that my workmen well understood my method, which was very different from that of the other masters of this craft, reassuring myself that I could trust them, then I turned to my furnace. This I had filled with many blocks of copper and others of bronze, placing them one upon the other so as to leave spaces between them for the flames, as the craft requires, so that the metal placed in the furnace more rapidly reaches a temperature at which it melts and liquefies. Then I called loudly to my workers to set fire to the furnace. So the pinewood was heaped on, and between its resins which fed the fire, and the excellent construction of my little furnace, the fire was so forceful that I needed to rush from one side to another, requiring an effort that was beyond my strength; and yet I forced myself. . . .

Cellini has become suddenly and critically ill. Unable to continue work on the statue, he instructs his workmen to carry on, while he returns home and throws himself on his bed, certain that he was near death.

LXXVI. . . . Lost in this bottomless torment, I seemed to see a man enter my bedroom whose figure was twisted into a capital letter S. In a voice mournful and distressed, like that of one telling a condemned man on the point of death to commend his soul to God, he said: "O Benvenuto, your work is ruined, and there is no possible way to save it!" As soon as I heard the words spoken by this wraith, I let loose a scream so piercing that it might have been heard on the moon.[37] I leapt up from my bed, seized my clothes and began to dress, kicking and punching the servants, my boy, and anyone who approached to assist me, while screaming at them, "You traitors, you schemers! What malicious treachery! But I swear before God that I shall make your evil known, and before I die I shall inform the whole world of your astounding treachery." When I had finished dressing, I ran to the workshop in a vicious frame of mind. There I saw all those who had been so sure of themselves when I left them, standing around panicked and stupefied. I said, "Now hear me, since you did not know how to or did not want to obey my instructions, obey me now that I am here with my work before me; and let no one contradict me, because what is needed now is action and not chatter." . . .

I went right to the furnace, and saw that the metal had set, forming a kind of baked pudding. I sent two of the workers across the way to the house of the butcher Capretta to get a bunch of young oak logs, which had dried for more than a year, which Ginevra, Capretta's wife, had offered me, and as soon as the first pieces arrived, I began to fill the brazier. . . . Since this sort of oak produces the most robust fire of any other sort of wood, . . . when the set metal began to feel that fierce fire, it began to glow and send off sparks. Meanwhile I took care of the air channels, and sent others up to put out the fire on the roof, which had flared up with the heat of the intensified fire; and had boards, rugs, and other hangings set up outside to keep the rain from getting inside.

LXXVII. After I had managed all of these tempests, at the top of my voice I shouted now to this man and now the other, "Bring that here, put that there!" Now that the workers saw that the caked metal began to liquefy, they all obeyed me with such determination that each man did the work of three. Then I grabbed a half a lump of tin weighing about 60 pounds, and threw it into the pudding inside the furnace. With this addition, and with other applications of wood and proddings with pokers and iron rods, it soon melted. Now that it was clear that I had achieved a resurrection, overcoming the doubts of all these idiots, such vigor returned to me that I forgot all about my fever and no longer feared death. But then there was an explosion, and huge flames shot up, as though a thunderbolt had struck right there in our midst, paralyzing us all with fear and terror, me even more than the rest.

Once the clamor and flashing light had passed, we began to look each other in the face again. Finding that the cap of the furnace had exploded and

---

37. Literally, the "sphere of fire": in the geocentric Ptolemaic system, the sphere between that of air and the first heaven of the moon: see Bellotto ed., LXXVI n6.

the bronze rose up and overflowed, I quickly opened the mouths of my mold, and hammered in two plugs to contain the melted bronze. As the metal did not flow as readily as it should, I concluded that the cause was probably that the tin had been consumed by the heat of that ferocious fire. So I grabbed all my tin plates, bowls, and saucers, of which I had about 200, and one by one I inserted some into the canals, and threw the rest directly into the furnace. . . . Instantly my mold filled up. I fell to my knees and with all my heart gave thanks to God. . . .

Cellini celebrates with a good meal, and pays his jubilant workers for their efforts. His rivals again seek to minimize his triumph and to poison the Duke against him—unsuccessfully, as will be seen.

LXXVIII. Having left my statue to cool for two days, I began to uncover it bit by bit. I found first of all the head of the Medusa, which had come out splendidly because of the air-vents, since as I had explained to the Duke it is the nature of fire to ascend. Then I proceeded to uncover the rest of the statue, and found the other head, that of Perseus, which had succeeded equally well—and this really amazed me, because it is positioned well below that of the Medusa. . . . Miraculously, no fragments remained in the canals, nor was anything at all lacking in the statue, which seemed truly to be a miracle, guided and directed by the mind of God. . . . Now that my work had been fully accomplished, I departed right away for Pisa to find the Duke, who received me with the most cordial welcome that could be imagined; and so likewise did the Duchess. . . .

Chapter 7: Humanism and Religion

Introduction

Humanism, to many, is a term implying hostility to religion. It is often used in this way in the popular media, sometimes coupled with the modifier "secular." "Secular humanists" are described as being—depending on the point of view—scientifically-minded rationalists who stand up to superstitious beliefs, or soulless opponents of family, community, and tradition, as well as the churches that bolster all three.

Leaving aside the merits or failings of the "secular humanist" position in the present moment, it is important to recognize that Renaissance humanism, an intellectual movement that melded elements of Christian and classical civilization, was not "secular." Humanism not only took form within a Europe that was profoundly religious—and religious in a dynamic and vital way, brimming with new initiatives and perspectives—but the humanists themselves participated in that religious fervor, before, during, and after the critical moment when Luther broke with the Roman church.

Of course, there were skeptics among the humanists, with most of that skepticism targeting the official church, which had faced institutional crisis in the fourteenth and early fifteenth centuries, and whose leaders had nakedly pursued wealth and power from the fifteenth to the sixteenth in the face of repeated calls for reform. More frequently, the humanists were themselves reformers—some of them were even clerics—calling for institutional restoration and spiritual renewal. Erasmus is an overwhelming presence: his critique of ignorant and greedy churchmen and of empty ritual observances, along with his call for sincere, interior religious commitment, runs through most of his works, which were best-sellers across Europe. In Chapter 5 of this volume, it was seen how his insistence on a new religious outlook saturates his recommendations for the formation and regime of a Christian prince.

Prior to Luther's break with the Roman church, humanist participants in religious reform and renewal were necessarily Catholic. After that watershed—which did not occur in a single moment, but over a full generation—some were Catholic, and others identified with one or another of the Reformation denominations or sects. The great majority of the leaders of the Protestant Reformation had received humanist educations, even though, once embarked on their reform careers, their humanist pursuits took second place to their Reformation agendas.

In sum, the relationship is complex between the humanist movement and the surge for religious renewal and reform both within the Catholic church and in the new Reformation churches. Earlier chapters have already highlighted some cases of interest. These include Olympia Morata's German exile, as an Italian refugee and Protestant convert; Luigi Guicciardini's narrative of the Sack of Rome, an assault on the institutional church by a secular state, which numbered among its military personnel ardent opponents of the papacy; and, as early as the fourteenth century, Boccaccio's defense of the study of pagan literature over religious objections. This chapter presents four additional texts that illustrate different patterns in the intersection between humanism and the surge of religious reform and renewal that is a hallmark of the era of the Renaissance.

First, Lorenzo Valla (1407–1457), a humanist of particularly acute intellect, in his critical dissection of the forged eighth-century document known as the "Donation of Constantine," employs a full range of historical, philological, and linguistic tools to eviscerate the papal claim to territorial as well as spiritual sovereignty, both in Rome and throughout Europe. His elegant Latin exposé of the papal grab for wealth and power should be viewed in the context of his other works also addressing religious issues, especially his careful study of the scriptural text in all its original languages, which would have an immense impact on the two great northern reformers, Erasmus and Luther.

Second, Jacques Lefèvre d'Étaples (c. 1455–1536), as seen in the preface to his translation of the four Gospels—a translation that was in itself a radical act—combines humanist expertise with a humanist faith in language as a civilizing force. For Lefèvre, the personal, interiorized reading of scripture is the key to genuine religious observance—from which comes the necessity of translation into the language that is closest to the reader.

Third, Bernardino Ochino (1487–1564), in his *Dialogue about the Thief on the Cross*, employs the persuasive rhetorical device of the dialogue to make a compelling case for the Reformation doctrine of justification by faith. A theologian and a friar who rose to the leadership of the Observant branch of the Capuchin Order, Ochino traveled in Italian evangelical circles, characterized by salon-like gatherings amid elaborate networks of high-ranking clergy and aristocratic patrons, especially women.

Fourth, Gasparo Contarini (1483–1542), the lead author of a set of recommendations for the reform of the Catholic church commissioned by the papacy, identifies twenty-six abuses that required correction as an essential step toward the revitalization of the church. A member of the same evangelical circles in which Ochino traveled, Contarini was recruited late in life while still a layman to the cardinalate. Despite his own profound convictions,

which included the acceptance of the critical reformed doctrine of justification by faith, Contarini still aligned himself with the more modest goals of
institutional reformers. Their aim—still a radical one in the setting of papal
Rome—was the correction of practices that had become corrupted, which
were barriers to the piety and trust of the Christian public. Respectful of
institutions, as befit his Venetian upbringing, Contarini accepted the goal
of reforming the church without dismantling it, distinguishing himself from
contemporary Protestant reformers with whom, nonetheless, he had contact
and shared some sympathies.

These four writers, for all the diversity of their aims and methods, ardently
sought the reform of the church. All four came to maturity before Luther's
break with the church—Valla nearly a century before—and only Ochino
lived to see the creation of autonomous Protestant churches. By that time, the
humanist participation in religious debate vanished, yielding to the partisan
polemics that characterized the Reformation era. But the humanist contribution to the reform effort had been notable. Humanists unpacked the text of
the Bible, accessing ancient languages with new philological skill, to which
they added a serious understanding of history and the law. These were the
intellectual foundations of the movements we know as the Reformations,
both Protestant and Catholic, which remade Europe for the modern era.

Lorenzo Valla

Lorenzo Valla (1407–1457) had, arguably, the most acute critical mind
of the Italian humanists, and perhaps of humanism as a whole, with the
possible exception of Erasmus. He applied it to many matters: to the Latin
language, ancient history, classical texts, and moral philosophy, but above
all to religion. In that arena, he wrote against the monastic life; critiqued
the fourth-century Latin translation of the New Testament[1] by contrasting
it to the Greek original; examined the tension between notions of free will
and divine providence; and exposed as a forgery the so-called Donation of
Constantine, which was used to authorize papal dominion over much of
Europe. His disciplined and well-grounded confrontation of the pretensions
of the church shocked and fascinated his readers, and profoundly influenced later thinkers, including Erasmus and Luther—and so had a role in the
Protestant revolution of the sixteenth century. Yet he was himself a Christian,

---

1. By Saint Jerome, known as the Vulgate, the version commonly used in Catholic Europe
until the sixteenth century and beyond.

a priest, and an apostolic secretary,[2] and lies buried in an elegant tomb in Saint John Lateran, the papal basilica in Rome.

Valla is best known for his unprecedented *tour de force*, the deconstruction of the supposed Donation of Constantine, of which excerpts are given here. It is a lean, angry, and meticulously crafted argument that in brief compass dismantles papal pretensions to territorial rule, and so strikes at the basis of church wealth and power. Created in the eighth century, the Donation purports to be a document of the fourth century, recording the gift by the Roman emperor Constantine (r. 306–337) to the pope Sylvester I (r. 314–335), in gratitude for the latter's having cured him of leprosy, of the territories of the Western empire. Over the centuries that followed, the popes used the Donation document to justify interventions in secular politics, especially in Italy itself, where an entire swath of cities and countryside were under direct papal governance. In 1439 to 1440, it has often been noted, while Valla was writing his manifesto, he was resident at the court of Alfonso, king of Naples, upon whose sovereignty the reigning pope Eugene IV had designs—as did Alfonso on his. This circumstance alone does not explain Valla's position, of course, since it is wholly consistent with his other work, which generally provoked fundamental reevaluations of whatever issue he engaged.

Given here are sections from the introduction and conclusion, in which Valla lays out and closes his principal arguments. Between these two fence posts stretch more than 20,000 words of crisp analysis, presented with taut and mordant argumentation, and buttressed by apt references to scripture, law, and history.

Valla opens with a disarming statement of intent. He has provoked his readers before, and will outrage them again now, aiming his attack at the highest official of the most powerful institution in Christendom. He will not be deterred, however, by the imposing might of the church, because he knows that he is in the right and trusts in God: "Many have risked their lives in defense of their earthly fatherland; shall the fear of death cause me to shy away from the pursuit of a heavenly fatherland—which belongs to those who please God, not men?" His readers have long expected him to detail some charge against the pope, and now he will: "It is indeed an egregious crime, prompted by gross ignorance, perhaps, or by boundless greed, . . . or by lust for power." Long ago, the papal bureaucrats either overlooked the fact that the Donation document was forged, or they forged it themselves; and their successors have perpetuated the fraud. They claim that the papacy received from Constantine a gift of all of the West—all the lands of what are now Italy, Spain, Germany, France, and Britain. "Does that make all these things yours, supreme pontiff?" Valla writes mockingly; "Were you planning to take them all back?" In his quest for territorial aggrandizement, the pope will recognize no limit.

---

2. An employee in the papal bureaucracy, or *curia*.

These papal pretensions Valla will emphatically disprove. Constantine did not in fact have the power or the right to transfer these imperial lands to the pope, and neither did Sylvester have any desire or right to receive them. Constantine had earlier made a donation of some properties to a prior pope, but this was a minor grant. Even if the desire and capacity had been present in both emperor and pope to execute so large a transfer of lands, in fact they were not transferred, for they are found after the time of the supposed Donation solidly in the hands of the Roman emperors. Nor does the document itself survive where the papal secretaries say it may be found. It is not included among the papal decrees compiled by the twelfth-century jurist Gratian in his *Decretum* (the *Concordance of Discordant Canons*). Neither does it appear in the account of the life of Sylvester I included in the *Book of the Popes* (*Liber pontificalis*), which recorded the reign of each pope into the fifteenth century—a wholly unreliable source in any case, Valla adds. Finally, after the lapse of so many centuries, even if Sylvester had taken possession of some of the lands in question but later popes had lost it, title to those lands could not be reclaimed; indeed, no assignment of property made so long ago can be said to validate the pope's title to lands he currently holds. And even if none of these points held true, still the crimes committed by the popes in their pursuit of territorial power cancel out any right they might have to hold it.

The popes, Valla charges in conclusion, have not been good shepherds of the church they are charged to be, but they devour the wealth and property of God's children, "while Christ in the person of the myriads of the poor is dying of hunger and cold," stir up wars and discord, and baldly claim the gift purportedly given by Constantine, "as though its repossession will bring any benefit to the Christian religion, rather than more suffering from all forms of shameful and libidinous excess—as though it could suffer any more than it already has, and if there is room for any as yet undiscovered kind of wickedness."

Perhaps, Valla concludes, the pope will listen to the admonishments of reasonable advisors. Perhaps he has already realized his errors, and is ready to cease his depredations, so that the din of Christians fighting each other will no longer be heard—a theme that Erasmus will later develop. "At that time, the pope will not only be called 'holy father,' but will be so in fact, father of all, father of the church."

Thus quietly, Valla draws to a close a fiery work that provides to later reformers a platform for the repudiation of the papacy itself, and not just the supposed Donation of Constantine. His refutation of that document is itself irrefutable. Valla has not merely raised but hurled his pen against the papacy, and drawn blood.

Lorenzo Valla, *On the Donation of Constantine* (1440)

I have sent forth into the world many books, a great many, in nearly every branch of knowledge. In these I have dissented from what was said by numerous authors, who have long been revered over the ages. Since there are some who are angered by what I have already written, and charge me with impertinence and sacrilege, what do we imagine they are going to do now? How passionately they will rage against me, and if they are able, how eagerly and swiftly will they convey me to the hangman! For I am writing against not only those who have died, but also those who still live; not only this person or that one, but a multitude; not only private persons, but even high officials! And what officials! None other than the supreme pontiff, armed not only with the temporal sword like kings and princes, but also the ecclesiastical,[3] so that the shield of no prince can protect you from him, so to speak, nor can you escape his weapons of excommunication, anathema, or malediction. . . .

But there is no reason why this twofold[4] threat of danger should shake me or deter me from my plan. For the pope may not bind or release anyone contrary to human or sacred law; and to offer one's life in the defense of truth and justice is the height of virtue, of honor, and of glory. Many have risked their lives in defense of their earthly fatherland; shall the fear of death cause me to shy away from the pursuit of a heavenly fatherland—which belongs to those who please God, not men? So away with fear, let trembling cease, let trepidation depart! With a bold spirit, great confidence, and firm hope, must we defend the cause of truth, the cause of justice, the cause of God! No one should be deemed a true orator because he can speak well, unless he dares also to speak out. Let us therefore boldly accuse him, whoever he may be, who commits deeds that warrant accusation; and let him who sins against all be brought to justice by the voice of one who speaks for all. . . .

I do what I do not because I want to persecute anyone, as though I were lambasting him with Philippics[5]—may such a thing be utterly foreign to me—but so I may root out error from the minds of men, and by urging and prodding turn them away from vice and wickedness. . . .

For a long time now, I know, the ears of men have longed to hear what crime it was of which I would accuse the popes of Rome. It is indeed an

---

3. In medieval political theory, authority was conceived as having two aspects, or "swords": the emperor and other princes wielded the secular sword, the pope the ecclesiastical.

4. That is, both temporal and ecclesiastical.

5. The Roman statesman and orator Cicero delivered a series of denunciatory speeches against Mark Antony in 44 BCE, called Philippics after the series of speeches the fourth-century BCE orator Demosthenes delivered to the Athenians to spur them to resist the advance of Philip of Macedon.

egregious crime, prompted by gross ignorance, perhaps, or by boundless greed, which is the sin of idolatry,[6] or by lust for power, whose constant partner is cruelty. Centuries ago, these pontiffs either failed to see that the Donation of Constantine is a fabrication and forgery, or they forged it themselves; while their descendants, following the fraudulent path of those who came before, defended as true what they knew to be false—thus dishonoring the majesty of the pontificate, dishonoring the memory of the ancient popes, dishonoring the Christian religion, and defiling all they touch with carnage, catastrophe, and crime.

They say that the city of Rome belongs to the pope; likewise the kingdom of Sicily and Naples and the whole of Italy; so too the Gauls, the Spanish, the Germans, the Britons, in sum, the whole of the West;[7] all these possessions, they claim, are named in the pages of that supposed donation. Does that make all these things yours, supreme pontiff? Were you planning to take them all back? To seize the cities of all the kings and princes of Europe, was that your intent, or to force them to pay you an annual tribute? On the contrary, it seems to me that those princes have a better right to despoil you of all that you possess. For as I shall show, that donation, from which document the supreme pontiffs derive their claims, was unknown both to Sylvester and to Constantine.[8]

But before I proceed to refute the document of Donation—the sole authority for their pretensions, which is not only a forgery but a crude one—it is necessary to lay the argument out from the beginning. So first I shall show that Constantine and Sylvester were not such men that the former would wish to make any such donation; nor would he have the legal right to do so; nor would he have the power to transfer these lands to another; and the latter, likewise, would not wish to accept such a donation, nor would he have the legal capacity to do so. Second, I shall show that even if these conditions did not exist, although they are perfectly true and self-apparent, still it is the case that Sylvester did not accept, nor did Constantine confer any title to the things that were said to have been donated, but they remained always in the authority and control of the Caesars.[9] Third, I shall show that while nothing was given by Constantine to Sylvester, there was a donation by

---

6. *servitus idolorum*: Galatians 5:20 (Vulgate); the passage names idolatry as one of the several forms of immorality detailed in verses 19–21.

7. In Valla's day, all these regions were understood to be encompassed by the Donation of Constantine, although at the time of the composition of the forgery (eighth century CE), probably only the regions of Italy were intended; see Christopher B. Coleman, *The Treatise of Lorenzo Valla on the Donation of Constantine* (New Haven: Yale University Press, 1922; rept. Toronto: University of Toronto Press in association with the Renaissance Society of America, 1993), 27n6.

8. Pope Sylvester I (r. 314–335) and the emperor Constantine (r. 306–337).

9. That is, the Roman emperors.

Constantine, before his baptism, to a prior pope, consisting of small grants intended to support that pope during his lifetime. Fourth, I shall show that the claim is false that a copy of the Donation is found among the papal decrees[10] or, equally, that it appears in the *History of Sylvester*,[11] since it is not discovered there or in any other history comprising the *Book of the Popes*,[12] which contains only contradictions, impossibilities, stupidities, barbarisms, and nonsense. Furthermore, I shall speak of donations by certain other emperors which were either fictitious or worthless. Then I shall add this argument on top of all the others: if Sylvester had taken possession of anything from such a donation, and if either he or any other pope had lost it, after so long a lapse of time, under either divine or human law,[13] title could not be regained. Finally, I shall show that no assignment of ownership, after so long a period of time, can validate possessions now claimed by the supreme pontiff.

There intervene between the excerpts from Valla's introduction, above, and his conclusion, which follows, more than 20,000 words of systematic refutation of the Donation of Constantine along the pattern the author has set forth.

But what more is there necessary to say about a matter so perfectly clear? I contend not only that Constantine did not donate such extensive territories, nor that the Roman pope could not have held them as a result of such donation, but that also, even if these things had happened, still the crimes of the possessors would have cancelled their right to them—for it is evident that the destruction and devastation of all Italy and many other regions have flowed from this one source. . . . Can we accept the principle of papal power, when we see that it has been the cause of so much wickedness and of so many crimes of every description?

Wherefore I declare and proclaim—for trusting in God, I do not fear men—that no one in my time who has held the office of supreme pontiff has been either "a faithful or prudent steward," as the gospel commands;[14] but they have so far failed in their duty to feed the children of God, that they have

---

10. G. W. Bowersock identifies these as imperial decrees in his edition of *Valla On the Donation of Constantine* (Cambridge, MA: Harvard University Press, 2007), 8; but the sense clearly implies papal decrees, at this era incorporated in Gratian's *Decretum*; see also Coleman ed., 29.

11. Here Valla refers to the account of the reign of Pope Sylvester I in the *Liber pontificalis*, which contains brief accounts (that Valla calls "histories") of each pope's reign into the fifteenth century.

12. That is, the *Liber pontificalis*.

13. The Middle Ages inherited the corpus of Roman law, from which was developed, especially from the eleventh century forward, the law of the church, called "canon law." Canon law provided basic principles that other forms of civil law, whether promulgated by king, prince, or city, followed to a greater or lesser extent. These two forms of law are here referred to as, respectively, divine and human, terms also used by the ancient Romans.

14. Luke 12:42; Bowersock ed., n116.

rather fed on them instead, like a crust of bread.[15] The pope himself wages wars against peaceful nations and sows discord between cities and princes. The pope both thirsts for the wealth of others and consumes his own. . . . The pope does not defraud merely a republic, which neither Verres nor Catiline nor any other embezzler dared to do, but robs the Church itself and the Holy Spirit, from which sin even the mountebank Simon the Magician shied away.[16] And when he is admonished for all this, and reproached by a few good men, he does not deny his crimes, but openly confesses and glories in them. For he claims the right to extort from its present occupants by any means the patrimony bestowed by Constantine on the church; as though its repossession will bring any benefit to the Christian religion, rather than more suffering from all forms of shameful and libidinous excess—as though it could suffer any more than it already has, and if there is room for any as yet undiscovered kind of wickedness.

Then so as to recapture the other pieces of the supposed donation, he has viciously stolen money from good people and more viciously dispensed it to support the military forces, equestrian and pedestrian, which bring only destruction, while Christ, in the person of the myriads of the poor, is dying of hunger and cold. He does not realize—a shameful crime!—that while he snatches from secular rulers what belongs to them, they in turn, either because they are induced by his awful example or are forced by necessity, even if not a real necessity, to steal from the church. Religion, then, is nowhere to be found, no holiness, no fear of God, but, horrible to say,[17] evil men excuse themselves for all their crimes because the pope has led the way—for he and his courtiers have modeled every kind of wickedness. . . . How can anyone who calls himself a Christian tolerate this?

But in this first discourse of mine I do not urge princes and nations to restrain the pope from rushing forward in his unleashed frenzy and to compel him to stay within his limits. But I do ask them to admonish him, who has perhaps already recognized the truth, and will on his own return from an alien place, with its wild currents and savage storms, to his own safe harbor. But if he refuses, then I shall gird up for a second and much bolder discourse. If only, if one day I may see—may it not be long before I see this, especially if my words have made it happen—that the pope behaves solely like the vicar

---

15. Psalm 53:4: "They devour my people as though eating bread" (New International Version, or NIV); Bowersock ed., n117.

16. Verres defrauded the people of Sicily and was prosecuted by Cicero; Catiline conspired against the Roman state and was condemned by the Senate at Cicero's urging; perhaps Valla means that, although they committed crimes, they were not crimes of embezzlement. Simon the Magician makes an appearance in Acts 8:9–13.

17. *referens horresco*: Virgil, *Aeneid*, 2:204; Bowersock ed., n119.

of Christ and not also like the vicar of Caesar. If only we might no longer hear the terrible cries, "We fight for the church," or "We fight against the church"; or that the church has turned its fire against the citizens of Perugia or the citizens of Bologna.[18] It is not the church that fights against Christians, but the pope; the church fights "spiritual sins on high."[19] At that time, the pope will not only be called "holy father," but will be so in fact, father of all, father of the church. Then he will no more incite wars between Christians, but those incited by others, by his apostolic judgment and papal majesty, he will pacify.

Jacques Lefèvre d'Étaples

Jacques Lefèvre d'Étaples (c. 1455–1536), the most important advocate of church reform in France before the Reformation, is the quintessential Christian humanist: a humanist learned in ancient languages and thought who bent his knowledge wholly to the cause of Christianity; a Christian thinker for whom the key to all theological understanding is the word: the words of the scriptural text, words that do not deceive, words that are written in the flesh and in the spirit, words that are themselves the law and the path to salvation, the word of God, the word incarnate in Jesus Christ. His single-minded determination in advancing this theme of the preeminence of the word distinguishes him from his contemporary, the more learned and more far-seeing Erasmus. His clarity, however, makes the letter that appears here, and many other similar works, especially valuable. There is no escaping the point. Words matter: as they did for the humanists, so they do, vitally, for Christians.

An ordained priest of modest parentage, Lefèvre studied at the University of Paris as a young man before making two extended visits to Italy, where he perfected his Greek and absorbed the prevailing humanist and philosophical culture, both Aristotelian and Platonist. In 1521, back in France, he joined the reform circle centered in the city of Meaux, which promoted improved clerical training and some evangelical ideas that skirted close to Lutheran doctrines but never broke with Catholicism. While resident there, he published, in 1523, his French translation of the Gospels, and in 1524–1525, of the remainder of the New Testament. These had been preceded by his translations of the psalms and the letters of the apostle Paul, and would be followed, in 1530, by his translation of the entire Bible into the

---

18. In this era, the church's military forces, and even the pope himself, engaged in warfare in Italy involving territorial claims. Valla may also be referring to the protracted struggles between the pro-church Guelphs and pro-imperial Ghibellines in an earlier era.

19. Ephesians 6:12; Bowersock ed., n122.

language of the people. His biblical translations exposed him to accusations of heresy, but he was protected by King Francis I and the latter's sister, the reform-minded and humanistically-trained Marguerite de Navarre. At her prompting, he took refuge in the town of Nérac in southwestern France in 1531, where he died five years later.

The "exhortatory epistle" that follows, addressed to his "brothers and sisters" in the faith, and written at Meaux around 8 June 1523, constitutes the preface to Lefèvre's translation of the Gospels, the first of the two parts of his New Testament. In it is expounded what might be called Lefèvre's theology of the word—since for him, the act of translation was in itself the exposition of doctrine, there being nothing so significant as the evident meaning of the plain word, the only barrier to understanding being that of language. By rendering the biblical text from Latin into French, in Lefèvre's view, the whole task of religious teaching is accomplished.

The day of redemption is come, Lefèvre announces at the outset of his letter; because here, at this time, "our Lord Jesus Christ, the only salvation, truth and life, wants his Gospel to be declared in all its purity to the whole world." Lefèvre's translation is itself the redemptive event, for when Christian people can read the word for themselves "in all its purity"—that is, unmediated by human interpretations and interpolations that are inherently distorting—they will receive the "grace, illumination, and salvation" that the author promises in his salutation. He has provided the plain text, "without adding or removing anything," so that those who can read only French and not the Latin of the Vulgate, the version utilized by the church, "can be as certain of the truth announced in the Gospel as are those who can read Latin."

In a series of statements tinged with Platonism and Neoplatonism, Lefèvre likens the translated word to light. Just as the material sun is the source of all light on earth, the immaterial or spiritual sun, Jesus Christ himself, is the source of all enlightenment. The words of the Gospel, which include all the words that Jesus himself was considered to have spoken, are therefore light, and clearly show the true path to God. Therefore, Lefèvre writes, "let us walk in the light of day, in the light of the holy Gospel, having full faith in the true path to the true sun, and doing so we shall never sin against God."

For Lefèvre, the words of scripture, which are the word of God, are patently true, whereas the words of human beings are likely to be false: "Know that men and their teachings are nothing, unless they are corroborated and confirmed by the word of God." Such men argue that the Gospel narrative needs to be altered for the understanding of ordinary folk, "with something added or removed or explained, which adjustments make them more elegant." This claim Lefèvre repudiates; rather, such alterations "misguide simple folk or deflect them from the truth." As for elegance, "what many admire as elegance among men is inelegance and falsehood to God."

The "beauty, excellence, and glory of the Gospel," Lefèvre continues, is directly communicated by "a ray from the true spiritual sun" to the "internal eye of the spirit," just as rays from the material sun are perceived by the external eye of the body. Such communication requires no mediation by learned men, but directly reaches even ordinary people: "it communicates itself many times more completely and spiritually to the simple folk, the humble and meek, than to clerics, the proud and mighty." Just as the Jews in ancient times, and even in the present day, read and know the law that is contained in the Old Testament, so Christians must have access to the law contained in the New: "We must not only read it and have it inscribed in material books, but possess it readily in our memory and have it inscribed on our hearts."

How vast is the gulf between the twenty-first century, where no truth is solid and no text is what it says, and the sixteenth, which Lefèvre inhabited, confident that words have both clear meaning and redemptive power!

Jacques Lefèvre d'Étaples, *Exhortatory Letter on Translating the Gospels into French* (c. 8 June 1523)

To all Christian men and women grace, illumination, and salvation in Jesus Christ!

When Saint Paul was on the earth preaching and declaring the word of God, along with the other apostles and disciples, he said: "Now is the time of God's favor, now is the day of salvation."[20] Now, indeed, that day is come; here, now, is the day of our redemption. For now the time has come when our Lord Jesus Christ, the only salvation, truth, and life, wants his Gospel to be declared in all its purity to the whole world, so that it is no longer obscured by the teachings of men who, as Saint Paul says, think they are something but are not, and so deceive themselves.[21] Because now we can say as he did: . . . Now, indeed, that day is come; here, now, is the day of our redemption.

So that each person who knows French but no Latin will be more receptive to the gift of grace, which God in his goodness, pity, and mercy offers us in this age in the sweet and loving person of Jesus Christ our only savior, I have by the grace of God translated the Gospels into the vernacular, following the commonly-used Latin text without adding or removing anything. With this translation, simple members of the community of Jesus Christ, having him in their own language, can be as certain of the truth announced in the Gospel as are those who can read Latin. And later, by the grace of God, they shall have the rest of the New Testament,[22] which is the book of life and the only guide

---

20. 2 Corinthians 6. Translation is NIV, here and henceforth.

21. Galatians 6:3: "If anyone thinks they are something when they are not, they deceive themselves."

22. Lefèvre's translation of the Gospels published in 1523 constitutes the first part of the New Testament. The second part, containing Acts, the Pauline and extra-Pauline epistles, and Revelation, was published in 1524/1525.

of Christians, which now already circulates in diverse regions and a diversity of languages to Christians across most of Europe, to stir the hearts of all by the spirit of our Lord Jesus Christ, our salvation, our glory, and our life.

Moreover, his infinite goodness shows us that it is necessary that all men, of high station and low, know the holy Gospel particularly in these times, when we are threatened by the enemies of our faith, the Turks, just as in ancient time the Babylonians were the enemies of Israel, guardian of the law.[23] This threat arises so as to correct the faults of Christendom, which are very great, and prompts us to return to him, abandoning entirely our insane faith in created things and merely human customs, which cannot save, and following only the word of God, which is life and spirit.

Let us all strive therefore to know his will through the holy Gospel, so that in this time of testing which is now upon us we be not numbered among the reprobate. Let us receive the sweet visitation of Jesus Christ, our only redeemer, in the heavenly light of the Gospel, which, as was said, is the guide for Christians, a guide for living, and a guide to salvation. And if there are any who would put forward or promote a different guide than this one which God has given, which is the Gospel alone, they are those, or like those, of whom Saint Paul speaks to Timothy by the spirit of Jesus Christ, saying: "The goal of this command is love, which comes from a pure heart and a good conscience and a sincere faith. Some have departed from these and have turned to meaningless talk. They want to be teachers of the law, but they do not know what they are talking about or what they so confidently affirm."[24] . . . Let us pursue, therefore, the wisdom of God, in which there can be no vanity, no lack of understanding, no affirmation of what is contrary to a truth which is evident to all who are not blind; but rather let us see with full knowledge and certainty that which passes beyond all understanding.

For is it not so that we see nothing at all unless it is day and the sun shines so brightly that the stars are hidden? How then on the day of Jesus Christ, who is the true sun, can one see by any light other than the light of his faith, which is set forth in the holy Gospel? Nor should anyone place faith and trust anywhere but in Jesus Christ concerning the life eternal which we hope for, which he has promised us who is himself infallible truth, for it is written: "Salvation is found in no one else."[25] But we still walk in darkness and do not see the light of the sun which illuminates all things below and absorbs all light

---

23. Lefèvre here draws a parallel between the situation of Christians facing the aggressive expansion of the Ottoman Turks through the Balkans and into Europe (fifteenth and sixteenth centuries) and of the Jews of the sixth century BCE, who were menaced and eventually conquered by the Babylonians.

24. 1 Timothy 1:5–7.

25. Acts 4:12: "Salvation is found in no one else, for there is no other name under heaven given to mankind by which we must be saved."

from above. Who is there who, in full daylight, can see the stars? Wherefore we still dwell in error and in the dark of night. As Jesus Christ tells us in the words of Saint John: "Anyone who walks in the daytime will not stumble, for they see by this world's light. It is when a person walks at night that they stumble, for they have no light."[26] . . . From which we understand that he who walks at night, for all that he can see the stars, if he takes them as his guide, he is lost.

Therefore, my brothers and sisters, let us walk in the light of day, in the light of the holy Gospel, having full faith in the true path to the true sun, and doing so we shall never sin against God: for he himself has told us so in the words of Saint John, as we have heard. So let us go to none other than our heavenly Father, through Jesus Christ and in Jesus Christ, as his word commands us, so that we may be children of God in him and by him, children of grace and light, children of the spirit and of life. Then we shall live through his spirit and through his life which is everything, and not through our spirit and our life, which are nothing. Let us leave behind the flesh, and choose the spirit. Let us leave behind death, and choose life. Let us leave behind the night, and choose the day. . . .

Know that men and their teachings are nothing, unless they are corroborated and confirmed by the word of God. But Jesus Christ is all: he is all man and all God; and a man is nothing, except in him; and the words of men are nothing, except in his word. Thus Saint John says in his second letter: "If anyone comes to you and does not bring this teaching, do not take them into your house or welcome them."[27] And what is this teaching, if not the Gospel of Jesus Christ?

If anyone seeking to misguide simple folk or deflect them from the truth presumes to say that it is better to read the Gospels when they have been altered, with something added or removed or explained, which adjustments make them more elegant, I can respond that I have not done so, nor have I resorted to paraphrase in order to explicate the Latin, for fear of . . . contaminating or replacing the word of God with the words of men. . . . For this reason, using paraphrase in translating the word of God is a perilous thing, particularly if any alteration is made to the word of God by adding something or taking anything away. And regarding those who believe that doing so makes the text more elegant, clearly their view of holy Scripture is presumptuous. Do they wish to be more elegant than the Holy Spirit? . . . Know that what many admire as elegance among men is inelegance and falsehood to God, and that the word of God in its innocence and simplicity of spirit is true elegance to God and to those who see with spiritual eyes, whom he alone enlightens.

---

26. John 11:9–10.
27. 2 John 1:10.

Further, they will say that presenting the Gospels in this way will leave many things difficult and obscure, so that simple folk will not be able to understand them, and so may fall into error. . . . But for the same reason, the Gospels should not have been translated into Greek for the Greeks, or into Latin for the Romans; which versions have many difficult and obscure passages, which neither the Greeks nor the Romans can understand. Wherefore it is sufficient that they believe, as our Lord commands, saying "Repent and believe the good news!"[28] . . .

Everyone knows that it is futile to teach a blind man to see the beauty, excellence, and magnificence of the material sun. It is even more impossible to explain in mere words the beauty, excellence, and glory of the Gospel, which is the word of God, a ray from the true spiritual sun which contains within it all beauty, excellence, and glory, and all preeminent goodness. That goodness cannot be known in itself and is made manifest here below only to the internal eye of the spirit—just as the material sun cannot be known by itself nor is it perceived without the external eye of the flesh. But just as the material sun communicates itself through its own natural goodness, so the spiritual sun communicates itself through its supernatural goodness, but much more powerfully, since it is inestimably more beautiful and finer than the material sun. And it communicates itself many times more completely and spiritually to the simple folk, the humble and meek, than to clerics, the proud and mighty, as we know from the word of our Lord spoken through the evangelist Saint Matthew: "I praise you, father, Lord of heaven and earth, because you have hidden these things from the wise and learned, and revealed them to little children."[29] . . .

If there are those who wish to discourage or prevent the people of Jesus Christ from having the Gospel, which is God's own teaching, in their own language, they should know that Jesus Christ commands otherwise, saying through the words of Saint Luke: "Woe to you experts in the law, because you have taken away the key to knowledge. You yourselves have not entered, and you have hindered those who were entering."[30] . . . And did he not make the same point through the words of Saint Mark? "Go into all the world and preach the gospel to all creation."[31] . . . And through the words of Saint Matthew? "[Teach] them to obey everything I have commanded you."[32]

---

28. Mark 1:15. The phrase "good news" is a translation of the word that also means "the Gospel."

29. Matthew 11:25.

30. Luke 11:52.

31. Mark 16:15.

32. Matthew 28:19–20: "Therefore go and make disciples of all nations, baptizing them in the name of the Father and of the Son and of the Holy Spirit, and teaching them to obey everything I have commanded you. And surely I am with you always, to the very end of the age."

And how can they preach the Gospel to all creation, how can they teach the faithful to obey everything that Jesus Christ has commanded, if they prevent simple folk from seeing and reading God's Gospel in their own language? For this obstruction, they will be called to account before the tribunal of the great Judge on the day of judgment, and equally, if they have deceived the people by preaching what they said was the word of God, and it was not.

God says through Esdras, speaking of the Old Law: "Let them read it, both the worthy and the unworthy."[33] . . . Are Christians, the children of God, to be considered less worthy to read the New Law, the law of life and grace, than the ancient Jews, who were slaves? Should we be less worthy to read our Law than are the Jews of this present day to read theirs, who, whenever they are questioned about some passage of their Old Law, can promptly respond? But God speaks of Christians in these words of Jeremiah: "I will put my law in their minds and write it on their hearts."[34] . . . And what is this law, according to the Gospels and the writings of the New Testament? We must not only read it and have it inscribed in material books, but possess it readily in our memory and have it inscribed on our hearts, so that "[our] feet" may be "fitted with the readiness that comes from the gospel of peace."[35] And finally, my brothers and sisters in Jesus Christ, just as this letter began with Saint Paul, so also does it end with Saint Paul. Let us pray as he prayed for the Corinthians that the grace of our Lord Jesus Christ, and the love of God the Father, and the fellowship of the Holy Spirit, be with you all.[36] Amen.

Bernardino Ochino

Where Lefèvre d'Étaples committed himself to the plain text, believing that words alone, if translated into a language the audience could understand, would satisfactorily convey theological meaning, for Bernardino Ochino (1487–1564), the plain text was but a taut skin beneath whose surface lay multiple strata of meaning ready to be probed. He did so most famously in his *Seven Dialogues*, composed separately in the late 1530s and first

---

33. Esdras 4:45: "*Et factum est, cum completi essent quadraginta dies, locutus est Altissimus dicens: priora quae scripsisti in palam pone, et legant dignit et indigni.*" See G. H. Box, ed., *The Ezra-Apocalypse: Being Chapters 3–14 of the Book Commonly Known as 4 Ezra (or II Esdras)* (London: Sir Isaac Pitman and Sons, 1912), 362. Esdras forms part of the biblical apocrypha. The Vulgate book 4 Esdras appears as 2 Esdras in other biblical translations.

34. Jeremiah 31:33.

35. Ephesians 6:15.

36. 2 Corinthians 13:13, verbatim.

published as a volume in 1542. In these little verbal gems, brilliant and sharp-edged as diamonds, he presents a mix of Franciscan mysticism, Reformation Christology, and humanist interiority, all in a distinctly Italian accent. His medium is simple and accessible; the message conveyed is complex and bottomless.

Ochino was a major figure of Italian evangelism, an indigenous reform movement of the early sixteenth century, which also included such notable figures as the Spanish nobleman and humanist, Juan de Valdés, its avatar; high-ranking clerics like Cardinal Gasparo Contarini, the author of the excerpt following this one; and noblewomen like Vittoria Colonna, Giulia Gonzaga, and Caterina Cybo, pious seekers and patrons of those who could guide them. The movement predates Lutheranism and parallels it on some points of doctrine, especially on the critical one of justification by faith. But in part due to its geographical setting, in the land where the pope personally reigned, and in part to the high social rank of many of the leading participants (although Ochino himself was a commoner), the Italian evangelicals did not join the reformers beyond the Alps in parting with the established church. With the establishment of the Roman Inquisition in 1542, most of the evangelicals conformed; a few were captured and persecuted; and some, as did Olympia Morata (see Chapter 4), fled north to Protestant strongholds. Ochino was one of those who fled, departing for Geneva, where John Calvin presided. He journeyed later to England, where he enjoyed a warm reception until, in 1553, a Catholic monarch returned to the throne, and finally to Poland, where, having departed from Protestant as much as from Catholic orthodoxy, he died in isolation.

The Italian evangelicals, while they certainly advocated the reform of corrupt church institutions, were primarily intent on pursuing an inward piety: the examination of the self, and a personal communion with the divine. To this extent, they were Erasmians, for Erasmus' criticism of church practices and promotion of a deeply personal piety were widely read throughout Europe, despite attempts to censor his works. But in Italy this Christian humanism was also tinged by mysticism, a strong current in that region, and by a new Christology similar to that advanced by Luther's followers. Christ's suffering on the cross won for all the faithful the expiation of sins; those who repented, confessed their sins, and affirmed their faith were "justified"—that is, made just, though they had behaved unjustly. The crucified Christ was the center of this doctrinal innovation, as he had been the object of veneration by medieval mystics.

The crucified Christ, and the related doctrine of justification by faith, is the subject as well of Ochino's fourth dialogue, excerpted here.[37] A favored humanist genre encountered earlier in this volume in Alamanno Rinuccini's *On Liberty* (see Chapter 3), the dialogue permitted an interplay of ideas that

---

37. First published in 1540; all seven dialogues were printed together for the first time in 1542; in both cases by the Venetian printer Zoppino.

fostered a complexity and openness not found in, for instance, the treatise, or even the letter. Ochino's dialogue, mirroring the conversational culture of Italian evangelicism, which unfolded in domestic gatherings, presents a drama where the less-vocal interlocutor, seeking guidance, is drawn into a deeper understanding of the matter at hand by a skilled and persuasive companion. The guide—in the fourth dialogue identified only as "a man"—is an expert, as Ochino was: a Franciscan preacher who went on to join the new Capuchin order, rising to become its Vicar General. His interlocutor, identified as "a woman," asks the question that triggers the discussion and comments along the way. But the coaxing voice of the man is dominant, and his words win the woman over to a deeper faith, much as in the real world the evangelical Ochino won over his patroness Caterina Cybo.

The dialogue opens with the woman's statement that she is "stupefied" by the "abyss" that is the scene at the cross: Jesus is alone, his lacerated body hanging from the cross, placed between two others on which common criminals hung; he has been "denied by Peter, betrayed by Judas, deserted by his followers, persecuted by the Jews, scorned by the Gentiles, discredited before all. . . ." Only his mother and the other women remained with him. While those who had known him, heard him, and witnessed his miraculous powers lost their faith in Jesus, one "wretched thief, stupid and ignorant," acquired his. The woman asks the man to explain how this came to be. The man does so, engaging in an extended meditation on Luke 23:39–43, the few brief lines of scripture that sketch these events.

The suffering of Christ triggers the thief's compassion: he is in anguish, "but without perturbation, rather with a look of elation: he seemed to rejoice in the shedding of his blood." The thief realizes that Jesus is truly the son of God, and when he turns to Christ in his weakness and humility, "Christ, responding, illumined him." For the evangelicals, as for some mystics and heretics of this era, who were variously referred to in Italy and Spain as *illuminati* or *alumbrados*, that is, "illuminated ones," the person who received divine grace was "illumined" by God. Artfully, Ochino introduces this concept here: the dying Christ, physically powerless but all powerful in his divinity, can with his glance "illumine," or confer grace upon, the distraught and needy thief.

At this point, Ochino introduces another theological principle: that of election. The "good" thief, the one who in his extremity turns to Christ, hangs on the cross at Christ's right side, and is identified with the multitude of the elect who will be saved not because of their merits but by the grace of God (an explicitly Lutheran concept); the unrepentant thief, in contrast, who mocks Jesus and feels no compassion for him, hangs at his left, and is identified with the multitude of the reprobate who for their sins will be consigned to eternal damnation. The good thief is saved at the moment when he acknowledges, in one breath, his own sinfulness and Christ's perfect innocence (Luke 23:40–41): "And so he stands for all the elect who are saved only by the goodness, kindness and mercy of God."

By confessing his sin, the good thief "showed that his suffering was just, while the innocent Christ's was not," and that Christ suffered, not for his sin, but for all sinners. Calling him "Christ" and "Lord," the thief acknowledges his divinity and so makes his plea: "remember me, when you have come into your kingdom" (Luke 23:42). How humble is his request! It is as though the thief says: "I do not deserve to be in heaven at your side, with the other saints, nor to live in paradise with the blessed; it will be enough for me if you do only this, hold me living in your memory; and even if I shall be damned, remember from time to time me; and if I know that you will remember me, I shall consider myself blessed, even if I am condemned to be punished eternally."

Christ responds to the thief's great humility, bypassing and forgiving his sins: "Truly, I tell you that today you will be with me in paradise" (Luke 23:43). The "man" comments, explicating the significance of Christ's promise: "See what a great gift he bestows: for the thief asked only to be remembered, but Christ promised him paradise. And when? That very same day. And with whom? With Christ—oh, what a companion! And for how long? For all eternity. And to whom was this great promise made? To a depraved thief. . . ."

He expands further: the thief will accompany Christ when he descends to Limbo to rescue the saints of the Old Testament; will ascend with him into the heavens; will enjoy his triumph and glory for all eternity. "Was it not a prodigious thing that on that holy Friday, when the windows of heaven were thrown open to reveal the divine treasure, and when Christ so fervidly spent his blood, spilling out from his wounds the new wine of divine love and pouring forth his grace in such abundance, that a thief was illumined and saved?"

This haunting dialogue, with its probing exploration of the mind of the penitent thief and the merciful Christ, draws on mystical and reform traditions alike. It interlaces a highly visualized drama with the theology of illumination and election and above all, of the salvation of sinners by divine grace only, their justification by faith alone.

Bernardino Ochino, *Dialogue about the Thief on the Cross* (1540)

SPEAKERS: A MAN AND A WOMAN[38]

WOMAN: Who is not stupefied at the abyss that God ordained? Christ on the cross, his body torn and close to death; denied by Peter, betrayed by Judas,

---

38. The speakers may be identified as Ochino himself and his pupil and protector, Caterina Cybo, duchess of Camerino.

deserted by his followers, persecuted by the Jews, scorned by the Gentiles, discredited before all, except only his stricken mother, the glorious Virgin Mary? Yet at that very moment a wretched thief began to believe in him, when the others ceased to believe: those who had spoken with Christ, heard his promises, seen his sinlessness and power, his overflowing love, his matchless, holy, and profound humility, his prodigious signs and miracles. They had read the prophets and studied the Scriptures and plumbed their meaning and seen all this revealed in Christ; and with all this, still they lost faith in him. For he hung from the cross without performing miracles, and failed to glorify himself by acting like God. And yet this one wretched thief, stupid and ignorant, who had read nothing nor studied the Scriptures, who had seen no signs or miracles and had no other proofs, not having seen Christ, or heard him speak, yet he, in pain and anguish on the cross and seeing Christ in such great suffering and on the edge of death, believes that he is God and hopes to gain paradise from the one who cried on the cross, "My God, my God, why have you forsaken me?"[39] Please explain to me how he came to have such great faith. . . .

MAN: Looking at Christ, the good thief sees that he suffered greatly but without perturbation, rather with a look of elation: he seemed to rejoice in the shedding of his blood. He saw Christ's burning tears fall to the earth, and his ardent, flaming sighs rise to heaven. He heard his impassioned words; observed his godly deeds and acts, his wonderful patience, his boundless love, his endless perseverance, and his other divine virtues. All these aroused in him the belief that truly, this was the son of God. God does not disappoint those who turn to him. In his weakness, the thief turned to God, and Christ, responding, illumined him. If the other thief had turned to God as much as he could, enabled by divine grace, which never fails, he too would have been illumined, because just as Christ, like a true and divine sun, was born and lived for all, so also he died for all. He looked on the thief to his right with his eye of mercy, and perhaps also his bodily eye, just as he had looked at Peter.[40]

Accordingly, the thief also represents the elect who will be on Christ's right when they ascend to paradise not because of their merits but because of those of Jesus Christ, while the doomed will be on the left, having damned themselves by their sins.[41] Yet no one should despair on this account, seeing that

---

39. Matthew 27:46. All biblical quotations are from the NIV.

40. Ugo Rozzo, in his edition of Ochino's *I dialogi sette e altri scritti del tempo della fuga* (Turin: Claudiana, 1985), followed by Rita Belladonna, in her translation of the *Seven Dialogues* (Ottawa, Canada: Dovehouse Editions, 1988), interpret this comment about Peter as referring to Acts 5:15, where Peter's shadow cast on the ill cures them, but the text does not seem to support this reading.

41. A theological point: the elect win salvation because of Christ's sacrifice, not their own works, while the damned suffer for the sins they have committed; but if the thief on the cross can be forgiven, such grace is possible for all.

this thief, in all his depravity, at the very last minute was saved—who had truthfully said to Christ, as he hung on the cross, as is read in the gospel of Luke: "We are punished justly, for we are getting what our deeds deserve. But this man has done nothing wrong."[42] And so he stands for all the elect who are saved only by the goodness, kindness, and mercy of God.

Was it not a prodigious thing that on that holy Friday, when the windows of heaven were thrown open to reveal the divine treasure, and when Christ so fervidly spent his blood, spilling out from his wounds the new wine of divine love and pouring forth his grace in such abundance, that a thief was illumined and saved? Oh how great was his faith, his hope, and his love! He offered to Christ his heart and all his love, his thoughts, his tongue that spoke, the words he said; and he offered all these while hanging on the cross, first confessing his sins and not only his, but those of all sinners, for in his person he stood for all of them.[43] . . .

The good thief, while on the cross, by confessing his sin showed that his suffering was just, while the innocent Christ's was not: "This man has not sinned, but suffers for us and for our sins, out of his pure goodness and super-abundant love. We must therefore grieve for him, and thank him, because it is for us and not for himself that he suffers, and by praying for us, he forgives us." And the penitent thief continued, rebuking the other thief: "Do you not fear God, even on the cross and near to death?"[44] And then he prayed: "Christ, Lord, remember me, when you have come into your kingdom."[45]

See how, by calling him "Lord," the thief announces his divinity. See how his faith is full of divine wisdom: he did not ask for a meaningless but for a divine thing, only that he might be remembered. See how profound is his humility, as if he had said: "I do not deserve to be in heaven at your side, with the other saints, nor to live in paradise with the blessed; it will be enough for me if you do only this, hold me living in your memory; and even if I shall be damned, from time to time remember me; and if I know that you will remember me, I shall consider myself blessed, even if I am condemned to be punished eternally."

---

42. The text reads, incorrectly, Matthew 27, but the only fitting passage is Luke 23:39–41: "One of the criminals who hung there hurled insults at him: 'Aren't you the Messiah? Save yourself and us!' But the other criminal rebuked him. 'Don't you fear God,' he said, 'since you are under the same sentence? We are punished justly, for we are getting what our deeds deserve. But this man has done nothing wrong.'"

43. Just as Christ, in saving the thief by his mercy, bestows salvation on all the elect, so the thief, in confessing his sins and turning to Christ in his last moments, wins salvation not only for himself but also for all sinners.

44. Cf. Luke 23:40, given above, note 42.

45. Luke 23:42: "Then he said, 'Jesus, remember me when you come into your kingdom.'"

Oh, what great courage and constancy, that while he hung from the cross in such torment, he raised himself upwards not thinking of himself but only of Christ! How modestly he submitted to the divine will, distributing all with perfect justice:[46] to God, glory and honor; to himself, the loss and pain and punishment merited by the worst of thieves. For this reason, Christ replied to him most sweetly: "Truly, I tell you that today you will be with me in paradise." Not only did Christ promise him paradise, but so as to affirm the promise also added: "Truly," as though to say: "You may be certain, do not doubt, you have been a wretch and a thief, and you see me suffering on the cross, but nonetheless, you shall be with me today in paradise."[47] See what a great gift he bestows: for the thief asked only to be remembered, but Christ promised him paradise. And when? That very same day. And with whom? With Christ—oh, what a companion! And for how long? For all eternity. And to whom was this great promise made? To a depraved thief, who hung on a cross for his crimes, and who not long before had mocked his savior. And for what reason was he promised paradise? Because he had asked only to be remembered.

WOMAN: This thief, I am certain, is in paradise, because Christ has said so. And I think, too, that he is a great saint, who is specially favored.

MAN: First of all, he alone of all the elect merited to suffer with Christ the torment of the cross and be his companion. He alone with his whole heart joined the Virgin Mother in trusting in Christ and feeling his pain. He alone, on that day when all the others fled, fearlessly and publicly preached from the pulpit of the cross Christ's innocence and divinity. . . . He asked for grace while Christ was pouring it out for all, and when, by dying, gave it to all, and so it is likely he received it in abundance. . . . And is the first of all the elect; for I believe that he stands next to Christ in glory, as he hung next to him on the cross. . . .

This is what the thief on the cross meant to say: "When you will come into your kingdom, to which you are the natural heir and which you won for us with your precious blood, when you will be, I do not say great as in the present life, since your kingdom is not of this world, but when you will be in your heavenly realm, remember me—not my sins, not my failings, not my wretchedness, not the crimes I have committed, but remember that I am a weak and lowly man, that I am your creature bearing your image and likeness and formed by you for blessedness; remember that you created everything for me, that for me you clothed yourself in human flesh, for me you preached,

---

46. Interestingly, the two virtues named in this phrase—*temperanza* and *giustizia*—are two of the four cardinal virtues, whose origins are classical, not Christian.

47. Luke 23:43.

you fasted, you prayed, you slept on the ground, you wore yourself out, and for me you have suffered these thirty-three years; remember that I am your kin and that you will die for me.

"I do not ask for much, because I am not worthy of much. I am too ashamed to beg that so great a villain as I am be admitted to paradise. I know that that is not a place for me and that you have a thousand reasons not to want me there. I don't ask to be allowed to go there to wait on the citizens of heaven, for I do not merit that. I ask only to inhabit your memory. You must not forget those for whom you shed so much blood and suffer so much pain, for your companions on the cross. Do not consider my wickedness, but only your supreme goodness, which open the window to your treasury.

"But hoping to obtain grace, I ask for your charity. If it were only possible I would wish, at this last hour, to steal heaven, just as I have in this life stolen the things of this world. I have heard you pray to the Father for those who have nailed you on the cross, forgiving them with such sweetness, saying that they do not know what they do;[48] so you should not be surprised that I cry out in prayer to you. I have seen that you have appointed your mother the mother of all sinners,[49] so that from her abundant love she may thirst for our salvation; so I have summoned up the courage to ask. I am on the cross as you see, and I have three crosses in my heart more bitter than this one. One is the sorrow I have for my companion, who does not repent. A second is the fear I have of hell. The third is the sorrow I feel for you and for your mother. If only I knew that, in heaven, you would remember me, all the crosses would be sweet to me."

Then Christ replied: "Today is that day of eternity where nothing is, or was, or will be, but all is present in this moment. You will—because now we are still within the realm of time—be with me in paradise; you will see my divine essence, you will see me rescue from Limbo all the saints of the Old Testament,[50] and with the heavens opened wide, you will ascend with me into the Empyrean[51] with all the other saints, and there you will rejoice with me forever in triumph and glory." . . .

---

48. Luke 23:34: "Father, forgive them, for they do not know what they are doing."

49. A reference to the Catholic teaching that the Virgin Mary takes pity on sinners and intercedes for them with her son Jesus.

50. It was generally believed that the souls of unbaptized infants and of the just who died before the coming of Christ lived in the otherworldly abode of Limbo. Traditionally it was understood, based on the apocryphal gospels of Bartholomew and Nicodemus, that Christ, having descended into hell after his crucifixion, released the Old Testament saints and took them with him into heaven. See Belladonna ed., 92n22.

51. For the Greeks, the fiery sphere of the highest heaven; for the Christians, the heavenly home of God and his angels.

We too, like Christ, shall find ourselves on the cross of those who suffer the torments of death, placed between two thieves, that is, the good angel and the bad,[52] and often our relatives who hover nearby like real thieves, for they hunger for our goods and care nothing for our souls—which is why it is better to give them away and prepare oneself now, because on the point of death it is difficult to dispose of them.[53] But the conversion of the thief, just as it was the last miracle Christ performed, so too was it his greatest; which is why, your Excellency,[54] you should not delay, nor should you despair, when you find yourself in a similar situation. Therefore, following the example of this good thief, seek to live always in the memory not of those of this world, which cannot profit you, and in this way you will end in oblivion, but seek to live joyfully in the memory of Christ, through love and virtue. Christ in glory will not forget us if we always hold in our memory his bitter suffering on the cross.

Gasparo Contarini *et alii*

Nearly a century after Lorenzo Valla threw down a gauntlet, challenging the historical and legal basis for papal claims to authority, the Venetian humanist, statesman, and Cardinal Gasparo Contarini (1483–1542), as head of a committee appointed to propose a reform agenda, threw down another—a velvet one, with no iron fist inside—and communicated in well-mannered tones, without denunciations or fulminations. The *Report on the Reform of the Church*, detailing twenty-six improprieties and abuses and presented to Pope Paul III in March 1537, became a key document of Catholic reform. Its recommendations were incorporated in the decrees that would issue from the Council of Trent, an assembly that met intermittently from 1545 to 1563 to reinvent the church for the challenges of the next several centuries.

The report, of which excerpts are given here, opens with an expression of confidence in the pope's intention to lead the reform of the church, and describes the charge given to Contarini's committee. It then proceeds to the longest part of the document, which identifies a number of improprieties[55]

---

52. In the *ars moriendi* ("art of dying") tradition at this time popular among pious lay Christians, at death, a good angel struggles for possession of the soul, and a bad angel tempts the dying person to sin.

53. A tradition of literature *de bene moriendi*, advising "how to die well," urged Christians to prepare for death by giving away belongings and preparing their souls.

54. The Duchess Caterina Cybo of Camerino, the interlocutor termed the "Woman."

55. The later discussion makes clear that these are labeled as "abuses."

widely practiced by the clergy at all levels and tolerated by their superiors. These include the ordination[56] of persons unsuited for the priesthood, and, by a variety of devices and subterfuges that the committee details, the appropriation of church revenues by individual clergymen.

A second category of abuses concerns the direction, too often descending to misdirection, of lay Christians by clerics. Bishops and priests who do not reside in their diocese or parish are guilty of such malfeasance, as are Cardinals who absent themselves from the Curia, and so fail to perform their responsibilities as papal servants. Also at fault are the rules and practices that impede bishops from correcting corrupt clergy, and the scandalous laxity of some of the religious orders. The public teaching of false doctrine by school teachers and university professors is likewise lamented, as well as the instruction of the young in Latin from the *Colloquies*, a series of dialogues written by Erasmus—which meanwhile introduce heretical notions into innocent minds. Notably, the tendency to suppress free expression that would be endorsed at Trent is already conspicuous here, in a document that otherwise would have been approved by reformers anywhere in Europe.

A third set of problems concerns privileges granted by the pope for a variety of purposes: allowing clerics to discard their clerical habit or to marry, or allowing laymen barred by consanguinity to marry, and such like. A final category of abuses concerns the governance of the city of Rome, over which the pope has titular authority: the sloth and untidiness of the priests of St. Peter's, the papal church; the parading of prostitutes in public places; riotous outbreaks of enmity between different citizen factions; the care of widows and orphans in the city's hospitals—all require the exercise of papal authority through the cardinals of his church.

Contarini and his colleagues have gathered under these headings some of the kinds of behavior that horrified some and amused others, but which no onlookers could deem acceptable or accordant with the mission of the Roman church. In doing so, they offer the pope and the participants in the Council of Trent a recipe for reform.[57] They do not, however, to any extent address deeper forms of spiritual dissatisfaction that had arisen well before Martin Luther raised his stentorian voice and forced the church to take note. The craving for authenticity, heard already in Valla; the yearning for a deep experience of union with the divine, voiced by innumerable saints and mystics from the fourteenth to the sixteenth centuries; the demand for a direct encounter with the Biblical text, and through it the word of God, of which Lefèvre so eloquently spoke; the hunger for justification and redemption,

---

56. Priests were admitted to their duties and privileges, which included the power to celebrate the Mass, the central ritual of Catholic worship, by the sacrament of ordination.

57. Contarini's own earlier work *De officio viri boni et probi episcopi* (On the Office of the Bishop, 1516), edited and translated by John Patrick Donnelly as *Office of a Bishop* (Milwaukee: Marquette University Press, 2002), also placed hope for the regeneration of the church in the proper performance of the clergy.

which drove the Lutheran movement, and which is captured in the words of Ochino: these are ignored by the reform commission of 1537.

But they are not unaware of them—at least, Contarini is not. In his long and varied career as an author of humanist works,[58] a polished statesman, and a recruit unsullied by ecclesiastical intrigues to the high office of cardinal, Contarini had known profoundly inspired pioneers of Christian reform—conspicuous among them, his two close friends Tommaso Giustiniani and Vincenzo Quirini,[59] who had abandoned their successful political careers to undertake lives of spiritual retreat, repentance, and renewal. And Contarini himself leaned in that direction, believing more, as a result of a youthful spiritual crisis, in the route to salvation offered by divine grace than by external works. He participated in the evangelical movement of the *Spirituali* ("Spirituals") and supported the Theatines, a circle of clerics calling for the renewed commitment of those holding religious office. And in 1541, sent by the pope to the conference held at Regensburg that was a last attempt to reunite Protestant insurgents and Catholic loyalists, Contarini strayed from strict Catholic positions on such issues as justification by faith and the nature of the Eucharist, and very nearly accepted Protestant ones. In 1542, soon after he returned to Italy, he died. At that time and ever since, many have suspected that this consummate papal servitor—as it would be appear from the Catholic standpoint—had himself veered into heresy.

That heretical predilection, certainly, was in no way evident in the text of the *Report on the Reform of the Church*, composed just five years earlier. Rather it mapped a conservative path to reform, prescribing incremental steps to be taken toward the rectification of wrongs, without confronting the heartfelt longings of the many Christian faithful who had already, by this time, left the old church behind.

Gasparo Contarini *et alii, Report on the Reform of the Church* (1537)

Most Holy Father, we do not have the words to express the enormous gratitude that Christendom[60] owes to Almighty God for having named you pope, and made you, in these times, the pastor of his flock; and for having formed in your mind that intention you have, we cannot even begin to imagine how

---

58. Contarini is perhaps best known for his treatise on the Venetian constitution: *La republica e i magistrati di Vinegia* (The Republic and the Magistrates of Venice, 1520), of which a facsimile edition, with valuable introduction, has been edited by Vittorio Conti (Florence: Centro editoriale toscano, 2003). In his youth, he had received a thorough classical education at the university of Padua, along with a philosophical and theological one.

59. Contarini's relationship with these reformers is detailed in the classic article of J. B. Ross, "Gasparo Contarini and His Friends," *Studies in the Renaissance,* 17 (1970): 192–232.

60. Contarini's phrase is literally the "Christian republic."

great must be our gratitude. For the Spirit of God . . . has decreed that you will rescue the church of Christ which is now crumbling—or rather, it has wholly collapsed—and undertake the repair of this ruin, as we now see you doing, lifting it up to its pristine sublimity and restoring its pristine splendor. We intend to execute to the letter this divine decree: we whom you have called upon to identify, without regard for your ease or for any other consideration, those abuses, or really, those deadly plagues, which have long afflicted the church of God and especially this Roman curia,[61] which increasingly infected and overcome by these pestiferous ills, have become the hopeless morass now before us. . . .

> *These evils have come about because earlier popes allowed themselves to be misled; but the present pope is determined to exert leadership over the church, and correct them.*

You have sent, then, for us, though inexperienced and unprepared for so great a mission, yet inflamed with more than a little zeal both for your honor and glory and above all for the restoration of the church of Christ; and you have commanded us in weighty words to catalogue all the abuses and reveal them to you, warning that we shall be held to account if we are negligent or insufficient in performing this task required of us by Almighty God. And so that we can speak of all these matters freely among ourselves and convey them to you, you have bound us by an oath, under pain of excommunication, not to divulge any of our deliberations to anyone. . . .

> *The compilation that follows of problems to be resolved mostly concern the universal church, over which the pope rules; but some matters having to do with the local situation in Rome, over which the pope is also ruler, will also be noted. Before beginning, the point needs to be established that the law must be obeyed, and must not be set aside without due cause.*

So with this principle established, we may proceed. Now your holiness manages the church of Christ with the assistance of many agents, through whom you act. These are all clerics, however, to whom is entrusted the worship of God: namely many priests and their curates and above all bishops. Accordingly, if the governance of the church is to be carried on rightly, care must be taken that these agents are suited for the office they must perform.

The first abuse in this category is the ordination of clerics and especially priests, where no care has been taken, no diligence applied, lest any ignorant, basely-born, immoral, or under-aged candidates happen to be admitted to holy orders and especially to the priesthood, in which office they must

---

61. The prelates and bureaucrats surrounding the pope and constituting the central administration of the church.

absolutely be fit to serve as the representative of Christ. This laxity results in numerous scandals, in contempt for the clergy, and in not merely the diminution but the utter extinction of reverence for divine worship. . . .

A recommendation is made for proper supervision of the process of the selection of candidates for ordination.

A second abuse of great consequence concerns the assignment of ecclesiastical benefices, especially of parish benefices and above all of bishoprics, so as increasingly to profit those upon whom the benefices are conferred, rather than the people or church of Christ. In conferring these benefices on parish priests, therefore, but even more on bishops, care must absolutely be taken to give them to good and learned men, who can adequately perform by themselves the offices they hold—and on those, in addition, who will actually live in residence where they are assigned, so a benefice in Spain or Britain should not be conferred on an Italian, or vice versa. . . .

Another abuse concerns the payment of income from benefices which are conferred or transferred to others—indeed, often the person ceding the benefice reserves all the income for himself! . . . To seize and reserve all the income which should be given for the support of the worship of God and of the person holding the benefice is a great abuse. So also, certainly, is the granting of pensions to wealthy clerics who can comfortably and respectably live on their income. Both abuses must end.

Another abuse arises from the transfers of benefices done by secret agreements, which are all simoniacal,[62] having no purpose other than profit.

Another abuse to be rooted out, devised by some crafty operators, is now spreading in the Curia. While the law forbids benefices from being bequeathed by will, since they do not belong to the testator but to the church, and so that ecclesiastical property be preserved for the common good of all, and not diverted into private hands, yet human skill—certainly not divine—has invented various devices by which this law may be foiled. . . .

Various devices currently in practice for retaining benefices even after they have been resigned, in effect appointing an heir; for passing a benefice on to a son; and for reserving the right to a benefice in expectation of the present holder's death; and for holding several benefices at once, a "plurality of benefices."

Another growing abuse is the practice of conferring bishoprics on cardinals, or worse, that of conferring not merely one but several. We think that this practice, most Holy Father, is of great moment in the church of God—principally because the offices of cardinal and bishop are incompatible. For the

---

62. Simony is the practice of the sale of church offices.

office of the cardinal is to assist your holiness in governing the universal church, while the office of the bishop is to tend to his flock, which he can scarcely perform well and properly unless he lives with his sheep, as a shepherd with his flock. . . .

> *This practice is especially harmful because the cardinals are principal members of the church hierarchy and must set an example for others; moreover, if they solicit bishoprics from princes of states, they cannot properly exert authority over those rulers.*

With these abuses corrected, which pertain to the management of your agents, through whom as through instruments both the worship of God can be carried on properly and Christian folk can be instructed and guided in the Christian way of life, we must now approach those matters concerning the governance of Christ's people. On that issue, most Holy Father, this abuse must be corrected first and foremost: neither bishops, above all, nor even parish priests should be absent from their churches and parishes, except for some grave cause, but live in residence; especially bishops, as we said, because they are the bridegrooms of the churches entrusted to them.

> *Because of such absences of their pastors from churches, the churches themselves are emptied of worshipers. The rule should be established that a bishop may not be absent from his church for more than three Sundays.*

It is also an abuse that so many cardinals are absent from this Roman curia, and in no way perform the duties required of them as cardinals. . . .

Another great abuse which must not be tolerated, which scandalizes all Christian people, stems from the obstacles faced by bishops in governing their flocks, which impede them from correcting and punishing corrupt clergy. . . . It is impossible to express, most Holy Father, how greatly this scandal outrages the Christian public. Put an end to these practices, we beg your holiness by the blood of Christ, so as to redeem your church and cleanse it in that same blood; put an end to these crimes, which if they were to infect any secular state or realm, it would immediately fall into ruin and could no longer stand; and yet we permit these monstrosities to corrupt our state of Christendom.

Another abuse that must be corrected concerns the religious orders, of which many have deteriorated to such an extent that they scandalize the laity and injure everyone by their example. . . .

> *"All conventual orders" should be done away with, by not admitting newcomers, and releasing all resident boys who have not yet taken vows. Clearly, this instruction applies not to all monasteries but the less strict mendicant ones, often called "conventual" because of the branch of the Franciscans known as*

the "Conventuals." Also recommended is the careful screening of mendicant friars allowed to become priests or confessors; the barring of personal enrichment by the papal representatives called legates and nuncios; and the stricter supervision of nuns.

Another great and pernicious abuse is found in the public schools,[63] especially in Italy, in which many professors of philosophy teach impious doctrines. They hold impious disputations in churches—or, if not impious, still they concern religious matters, which are improperly discussed by laymen in these public settings. We recommend, therefore, that in those dioceses where these public schools are found, the bishops be ordered to caution the instructors not to teach the youth such impieties, but rather declare the inadequacy of natural reason in matters pertaining to God—such as whether the universe is created or eternal, and such like[64]—and direct them in the path of piety. Likewise, disputations about such issues should be banned, or about any theological matters, for they arouse the disrespect of the laity, but all disputations about these matters should be private, and public disputations should be confined to the discussion of the natural sciences.[65] And all other bishops should be similarly charged, especially those presiding in the major cities, where these sorts of disputations are frequently held.

The same diligence must be exercised also with regard to the printing of books.[66] All rulers should be instructed in writing to take care that books not be indiscriminately printed in their jurisdictions, but that such activity should be subject to clerical supervision. And since schoolboys are now often taught Latin from the *Colloquies* of Erasmus,[67] in which there are many things

---

63. Not "public" in our sense, in the United States of the twenty-first century: these were lay schools endowed by city or princely governments, or managed by individual teachers who received tuition payments from their pupils, or universities chartered by the church but usually governed by the state. The "professors" are not necessarily university-level teachers, and "philosophy" in this era includes an omnibus of liberal arts subjects.

64. The notion of the eternity of the world was much discussed in the fourteenth through sixteenth centuries in the wake of the introduction of the works of the Arab philosopher Averroes to the university curriculum, but was deemed heretical, since it obviated a divine creation.

65. In the terms of that era, to "physics" or "natural philosophy," leaving metaphysics and theology out of the public sphere.

66. At this moment, printing was nearly a century old, and books were flying off the presses, especially in Italy, the homeland of the church, which struggled with secular authorities to retain control of granting permission to print.

67. The *Colloquies* of Erasmus, first published in 1518, consisted of a series of dramatic conversations, written in a lively Latin prose that introduced schoolboys to Latin grammar and vocabulary, while encouraging them at the same time to question the abuses and contradictions of contemporary church practice.

which teach impiety to young learners, that book and others like it should be prohibited in the grammar schools.[68]

> *Another category of abuse is that of papal privileges, granted to particular groups in contravention of established rules. Among them, the granting of these privileges should most particularly be halted: allowing monks and friars not to wear the habit of their order; allowing someone in Holy Orders to take a wife; allowing marriages between persons closely related by blood; absolving those guilt of simony (the sale of church office); permitting the alteration of testaments to divert to individuals wealth bequeathed to pious causes; and the bequest of ecclesiastical property.*

Having explained in brief as best we could all matters which pertain to the pope as head of the universal church, it remains to make a few points about his role as bishop of Rome.[69] The city and church of Rome is the mother and teacher of all other churches; here, accordingly, the worship of God and propriety of morals must both strongly flourish. For this reason, most Holy father, visitors to the church of St. Peter are shocked when they enter to find that the priests celebrating mass there are disheveled, uncouth, and clothed in paraments and robes not even suitable for the lowliest churches. All consider this a great scandal. . . .

In this city, as well, prostitutes walk through the streets as freely as do respectable matrons, or ride about on mules, attended in broad daylight by members of the households of cardinals, both noblemen and clerics.[70] In no other city do we see this corruption except in the one which should set an example for all. These whores also live in splendid houses. This shameful abuse must be corrected.

Hatred and conflict among the private citizens also prevail in this city, which it is especially the interest of the bishop to resolve and reconcile.[71] For this purpose he may call upon those cardinals who are themselves Roman, who are especially suited to settle these enmities and soothe the passions of the citizens.

The oversight of the hospitals and the care of orphans and widows are a principal concern of the bishop and of the city government. Your Holiness,

---

68. Grammar schools were those where Latin and sometimes Greek were taught to students likely to advance to the university or to administrative positions in church or state.

69. The pope was at once the head of the "universal church," the Roman church in Western Europe (and now worldwide), and the bishop of Rome, the city in which the papacy resided.

70. The cardinals, aptly called the "princes" of the church, maintained large palaces staffed by lay and clerical assistants, who in the sum made up their "household."

71. Often violent quarrels among the noble families of Rome were enduring and endemic.

therefore, can easily manage these responsibilities through the worthy men who are your cardinals.

These are the abuses, most Holy Father, which we have identified at present, so far as we have been able, and which we believe must be corrected. Now you, by your goodness and wisdom, will take the lead. Although the magnitude of the task far exceeds our capacity, yet we certainly have satisfied our consciences, and nurture the greatest hope that under your leadership we may see the church of God purified, as lovely as a dove, at peace within itself, unified in purpose, to the eternal memory of your name. You took for yourself the name of Paul;[72] we hope you will imitate the love of Paul. He was chosen as the vessel to bring the name of Christ to all people;[73] you, we hope, have been chosen to restore in our hearts and our works the name of Christ, now forgotten by all peoples and all churchmen, to heal our diseases, to guide the sheep of Christ into one fold, and to avert from us the wrath of God and his vengeance, which we deserve, which is already prepared and soon descends upon our heads.

The names of nine signatories follow, with that of Cardinal Gasparo Contarini, as president, at the head.

---

72. Upon being raised to the papacy, each pope chooses a new name, generally one held by his predecessors or by the apostles.

73. Acts 9:15.

Chapter 8: Humanism, Science, and Philosophy

Introduction

In the previous chapter, it was seen that humanism, though often considered hostile to religion, in fact was deeply engaged with contemporary religious movements, while humanist works often gave expression to profound religious feeling. In the same way, humanism is often seen as indifferent or even adverse to contemporary developments in science and philosophy. But as this chapter shows, humanism was intertwined in complex ways with these seemingly incompatible intellectual movements.

The perception that humanism was antithetical to science and philosophy has some basis. Humanism was enamored of words. Along with the recovery of ancient texts, the imitation of classical models of verbal expression was a key pursuit of the humanists, who were generally interested far more in the analysis of language than in the observance of natural events. Science (the term was not yet used, but by the sixteenth century some intellectuals were engaged in investigations that in hindsight many would consider to be scientific) does the reverse. It is concerned with *things* more than with *words*: what things are made of, how they function, how they interact.

Philosophy, like humanism, is concerned with language—again, the term philosophy had a broader meaning in the Renaissance than it does in modern times, precisely because of the contributions of seventeenth-century philosophers. But philosophy uses language to describe vast systems to which the humanists were largely indifferent: systems we would today call metaphysical, ontological, epistemological, and so on. While philosophers asked about the nature of the universe, of being, and of knowledge, humanists were concerned with matters nearer by: the history of Florence, or the purpose of marriage, or the duties of the ruler. And while philosophers sought to build systems that were all-encompassing and explained everything, humanists avoided systems and focused on particulars. Moreover, humanists detested the language of the philosophers; for as the latter molded language to the technical needs of their craft, they denuded it of the stylistic niceties the humanists cherished.

Yet the pursuits of humanism, science, and philosophy intersected each other at key moments as they developed from the late fifteenth to the early seventeenth centuries. Four exemplary cases are presented in this chapter, ranging from 1473/1474 to as late as 1637, chronologically the outer limit of the texts considered in this volume. These dates take us from the heart of the Italian Renaissance to approximately that point when it can be said the Renaissance had waned and modernity had begun.

Marsilio Ficino (1433–1499), the first of these figures, is both wholly a philosopher and wholly a humanist. As a philosopher, he translated into Latin the complete works of the Greek philosopher Plato, previously unavailable to most of the European intellectual elite. He also wrote commentaries on several of the Platonic dialogues, and in his original treatises, integrated the Platonic philosophical legacy with Neoplatonism and other late-ancient and medieval streams of thought and, even more ambitiously, with Christianity. The linguistic skills he required to perform this mammoth work of intellectual synthesis derived, of course, from his humanist training. As a humanist, he also lived the intellectual issues that Plato raised, gathering about him in the flesh and through his correspondence a large circle of humanists and humanistically-trained statesmen, diplomats, and clerics, creating a community of intellectual endeavor not yet fractured by the collapse of religious and cultural unity in the sixteenth century.

Nicholas Copernicus (1473–1543), a cleric, canon lawyer, mathematician, and astronomer, who wrote little before his monumental *On the Revolutions of the Celestial Spheres*, published in the year of his death, was no humanist, yet was indebted to humanism. He had encountered humanism in the Italian universities where he spent some years of his youth, far from his home on the German-Polish border. He studied Greek, and he scoured the books of ancient Greek astronomers to find the key to the problem he posed for himself: how to resolve the contradictions and imperfections of the then-prevailing Ptolemaic world system. While his humanistic inquiry triggered his thinking, however, it was his empirical and theoretical work that in time yielded the new Copernican hypothesis.

Galileo Galilei (1564–1642), reared in the cultural world Ficino had known and helped form, was the product of a thoroughly humanistic education, and drew on that resource when, over the course of thirty years, he poured out a flood of treatises, dialogues, and letters, in Latin and Italian, on subjects ranging from sunspots to the strength of materials to the proper interpretation of the Bible. Yet he was above all a scientist, on the frontier of modern scientific method, who approached the problem of the motion of terrestrial bodies by performing empirical experiments, and that of the motions of celestial bodies by probing the heavens with a telescope, a device of his own invention. By these methods, he validated the Copernican hypothesis, provoking the hostility of churchmen who could not tolerate so eloquent a defender of a new world system.

René Descartes (1596–1650), finally, had received at a Jesuit school an education as profoundly humanistic as Galileo's—a humanism reflected in the chatty, autobiographical passages of his *Discourse on Method,* which states in a nutshell the metaphysics he would develop in full in later works. The *Discourse* strikingly opens with an extended display of self-exploration—much in the mode of Descartes' humanist predecessors Petrarch and Montaigne—which culminates in the establishment of a new metaphysics on the basis of the stability and certainty of the self's existence. In these pages we traverse over the chasm between humanist narrative and philosophical demonstration. Equally striking is the prominence given in this work—as it is in the rest of Descartes' philosophical system—to reason, which is characterized in virtually the same terms as it had been by the humanists, as the faculty which distinguishes men from beasts. Descartes, like Copernicus and Galileo, is no humanist; but humanist perceptions reverberate in his *Discourse on Method.*

Scholars have spilled much ink in an attempt to resolve the conundrum of the relationship of humanism and philosophy, or of humanism to science, philosophy's early modern offspring. That puzzle is not resolved here, but highlighted. Humanism is not divorced from science any more than words are the opposite of things, for words are the medium by which things are known. And humanism does not relate to philosophy as rhetoric does to logic, or symbol to system, for rhetoric constitutes a kind of logic, and system itself is a kind of symbol. Humanism bestows a heritage on the investigators of new forms of knowledge as the era of the Renaissance gives way to modernity, a heritage without which their achievements would have been naught.

Marsilio Ficino

The humanist, philosopher, and priest Marsilio Ficino (1433–1499) is remarkable, above all, for his translation of the works of the ancient Greek philosopher Plato into Latin. Through his Latin translation the intellectuals of Western Europe had access for the first time to the full range of Platonic thought, unmediated by Hellenistic, Arabic, or Christian interpretations. To the extent that, as Alfred North Whitehead famously commented, the whole European philosophical tradition "consists of a series of footnotes to Plato,"[1] Ficino's translation was pivotal in its construction.

Ficino contributes not only to the mainstream of Western thought, however, but also to the microcosm of Renaissance culture: to humanism above

---

1. Alfred North Whitehead, *Process and Reality* (New York: Free Press, 1979), 39.

all, but also to religion, science, art, and literature. His translation of Plato's words into Latin was accompanied by a transposition of Platonism into the contemporary cultural milieu. Plato's concepts of the reality of ideal forms and, conversely, the unreality of human perception; of love as a binding universal force generated by the desire for ever-higher manifestations of the beautiful; of conversation, the informal exchange of ideas in dialogue and symposia, as the framework for the discovery of truth—all these Ficino brought to life in the setting of Renaissance Florence, energizing a circle of thinkers, patrons, friends, and visitors, who met with him in the precincts of the so-called Platonic Academy that he headed and who corresponded with him in volumes of letters that are themselves rich with philosophical matter. In his commentaries on Plato, moreover, especially those on the *Symposium*, and in his works *On the Christian Religion* (1474–1476) and the *Platonic Theology on the Immortality of the Soul* (1469–1474), the Ficinian synthesis of Platonic with Christian, Neoplatonic, and Hermetic ideas circulated throughout Europe, feeding its literary and artistic as well as intellectual traditions into the eighteenth century.

The son of the physician to Cosimo de' Medici, the unofficial ruler of Florence from 1434–1464, Ficino grew up in the Medici orbit, where he early caught Cosimo's eye and subsequently enjoyed his patronage. Having studied Greek with one of the refugees from the takeover of Constantinople by the Ottoman Turks, a scholar then teaching at the university in Florence, Ficino undertook in the 1460s the translation of the Platonic corpus (completed in draft by 1468–1469, though not printed until 1484). During these years as well, he was tutor to Lorenzo de' Medici (his correspondent in two of the letters given here) and to Giovanni Pico della Mirandola, the author of the *Oration on the Dignity of Man* previously considered (see Chapter 2). Meanwhile, at the Medicean villa at Careggi, made available to him for this purpose, he gathered his students and friends about him—among the latter, the leading intellectuals of Florence and Italy—for conversations about the soul, the mind, and immortality.

Ficino's letters emerge from this milieu, and illuminate it vividly. For editor Sebastiano Gentile, they constitute "the most faithful mirror" of Ficino's intellectual life and are "intimately connected" to his work of translation, commentary, and original composition.[2] Occupying two volumes in their Latin edition, they include exchanges with such contemporaries as the intellectuals Giovanni Cavalcanti and Angelo Poliziano, and the statesmen Bernardo Bembo and Bernardo Rucellai.

The four letters presented here provide a snapshot of Ficino's cultural world, affording a view of his ideas in action as they unfold in interaction with friends. The first three brief ones form a group centered on the figure of

---

2. Sebastiano Gentile, ed., *Lettere*, 2 vols. (Florence, Leo S. Olschki, 1990, 2010); Introduction, 1:xiii, xvi.

Lorenzo de' Medici, Ficino's student and patron.[3] The fourth, more expansive letter presents Ficino's concept of the soul, of a piece with his more formal and extended discussion of the soul in his major works.

The first group of three consist of a letter of Lorenzo's to Ficino, Ficino's response to Lorenzo, and Ficino's rhapsody on Lorenzo's fine qualities in a letter to another friend, the Florentine Niccolò Michelozzi, a loyal secretary and agent of the Medici family. In the first of these, Lorenzo explicitly declares his love for Ficino: he had just received Ficino's letter, "full of that sweetness which had awakened in me so ardent a longing"; Ficino no longer belongs now to himself, "to Marsilio, but to your Lorenzo, who is no less yours than you are your own."

The modern ear readily detects the homoerotic tones of this discourse—something not at odds with the homosexual culture of ancient Athens shared by Socrates and Plato, or that of contemporary Florence, where male homosexual activity was commonly understood to be an aspect of a transitional phase between youth and adulthood.[4] But that ear should judge cautiously: for this love relationship can also be understood as philosophical, a coded simulacrum of the oneness between souls united by their shared intellectual commitments—Platonic lovers, in effect. Ficino, among his other achievements, is the architect of the notion of "Platonic love" that threads through European literature and art from this time forward.

Tonalities of that Platonic love, expressed by a teacher to his student, are heard in Ficino's response to Lorenzo. He is not so much the lover as the servitor, or at least approving mentor, who notes that Lorenzo, a "wealthy citizen," a "powerful man" and a man of "many responsibilities," is the "hope of our city" and a mainstay of the Ficinian Academy. This one, whatever may have been the missive to which it responds, is not a love letter.

Similarly, while Ficino lauds Lorenzo most generously in his letter to Michelozzi, he speaks here as an approving mentor: "Tell me, my friend, I ask you: Who speaks more elegantly? Who argues more astutely? Who plays more sweetly? Who persuades more forcefully?" Indeed, Ficino, as an old man who must step aside for an "eager newcomer," is almost envious of Lorenzo. He closes with the language of Platonic love: "for Lorenzo is mine, . . . And I, too, am Lorenzo's . . . : he has purchased me at a high price, which is, himself."

Quite different in tone is Ficino's letter to Giovanni Cavalcanti, which within the framework of a letter to a friend is a miniature treatise on questions concerning the soul: whether it can exist and function when separated from the body; and whether, if so separated, it is capable of clear understanding. The answer to both questions is yes. To the first: the soul, or mind,

---

3. For Ficino's relationship with Lorenzo, see Gentile's introduction to the *Lettere*, at 1:xlvi–lxii.

4. For which see especially Michael Rocke, *Forbidden Friendships: Homosexuality and Male Culture in Renaissance Florence* (New York: Oxford University Press, 1996).

when separated from the body "will be able to perceive through itself much more easily and amply," and "be able both to exist and to live." To the second: "the soul will clearly see itself through itself, more acutely seeing the light perceived by the intellect than it now sees that lesser light perceived by the senses through the glass windows of this bodily prison"; indeed, it will see things as they really are, and not the shadowy images that are perceived through bodily sense. The message Ficino conveys is emphatically Platonic, conveyed in a language that is both technical and highly allusive—more opaque, arguably, than that of the ancient philosopher.

These letters capture Ficino as he acted within the world of Florence: a bookish sage, an original and complex thinker, a convivial friend, a patriotic citizen, at home with power.

Marsilio Ficino, *Letters* (1473/1474)

#24: Expressions of love (Pisa, 19 January 1474)[5]

From Lorenzo de' Medici to Marsilio Ficino, Platonist, greetings.

I believe now, most learned Marsilio, that what Plotinus—if I remember the name correctly—said about the soul was true, which you also posit in your book of Theology:[6] that is, that our souls are everywhere at any moment of time. For that point you proved in your book with extensive arguments is now clearly confirmed in action: for scarcely had I sealed up my latest letter to you, than I received from you the letter which I had so much desired, full of that sweetness which had awakened in me so ardent a longing. I believe that when you were away, and you read my letters which complained of your tardiness in writing, you were prompted to delay your reply no longer. However that may be, I feel no need now to inquire about why or how you wrote. It is enough that your letter has come; nothing could be more pleasing or delightful to me. I see again what I had already known: that you would not disappoint me. For my long expectation made the sweetness of your letter somehow more sweet, as often happens also to those who suffer a great thirst.

Now reading your letter, I find it to be in no way unlike Marsilio—if the expressions of gratitude are excepted. For those thank-yous do not accord either with our friendship, nor with that man who gave himself so fully to me that nothing remained that was his. . . . Now, truly, you do not belong to Marsilio, but to your Lorenzo, who is no less yours than you are your own. If you care to recover yourself for yourself, therefore, know that henceforth it

---

5. For date, Gentile ed., 1:li n101, cclix.

6. *Platonic Theology on the Immortality of the Soul*, ed. and trans. Michael J. B. Allen and James Hankins, 6 vols. (Cambridge, MA: Harvard University Press, 2001–2006).

will be on the condition that you may do nothing concerning yourself without at the same time also considering me. For those whom immortal God has joined together, let no man separate. To return to the matter of gratitude, I do not want you to mention it any more in your letters to me. For if the thanks you give are not yours, you give me nothing at all; if they are yours, as I have already said, you have already given me yourself and all that belongs to you.

Farewell, and love yourself, by doing which, you will also love me. This our extraordinary love demands—which I may frankly tell you, since in that book which you have written about love,[7] you describe all the passions of love so artfully that there is nothing to be said about the nature of love that may not be read in that book, and nothing is contained in your book that is not also a part of love.

Again, farewell.

#25: God, not man, is the author of wondrous things (21 January 1474)[8]

From Marsilio Ficino to the great-souled Lorenzo de' Medici, greetings

What I am to do now, Lorenzo, I do not know. Your wonderful letter compels me to admire you enormously, but the modesty that befits a philosopher prohibits my saying so. Your rare humanity and nobility of soul calls for the expression of boundless gratitude, but your letter instead forbids it. Let me at least thank God, my Lorenzo, I pray you, that he has given us in our time a wealthy citizen whose character is modest and whose intellect is lofty; a young man of private condition, who possesses both prudence and power; a powerful man, with the capacity for self-control as well as liberality; a man with many responsibilities, who yet diplays wisdom illumined by eloquence.

You have greatness within you, Lorenzo, greatness without a doubt. And lest any suspect me of the vice of too much adulation, which should be absolutely foreign to a man who is a philosopher and your friend, I have said that there are great things within you, not because of you: for only God Almighty creates wonders. O excellent man, you are an instrument of God, prepared, and I know what I say, to do magnificent things. So long as you are obedient to the divine creator, you will accomplish splendid and remarkable deeds. Your obedience will be perfect, if you pray to him often—believe me—asking him to show you how to obey. He will surely respond to your prayer, since even before you turn to him, he encourages you to do so, and shows you for what and how you are to pray.

---

7. *Symposium: Commentary on Plato's Symposium on Love*, trans. Sears Jayne (Dallas, TX: Spring Publications, 1985).

8. For date, Gentile ed., 1:li n101, cclix.

A warm farewell, hope of our city.[9] Before I close, my Lorenzo, I beg you, both for the sake of the Academy[10] which flourishes because of you, and for the sake as well of this city of yours that you cherish before all things, to take care of your health. For unless you are well, I think that neither the Academy nor our city, in these times, can prevail.

#26: The greatness of Lorenzo de' Medici (21 January 1474)[11]

From Marsilio Ficino to Niccolò Michelozzi, a true man, greetings

How difficult it is, my Niccolò, how difficult not to be overcome by envy! If those qualities that Lorenzo possesses were not also mine, perhaps I could not stem my envy that such fine, so great, and so many virtues normally found only in the old are to be found in this youth? Tell me, my friend, I ask you: Who speaks more elegantly? Who argues more astutely? Who plays more sweetly? Who persuades more forcefully? Poets long since yielded to him their laurel crowns; orators have recently done so; and now we philosophers must yield. By Jupiter, how is it that we lazy old hands should be so quickly, so easily, and so totally surpassed by this eager newcomer?

But while other men might give in to envy in this situation, and explode with spite, I shall wondrously rejoice in and enjoy him: for Lorenzo is mine, on account of his incredible goodness. And I, too, am Lorenzo's, on account of his remarkable qualities of soul: he has purchased me at a high price, which is, himself—may God so love me!

Niccolò, I say what I feel: no one was closer to me than the great Cosimo, no one more beloved. I knew in that old man no merely human, but a heroic virtue. Now I see him once again in this youth, I see the whole of that old man: I see the phoenix in the phoenix,[12] the light of the sun in the sunbeam. Now there shines forth daily from our Lorenzo the splendor of Cosimo in so many ways: a light to lighten the Latin peoples, and the glory of the Florentine Republic. . . .[13]

Farewell.

---

9. The word *patria* is often translated "fatherland," but in the cultural setting of the Italian Renaissance, "city" is more appropriate.

10. The so-called Platonic Academy, discussed in the introduction to this section.

11. For date, Gentile ed., 1:li n101, cclix.

12. The phoenix was a symbol of resurrection.

13. No doubt an allusion to Luke 2:32: "A light to lighten the Gentiles, and the glory of thy people Israel" (King James Version).

#38: Serious thoughts for Giovanni: the soul can think after death, and more clearly than when in the body (1473/1474?)[14]

Marsilio Ficino to his special friend Giovanni Cavalcanti, greetings.

I have written you several times, my best of friends, in which I employed the language of love, which not only befits our friendship, but also accords with that noble freedom that existed between Socrates and Plato. But now moving past these amatory tropes of the Platonists (for Plato introduced his works in this way), we may come to serious matters. Hear now about my recent discussion about the mind with those excellent citizens and experts in law Bernardo Giugni and Bartolomeo Fortino.

We mortals have two principal questions about the mind. The first is, whether the intellect may be disjoined from the body, and thus separated from the body, still live and act. The second is whether it is then capable of understanding, and whether it understands clearly or not. I shall now respond to these questions as briefly as possible, for these and similar matters are discussed at length in my *Theology concerning the immortality of the soul.*[15]

It is understood that the intellect can think about many incorporeal things: for instance, God, angels, souls, virtues, numerical proportions, universal archetypes and causes. Nonetheless, we are unable by our bodily sight to perceive invisible things, nor can we by any bodily instrument think about incorporeal things; neither can we, through a nature that is bounded by body, place, and time, explore, inquire, know, or comprehend things that are unlimited by matter, place, or time. But if the mind, while it still holds dominion over the body, can so gather itself to itself that it can perceive an object through itself alone, it follows that when separated from the body, it will be able to perceive through itself much more easily and amply. If it can function thus by itself, then also by itself it will be able both to exist and to live.

So we turn now to the second question: Will the soul apart from the body be able to know whatever objects are offered to it internally more clearly than the senses now perceive those offered to them externally? and more clearly to the same degree that sight is sharper and faster than hearing and the other senses? and equally, to the extent that the mind is more noble than the senses, so also is the object of mind more excellent than the object of sense?

That the mind is more excellent than the senses no one who has experienced its power doubts: for he sees that the mind is the judge of the senses, and since it is more valuable, it is bestowed less often, is trained more slowly, and employed more rarely. This superiority of mind also shows that the objects of the mind will be more sublime than the objects of the senses, for the for-

---

14. For date, Gentile ed., 1:cclx.

15. The *Platonic Theology.*

mer are universal, boundless, and eternal, and the latter particular, finite, and mortal. In addition, the more greatly the exterior senses are employed, to the same extent the interior sense withdraws, and vice versa. For he who more attentively looks at and listens to external objects can scarcely at the same time imagine internal ones; and he who actively employs his imagination scarcely sees or hears external stimuli. The same relations hold for the intellect as for the imagination.

The soul while in this body suffers two great impediments. First, it is involved in many activities, which interfere with and weaken each other, since it is difficult to manage many things at the same time, causing in turn much perturbation. Second, both because the soul dwells in a lowly habitation, and because it must tend to bodily needs for the span of time allotted to human existence, it is engaged in inferior actions earlier, more energetically, and more often than superior ones. So it happens that when we wish to reflect on incorporeal things, we do so stupidly and clumsily, as though we are walking in a fog. But when we refrain entirely from eating, growing, sensing, and imagining, or we decrease these activities, then our mental capacity sharpens to that point that whatever the mind perceives, it perceives more clearly as though by a light. For then the soul will clearly see itself through itself, more acutely seeing the light perceived by the intellect than it now sees that lesser light perceived by the senses through the glass windows of this bodily prison. In tranquillity, through its own still and crystalline serenity, it will view the finest visions by the light of the divine Sun—a light so brilliant that the light of the earthly sun will seem to be only shadow, and so radiant that, invisible to impure eyes, it shines only for those that are pure. For what it sees are not pallid images, but reality itself, of which all other things are images.

When in sleep the actions and motions of the external senses cease, then the imagination, which is fed by those other faculties, is so strengthened that it creates internal images which seem to be representations of real things. What then will the intellect do, which is so much more powerful than the imagination, when it shall be liberated from its restraints far more greatly than is the imagination of one who sleeps, and it will perceive at the zenith of truth and reason the first principles of all things? Then, surely, it will depict within itself all that is true with perfect accuracy—or rather, it will be imprinted by all universal truths everywhere. But precisely by what? By the mind of minds, by the light of all light. And how easily will this be done? With perfect ease, and suddenly: for, by way of a certain natural kinship, visible light illumines the corporeal light as soon as it becomes serene and pure, forming it with its own form, and thus with the forms of all visible things. Similarly the intelligible light—the more than intelligible light, which is God—forms the light of the intellect as soon it becomes serene, forming it with its own form, that is, its divine form, which contains and transmits the forms of all intelligible things.

For just as God has already provided us with vital warmth and joy, so he now confers on us the great benefit of his light, and so liberates life from death. And just as he pours forth light to counter darkness, and beyond the limit of whatever span of time he chooses, he pours light into the mind, by which it ascends from the mutability of time to the permanence of eternity. More, he nourishes us with goodness to the limit of our desire, and filling us with beauty awakens our appetite, and in awakening, fills it. There we have fullness without satiety, where there is good without evil, and where infinite goodness creates also an infinite capacity for goodness. Infinite goodness and beauty, therefore, the source of countless good and beautiful manifestations, arouse our desire and likewise satisfy it throughout eternity.

Nicholas Copernicus

The publication in 1543 of *On the Revolutions of the Celestial Spheres* by Nicholas Copernicus (1473–1543) is arguably the zero point for what many scholars call the Scientific Revolution: the moment of its birth. Removing the earth from its fixed and central position, *On the Revolutions* reconstructs the model of the universe that had prevailed for almost fourteen centuries. Its author, a German-Polish astronomer, physician, and cathedral canon, intended only to provide a more accurate explanation of the observed movements of the heavenly bodies than that offered by traditional Ptolemaic theory. That he did; and collaterally, he opened the pathway to modern astronomy, physics, and mathematics.

He did so during the peak years of the Renaissance, when the humanism and art of the Italians had begun to diffuse northward over the Alps to all corners of Europe, including the remote corner where Copernicus dwelled on the shore of the Baltic Sea. Born into a wealthy merchant family but raised by his maternal uncle, a prominent figure in the Church and in political, diplomatic, and cultural circles, Copernicus had journeyed when young in the opposite direction—southward over the Alps to study at the Italian universities of Bologna and Padua. Here he pursued the disciplines for which they were renowned: medicine (which included mathematics and astronomy as then understood) and law (which included ecclesiastical or canon law, in which he took a degree). And here, too, although already fluent in Latin, as were all the educated elites of Europe, he learned Greek, which was acquired by only the most advanced scholars. It has been seen in this volume how Petrarch and Boccaccio yearned to gain access to Greek literature and could not, while their fifteenth-century successors gradually mastered the Greek language and literary canon. By the late 1400s, Greek learning was well-established at the Italian universities, and infused the curriculum in arts, medicine, and philosophy. Copernicus' scrutiny of ancient Greek texts sparked him to envisage his new theory, thereafter named for him: the Copernican, or heliocentric theory, according to which the Earth moved, and the Sun, not the Earth, stood at the center of the planetary system.

The mammoth phenomenon of Copernicanism took root, therefore, within a cultural world transformed by humanism, even if humanism had little to do with the decades of precise astronomical observation and mathematical calculation that Copernicus devoted to the full development of his theory. Ironically, the decentering of the Earth that Copernicanism accomplished would, in time, erode the foundations of humanism, whose fundamental cosmology, as it was articulated most concisely and elegantly by Pico della Mirandola (see Chapter 2), consisted of a world governed by divine providence in which, like the Earth in the Ptolemaic system, the human realm was central: placed a little lower than the angels, and above the animal, vegetable, mineral, and demonic regions of the lower and nethermost worlds.

After 1503, when Copernicus had finished his Italian studies, he returned to Royal Prussia, then part of the kingdom of Poland, where he served as secretary and physician to his uncle until 1510, and thereafter as canon of Frombork cathedral, a clerical position that offered lifetime security and income. By 1514, he had already adopted the heliocentric hypothesis, which he announced in a brief work without mathematical demonstrations, the *Commentariolus* (Little Commentary), and circulated only in manuscript among a select group of scholars. During the remaining decades of his life, he elaborated upon his hypothesis, making repeated astronomical observations—these without a telescope, which had not yet been invented—and laboriously developing a mathematical account of the celestial movements he recorded. Persuaded to publish his findings, he allowed his younger German friend Georg Joachim Rheticus, who had connections to the printing shops of Nuremberg, to make the arrangements. On the day he died, 24 May 1543, an advance copy of *On the Revolutions*, it is said, was placed in his hands.

On the Revolutions was controversial even before it was published. Copernicus' *Commentariolus* circulated among astronomers well before 1543, as did a separate description of his theory composed by Rheticus. After the publication of *On the Revolutions*, astronomers continued to be the main consumers of Copernican theory: one historian has investigated their copious marginal notations on many print exemplars during the next decades.[16] But the work was not widely discussed, or accepted, or understood as a serious threat to traditional thinking, until the turn of the next

---

16. For which see Owen Gingerich, *The Book Nobody Read: Chasing the Revolutions of Nicolaus Copernicus* (New York: Walker and Company, 2004).

century. By then, in 1596, the mathematician and astronomer Johann Kepler had published his *Mysterium cosmographicum* (Secret of the Universe), which accepted and validated the Copernican theory, which he would develop further in his own studies of planetary motion. Soon afterwards, Galileo Galilei, whose own struggles with a resistant public will shortly be considered, made the Copernican theory the central issue of European culture—and was silenced.

Copernicus had anticipated the controversy, as we learn from the astonishingly direct and confident Preface, which follows here. He dedicated it to a cultivated man, a product of the Italian Renaissance: Alessandro Farnese, Pope Paul III (r. 1534–1549), a figure of supreme authority and some knowledge: "For even in this far distant corner of the Earth where I pursue my work," Copernicus wrote, a bit hyperbolically, "you are held to tower above all others because of the dignity of your office and your love for all learning and even for astronomy." This choice of dedicatee is striking: there were many lesser men, both scholars and potentates, available for such a purpose. Possibly Copernicus foresaw the conflict between his hypothesis and the religious establishment that would eventually present itself—a possibility hinted at when he disparages those of his imagined detractors who would "venture a refutation based on some passage of scripture twisted to suit their purpose." A storm of such refutations not too much later greeted the work of Galileo, as will be seen.

Although Copernicus anticipated there would be detractors, he did not seem to fear those defending the authority of the Bible so much as those defending the authority of Ptolemy. For the Ptolemaic model of the universe had stood the test of time. Presented in Ptolemy's *Almagest* (c. 150 CE), it compiles the best of earlier Greek cosmology with Ptolemy's own mathematical calculations and astronomical observations.[17] Upon it rests the classical, Arabic, and Christian astronomical investigations of medieval scholars. Its monumental presence weighs on Copernicus: the pope himself might wonder "how it ever came into my head, against the established view of the astronomers, and virtually against common sense, to be so bold as to imagine the possibility of terrestrial motion"; it would be seen as an "absurd notion" that would likely be met with "a great blast of disapproval," and he feared the contempt that might descend on him "because of the novelty and disruptiveness of my theory." Not only do his words give voice to this caution and fear, but so too does the record of his career, which shows that he held back from a full demonstration of his theory for some three decades, delaying it almost to the moment of his death.

---

17. Claudius Ptolemy (c. 90–168 CE), a Greek mathematician who lived in Roman Egypt, then a flourishing cultural center, and author of the *Syntaxis*, a textbook of mathematical astronomy. The *Syntaxis* was known later generally by its Arabic title, the *Almagest*, reflecting the appropriation of the work by Arabic scholars during the Middle Ages, when the work was no longer read in Greek in most of Western Europe.

Yet Copernicus is emboldened by the logic of his case, buttressed by his own meticulous observations and mathematical proofs. His confidence rests on the undoubted fact that the Ptolemaic model, for all its grandeur, did not work: it did not accurately and completely describe what centuries of astronomers could see with the naked eye. As Copernicus notes, to make the system work—to "save" the "phenomena," as the experts of the time said—it was necessary to interpolate various subsidiary systems of circular motions: the equants, homocentrics, eccentrics, and epicycles that were layered onto the Ptolemaic substratum. Nor could the experts agree on just which assortment of such devices was best able to save the phenomena, and yield an account of what actually transpired in the regions beyond the moon. They did not believe in their own manipulations, but retained unwavering faith in the underlying Ptolemaic theory.

Copernicus proposes an astonishingly simple solution, a single changed assumption that removes the difficulties astronomers had long faced and whisks away the entire concoction of subsidiary equants and epicycles. If it is the Earth that moves, the motions of Sun, Moon, and five known planets fall into place: they are uniformly circular, and constitute a hierarchy of lengths of revolution based on their distance from the sun. The universe is shown to be coherent and systematic throughout—a welcome outcome. It is also much larger than was thought: the distance between the Earth and the Sun is but a small fraction of that between the Sun and the outermost sphere of the fixed stars. Once motion is attributed to the Earth, therefore, Copernicus writes in his preface to Pope Paul III, "I found at last that if the motions of the other planets are correlated with the Earth's circulation in its orbit, and are computed for the revolution of each planet, not only do their observed phenomena follow therefrom, but also the order and size of all the planets and spheres and of the cosmos itself so arrange themselves into a system, so that no part of it can be transposed without causing confusion elsewhere and so throughout the entire universe."

Copernicus was cautious, but also courageous: a Renaissance man who dared to reexamine what lay before his eyes; an aesthete who required an elegant and coherent solution for the problem he identified; and a disciplined scientist who spent decades gathering the observations and calculations that would defend his revolutionary vision. The modern world whose foundations he laid, however, was no longer compatible with the humanist and Christian synthesis that characterized the Renaissance. The outcome of the Copernican moment would be to challenge the cultural construct of the Renaissance world from which it had emerged.

Nicholas Copernicus, Preface to *On the Revolutions of the Celestial Spheres* (1543)

NICHOLAS COPERNICUS, PREFACE TO HIS BOOK ON THE REVOLUTIONS OF THE HEAVENLY BODIES, TO HIS HOLINESS, POPE PAUL III[18]

I can imagine vividly, most holy Father, that as soon as it is recognized that this book of mine on the revolutions of the heavenly spheres attributes motion to the Earth, I shall be greeted with a great blast of disapproval. Nor am I so pleased with my own theories that I do not seriously consider how others will judge them. And although I do recognize that the cogitations of the philosopher should be exempt from the judgment of the mob, since his purpose is to seek what is true in all matters to the extent that God has permitted human reason to do, still I grant that entirely wrong-headed ideas should be avoided. I mulled over in my mind, therefore, what an absurd notion others would think it—aware that for many centuries it has been deemed a certainty that the Earth rests immobile in the middle of the universe, as though set at its center—if I, on the contrary, were to assert that the Earth moved. I held back, uncertain whether I should publish what I had written to demonstrate terrestrial motion, or whether it would be enough, following the example of the Pythagoreans and some other philosophical schools, who transmitted their theories not in writing but by word of mouth only among a close circle of their friends and associates. . . . As I weighed these matters, the contempt that I feared would descend upon me because of the novelty and disruptiveness of my theory nearly caused me to give up all thought of publication.

But my friends, though I delayed and even resisted, drew me back to the task. Among these, the first was Nicholas Schönberg, the cardinal of Capua, renowned in every kind of learning.[19] After him was my very close friend, Tiedemann Giese, the bishop of Chelmno, a devotee of both sacred and secular letters.[20] He constantly urged and exhorted me, spurring me on with occasional reproaches, to let it see the light at last, and to publish the book that had lain hidden on my desk not for a mere nine years, but now as much as four times nine. Quite a few other very eminent and learned men likewise pressed me, imploring me to delay no longer, on account of my imagined fears, in making my work available to the community of learned astrono-

---

18. Alessandro Farnese, who reigned as Pope Paul III 1534–1549.

19. For Schönberg, see Edward Rosen, *Nicholas Copernicus on the Revolutions: Translation and Commentary* (Baltimore: Johns Hopkins University Press, 1992), XVII, 338n to 3:31.

20. For Giese, see Rosen, *Nicholas Copernicus*, XVII, 338n to 3:33.

mers. It might be, they proposed, that to the extent that my theory about the Earth's motion is now seen by many as absurd, so much greater will be the admiration and approval it will receive once the work is published, and the fog of absurdity is diffused by the exquisite clarity of the proofs. Persuaded by these advisers and the hope they offered, I permitted my friends at last to publish the work as they had long begged me to do.

Perhaps your Holiness will not be surprised so much that I have dared to publish these theories of mine after I had devoted so much effort to develop them, not hesitating even to commit to print my thoughts on the motion of the Earth, but rather may wonder how it ever came into my head, against the established view of the astronomers, and virtually against common sense, to be so bold as to imagine the possibility of terrestrial motion. I shall not then conceal from your Holiness that what impelled me to consider a different explanation of the movements of the heavenly spheres was this: I observed that the astronomers do not agree among themselves in their investigations of this matter. First of all, they are so uncertain of the motions of the Sun and the Moon, that they cannot calculate or establish a set magnitude even for the tropical year.[21] Secondly, in determining the motions of these two bodies along with those of the other five planets,[22] they do not employ the same principles and assumptions or explanations of the revolutions and motions that are observed. For some employ only homocentric circles, and others eccentrics and epicycles, yet with all these artificial constructs they still do not attain the desired resolution.[23]

For those who trusted in homocentrics, and using them could describe certain aberrant motions, were nonetheless unable successfully to explain the observed phenomena. Those who worked with eccentrics, on the other hand, were able to account mathematically for the most of the oberved planetary motions, but in so doing they introduced other notions which contradicted the first principles of uniform motion. Moreover, they were unable to discover or deduce what is of paramount importance, the structure of the cosmos and the particular symmetry of its parts. Rather it was as if someone had ordered from various sources depictions of hands, feet, the head, and other bodily parts, splendidly drawn perhaps, but not belonging to any one body,

---

21. The "tropical," or "solar year," is the time required for the Sun to make one full seasonal circuit—for example, from vernal equinox to vernal equinox. It is not quite the same as the "sidereal year," the time it takes the Earth to make one full orbit around the Sun as measured by its position relative to the fixed stars.

22. The classical planetary system consisted of Sun and Moon and the five other planets called "wandering stars" because they appeared to the eye to "wander" through the zodiacal signs: Mercury, Venus, Mars, Jupiter, and Saturn.

23. Homocentrics, eccentrics, and epicycles, devised by Aristotle and Ptolemy, are theoretical constructs of planetary motion that astronomers utilized to explain the observed paths of celestial bodies. See also Rosen, *Nicholas Copernicus*, 340–41n to 4:12.

and so all out of proportion with each other, as though they might combine to form a monster, but not a man. In the process of demonstration, therefore, . . . they either omitted something necessary, or introduced something unnecessary and largely irrelevant. They would not have fallen into these difficulties if they had obeyed proper principles. For if their assumptions had not been fallacious, everything that followed would have been verifiable beyond a doubt. What I am saying here may seem obscure, but it will become clearer in due course.

I reflected at length, therefore, on this weakness of received astronomical knowledge in explaining the motions of the heavenly spheres, becoming frustrated that no more rational explanation of the operations of the cosmic machine, created for us by that greatest of all Artisans, and most rational, had been offered by the philosophers who otherwise examined with such exquisite care matters of far lesser magnitude than the system of the universe. For this reason I undertook the task of rereading the books of all the philosophers that I could lay hold of to find out whether any of them ever had hypothesized that the movements of the heavenly spheres were different than those put forth by the professors of astronomy. And so I found that, first, according to Cicero, Hicetas[24] believed that the Earth moved; and that, second, according to Plutarch,[25] others were of the same opinion. . . .

These discoveries providing an entryway, I, too, began to consider the possibility of terrestrial motion. While the theory seemed absurd, yet I knew that others before me had been granted the freedom to plot all the circles they wished in an attempt to explain astronomical phenomena. I judged that I, too, might freely explore whether, by positing some kind of terrestrial motion, more plausible explanations could be found than those others had proposed for the revolution of the heavenly spheres.

And so having attributed certain motions to the earth which are described later in this work, after many repeated calculations, I found at last that if the motions of the other planets are correlated with the Earth's circulation in its orbit, and are computed for the revolution of each planet, not only do their observed phenomena follow therefrom, but also the order and size of all the planets and spheres and of the cosmos itself so arrange themselves into a system, so that no part of it can be transposed without causing confusion elsewhere and so throughout the entire universe. Accordingly, I follow the

---

24. Cicero, *Academic Questions*, II.39.123. Hicetas, or Nicetas, of Syracuse, was a Pythagorean, who lived c. 400 BCE. See Rosen, *Nicholas Copernicus*, 341n to 4:45.

25. *The Opinions of the Philosophers*, III.13, a pseudo-Plutarchan work considered in Copernicus' day to be part of Plutarch's compilation of the *Moralia*. See Rosen, *Nicholas Copernicus*, n342 to 5:1. Other ancient Greek heliocentrists, from the fifth through third centuries BCE, were Philolaus, Heraclides Ponticus, and Aristarchus of Samos.

same order in the structure of this work. In the first book, I describe the system of all the spheres, along with that of the Earth and the motions I ascribe to it, so that this book defines as it were the whole structure of the universe. Then in the remaining books, I correlate the motion of the other planets and spheres to the motion of the Earth, showing from these calculations to what extent the motions and appearances of the other planets and spheres may be saved by so doing [—showing, that is, that their phenomena follow directly if the motion of the Earth is posited.][26] I have no doubt that capable and learned astronomers will agree with me, if they choose to examine carefully and thoroughly, as this branch of philosophy requires, and not superficially, the data I have provided in this work to support the demonstration of my theory. But so that the learned and unlearned alike may see that I wish in no way to escape judgment, I have chosen to dedicate these theories of mine to your Holiness, rather than to any other person. For even in this far distant corner of the Earth where I pursue my work, you are held to tower above all others because of the dignity of your office and your love for all learning and even for astronomy, whereby you may easily by your authority and judgment forestall the bite of the calumniators—for as the proverb says,[27] there is no remedy for the bite of sycophants.

There will be those fools, perhaps, who though they are entirely ignorant of astronomy yet will venture a refutation based on some passage of scripture twisted to suit their purpose, who will dare to insult and attack my work. I shall not waste my time on them, but only deplore their rude ignorance. . . . Astronomy is written for astronomers. To them these labors of mine, if I am not mistaken, will be seen also to be valuable to the Church, of which your Holiness is now supreme head. For not long ago when under Pope Leo X there was discussion at the Lateran Council about reforming the ecclesiastical calendar,[28] no progress could be made because the lengths of years and months, and the motions of the Sun and Moon, had not yet been satisfactorily measured. Since that time, however, prompted by that most excellent man Paul, the bishop of Fossombrone,[29] who then headed up this effort, I have investigated these things and made the accurate observations required.

---

26. Copernicus alludes to the necessity for astronomers of "saving the phenomena," that is, finding explanations for the physical events that they observed, and so respecting, or "saving," those realities. I have interpolated the bracketed phrase to clarify this point for the reader.

27. Ultimately a saying from the Greek comedian Aristophanes, by way of Erasmus and Copernicus' friend Giese; see Rosen, *Nicholas Copernicus*, 342n to 5:36.

28. For the circumstances of this discussion, see Rosen, *Nicholas Copernicus*, 343n to 5:47.

29. In 1513, Paul of Middelburg, Bishop of Fossombrone, invited Copernicus, along with other astronomers, to make these observations. Although the Gregorian Calendar was not instituted until 1582, its emendations were based on astronomical tables compiled in part from Copernicus' observations.

To what extent I have succeded in that endeavor, I leave to the judgment of your Holiness above all, and to that of all the other learned astronomers.[30] And now, so that I do not appear to promise your Holiness more concerning the utility of this work than I can accomplish, I turn to the work at hand.

Galileo Galilei

Like Ficino, and more so than Copernicus, Galileo Galilei (1564–1642) emerged from the cultural world of the Renaissance. Born in Pisa, then part of the Grand Duchy of Tuscany of which Florence was capital, the epicenter of Italian humanistic and artistic innovations, Galileo moved in elite intellectual circles in Pisa, Padua, Florence, and Rome. Initiating modern physics by his utilization of the experimental method in the investigation of moving bodies, and continuing the Copernican revision of astronomy by his observations and by his literary defense of a new world system, he ultimately undermined the Christian and humanist synthesis, grounded in texts of ancient origin, and fundamental to Renaissance culture. Copernicus, too, had undermined that synthesis, as has been seen, by decentering the Earth, and with it the claim of the human species for dominance in nature and of the human mind for cosmic preeminence. Galileo would do so by defining scientific investigation as a realm of human knowledge distinct from that of scriptural statement and theological interpretation—a realm of things, not words—and free from the limits it imposed. To do so, he confronted the immense power of the church not only in his theoretical works, but in his actions.

Exemplifying a range of humanist genres including the treatise, the letter, and the dialogue, Galileo's works introduced not just professional mathematicians but a whole lay public to the Copernican hypothesis and a new physics of moving bodies. Writing sometimes in Latin and sometimes in Italian, for the greater diffusion of his views, his achievement included the two monumental publications of 1632, the *Dialogue on the Two Chief World Systems, Ptolemaic and Copernican,* and 1638, *The Two New Sciences,* which lays the foundations of modern physics. These two works came toward the end of his career, after the struggles and controversies of earlier years, documented in many briefer works including the one excerpted here: the 1615 letter to Christina of Lorraine, the dowager duchess of Medici grand duke Ferdinando I and mother of his successor, Cosimo II. Here Galileo

---

30. Copernicus' inclusion of Pope Paul III among the community of "learned astronomers" Rosen calls a "polite flattery": *Nicholas Copernicus,* 343n to 6:7.

anticipates the attempt by churchmen to silence him and to obstruct the whole project of the scientific investigation of the natural world.

Galileo's struggle with the church would peak at two moments: in February to March, 1616, when the Roman Inquisition instructed the respected intellectual Cardinal Bellarmine to warn Galileo to abjure his Copernican views—a warning which was issued and to which Galileo acquiesced; and in the spring of 1633, when Galileo was tried before the Inquisition, threatened with torture, ordered to abjure his views, and condemned to imprisonment, with his sentence gradually reduced to lifelong house arrest. Much as the church has suffered the outrage of moderns who view its proceedings as repressive and reprehensible, Galileo, too, has received some blame for committing the "crime" of acceding to church authorities.[31]

Galileo did not seek the martyrdom that he suffered. Unlike Copernicus, who avoided any confrontation with the church as he carried on his astronomical investigations, Galileo was pursued, as he put it, by "professors of theology." It is their opposition which is the context of Galileo's letter to the Grand Duchess Christina, written to this literate and powerful member of the Medici household as a way of publicizing and dignifying his argument for the independence of scientific investigation.

Galileo performs two related tasks in his long letter to Christina, of which excerpts are given here: first, he lambasts the professors who criticize his work; second, he defines the realm of scientific inquiry as other than, and rightly independent from, that of scriptural interpretation. The attacks by his critics are writings "full of useless arguments," Galileo complains, "studded with attestations from the Holy Scriptures," which they do not understand well and misapply. "Embittered," they shield themselves "with a zealous but simulated piety." They piously assert that "Holy Scripture can never lie," which is surely true, "so long as its real meaning has been understood"; but in insisting on the literal truth of Scripture—which has long been known to require careful interpretation by experts—they distort it, and if they had the power to do so, would force others "to accept as true conclusions that are refuted by logical demonstration and the evidence of the senses." This is an abuse, Galileo charges, which if permitted to stand—"may God forbid!"—would soon "lead to the prohibition of all the speculative sciences."

There is the danger: this crowd of professorial busybodies may stifle the pursuit of positive knowledge in areas that have nothing to do with Holy Scripture: "to extend, if not to say abuse their authority," insisting "that even in matters concerning nature, not faith, it is necessary totally to abandon the use of the senses and rational argument. . . ." But Holy Scripture and natural truth, while they have the same origin, have different aims and functions: "Both Holy Scripture and nature, equally, proceed from the Word of God: the first as dictated by the Holy Spirit, the latter as scrupulous executrix of

God's laws." But while the aim of Scripture is to obtain salvation for the faithful, and so, in order to communicate to those without learning, may sometimes depart from absolute truth, nature ". . . is inexorable and immutable, never trespassing the boundaries that God's laws impose upon it, and does not care whether the human mind can or cannot fathom its recondite principles and operations." Scriptural meanings should not be distorted so as to compel an understanding of nature that is demonstrably false. To do so would be tantamount to "extinguish[ing] the human mind."

Galileo does not deny the truth of Holy Scripture, written at the dictation of the Holy Spirit, in its domain. But in the domain of nature, truth derives from "sense experience and of demonstrations based upon them," which yield knowledge that is absolutely true. Such truth may be suppressed, but it cannot be falsified or negated. Despite his own personal humiliation and silencing, Galileo advances in his letter to the Grand Duchess Christina the theory of the independence of scientific inquiry as a path to verifiable truth.

Galileo Galilei, *Letter to the Grand Duchess Christina* (1615)

A few years ago, as your most serene highness knows well, I discovered some objects in the sky that had been invisible until this age. Because of their novelty, and because of the implications proceeding from their appearance, which challenge some propositions of natural philosophy commonly accepted in the schools, their discovery stirred up no small number of professors against me—as if with my own hand I had arranged these objects in the sky in order to agitate both nature and the world of learning! These professors have somehow forgotten that a diversity of truths contributes to the investigations of the learned disciplines, and to their growth and success, rather than to their diminution or destruction. And at the same time, they have demonstrated that they are fonder of their own opinions than of the truth. For they have raced off to deny and indeed to annihilate these new phenomena, the existence of which their own senses, had they wished to pay attention, could have convinced them. To do so, they have produced all sorts of things, and published various writings full of useless arguments, and what is worse, studded with attestations from the Holy Scriptures, excerpted from passages they do not properly understand and far afield from the matter at hand. . . .

With the passage of time, moreover, the truth of what I had first presented has been gradually revealed to all, and at the same time, along with the establishment of the facts, the division between the views of those who frankly and without any rancor had rejected at first the truth of these discoveries, and those to whose incredulity was added a touch of hysteria. Accordingly, joining those most knowledgeable in astronomy and physics who were persuaded by my first announcement, is another group of those whose objections have subsided bit by bit: those who were not determined to oppose my discoveries, or who doubted only because of their surprising novelty, and because they had not had the opportunity to experience the phenomena with their own senses. But there is yet another group who, beyond their infatuation with their original error, are driven by I could not say what other fanciful concern, which renders them hostile not so much to the discoveries as to the author. To the former, since they are unable any longer to deny their truth, they respond with a stony silence. As for the latter, guided by their fantasies and embittered more than ever by the same realizations that have softened and soothed the resistance of others, they try to harass me in every way.

Truly, I would give their attacks no greater heed than I gave earlier opposition, . . . if I had not seen that the new calumnies and persecutions do not amount merely to a squabble over who knows more or less, which I would ignore, but they extend to an attempt to slander me with charges which should be and are more abhorrent to me than death. Nor can I content myself that these charges will be recognized as unjust not only by those who know both me and my opponents; they must be proved false to everyone else as well. My critics persist, therefore, in their primary intention of employing every possible means to destroy me and my work, knowing the principles I hold in my studies of astronomy and philosophy concerning the constitution of the parts of the cosmos: which are, that the Sun does not change position, but remains in the center of the system of encircling celestial spheres; and that the Earth, rotating on its own axis, circles around the Sun. Further, they see that in proving my view I not only contradict the thinking of Ptolemy and Aristotle, but produce much evidence against them: some pertaining to physical effects, in particular, whose causes seemingly cannot be otherwise explained; and some astronomical effects, the outcome of repeated observations of the new celestial discoveries, which plainly confute the Ptolemaic system but marvelously accord with and prove the other cosmic model presented above. Now these critics . . . are resolved to disguise the fallacies of their discussions with the cloak of feigned piety and with the authority of Holy Scripture, which they ignorantly wield to confute arguments they have not grasped or understood.

So at first, they sought on their own to spread the rumor everywhere that these astronomical principles are contradicted by the Holy Scriptures, and consequently damnable and heretical. And then . . . it was not difficult for them to find someone who has brazenly preached, even from the pulpit, that they are indeed damnable and heretical, impiously and recklessly endangering not only these ideas and those who embrace them, but all of mathematics and mathematicians. Thereupon, swollen with confidence, and foolishly hoping that this seed which first took root in their hypocritical minds might stretch out its branches and reach up to heaven, they go about whispering to the people that these ideas will soon be condemned by the supreme authority. And knowing that such a judgment would demolish not only the two points stated earlier, but would label as damnable all other related astronomical and physical observations and propositions, to lighten their task in pressing this business they strain to make it appear, at least to the public, that these ideas are new and specifically mine—pretending not to know that Nicholas Copernicus was their author, who discovered and proved them. . . .

Galileo bemoans the criticism by his enemies of Copernicus, whose work he
praises, and whose ready acceptance by the church he exaggerates.

Now, because of the libels that these fellows want so unjustly to hang around my neck, if I am to defend myself to the public, of whose judgment and good sense when it comes to religion and to reputation I have the highest estimation, I must comment on the allegations that they turn up to disparage and discredit my position—to proclaim them, in short, not merely false, but heretical. Always shielding themselves with a zealous but simulated piety, and co-opting Holy Scripture, making it a sort of agent of their hypocritical pronouncements, they want, moreover, to extend, if not to say abuse their authority, if I am not mistaken, against the intention of both Scripture and the Church Fathers: for they insist that even in matters concerning nature, not faith, it is necessary totally to abandon the use of the senses and rational argument in favor of some scriptural passage, whose superficial message may neglect another, quite different meaning.

In return, I hope to demonstrate that I proceed with far greater piety and faithful zeal than they do, proposing not that they should not condemn this book of Copernicus', but that they should not condemn it, as they wish to do, without understanding it, or listening to it, or even looking at it. They would find that its author never treats of things related to doctrine or faith, nor employs arguments in any way pertaining to the authority of Holy Scripture, which he might perhaps improperly interpret, but he always bases what he says on physical evidence regarding celestial motions, developed with astronomical and geometrical demonstrations, derived above all from sense experience and the most accurate possible observations. It is not that he was unconcerned with sacred letters; but being absolutely certain that his arguments were grounded in demonstrated fact, he knew that they could not contradict Scripture when it is properly understood. . . .

Affirming his deference to church authorities in matters pertaining to faith,
Galileo returns to his critics' agenda to challenge scientific propositions that,
in his view, should not be subject to their scrutiny.

This, then, is they reason they produce for condemning the hypothesis of the Earth's movement and the Sun's stability: that in many places in Holy

Scripture, it is the Sun that moves and the Earth that stands still. And since Scripture can never lie or err, it follows necessarily that the opinion of those who assert that the Sun itself is immobile, but the Earth mobile, is erroneous and damnable.

Concerning this argument, it must first be observed that it is most devoutly said, and most wisely established, that Holy Scripture can never lie—so long as its real meaning has been understood. Yet I think it cannot be denied that its meaning is often recondite, and very different from what seems to be the plain significance of the words. From which it follows that if each time someone expounding a scriptural passage goes no further than its literal sense, and if that reading is wrong, he can introduce to Scripture not only contradictions and untrue statements, but even grave heresies and blasphemies. For we would need to equip God with feet and hands and eyes, not to mention bodily sensations and human feelings such as anger, remorse, hatred, and also at times the forgetfulness of things past and the ignorance of future ones. . . .

Galileo suggests that such scriptural passages were written so as to accommodate popular understanding, and are not to be understood literally; and in the same way, other passages describing natural phenomena, that have nothing to do with matters of faith or the salvation of souls, should not be subject to a literal reading.

Since things stand thus, it seems to me that in disputes about natural phenomena one must not turn immediately to passages of Scripture, but rather utilize the evidence of sense experience and of demonstrations based upon them. Both Holy Scripture and nature, equally, proceed from the Word of God: the first as dictated by the Holy Spirit, the latter as scrupulous executrix of God's laws. However, in order to be accessible to popular understanding, Scripture necessarily says many things that, in the tone and tempo of the literal signification of the words, diverge from absolute truth; but nature, on the contrary, is inexorable and immutable, never trespassing the boundaries that God's laws impose upon it, and does not care whether the human mind can or cannot fathom its recondite principles and operations. So it seems that whatever natural processes or the experience of the senses puts before our eyes, or whatever demonstrations based upon them conclude, should not in any way be cast in doubt, much less condemned, by passages of Scripture that appear to have a different meaning. For not every dictum of Scripture is bound by restraints as severe as bind each natural process, and God reveals himself no less splendidly in nature as in the sacred words of Scripture. . . .

That said, I do not wish to suggest that we should not have the highest regard, for passages of Holy Scripture. . . . I propose rather that the authority of Holy Scripture has the goal principally of conveying to men those articles and propositions which, transcending all human understanding, could not have been derived by any learned discipline or by any other means than from the mouth of the Holy Spirit. . . . But this I do not think it is necessary to believe: that the same God who has endowed us with our senses, with language, and with intellect, has wished us to set these capacities aside, and give us some other means of knowing that which we can discover for ourselves . . . and especially in those disciplines concerning which there is scarcely a jot that can be read in Scripture. . . .

> *This observation especially applies to astronomy, Galileo argues, about which Scripture says little—not even naming the planets other than the Sun and Moon and, once or twice, Venus—perhaps because such matters are of no use in guiding human beings to salvation. The truths yielded by philosophical investigation are not negated by the truths of Scripture: both are true, but in different domains.*

Indeed, . . . I believe that it would be wise to bar any engagement with scriptural passages, forcing them somehow to confirm the truth of this or that scientific conclusion, if sense experience and rational proofs and demonstrations could ever determine the contrary. Who wants to extinguish the human mind? Who will maintain that everything in the world that can be investigated by the senses or apprehended by the mind has already been seen and known? . . . Certainly not, it seems to me, one must not . . . obstruct the path to free thought about the world and the processes of nature, as if they all had already been explained with certainty and thoroughly revealed. Nor should it be called temerity to question views which are generally accepted, nor should anyone seethe with indignation if, in disputes about the natural world, another disagrees with the opinion he prefers, especially concerning problems that have been argued by the greatest philosophers over thousands of years—such as that of the Sun's immobility, and the Earth's motion. . . .

> *Galileo provides examples of the divergent views on these matters of ancient philosophers.*

Given all this, beyond those articles concerning salvation and the foundations of the Faith, against whose massive strength there is no danger whatever that any valid or effective doctrine could be launched, it would be a most wise and useful plan to add no others unnecessarily. Accordingly, confusion would surely result from adding any articles proposed by persons who, while we do not know whether their views are divinely inspired, yet, as we do know, lack the intelligence required first to understand, and secondly to challenge the demonstrations by which, in the most advanced fields of knowledge, such conclusions are proved. I would add, if I am permitted to offer my opinion, it might perhaps better serve the decorum and majesty of Holy Scripture to bar these lightweight and vulgar scribblers from legitimating their compositions, spun too often from their empty fantasies, by strewing them with biblical passages interpreted, or better twisted, to mean something as remote from the plain intention of Scripture as they are close to the absurdity of those who pompously employ them to adorn their work. . . .

Galileo provides two examples of such misinterpretation.

The result, manifestly, is that these authors, having failed to penetrate the real meaning of Scripture, would have required others, had they wielded any real authority, to accept as true conclusions that are refuted by logical demonstration and the evidence of the senses. If this abuse—may God forbid!—took root or took charge, it would soon lead to the prohibition of all the speculative sciences. For in that the number of men incapable of a perfect understanding of Holy Scripture, or of any learned discipline, is by nature greater than the number of the mentally competent, the former, dashing through the biblical texts, would arrogate to themselves the authority to decide all natural questions on the strength of some word or other they have misconstrued, and that had been used in quite the opposite sense by the sacred authors; nor could the tiny remnant of the intelligent withstand the raging flood of the ignorant, who will have gathered as many new followers as it is sweeter to acquire a reputation for wisdom without study or effort than to consume oneself in the ceaseless pursuit of the most demanding disciplines. . . .

René Descartes

The *Discourse on Method* by René Descartes (1596–1650) is, chronologically, the latest of the texts examined in this volume, as well as the one seeming to have the most tenuous connection to humanism. For Descartes was a philosopher—often called the "father of modern philosophy"—in a sense that was not true of Ficino or Pico della Mirandola, or even Copernicus or Galileo: Descartes detaches philosophy from the disciplines with which it had been bundled since antiquity. He builds a metaphysics informed, necessarily, by the ancient Greeks and later thinkers, but which is independent, a system of his own creation. And although he is also interested in mathematics, closely related to his metaphysical investigations, he had in his maturity little interest in classical texts.

Yet Descartes has a place in this exploration of humanism. At the Jesuit school where he studied from age eleven to nineteen (from 1607 to 1615), he was steeped in the Greek and Latin classics, which he read in their original languages. Then during the transformational years of 1618 to 1619, when he traveled abroad as an enlisted officer during a quiet phase at the outset of the Thirty Years War, he engaged in an examination of self, described in the *Discourse*, that was deeply humanistic in quality and strongly reminiscent of the work of Petrarch and Montaigne. Most significantly, the centrality Descartes gives in his metaphysics to the faculty of reason is a heightened expression of the humanist understanding of reason as the distinguishing feature of human nature. Descartes' characterization of reason in Part One of the *Discourse* perfectly echoes this humanist principle: reason alone "makes us men and distinguishes us from the beasts" and "exists whole and entire in each of us." Reason makes us human, and every human possesses it. Here is the fulcrum of Descartes' whole philosophy, which envisioned a universe made up of only two substances: matter, the substance of all things, and mind, which acts upon it, vivifies it, and understands it.

After the critical years 1618–1619, Descartes traveled for nine years, then in 1628 left his native land to live, mostly in solitude, in the Netherlands. There, beginning in 1637 with the publication of the *Discourse on Method*, which anticipates his fully-developed metaphysics, he wrote most of his many works. He left the Netherlands only for brief journeys until 1649, when at her invitation he joined the court of Queen Christina of Sweden, then died several months later. It was a quiet career, replete with thinking, as befits a man for whom the rational mind was the key universal actor.

The *Discourse on the Method for Conducting One's Own Reason Well, and for Seeking the Truth in the Sciences,* to give its full title, unfolds in six parts carefully outlined by the author in his brief preface. Given here are brief excerpts from the first four parts of this substantial work of more than 20,000 words, which suffice to give a sense of Descartes' project.

In Part One, Descartes posits that all human beings possess the faculty of reason, and that there is no obvious difference between the rational capacities of one human being or another: for reason, as quoted earlier, "exists whole and entire in each of us." There are naturally differences in customs, experience, and education, and Descartes reflects on his own excellent education, at the culmination of which, nonetheless, he found himself "confounded by so many doubts and errors" that he turned to study "the book of the world." After some years of travel and rumination, he resolved "to study within myself too and to spend all the powers of my mind in choosing the paths that I should follow." That inward journey is then recounted in the following parts of the *Discourse*.

In Part Two, Descartes reflects on a moment in his youth when he found himself isolated in a warm and pleasant room, and embarks on a quest for certain knowledge. He sets for himself four principles: first, to accept only those truths of which he was certain; second, to divide each problem into parts for their better resolution; third, to proceed in an orderly manner from smaller to larger matters; and fourth, to regularly review and check all that he had gleaned from his inquiries. He is pleased that by this method he is able to perceive the objects of his mind "more rigorously and more distinctly."

In Part Three, Descartes adds to the principles of his method three moral guidelines that he will follow: first, not to deviate from the laws, customs, and religion of his homeland; second, to be firm and resolute even in pursuit of doubtful matters; and third, to remain self-sufficient despite circumstances, since "there is nothing that is completely within our power except our thoughts." He decided, moreover, to continue in the mode of life he then enjoyed, that of an intellectual whose joy lay in the discovery of truth, and so removed himself from his own country to another, where he could find the necessary well-ordered solitude.

In Part Four, after all these preliminaries, Descartes swiftly lays down the foundations of his metaphysics. Systematically rejecting as untrue the opinions about things he had received, he observed that there was one truth that irrefutably existed: that it was his mind that was engaged in that process of refutation, which meant that he himself indubitably existed. Descartes' concise formulation of this realization is understandably famous: "I think, therefore I am." Since the *Discourse* was published in French, Descartes actually wrote "Je pense, donc je suis," giving also the even briefer Latin, "Cogito, ergo sum." All possible thoughts are reduced to this one alone that is true: and it rests on the unconquerable reality of the thinking mind, identified as undying soul. Proceeding from this first principle, Descartes proceeds to a second. He himself, beset by doubts, was clearly imperfect; but his very imperfection implied the existence of a being who was perfect: "I decided to search for the source from which I had learned to think of something more perfect than I was; and I plainly knew that this had to be from some nature that was in fact more perfect." That being is God.

God remains a presence in Descartes' lonely universe, but the more potent presence is the human mind, which has the power to know and dominate nature. This is not humanism, but it is descended from it.

René Descartes, *Discourse on Method* (1637)[32]

PART ONE

Good sense is the best distributed thing in the world, for everyone thinks himself to be so well endowed with it that even those who are the most difficult to please in everything else are not at all wont to desire more of it than they have. It is not likely that everyone is mistaken in this. Rather, it provides

---

32. From Descartes, *Discours de la méthode*, trans. Donald Cress, in René Descartes, *Philosophical Essays and Correspondence*, ed. Roger Ariew (Indianapolis, IN; Cambridge, MA: Hackett Publishing Co., 2000), 46–82.

evidence that the power of judging well and of distinguishing the true from the false (which is, properly speaking, what people call "good sense" or "reason") is naturally equal in all men. . . .

For myself, I have never presumed that my mind was in any respect more perfect than that of ordinary men. In fact, I have often desired to have as quick a wit, or as keen and distinct an imagination, or as full and responsive a memory as some other people. And other than these I know of no qualities that serve in the perfecting of the mind, for as to reason or sense, inasmuch as it alone makes us men and distinguishes us from the beasts, I prefer to believe that it exists whole and entire in each of us. . . .

> *Descartes considers himself fortunate to have employed his mind since his youth in seeking out truth, for which task he has developed a method that he will explain in this essay. His excellent education was a good foundation, but not in itself sufficient.*

I have been nourished on letters since my childhood, and because I was convinced that by means of them one could acquire a clear and assured knowledge of everything that is useful in life, I had a tremendous desire to master them. But as soon as I had completed this entire course of study, at the end of which one is ordinarily received into the ranks of the learned, I completely changed my mind. For I found myself confounded by so many doubts and errors that it seemed to me that I had not gained any profit from my attempt to teach myself, except that more and more I had discovered my ignorance. And yet I was at one of the most renowned schools of Europe, where I thought there must be learned men, if in fact any such men existed anywhere on earth. . . .

> *Descartes pursued all the disciplines taught in school, and explored others as well. He delighted in mathematics, respected theology, and studied philosophy, but did not find that any offered him certainty. Nor was he willing to accept as true those things accepted by many people as custom.*

But after I had spent some years thus studying in the book of the world and in trying to gain some experience, I resolved one day to study within myself too and to spend all the powers of my mind in choosing the paths that I should follow. In this I had much more success, it seems to me, than had I never left either my country or my books.

PART TWO

I was then in Germany,[33] where the occasion of the wars which are not yet over there had called me; and as I was returning to the army from the coro-

---

33. In 1618 to 1619, during the Thirty Years War, Descartes served under Prince Maurice of Nassau (the Netherlands) and Duke Maximilian I, Elector of Bavaria, which involved travels

nation of the emperor, the onset of winter detained me in quarters where, finding no conversation to divert me and fortunately having not worries or passions to trouble me, I remained for an entire day shut up by myself in a stove-heated room, where I was completely free to converse with myself about my thoughts.

> *Here Descartes begins the meditations that lead to his discovery of his method for seeking truth. He muses on the greater excellence of projects guided by one master, rather than many, and thereupon concludes that the reasoning one pursues in one's own mind is superior to that built on the opinions of others— opinions from which he now proceeds to free himself. He sets himself a set of four rules to follow in his quest for certain knowledge.*

And since the multiplicity of laws often provides excuses for vices, so that a state is much better ruled when it has but very few laws and when these are very strictly observed; likewise, in place of the large number of precepts of which logic is composed, I believe that the following four rules would be sufficient for me, provided I made a firm and constant resolution not even once to fail to observe them:

The first was never to accept anything as true that I did not plainly know to be such; that is to say, carefully to avoid hasty judgment and prejudice; and to include nothing more in my judgments than what presented itself to my mind so clearly and so distinctly that I had no occasion to call it in doubt.

The second, to divide each of the difficulties I would examine into as many parts as possible and as was required in order better to resolve them.

The third, to conduct my thoughts in an orderly fashion, by commencing with those objects that are simplest and easiest to know, in order to ascend little by little, as by degrees, to the knowledge of the most composite things, and by supposing an order even among those things that do not naturally precede one another.

And at last, everywhere to make enumerations so complete and reviews so general that I was assured of having omitted nothing.

Those long chains of utterly simple and easy reasonings that geometers commonly use to arrive at their most difficult demonstrations had given me occasion to imagine that all the things that can fall within human knowledge follow from one another in the same way, and that, provided only that one abstain from accepting any of them as true that is not true, and that one always adheres to the order one must follow in deducing the ones from the others, there cannot be any that are so remote that they are not eventually reached nor so hidden that they are not discovered. And I was not very

---

through the German lands. Emperor Ferdinand II was crowned on 9 September 1619, in Frankfurt.

worried about trying to find out which of them it would be necessary to begin with; for I already knew that it was the simplest and easiest to know.

He begins, therefore, with mathematics, specifically geometrical analysis and algebra, and was confident that he was making steady progress toward achieving certain knowledge.

But what pleased me most about this method was that by means of it I was assured of using my reason in everything, if not perfectly, at least as well as was in my power; and in addition that I felt that in practicing this method my mind was little by little getting into the habit of conceiving its objects more rigorously and more distinctly. . . .

PART THREE

And finally, . . . in order not to remain irresolute in my actions while reason required me to be so in my judgments, and in order not to cease to live as happily as possible during this time, I formulated a provisional code of morals, which consisted of but three or four maxims, which I very much want to share with you.

The first was to obey the laws and customs of my country, constantly holding on to the religion in which, by God's grace, I had been instructed from my childhood, and governing myself in everything else according to the most moderate opinions and those furthest from excess. . . .

My second maxim was to be as firm and resolute in my actions as I could, and to follow the most doubtful opinions, once I had decided on them, with no less constancy than if they had been very well assured. . . .

My third maxim was always to try to conquer myself rather than fortune, and to change my desires rather than the order of the world; and generally to accustom myself to believing that there is nothing that is completely within our power except our thoughts, so that, after we have done our best regarding things external to us, everything that is lacking for us to succeed, is, from our point of view absolutely impossible. . . .

Finally, to conclude this code of morals, I took it upon myself to review the various occupations that men have in this life, in order to try to choose the best one; and, not wanting to say anything about the occupations of others, I thought I could not do better than to continue in that very one in which I found myself, that is to say, spending my whole life cultivating my reason and advancing, as far as I could, in the knowledge of the truth, following the method I had prescribed to myself. I had met with such extreme contentment since the time I had begun to make use of this method, that I did not believe one could obtain any sweeter or more innocent contentment in this life; and, discovering every day by its means some truths that to me seemed quite important and commonly ignored by other men, the satisfaction I had from them so filled my mind that nothing else was of any consequence to me. . . .

> *Having established his code of morals, Descartes embarked over the next nine years on the next phase of his career, in which he traveled and conversed with learned men, while freeing himself of the burden of inherited opinions. Then, he withdrew from society to pursue his meditations.*

And it is exactly eight years ago that this desire [to make himself worthy of the reputation for wisdom he had gained] made me resolve to take my leave of all those places where I might have acquaintances, and to retire here,[34] to a country where the long duration of the war has led to the establishment of such well-ordered discipline that the armies quartered here seem to serve only to make one enjoy the fruits of peace with even greater security, and where in the midst of the crowd of a great and very busy people who are more concerned with their own affairs than they are curious about those of others, I have been able, without lacking any of the amenities to be found in the most bustling cities, to live as solitary and as withdrawn a life as I could in the remotest desert.

PART FOUR

I do not know whether I ought to tell you about the first meditations I engaged in there; for they are so metaphysical and so out of the ordinary that perhaps they will not be to everyone's liking. And yet, in order that it should be possible to judge whether the foundations I have laid are sufficiently firm, I find myself in some sense forced to talk about them. For a long time I had noticed that in matters of morality one must sometimes follow opinions that one knows to be quite uncertain, just as if they were indubitable, as has been said above; but because I then desired to devote myself exclusively to the search for the truth, I thought it necessary that I do exactly the opposite, and that I reject as absolutely false everything in which I could imagine the least doubt, in order to see whether, after this process, something in my beliefs remained that was entirely indubitable. Thus, because our senses sometimes deceive us, I wanted to suppose that nothing was exactly as they led us to imagine. And because there are men who make mistakes in reasoning, even in the simplest matters in geometry, and who commit paralogisms, judging that I was just as prone to err as any other, I rejected as false all the reasonings that I had previously taken for demonstrations. And finally, considering the fact that all the same thoughts we have when we are awake can also come to us when we

---

34. Descartes moved more or less permanently to the Netherlands in 1628, nine years after his stay in Germany.

are asleep, without any of them being true, I resolved to pretend that all the things that had ever entered my mind were not more true than the illusions of my dreams. But immediately afterward I noticed that while I wanted thus to think that everything was false, it necessarily had to be the case that I, who was thinking this, was something. And noticing that this truth—*I think, therefore I am*—was so firm and so assured that all the most extravagant suppositions of the skeptics were incapable of shaking it, I judged that I could accept it without scruple as the first principle of the philosophy I was seeking.

Then, examining with attention what I was, and seeing that I could pretend that I had no body and that there was no world nor any place where I was, I could not pretend, on that account, that I did not exist at all; and that, on the contrary, from the very fact that I thought of doubting the truth of other things, it followed very evidently and very certainly that I existed; whereas, on the other hand, had I simply stopped thinking, even if all the rest of what I had ever imagined had been true, I would have had no reason to believe that I had existed. From this I knew that I was a substance the whole essence or nature of which is simply to think, and which, in order to exist, has no need of any place nor depends on any material thing. Thus this "I," that is to say, the soul through which I am what I am, is entirely distinct from the body and is even easier to know than the body, and even if there were no body at all, it would not cease to be all that it is.

After this, I considered in general what is needed for a proposition to be true and certain; for since I had just found one of them that I knew to be such, I thought I ought also to know in what this certitude consists. And having noticed that there is nothing at all in this *I think, therefore I am* that assures me that I am speaking the truth, except that I see very clearly that, in order to think, it is necessary to exist, I judged that I could take as a general rule that the things we conceive very clearly and very distinctly are all true, but that there is merely some difficulty in properly discerning which are those that we distinctly conceive.

Following this, reflecting upon the fact that I doubted and that, as a consequence, my being was not utterly perfect (for I saw clearly that it is a greater perfection to know than to doubt), I decided to search for the source from which I had learned to think of something more perfect than I was; and I plainly knew that this had to be from some nature that was in fact more perfect. As to those thoughts I had of many other things outside me, such as the heavens, the earth, light, heat, and a thousand others, I had no trouble at all knowing where they came from, because, noticing nothing in them that seemed to me to make them superior to me, I could believe that, if they were true, they were dependencies of my nature, insofar as it had some perfection; and that, if they were not true, I obtained them from nothing, that is to say, they were in me because I had some defect. But the same could not hold for the idea of a being more perfect than my own, for it is a manifest contradiction to receive this idea from nothing; and because it is no less a contradiction that something more perfect should follow from and depend upon something less perfect than that something should come from nothing, I could not obtain it from myself. It thus remained that this idea had been placed in me by a nature truly more perfect than I was and that it even had within itself all the perfections of which I could have any idea, that is to say, to explain myself in a single word, that it was God.

Chapter 9: Women and Humanism

Introduction

Humanism was an essentially male phenomenon. It required the mastery of Latin texts at a high level, and in European culture Latin had always been a male preserve. Male clerics—priests, monks, and the higher clergy—had access to it, being taught mainly in monastic and cathedral schools. So too did the laymen (notaries, secretaries, lawyers), particularly in Italy, who required Latin for their professional tasks, and learned it in secular schools under independent or publicly-appointed masters. The early humanists followed in that path. Ironically, that secular Latin schooling only made humanism more specifically male-gendered; for within the church, at least, in convents and other female communities, a few women learned Latin sufficiently to keep records, write chronicles, and create original works, while there was no such institutional context for female intellectual activity within the humanist domain. The classical works the humanists so admired, finally, and that so powerfully fired their imaginations, to a great extent concerned those quintessentially masculine forms of activity, political rule and military achievement. Why, and how, would women enter into the world of the humanists?

But in fifteenth-century Italy—the Quattrocento, or "400s," as it was called, the preeminent century of early humanism—they did. There were not many female humanists, only a dozen or so in this era, all born into the professional or aristocratic elites, who by some accident of family structure or heritage acquired a Latin education. Thereupon they hungrily and irrepressibly participated in humanist intellectual circles, and composed works in the usual humanist genres: letters above all, but also orations, dialogues, treatises, and poems. Surprisingly, despite some misogynistic responses, they were on the whole welcomed, their merits acknowledged by major humanist arbiters whose validation of the efforts of these fledgling authors opened the doors through which they could enter into the discourse that transpired in male intellectual circles. Yet once admitted to these enclaves, what they spoke and wrote about, strikingly, was themselves—not as individuals, but as women. The misogyny of the inherited intellectual tradition was so potent a force that these women, equipped with the tools of learning and eloquence, felt compelled to confront it.

Excerpts from the works of the three major female humanists of the Italian Quattrocento are included here: Isotta Nogarola (1418–1466), Laura Cereta (1469–1499), and Cassandra Fedele (1465–1558). Nogarola, the author of letters, orations, and a dialogue, directly addresses the gender bias inherent in Christian thought in her *Dialogue* on the relative culpability of Adam and Eve for Original Sin. Cereta, the author of letters and an oration, uses the humanist letter as a vehicle for the defense of female intellectual activity. Fedele, the author of letters and orations, defines the importance of the liberal arts, and extends their utility for men alone, who will employ them in their professional lives, to women as well. A fourth major Italian woman humanist, Olympia Morata, encountered earlier in this volume (Chapter 4), belongs to the sixteenth century and the Reformation crisis that characterized it.

In the sixteenth and seventeenth centuries, as humanism diffuses throughout Europe and impacts upon nearly every branch of learning, the humanist defense of female learning intersects with a wider European discussion of the worth of women: a debate, often referred to by the French phrase *querelle des femmes*, involving both male and female advocates of female merit. That debate culminates in the seventeenth-century works of the Dutch writer Anna Maria van Schurman, whose defense of education for women circulated widely in several languages, and the French writer Marie Le Jars de Gournay (1565–1645), whose brilliantly concise essay on *The Equality of Men and Women* seems to gather up all the strands of thought about women's intellectual capacity and announce a final resolution: that in mental capacity and essential dignity, men and women are equal, differing only in physiology so as to propagate the species. This chapter ends with selections from Gournay's influential work.

Humanism was not the only realm in which learned women were active from the fifteenth to seventeenth centuries. Before the Italian women humanists raised their pens, the French author Christine de Pizan had already composed her *Book of the City of Ladies* in 1405, a response to Boccaccio's encyclopedic compilation of *Famous Women* as well as to the whole tradition of male misogyny; it was not a humanist work, but a vernacular composition that emerged from the context of French courtly literature. And after the humanist Quattrocento, the sixteenth century would see an explosion of female-authored literary works, mostly in the vernacular: poems, letters, epics, plays, dialogues, and treatises. But the specific contribution of the women humanists is their engagement on the theoretical plane with the inherited arguments against female learning, in unpacking which they lay the foundation for the claim of female equality with men.

Isotta Nogarola

The first major female humanist, Isotta Nogarola (1418–1466) wrote in three of the principal humanist genres: the letter, the oration, and the dialogue. These all attest to her mastery of the classical tradition, and her graceful and intelligent prose. Her one dialogue, however, towers in importance: for in her *Dialogue on the Equal or Unequal Sin of Adam and Eve*, she squarely confronts the theological arguments—in place for more than a millennium and still actively employed—for the subordination of women. Arguably, this single work is the gateway to the further achievements of learned women during the Renaissance and later periods. For without a challenge to the most fundamental beliefs of the scholarly and clerical elite regarding the moral worth of women, it would scarcely have been possible for women to progress.

Born to a noble family of the city of Verona, then subject to Venice, Nogarola's career path diverged conspicuously from that of most privileged women of the Italian Renaissance. She was, first of all, educated: not just at a rudimentary level, not just in the Italian vernacular, as was not uncommon, but in the latest humanist curriculum, delivered by a professional tutor who was himself the protégé of one of Italy's foremost Greek scholars. Second, while still an adolescent she was welcomed to the lofty humanist circles that had recently formed in Venice and its nearby university town of Padua, where her brothers had been students. Not only engaging in conversation with these luminaries, she also began her literary career, approaching them as correspondents and winning their approval. Finally, Nogarola chose not to marry—most unusual for a woman, whose only alternative to marriage, normally, was to enter a convent—but returned to her native Verona, took up residence with her widowed mother in the households, successively, of two brothers, and dedicated herself to a life of study. In this era, however, when it was not possible for a single woman of Nogarola's rank to live alone and move freely in society, only one acceptable role was available to her: that of a holy woman, a woman who lived at home but in religious seclusion. It seems that Nogarola chose this path. Without formally adopting any religious vocation, she surrounded herself with sacred objects, icons, and books, and turned her attention to religious and philosophical more than literary matters. The male intellectuals of Italy saluted and celebrated her.

None esteemed her more than Ludovico Foscarini (1409–1480), a Venetian nobleman, statesman, and humanist, whose official duties brought him often to Verona. In 1450–1451, and again in 1456–1457, he served as one of the two Venetian governors appointed to Verona, a subject city.

During the first of these periods of official residence, the deep friendship he had already formed with Nogarola was documented in an exchange of letters, of which only his survive. In 1451, as well, he and Nogarola engaged in what was possibly a public disputation on the subject of the relative culpability of Adam and Eve for the expulsion from paradise, or, more likely, an exchange of formal letters on that theme. He invited Nogarola to recast these exchanges as a dialogue, of which a section is given here. In it, both actors display their extensive knowledge of theology and law. In it, too, Foscarini evinces the confidence and authority that were his by reason of his great eminence; and Nogarola demonstrates her considerable ingenuity and tenacity in resisting the normative interpretation of Eve's role in the Garden of Eden, held by both the official church and by Foscarini, a man who was in love with her.

In an interpretation crafted by the late ancient Fathers of the Church and transmitted and approved in the thousand years thereafter, Eve was seen as the principal culprit in the loss of innocence and expulsion from Eden. A diabolic serpent tempted her to taste the forbidden fruit of the Tree of Knowledge that God had placed there; she in turn persuaded her husband, Adam, to eat. This was the Original Sin in Christian theology that led to the downfall of man, a fall from grace that could only be remedied by the coming of Christ. Both were punished—Adam by the sentence of mortality and compulsion to work, Eve by the curse of bearing children in pain—and expelled from the Garden. Their guilt devolved to all of their descendants.

Against this wall of condemnation, Nogarola hurls her arguments: Eve was morally and intellectually weaker than Adam, and therefore should be considered to have sinned less; the sin she committed, a yielding to the promise of pleasure, was less than Adam's, a defiance of God's command; her lesser sin is signified by her lesser punishment—the duty to birth children viewed as lesser than Adam's consignment to perpetual labor. The excerpt that follows lays out these arguments, which are developed further in subsequent exchanges between the two interlocutors. The critical point is that Nogarola defends Eve from the terrible responsibility for Original Sin by conceding her inferiority: "For where there is less intellect and less constancy, there there is less sin, and Eve lacked sense and constancy and therefore sinned less." She was a victim of her cravings: where Adam ate because he hoped to become like God, she did so "because she was weak and inclined to pleasure." In yielding to her appetite, she "harmed only herself and in no way endangered human posterity," while Adam, in his rebellion against God's law, "spread the infection of sin to himself and to all future generations."

Space does not permit the presentation of the full sequence of winding arguments and counterarguments, like an intricate dance in which this Renaissance couple replicates the relations between Adam and Eve. It is a bravura performance. As the dialogue approaches its close, Foscarini commends her: "So divinely have you encompassed the whole of this problem that your words seem to have been drawn not from the fonts of philosophy and theology but from heaven itself." And he invites her to write the dialogue from the fabric of their conversation: "and although others may find that my writings suffer from the defect of obscurity, if you, who are most brilliant, accept them and join them to what you and I have already written, our views will become known and will sparkle and shine amid the shadows." And so they have.

Isotta Nogarola, *Dialogue on the Equal or Unequal Sin of Adam and Eve* (1451)[1]

An honorable debate between the illustrious lord Ludovico Foscarini, Venetian doctor of the arts and civil and canon law, and the noble and learned and divine lady Isotta Nogarola of Verona, regarding the judgment of Aurelius Augustine: "They sinned unequally according to their sexes, but equally in pride."[2]

LUDOVICO begins: If it is in any way possible to measure the gravity of human sinfulness, then we should see Eve's sin as more to be condemned than Adam's because she was assigned by a just judge to a harsher punishment than was Adam, because she believed that she could become like God, which is considered an unforgivable sin against the Holy Spirit; because she provoked, and thus was the cause of Adam's sin—not he of hers; and because, finally, since it is an excuse, although a shameful one, if one is led into sin by a friend, yet she is not to be excused, since she is the one who enticed Adam to do wrong.

ISOTTA: But I see things—since you move me to reply—from quite another and contrary vantage point. For where there is less intellect and less constancy, there there is less sin, and Eve lacked sense and constancy and therefore sinned less. Knowing her weakness, that crafty serpent began by tempting the woman, thinking the man perhaps invulnerable because of his constancy. For it says in *Sentences* 2:[3] "Standing in the woman's presence, the ancient foe did not boldly persuade but approached her with a question: 'Why did God bid you not to eat of the tree of paradise?' She responded,

---

1. From Isotta Nogarola, *Dialogue on Adam and Eve*, in Nogarola, *Complete Writings: Letterbook, Dialogue on Adam and Eve, Orations,* ed. and trans. Margaret L. King and Diana M. Robin (Chicago: University of Chicago Press, 2004), 145–58.

2. Augustine, *The City of God,* 14:14; trans. John O'Meara (New York: Penguin, 1984). See also *De Genesi ad litteram,* 12:11.35 (PL 34:449).

3. Peter Lombard, *Sententiae in IV libros distinctae* 2.21.5.2 (PL 192:696).

'Lest we should die.' But seeing that she doubted the words of the Lord, the devil said, 'You shall not die,' but 'you will be like gods, knowing good and evil.'"[4]

Adam must also be judged more guilty than Eve, second, because of his greater contempt for God's command. For in Genesis 2 it appears that the Lord commanded Adam, not Eve, where it says, "The Lord God took the man and placed him in the paradise of Eden to till it and to keep it" (and he did not say, "that they might care for and protect it"), "and the Lord god commanded the man" (and not "them"): "From every tree of the garden you (singular) may eat"—and not "you" (plural)—"for the day you (singular) eat of it, you (singular)"—and not "you (plural)"—"will die."[5] God directed his command to Adam alone because he esteemed the man more highly than the woman.

Moreover, the woman did not eat from the forbidden tree because she believed she would become like God, but rather because she was weak and inclined to pleasure. It is written, "Now the woman saw that the tree was good for food and pleasing to the eyes. . . . She took of its fruit and ate it, and also gave some to her husband and he ate,"[6] and it does not say that she did so in order to be like God. And if Adam had not eaten, her sin would have had not consequences. For it does not say, "If Eve had not sinned Christ would not have been made incarnate," but "If Adam had not sinned," etc.[7] Thus the woman, but only because she had been first deceived by the serpent's evil persuasion, did indulge in the delights of paradise, but she would have harmed only herself and in no way endangered human posterity if the consent of the first-born man had not been offered. Therefore, Eve was no danger to posterity but *only* to herself; but the man Adam spread the infection of sin to himself and to all future generations. Thus Adam, being the author of all humans yet to be born, was also the first cause for their perdition. For this reason, the healing of humankind was celebrated first in the male and thereafter in the female sex of the human species; likewise, after Christ expelled the unclean spirit from the man, he went up from the synagogue and came to the woman to heal her.[8]

As for the argument that Eve was condemned by a just judge to a harsher punishment, it is evidently false, for God said to the woman, "I will greatly increase your pangs in childbearing, in pain shall you bring forth children,

---

4. Genesis 3:4, 5.

5. Genesis 2:15–17.

6. Genesis 3:6.

7. A variation on 1 Cor. 15:22: "For as in Adam all die, even so in Christ shall all be made alive" (First Authorized Version of King James Bible, hereafter cited AV).

8. Mark 5:1–32.

yet your desire shall be for your husband, and he shall rule over you."[9] But to Adam he said, "Because you have listened to your wife and have eaten of the tree of which I have commanded you (singular) not to eat (notice what is said, that God commanded Adam alone and not Eve), cursed be the ground because of you; in toil shall you eat of it all the days of your life; thorns and thistles shall it bring forth to you, and you shall eat the plants of the field. In the sweat of your brow you shall eat bread till you return to the ground, since out of it you were taken; for dust you are and unto dust you shall return."[10] Here it is seen that Adam's punishment is harsher than Eve's; for God said to Adam, "To dust you shall return," and not to Eve, and death is the most terrible punishment that could be assigned. Therefore, it is established that Adam's punishment was greater than Eve's.

I have written this because you wished me to. Yet I have done so with trepidation, since this is not a woman's task. But you are kind, and if you find any part of my writing poorly done, you will correct it.

LUDOVICO: You defend the cause of Eve most subtly, and indeed defend it so well that, if I had not been born a man, you would have made me your champion. But sticking fast to the truth, which is firmly rooted, I have set out to assault your fortress with your own weapons and shall now attack its foundations, which can be destroyed by the testimony of sacred Scripture, so there will be no lack of material for my refutation.

Eve sinned from ignorance and inconstancy, from which you conclude that she sinned less seriously. But ignorance—especially of those things that we are obligated to know—does not excuse us. For it is written, "But if any man be ignorant, let him be ignorant."[11] The eyes that guilt makes blind, punishment opens. He who has been foolish in guilt will be wise in punishment, especially when the sinner's mistake occurs through negligence. For the woman's ignorance, born of arrogance, does not excuse her. In the same way, Aristotle and the legal experts, who teach a true philosophy, find the drunk and ignorant deserving of a double punishment.[12] Nor do I understand how in the world you, who are so many ages distant from Eve, fault her intellect, when her knowledge had been divinely created by the supreme artisan of all things, and who, as you wrote, daunted that clever serpent lurking in paradise who was not bold enough to speak to her directly but approached her with a question.

Acts to inconstancy, moreover, are even more blameworthy than those due to ignorance. For to the same degree that the acts issuing from a solid

---

9. Genesis 3:16.

10. Genesis 3:17–19.

11. See 1 Cor. 14:38 (AV).

12. Aristotle, *Nicomachean Ethics*, 3.5.1113b.30–33.

and constant mental attitude are more worthy and distinct from the preceding ones, so should those issuing from inconstancy be punished more severely, since inconstancy is an evil in itself, and when paired with an evil sin makes the sin worse. Nor is Adam's companion excused because Adam was appointed to protect her, contrary to your contention that thieves who have been trustingly employed by a householder are not punished with the most severe punishment like strangers or those in whom no confidence has been placed. For the woman's frailty was not the cause of sin, as you write, but her pride, since the demon promised her knowledge, which leads to arrogance and inflates with pride, according to the apostle.[13] For it says in Ecclesiastes, "Pride was the beginning of every sin."[14]

And although the other women followed, yet she was the first since, when man existed in a state of innocence, his flesh was obedient to him and did not struggle against reason. The first impulse of sin, therefore, was an inordinate appetite for seeking that which was not suited to its own nature, as Augustine wrote to Orosius, "Swollen by pride, man obeyed the serpent's persuasion and disdained God's commands."[15] For that adversary said to Eve, "Your eyes will be opened and you will be like God, knowing good and evil."[16] Nor would the woman have believed the demon's persuasive words, as Augustine says in his commentary on Genesis, unless a love of her own power had overcome her, which love is a stream sprung from the well of pride.[17] I shall continue to follow Augustine in his view that at the moment when Eve desired to capture divinity she lost happiness. And those words, "If Adam had not sinned, etc." confirm me in my view. For Eve may have sinned in such a way that, just as the demons did not merit redemption, neither perhaps did she. I speak only in jest, but Adam's sin was fortunate since it warranted such a redeemer.

And lest I finally stray too far from what you have written, I shall turn to your argument that Adam's punishment was more severe than Eve's and his sin, accordingly, greater. But the woman suffers all the penalties inflicted on the man, and since her sorrows are greater than his, not only is she doomed to death, condemned to eat at the cost of sweat, denied entry into paradise by the cherubim and flaming swords, but in addition to all these things that are common to both, she alone must give birth in pain and be subjected to her husband.

But because in such a matter it is not sufficient to have refuted your arguments without also putting forward my own, I shall do so now. Eve believed

---

13. See 1 Cor. 1:27–29, 8:1.

14. Ecclesiastes 10:13.

15. Augustine, *Ad Orosium contra Priscillianistas et Origenistas liber unus* (PL 42:669–78), 671.

16. Genesis 3:5.

17. *De Genesi ad litteram* 11:30 (PL 34.445).

that she was made similar to God, and, out of envy, desired that which wounds the Holy Spirit. Moreover, she must bear responsibility for every fault of Adam because, as Aristotle testifies, the cause of a cause is the cause of that which is caused.[18] Indeed, every prior cause influences an outcome more than a secondary cause, and the principle of any genus, according to the same Aristotle, is seen as its greatest component. In fact, it is considered to be more than half the whole.[19] And in the *Posterior Analytics* he writes, "That on account of which any thing exists is that thing and more greatly so";[20] now since Adam sinned on account of Eve, it follows that Eve sinned much more than Adam. Similarly, just as it is better to treat others well than to be well treated, so it is worse to persuade another to evil than to be persuaded to evil. For he sins less who sins by another's example, inasmuch as what is done by example can be said to be done according to a kind of law. For this reason it is commonly said that "the sins that many commit are without fault." Thus Eve, who persuaded her husband to commit an evil act, sinned more greatly than Adam, who merely consented to her example.

And if Adam and Eve both had thought that they were worthy of the same glory, Eve, who was inferior by nature, more greatly departed from the mean and consequently sinned more greatly. Moreover, as a beloved companion she could deceive her husband, vulnerable because of his love for her, more easily than the shameful serpent could deceive the woman. And she persevered longer in sin than Adam because she began first and offenses are that much more serious (according to Gregory's decree) in relation to the length of time they hold the unhappy soul in bondage.[21] Finally, to bring my discourse to a close, Eve was the cause and the example of sin, and Gregory greatly increases the guilt in the case of the example.[22] And Christ, who could not err, condemned more severely the pretext of the ignorant Jews, because it came first, than he did the sentence of the learned Pilate, when he said, "They who have betrayed me to you have greater sin, etc."[23] All who wish to be called Christians have always agreed with this judgment, and you, above all most Christian, will approve and defend it. Farewell, and do not fear, but dare to do much, because you understand so many things so well and write so learnedly.

ISOTTA: I had decided that I would not enter further into a contest with you because, as you say, you assault my fortress with my own weapons. The

---

18. See Aristotle, *Posterior Analytics* 2:11–12.94a20–96a19.

19. *Posterior Analytics* 2:13.96a24–96b24.

20. A paraphrase of the line of thought expressed in the previous passage.

21. Saint Gregory, *Liber regulae pastoralis* 3:32 (PL 77:115).

22. Gregory, *Liber* 1.2 (PL 77:15–16).

23. Nogarola is extrapolating on the Gospel account here (my note).

propositions you have presented me were so perfectly and diligently defended that it would be difficult not merely for me, but for the most learned men, to oppose them. But since I recognize that this contest is useful for me, I have decided to obey your honest wish. Even though I know I struggle in vain, yet I will earn the highest praise if I am defeated by so mighty a man as you. . . .

> *Refuting Foscarini's assertion that because Eve sinned "out of ignorance and inconstancy" her sin was increased, since the law does not allow for these deficiencies, Nogarola shows that, rather, because these traits were inborn in Eve, the product of nature and not malice, her guilt was lessened. She further demonstrates that Adam, being more perfect than Eve, was more responsible for his sin; and that Eve, though she was guilty of "inordinate desire" for the knowledge of good and evil, that fault is slight, and does not amount to a desire "to be like God in power." She denies, as well, that Eve suffered greater punishment in proportion to her greater guilt, and affirms that Eve, as well as Adam, would be redeemed by Christ. Nor does Eve bear greater guilt, Nogarola argues, because she was the cause of Adam's sin; rather Adam, possessing free will, sinned independently by his own guilty choice.*

Let these words be enough for me, an unarmed and poor little woman.

LUDOVICO: So divinely have you encompassed the whole of this problem that your words seem to have been drawn not from the fonts of philosophy and theology but from heaven itself. Hence they are worthy of praise rather than contradiction. Yet, lest you be cheated of the utility you may experience from this debate, attend to these brief arguments that can be posed for the opposite view, that you may sow the honey-sweet seeds of paradise that will delight readers and surround you with glory. . . .

> *Foscarini returns briefly to each of Nogarola's previous arguments on Eve's behalf, to refute them.*

I have explained my views with these few words, both because I was ordered not to exceed the paper sent me[24] and because I speak to you who are most learned. For you do not need me to guide you, for whom, because of your great goodness, the path ahead is perfectly bright and clear. I am only one who has pointed a finger, so to speak, in the direction of the sources—a reflection on earth of the celestial life; and although others may find that my writings suffer from the defect of obscurity, if you, who are most brilliant, accept them and join them to what you and I have already written, our views will become known and will sparkle and shine amid the shadows. And if what I have written is clumsy, by your skill you will make it worthy of your mind, virtue, and glory, you who march forward ever to new battles to the

---

24. A conventional statement, alluding to the need not to write at too great length (my note).

sound of sacred eloquence (as do soldiers to the clamor of trumpets), always more learned and more ready. And you march forward against me, who has applied the whole sum of my thinking to my reading and in the same spirit to my writing, that I might present my case and defend myself against yours, although the many storms and floods of my obligations toss me about at whim. Farewell.

Laura Cereta

Where Nogarola attempts in the language of the learned—philosophers, theologians, lawyers, and humanists—to confront the intellectual tradition that denigrated women, Laura Cereta (1469–1499) is more forthright. When she is challenged by male scorn and female gossip, she addresses her accusers directly, assailing their arguments, lambasting their motives, and defending the right of virtuous women to commit themselves to the labors and joys of mental endeavor. Her voice, on this account, is exceptionally modern, even when her prose, ornate and allusive as was characteristic of the High Renaissance, challenges the modern ear.

Having completed elementary schooling at a nearby convent, Cereta was introduced to the study of the classics by her humanist father, a public official of the Venetian subject city of Brescia. Father and daughter were close; she became not only his apt student—and teacher of her younger siblings—but his secretary and companion. Married in late 1484 or early 1485 to a Venetian merchant, Cereta was widowed on her husband's sudden death in 1486. Her literary career, begun in 1485 while her husband still lived, lasted but three years, through 1488, during which time she wrote a series of eighty-two letters and one oration. After the latter date, we have no more from her hand, although she died eleven years later, at the young age of thirty. What caused her to withdraw from her literary pursuits? Was she discouraged by the opposition they provoked?

The extent of that opposition appears from her angry, impassioned responses, evident in the two letters given here. The letter to Bibolo Semproni responds to a male opponent of learning in women, while that to Lucilia Vernacula responds to women who, absorbed in their trivial and meaningless pursuits, disparage those who have committed themselves to a life of study. The names of both of these correspondents are likely fictional, although they may represent real antagonists. "Bibolo" suggests "bibulous": Cereta is calling him a drunkard. "Vernacula" suggests "vernacular," that is to say common or crude: so Cereta viciously characterizes the posturing women that she mocks.

Bibolo Semproni, as we infer from Cereta's response, had attacked learning in women and refuses to admit that they might be capable of intellectual activity: "your mouth has grown foul," she writes, "because you keep it sealed so that no arguments can come out of it that might enable you to admit that nature imparts one freedom to all human beings equally—to learn." Men are supposed to be strong, but instead they flee from intelligent women "like someone who has been frightened by the attack of a pack of wolves." Does he "tremble from fear alone of my name? . . . What is it you fear?" Well may he tremble, however, because she will defend herself: "Who will be surprised, do you think, Bibolo, if the lacerated and wounded heart of a girl who is filled with indignation bitterly rears itself up against your sarcasm and satire from this day on, now that your trifling arrogance has wounded her with bitter injuries?"

To his malice, she presents the evidence of a "noble lineage" of worthy women, unrolling a parade of them drawn from Boccaccio's *Concerning Famous Women*, an encyclopedia that fueled much early feminist thought and writing from the fourteenth to seventeenth centuries.[25] That so many prophetesses, goddesses, female poets, warriors, and rulers existed over the ages constitutes the evidence to refute Semproni's charges of female incapacity. The sequence ends with the naming of three contemporary figures, including two—Isotta Nogarola and Cassandra Fedele—who also appear in this chapter. They stand, Cereta writes, in the "shimmering light of silence," brilliant but ignored, as seems to be the fate of learned women.[26] Nonetheless, such women "harden their bodies with sobriety and toil, they control their tongues, they carefully monitor what they hear, [and] they ready their minds for all-night vigils. . . . For knowledge is not given as a gift but by study. For a mind free, keen, and unyielding in the face of hard work always rises to the good, and the desire for learning grows in depth and breadth." Women such as these she will defend against male detractors of the "republic of women":[27]

[I] . . . shall wear down and exhaust my pen writing against those men who are garrulous and puffed up with false pride. . . . And I shall strive in a war of vengeance against the notorious abuse of those who fill everything with noise, since armed with such abuse, certain insane and infamous men bark and bare their teeth in vicious wrath at the republic of women, so worthy of veneration.

---

25. Available most recently in the English translation of Virginia Brown, *Famous Women* (Cambridge, MA: Harvard University Press, 2001).

26. Diana Robin, editor and translator of Laura Cereta, *Collected Letters of a Renaissance Feminist*, ed. and trans. Diana M. Robin (Chicago: University of Chicago Press, 1997), comments on this phrase at 78n57: "Cereta apparently didn't think modern Italian women scholars like Nogarola and Fedele got the press they deserved."

27. A phrase editor Robin says she has not encountered elsewhere: see 80n62. It is the analogue, she writes at 74, of the widely-used term *respublica litterarum,* "a metaphor for the notion that there is an imaginary city of men who share a commitment to the study of literature that transcends geopolitical boundaries."

Even more wounding, perhaps, than the attacks of men "puffed up with false pride" are the attacks on learned women by small-minded women: those "gabbing and babbling women" who "can't stand to hear even the epithet 'learned women,'" and "burning with wine and drunkenness, harm with their petulant talk not only their sex but themselves" as they "hunt down with their bilious poison those women who rise to greater distinction than they." Having no real purpose of their own, they "occupy themselves with keeping watch over other people's business, and, like scarecrows hung up in the garden to get rid of sparrows, they shoot poison from the bows of their tongues at those who cross their paths."

Cereta will resist them—"I am not a woman who wants the shameful deeds of insolent people to slip through under the pardon of silence"—and defend herself: "even dogs are allowed to protect themselves from more aggressive fleas by crushing them with their nails." We should be "ashamed and disgusted" that such women have not taken up study of the "humane arts" themselves, "when they could easily acquire such knowledge with skill and virtue," but lost in the "sludge of low pleasures," they fail to "ascend to the understanding of difficult things." For learning requires effort and persistence: it is not "bequeathed to us as a legacy" nor given to us "as a gift," but it is "something that we ourselves acquire."

Thus Cereta draws a bright line between the common crowd of women mired in the "sludge of low pleasures" and those like herself who struggle to acquire knowledge and so participate in the true "republic of women." Her vision of a kind of alternate female society makes her indeed, as Diana Robin has named her, a "Renaissance feminist"[28]—or at least a proto-feminist: for here women will define themselves by their own actions and are not defined by male-determined norms.

Laura Cereta, *Letters to Bibolo Semproni* (1488) and *Lucilia Vernacula* (1487)[29]

To Bibolo Semproni (13 January 1488)

Your complaints are hurting my ears, for you say publicly and quite openly that you are not only surprised but pained that I am said to show this extraordinary intellect of the sort one would have thought nature would give to the most learned of men—as if you had reached the conclusion, on the facts of the case, that a similar girl had seldom been seen among the peoples of the world. You are wrong on both counts, Semproni, and now that you've

---

28. In the title of her volume of Cereta's *Collected Letters*.

29. From Cereta, *Collected Letters*, 74–82.

abandoned the truth, you are going to spread information abroad that is clearly false.

I think you should be deeply pained—no, you should actually be blushing—you who are no longer now a man full of animus but instead a stone animated by the scorn you have for the studies that make us wise, while you grow weak with the sickness of debilitating leisure. And thus in your case, it is not nature that goes astray but the mind, for which the path from the appearance of virtue to villainy is a fairly easy one. In this manner, you appear to be flattering a susceptile young girl because of the glory that has accrued to her—my—name. But the snare of flattery is seductive, for you who have always set traps for the sex that has been revered all throughout history have been ensnared yourself. And duped by your own madness, you are trying, by running back and forth, to trample me underfoot and smash me to the ground with your fists. . . .

In case you don't know, the philosopher sees with her mind; she furnishes paths with a window of reason through which she can ascend to a state of awareness. For Providence, the knower of the future, conquers marauding evil, trampling it with feet that have eyes. I would remain silent, believe me, if you, with your long-standing hostile and envious attitude towards me, had learned to attack me alone. . . . But I am angry and my disgust overflows. Why should the condition of our sex be shamed by your little attacks? Because of this, a mind thirsting for revenge is set afire; because of this, a sleeping pen is wakened for insomniac writing. Because of this, red-hot anger lays bare a heart and mind long muzzled by silence.

My cause itself is worthy: I am impelled to show what great glory that noble lineage[30] which I carry in my own breast has won for virtue and literature—a lineage that knowledge, the bearer of honors, has exalted in every age. For the possession of this lineage is legitimate and sure, and it has come all the way down to me from the perpetual continuance of a more enduring race.

We have read that the breast of Ethiopian Sabba, imbued with divinity, solved the prophetic riddles of the Egyptian king Solomon.[31] The first writers

---

30. The "noble lineage" of which she speaks, as becomes apparent below, is that of the learned women through the ages: see *Collected Letters*, 76n39.

31. Named in this and the following paragraphs are figures drawn from Boccaccio's *Concerning Famous Women*: the biblical Queen of Sheba (Cereta's "Ethiopian Sabba"); the Sibyl (prophetess) Amalthea; the prophetesses Eriphila and Nicostrata; the goddess Isis; the warrior and author Zenobia; the prophetess Manto; the goddess Athena; Plato's students Phyliasia and Lasthenia; the poet Sappho; the poet Leontium; the author Proba; the queen Semiramis; the poet Sempronia; the orator Hortensia; the poet Cornificia; the learned Roman aristocrats Tullia and Cornelia. Not from Boccaccio but from her current knowledge, Cereta closes by naming three near-contemporaries: Nicolosa of Bologna who purportedly attended university lectures;

believed that Amalthea, a woman erudite in the knowledge of the future, sang responses near the banks that surround the Avernus, not far from Baiae. She, who as a Sybil was worthy of the gods of this lineage, sold books full of oracles to Priscus Tarquinius. Thus the Babylonian prophetess Eriphila, looking into the future with her divine mind far removed, described the fall and the ashes of Troy, the fortunes of the Roman empire, and the mysteries of Christ, who would later be born. Nicostrata, too, the mother of Evander and very learned in prophecy as well as literature, attained such genius that she was the first to show the alphabet to the first Latins in sixteen figures. The enduring fame of Inachan Isis will flourish, for she alone of the Argive goddesses revealed to the Egyptians her own alphabet for reading. But Zenobia, an Egyptian woman of noble erudition, became so learned not only in Egyptian but also in Latin and Greek literature that she wrote the histories of barbarian and foreign peoples.

Shall we attribute illiteracy to Theban Manto, the prophesying daughter of Tiresias, and to Pyromantia, too, who was full of those Chaldaean arts when she spoke with the shades of the dead and foretold events in the future through the movements of flames, the flights of birds, and livers and entrails of animals? Where did all the great wisdom of Tritonian Pallas come from, which enabled her to educate so many Athenians in the arts, if it was not that she succeeded in unraveling the mysteries of the scriptures of Apollo, the physician, to the delight of everyone? Those little Greek women Phyliasia and Lasthenia were wonderful sources of light in the world of letters and they filled me with new life because they ridiculed the students of Plato, who frequently tied themselves in knots over the snare-filled sophistries of their arguments.

Lesbian Sappho serenaded the stony heart of her lover with tearful poems, sounds I might have thought came from Orpheus' lyre or the plectrum of Phoebus. Soon the Greek tongue of Leontium, full of the Muses, emerged and she, who had made herself agreeable with the liveliness of her writing, dared to make a bitter attack on the divine words of Theophrastus. Nor would I omit here Proba, noted both for her exceptional tongue and her knowledge; for she wove together and composed histories of the Old Testament with fragments from Homer and Virgil.

The majesty of the Roman state deemed worthy a little Greek woman, Semiramis, for she spoke her mind about the laws in a court of law and about kings in the senate. Pregnant with virtue, Rome bore Sempronia, who, forceful in her eloquent poetry, spoke in public assemblies and filled the minds of her audiences with persuasive orations. Hortensia, the daughter of

---

Isotta Nogarola (Isotta of Verona); and Cassandra Fedele (Cassandra of Venice). Nogarola and Fedele, of course, also appear in the present chapter. For Cereta's use and manipulation of Boccaccio, see *Collected Letters*, 76–78nn41–57.

Hortensius, and also an orator, was celebrated at a public meeting with equal elegance. Her grace of speech was so great that she persuaded the triumvirs, albeit with the tears of a loyal mother, to absolve the women of Rome from having to pay the debt levied against them. Add also Cornificia, the sister of the poet Cornificius, whose devotion to literature bore such fruit that she was said to have been nurtured on the milk of the Castalian Muses and who wrote epigrams in which every phrase was graced with Heliconian flowers. I will not mention here Cicero's daughter Tulliola or Terentia or Cornelia, Roman women who reached the pinnacle of fame for their learning, and accompanying them in the shimmering light of silence will be Nicolosa of Bologna, Isotta of Verona, and Cassandra of Venice.

All history is full of such examples. My point is that your mouth has grown foul because you keep it sealed so that no arguments can come out of it that might enable you to admit that nature imparts one freedom to all human beings equally—to learn. But the question of my exceptionality remains. And here choice alone, since it is the arbiter of character, is the distinguishing factor. For some women worry about the styling of their hair, the elegance of their clothes, and the pearls and other jewelry they wear on their fingers. Others love to say cute little things, to hide their feelings behind a mask of tranquility, to indulge in dancing, and lead pet dogs around on a leash. For all I care, other women can long for parties with carefully appointed tables, for the peace of mind of sleep, or they can yearn to deface with paint the pretty face they see reflected in their mirrors. But those women for whom the quest for the good represents a higher value restrain their young spirits and ponder better plans. They harden their bodies with sobriety and toil, they control their tongues, they carefully monitor what they hear, they ready their minds for all-night vigils, and they rouse their minds for the contemplation of probity in the case of harmful literature. For knowledge is not given as a gift but by study. For a mind free, keen, and unyielding in the face of hard work always rises to the good, and the desire for learning grows in depth and breadth.

So be it therefore. May we women, then, not be endowed by God the grantor with any giftedness or rare talent through any sanctity of our own. Nature has granted to all enough of her bounty; she opens to all the gates of choice, and through these gates, reason sends legates to the will, for it is through reason that these legates can transmit their desires. I shall make a bold summary of the matter. Yours is the authority, ours is the inborn ability. But instead of manly strength, we women are naturally endowed with cunning; instead of a sense of security, we are suspicious. Down deep we women are content with our lot. But you, enraged and maddened by the anger of the dog from whom you flee, are like someone who has been frightened by the attack of a pack of wolves. The victor does not look for the fugitive; nor does she who desires a cease-fire with the enemy conceal herself. Nor does she set up camp with courage and arms when the conditions are hopeless. Nor does it give the strong any pleasure to pursue one who is already fleeing.

Look, do you tremble from fear alone of my name? I am savage neither in mind nor hand. What is it you fear? You run away and hide in vain, for the traps that await you around every corner have been more cunningly set. Is it thus that you, a deserter, leave this city and our sight? Is it thus that, regretful of what you have done, you rely on flight as the first road to safety for yourself? May your shame then stay with you. . . .

Who will be surprised, do you think, Bibolo, if the lacerated and wounded heart of a girl who is filled with indignation bitterly rears itself up against your sarcasm and satire from this day on, now that your trifling arrogance has wounded her with bitter injuries? Do not think, most despicable of men, that I might believe I have fallen out of favor with Jove. I am a scholar and a pupil who has been lulled to sleep by the meager fire of a mind too humble. I have been too much burned, and my injured mind has accumulated too much passion, for tormenting itself with the defending of our sex, my mind sighs, conscious of its obligation. For all things—those deeply rooted inside us as well as those outside us—are being laid at the door of our sex.

In addition, I, who have always held virtue in high esteem and considered private things as secondary in importance, shall wear down and exhaust my pen writing against those men who are garrulous and puffed up with false pride. I shall not fail to obstruct tenaciously their treacherous snares. And I shall strive in a war of vengeance against the notorious abuse of those who fill everything with noise, since armed with such abuse, certain insane and infamous men bark and bare their teeth in vicious wrath at the republic of women, so worthy of veneration.

To Lucilia Vernacula[32] (1 November 1487)

I should think that the tongues should be cut to pieces and the hearts brutally lacerated of people whose minds are so wicked and whose envious rage is so incredible that they deny in their ignorant rantings the possibility that any woman might master the most elegant elements of Roman oratory. I would pardon the morally hopeless and even people destined for a life of crime, whom wagging tongues are accustomed to castigate with obvious fury. But I cannot tolerate the gabbing and babbling women who, burning with wine and drunkenness, harm with their petulant talk not only their sex but themselves. These mindless women—these female counselors who emerge victorious from the cookshop jar after a prodigious vote among their neigh-

---

32. Again, very likely a fictionalized name; the allusion to the common language, the "vernacular," suggests a woman who is common or vulgar (my note).

bors—hunt down with their bilious poison those women who rise to greater distinction than they. The bold and undisguised passion these women have for destruction and disgrace, this hunger of theirs for calamity, which strives to smear even those who are completely above reproach, deserves to bring a worse disgrace on itself. For the man who does not take care to have himself absolved of wrongdoing wants his own moral lapses to be excused.

Besides, these women, being idle with time on their hands and no interests of their own, occupy themselves with keeping watch over other people's business, and, like scarecrows hung up in the garden to get rid of sparrows, they shoot poison from the bows of their tongues at those who cross their paths. What after all is the purpose of honor if I were to believe that the barking roars of these sharp-tongued women were worth tolerating, when decent and cultivated women always extol me with honorable words? I am not a woman who wants the shameful deeds of insolent people to slip through under the pardon of silence, either so that in the end I'll be said to approve of what I'm silent about or so that the very women who lead their lives with shame will continue to entice a great many people into their licentiousness as accomplices. Nor would I want, because of my speaking out, someone to criticize me for intolerance; even dogs are allowed to protect themselves from more aggressive fleas by crushing them with their nails. . . .

Those insolent women are therefore silent about every law of honor who, burning with the fires of hatred, would silently gnaw away at themselves, if they didn't feast in their slanderous talk on others. Mildew of the mind afflicts [them, who] . . . can't stand to hear even the epithet 'learned women.' . . . Human error causes us to be ashamed and disgusted that those women who are themselves caught in a tangle of doubt have given up hope of attaining knowledge of the humane arts, when they could easily acquire such knowledge with skill and virtue. For an education is neither bequeathed to us as a legacy, nor does some fate or other give it to us as a gift. Virtue is something that we ourselves acquire; nor can those women who become dull-witted through laziness and the sludge of low pleasures ascend to the understanding of difficult things. But for those women who believe that study, hard work, and vigilance will bring them sure praise, the road to attaining knowledge is broad.

Cassandra Fedele

"*O decus italiae virgo!*"[33] O virgin, ornament of Italy! With these words from Virgil's *Aeneid,* with which the hero's opponent addressed the warrior maiden Camilla, the great Florentine humanist Angelo Poliziano, encountered earlier in Chapter 4 as the chronicler of the Pazzi conspiracy, opens his encomium of Cassandra Fedele (1465–1558).[34] Implicitly, he compares her to that ancient paragon of female beauty and capacity, a salute that he follows with an extended celebration of her achievements. They were remarkable: a flawless Latin stylist, she carried on a correspondence with famous humanists, like Poliziano, and contemporary rulers, most notably Isabella, queen of Castile (modern Spain). In addition, she composed and delivered three impressive orations to distinguished audiences at the University of Padua and the Venetian Senate, with the resplendent doge presiding.

Fedele's success came early in life. The daughter of a state secretary—a position of markedly high status in Venice, just short of the aristocracy—she was reared to be a prodigy: a learned woman from a family distinguished by its many men of learning. She quickly won fame and garnered praise; she was, as Diana Robin writes, "perhaps the best-known female scholar and humanist living in Europe": "Kings and queens courted her," and "[p]oets, university professors, and churchmen sought her imprimatur for their work."[35] So it was until her marriage in 1499, at the late age, for that era, of 34. After that event, she vanished from sight until, in 1520, her husband died. Now an impoverished and childless widow, she relied for decades more on the generosity of others. From this obscurity, she was called to deliver her last oration, in 1556, at age ninety-one, two years before her death.

In her youth, when her fortunes were at their peak, Fedele had many admirers, but little of the fire and determination of her predecessors Nogarola and Cereta. Her letters are formal paradigms of style, her orations affirmations of existing hierarchies in the worlds of learning and politics. Yet they notably advance the emergence of women in the world of learning simply by making the participation of women normal, as seen in the oration given here, her second of three. In it, she presents a synthesis of the humanist view of the liberal arts as it had evolved since the days of Petrarch, Boccaccio, and Vergerio, examined in Chapter 1 of this volume.

---

33. Virgil, *Aeneid,* XI.508.

34. Poliziano's encomiastic letter in Antonino Fedele's edition with facing Italian translation, *Orazioni ed epistole* (Venice: il Poligrafo, 2010), 384–89; also in Giacomo Filippo Tomasini, ed., *Epistolae et orationes* (Padua: Franciscus Bolzetta, 1636), 155–58.

35. Diana M. Robin, editor and translator of Cassandra Fedele, *Letters and Orations* (Chicago: University of Chicago Press, 2000), 3.

"I shall speak very briefly," she begins, "on the study of the liberal arts, which for humans is useful and honorable, pleasurable and enlightening since everyone, not only philosophers but the most ignorant man, knows and admits that it is by reason that man is separated from beast." Those educated in the liberal arts are more distant from the unlettered than are the shadows of men seen in mirrors or paintings from their real prototypes. Those who do not develop their capacity for reason can never achieve great things; "wandering aimlessly they walk in darkness," they are mere creatures of fortune. The learned, in contrast, "turn all their thoughts and considerations toward reason as though toward a target," are free of fortune's whims, and are prepared "in every way to live well and in happiness." They also assist others by offering their "energy and advice in matters public and private," thus filling the prescription Plato had given in Book V of the *Republic* that the best state is governed by philosophers. For all these reasons the liberal arts are given the "sweet appellation" of the "humanities," because by them our species becomes truly human; just as nature is beautified by the labor of men, "so are our natures cultivated, enhanced, and enlightened by the liberal arts."

All that Fedele says here pertains normally to men. But Fedele speaks about women as well—and about herself, as a woman. Her statements about women and learning are brief, and serve as bookends to the discourse about the liberal arts as they were understood in the male domain. She opens by acknowledging the encouragement of her mentor, the humanist Giorgio Valla,[36] to address the learned audience before her, made up of the senators and doge of Venice: he has encouraged her to consider what "immersion in scholarship might do for the weaker sex in general, since I myself intend to pursue immortality through such study." So she agreed to deliver a public oration, "though I blush to do so and am ever mindful that I am a member of the female sex and that my intellect is small." She trembles to speak before an assembly so "elegant and grand," made up of men so learned that "even . . . a man who was the soul of eloquence" would scarcely be able to say anything worthy.

Fedele returns at the end of her oration to the theme of female unworthiness, and her own determination nonetheless. She has spoken enough, she says, of the splendor of the liberal arts, which provide benefits that "are extremely pleasurable, fruitful, and lasting," to which she adds, on a personal note: "benefits that I myself have enjoyed." In contrast to the "lowly and execrable" tools with which women normally must make their way in the world—the distaff and needle, the instruments of the textile crafts that were women's main occupation—liberal studies, even if they offer women "no rewards or honors," yet women "must nonetheless pursue and embrace such studies alone for the pleasure and enjoyment they contain."

Thus concluding, Fedele inserts women into the mainstream of European intellectual life. Women as yet will make no claim for professional position

---

36. A native of Vicenza, Valla held a high position in Venice from 1485 to 1500 as a teacher of rhetoric at the San Marco school: see Robin, *Letters and Orations*, 165n21.

or leadership roles, as Fedele emphatically does not, and indeed will not do so for some three centuries after these words were spoken. But though their studies will bring them no monetary reward or enhanced status, such as men garner from their labors, still women know the "pleasure and enjoyment" to be gained from their efforts, and so will engage in the same intellectual pursuits heretofore reserved for men. Fedele defines the path that most learned women would follow until the age of revolutions.

Cassandra Fedele, *Oration in Praise of Letters* (c. 1487)[37]

An oration delivered before the doge Agostino Barbarigo and the Venetian Senate: in praise of letters

The great orator and philosopher Giorgio Valla, who has thought me worthy of his presence here, has urged and emboldened me, most honored prince, conscript fathers,[38] and learned senators, to ponder what the constant and debilitating immersion in scholarship might do for the weaker sex in general, since I myself intend to pursue immortality through such study. And so I decided to oblige him and to obey his repeated demands and finally his insistence that I deliver a public oration, though I blush to do so and am ever mindful that I am a member of the female sex and that my intellect is small. Thus not only should the boorish rabble be ashamed of itself, it should cease to make trouble for me because of my dedication to the exercise of my natural skills and talents. Therefore it should not seem beside the point to anyone that my mind and heart might quail at the start and that I might stutter. For when I reconsidered the magnitude of the subject on which I had decided to speak before this elegant and grand assembly, I knew that nothing so elegant, illuminating, and polished even from a man who was the soul of eloquence could be brought to you that would not seem dry, uninteresting, and crude in comparison with the greatness of your learning and your presence. For who has the intellectual power and gift of eloquence that enable him to be equal to delivering an oration on the praise of letters or doing so before such an erudite audience as you?

For this reason, mindful of the difficulty of the task and the deficiency of my powers, I could very easily shy away from this opportunity to speak, were it

---

37. From Cassandra Fedele, *Oration in Praise of Letters*, in Fedele, *Letters and Orations*, ed. and trans. Diana M. Robin (Chicago: University of Chicago Press, 2000), 159–62.

38. Fedele is imitating the ancient custom of calling the Roman senators "conscript fathers," that is to say, those inscribed on the roster of the Senate: see *Letters and Orations*, 166n22.

not that your magnanimity and kindness toward all people urged me to come before you, especially since I am well aware that it is not your wont to demand or expect anyone to take on a heavier load than the rationale for the occasion allows or than their shoulders would appear to proclaim that they can. Besides, two additional things persuade me to speak: your fitting affability, which in the beginning seemed to give me pause; and your kindness, which causes me to think no oration would be more pleasing to listen to or sweeter to men who are extremely erudite, as are the great majority of you, and also to men who are notably interested in education, than an oration whose subject is (in whatever way appropriate) the praise of literature and the liberal arts.

Stirred by these thoughts, since I see that you are listening to me attentively, I shall speak very briefly on the study of the liberal arts, which for humans is useful and honorable, pleasurable and enlightening, since everyone, not only philosophers but the most ignorant man, knows and admits that it is by reason that man is separated from beast. For what is it that enlightens men's minds the way that an education in and knowledge of literature and the liberal arts do? These two things not only remove men far above the realm of the beasts, but they so simply and easily separate educated men from the ignorant and uncultivated that in my opinion men in paintings and even men's shadows do not differ more from real human beings than do the uneducated and untaught from men who are imbued with learning. But if men who are boorish and unlettered have a natural yet undeveloped spark of reason and they leave it unstirred for the whole of their lives, they will force it from disuse and habit to die, and in so doing they will render themselves unable to undertake great things. For wandering aimlessly they walk in darkness no matter what the circumstances, and through imprudence, ignorance, and inexperience they run headlong into calamities, and they render the course of their lives accidental. These are men who make Fortune their god. They place all things in her lap, and when she favors them they kiss her and approve, and when she opposes them they accuse her loudly and grieve.

So many times Fortune, ruler of the world and my life, is the best soldier in battle, ready with her company. No need for prayers: seek now death with your sword. Fortune brought such prosperity to the great man when he kept the faith; but even him Fortune marked for death and at the summit of his career. In one cruel day she brought every disaster on men to whom she had given years free from harm. Pompey was a man who never understood that happiness is mixed with sorrow. Happy was he when no god disturbed him and wretched was he when none spared him. When Fortune for the first time struck him, the sands resounded with a blow long delayed.[39]

---

39. Fedele is alluding in this paragraph to the career of the great Roman general and senator Pompey, who nevertheless died at the hand of an assassin: see *Letters and Orations*, 166n23.

But erudite men who are filled with the knowledge of divine and human things turn all their thoughts and considerations toward reason as though toward a target, and they free their minds from all pain, though plagued by many anxieties. These men are scarcely subjected to fortune's innumerable arrows, and they prepared themselves in every way to live well and in happiness. They follow reason as their leader in all things; nor do they consider themselves only, but they are also accustomed to assisting others with their energy and advice in matters public and private.

And so Plato, a man almost divine, wrote that those states would be fortunate in which the men who were heads of state were philosophers or in which philosophers took on the duty of administration. He noted, I believe, that men well-endowed by fortune with physical advantages are more often drawn to vices and are more easily seduced than those who lack such advantages. But those who are born with intellectual advantages who fail to cultivate the learned disciplines and who make deficient use of their advantages he judged unlearned and unsuited to managing the affairs of state. Nor was he wrong in this. The study of literature refines men's minds, forms and makes bright the power of reason, and washes away all stains from the mind, or at any rate, greatly cleanses it. It perfects its gifts and adds much beauty and elegance to the physical and material advantages that one has received by nature. States, however, and their princes who foster and cultivate these studies become much more humane, more gracious, and more noble.

For this reason, these studies have won for themselves the sweet appellation, "humanities." Indeed, those who were uncultivated and had harsh natures became more cultivated and gentle through their immersion in these studies, while those whom nature has endowed with external goods and other gifts of the body, who for the most part are arrogant and petulant, acquire modesty, gentility, and a certain miraculous amiability toward all other men through their exposure to the liberal arts. Just as places that lie unused and uncultivated become fertile and rich in fruits and vegetables with men's labor and hard work and are always made beautiful, so are our natures cultivated, enhanced, and enlightened by the liberal arts.

But clearly Philip the king of Macedonia,[40] whose virtue and work increased the wealth of the Macedonians and enabled them to take power over so many peoples and nations, understood this. In a letter to the philosopher Aristotle in which he announced the birth of his son Alexander, he explained that he rejoiced still more that his son happened to be born in Aristotle's lifetime than that he had come into the world as the heir to a great empire. O excel-

---

40. Philip II, king of Macedon, was the father of the future conqueror Alexander the Great, for whom he had summoned to his court the philosopher Aristotle as tutor: see *Letters and Orations*, 164n8, 166n25.

lent words and elevated sentiments, worthy of so great a prince and emperor. That king and illustrious emperor, who was affected by having spent so long a time in his own life in the business of war and conquest, knew that an empire could by no means be ruled justly, prudently, and gloriously by a man who had not been trained in literature and the best arts.

This was later borne out by Alexander himself who, having become learned in the liberal arts under the tutelage of Aristotle, far surpassed all other princes and emperors who came before or after him in ruling, increasing, and protecting his empire. For this reason the men of antiquity rightly believed that all leaders who were uneducated, however experienced they were in military matters, were boorish and uncultivated.

But enough on the utility of literature since it produces not only an outcome that is rich, precious, and sublime but also provides one with advantages that are extremely pleasurable, fruitful, and lasting—benefits that I myself have enjoyed. And when I meditate on the idea of marching forth in life with the lowly and execrable weapons of the little woman—the needle and the distaff—even if the study of literature offers women no rewards or honors, I believe women must nonetheless pursue and embrace such studies alone for the pleasure and enjoyment they contain. . . . [41]

Marie Le Jars de Gournay

A long century of 135 years separates the essay of Marie de Gournay (1565–1645) *The Equality of Men and Women* from the last of the works examined earlier of the Quattrocento humanists Nogarola, Cereta, and Fedele. Between 1487, the most likely date for Fedele's oration on the liberal arts, and 1622, the first publication of Gournay's *Equality*, immense changes occurred not only in European civilization in general, shaken by the Reformations of the church on the one hand and the explorations of new worlds on the other, but also specifically in the status of women in the world of learning. Whereas in the fifteenth century, but a handful of women achieved advanced education and engaged in intellectual discourse, there were many who did so by the seventeenth. At the same time, a vastly expanded female readership had emerged, and a large array of works had become available for female consumption.

---

41. Some words are missing from the oration at the end; see *Letters and Orations*, 166n26 (my note).

Not only did the quantities change, but the tone as well, as seen in Gournay's work on female equality, of which excerpts are given here. Nogarola's daring but diffident testing of limits, Cereta's anger and anguish, Fedele's modest determination, give way to Gournay's self-assurance, her easy flow of words, her scornful impatience with the small-minded objections of male critics. She builds on the contributions of earlier female writers—from her humanist predecessors to the fierce advocates Moderata Fonte and Lucrezia Marinella—as well as male defenders of women, especially Henry Cornelius Agrippa von Nettesheim, and her contemporary Anna Maria van Schurman, a proponent of female education. To this now already-robust literary tradition, Gournay brings her own substantial knowledge of ancient authors, the Christian fathers, and the Bible. From these ingredients, she provides the one work no one had yet, or could have before this written: a plain and concise assertion of the equality between men and women. She turns the corner and enters the future.

Gournay lived by her pen: she had no family wealth, no male protector, no institutional shelter, no single, steady patron. She sought out important people, who assisted her; she elbowed her way into male intellectual circles; late in life, she was granted royal pensions, which sustained her until she died at age eighty, only four years after she published in a volume of 860 pages the third edition of her complete works. She wrote poems, essays, translations of classical texts, and autobiographical texts. In 1622—no longer a young woman trying to find her footing in the world but a white-haired woman nearing her sixtieth year—she published *The Equality of Men and Women.*

Equality, not difference: here is the core, the entirely unique claim of her work. The tradition of literary misogyny, the textual residuum of the belief in female inferiority, had endured for more than 3000 years. Then for a century or so, authors like Agrippa, Fonte, and Marinella had proposed as a counter-case female superiority: female "preeminence," in Agrippa's phrase; women's superior "merit" to men, in Fonte's; the "nobility and excellence" of women in contradistinction to the "defects and vices" of men, in Marinella's. To these outlandish claims, Gournay makes a more temperate yet unprecedented, more potent, and startling one: that of the equality between the sexes: "For my part, I fly all extremes; I am content to make [women] equal to men."

The "human animal," she continues—animal!—"is neither man nor woman"; a point Gournay reinforces by noting that "there is nothing more like a [male] cat on the windowsill than a female cat," a point more forceful in French where the words *chat* for the male creature and *chatte* for the female are, except for a single vocalized consonant at the end, identical. These two identical animals are characterized by the same distinctive trait—the humanist leitmotif once again—of rational capacity: "The unique form and distinction of that animal consists only in its rational soul." The physiological difference between them is incidental, and serves the sole purpose of sexual reproduction: "the sexes having been made double, not so as to constitute a difference in species, but for the sake of propagation alone."

These thunderous statements are embedded in a loosely structured text, from which three other points might be elicited. First, men ascend to high positions not because of innate superiority, but because women have not enjoyed their "advantages and privileges," especially that of education, which could easily close the gap in the performance between male and female. Second, men's courage and physical power may be countered by a consideration of the Amazonian women of whom history is full: women who fought, killed, and triumphed as well as men, such as the biblical Judith, assassin of her people's deadly enemy Holofernes, and Joan of Arc, the victor at Orléans, who single-handedly salvaged the monarchy of King Charles VII of France. Finally, as a pioneer in New Testament feminist criticism, Gournay points out several passages where esteem for women is expressed not only by Jesus Christ, but also the apostle Paul; and strikingly, she balances the masculine component of Christ's Incarnation with the feminine one of Mary's parturition. As for the notion that, because women should submit to men in marriage, as certain scriptural passages advise, they are to be considered on that ground less worthy, it is refuted by the fact, established by God, that women have equal access to divine grace: they are admitted to the "holy Eucharist, . . . the mysteries of the redemption of paradise, and . . . the sight—indeed the possession—of God." How then could they not be worthy of the "advantages and privileges" of men? "Would this not declare man to be more precious and more exalted than all these things, and hence commit the gravest of blasphemies?"

The human animal, both male and female, Gournay establishes, are inherently equal, each possessing the same distinguishing rational mind; they are equal, too, in the mind of God, who has established an equivalence between Christ's mother and Mary's son, and admitted women as much as men to the redemption that mother and son, together, have wrought.

Marie Le Jars de Gournay, *The Equality of Men and Women* (1622)[42]

Most of those who take up the cause of women, opposing the arrogant preference for themselves that is asserted by men, give them full value for money, for they redirect the preference to them.[43] For my part, I fly all extremes;

---

42. From Marie le Jars de Gournay, *The Equality of Men and Women,* in Gournay, *Apology for the Woman Writing and Other Works,* ed. and trans. Richard Hillman and Colette Quesnel (Chicago: University of Chicago Press, 2002), 72–95.

43. That is to say, most men who defend the worth of women, departing from the usual male pattern of vaunting their own superiority, instead make a case for the superiority of women.

I am content to make them equal to men, given that nature, too, is as greatly opposed, in this respect, to superiority as to inferiority. But what am I saying? It is not enough for certain persons to prefer the masculine to the feminine sex; they must also confine women, by an absolute and obligatory rule, to the distaff—yea, to the distaff alone.[44] Still, what may console them for this contempt is that it comes only from those men whom they would wish least to resemble—persons who would lend plausibility to the reproaches that might be spewed upon the female sex, if they were of it, and who feel in their hearts that they have nothing to recommend them but the credit of being masculine. Because they have heard it cried in the streets that women lack value, as well as intellectual ability—indeed, the constitution and physical make-up to arrive at the latter—their eloquence exults in preaching these maxims, and all the more richly for the fact that value, sufficiency, physical make-up, and constitution are imposing terms. They have not learned, on the other hand, that the chief quality of a dolt is to espouse causes on the basis of popular belief and hearsay.

Amid the chirping of their lofty conversation, hark how such intellects compare the two sexes: in their opinion, the supreme excellence women may achieve is to resemble ordinary men. They are as far from imagining that a great woman might style herself a great man, if her sex were simply changed, as from allowing that a man may raise himself to the level of a god. . . . But isn't it beyond belief that those who seek to exalt and strengthen themselves through the weakness of others feel compelled to insist that they can exalt or fortify themselves by means of their own strength? And the best of it is that they think themselves exonerated for their effrontery in vilifying the female sex when they employ equal effrontery to praise, or rather to gild, themselves. . . .

My God, doesn't the desire ever come upon these embodiments of sufficiency to furnish a smidgeon of a just and precise example and a fitting rule for perfection to that poor sex? And if I judge well, either of the worthiness or of the capacity of women, I do not propose at present to prove it with reasons, since the opinionated might dispute them, nor with examples, since they are too common, but indeed only by the authority of God himself, of the Fathers—the buttresses of His Church—and of the great philosophers who have served as a light to the universe. Let us rank those glorious witnesses in front and reserve God, then the holy Fathers of his Church, for the innermost, as the treasure.

---

44. The distaff, or spindle used by women in spinning thread, was in former times a metonymy for all things pertaining to women, and, by extension, to the maternal lineage. Recall Fedele's lament about the "execrable weapons of the little woman—the needle and the distaff."

Gournay begins with Plato, and through him Socrates, whose views Plato interprets, on the subject of women, whose abilities they esteem: indeed, they "attribute to women the same rights, faculties, and functions in their Republics, and everywhere else."[45] In their view, women have sometimes surpassed men as inventors of useful arts and in oratory and philosophy. She also celebrates ancient female worthies, including the Queen of Sheba, the priestess Diotima, and the poet Sappho. She mentions in passing as well her contemporary Anna Maria van Schurman, author of a widely-circulated work arguing for women's education.[46]

If, therefore, women attain less often than men to the heights of excellence, it is a marvel that the lack of a good education—indeed, the abundance of outright and blatantly bad education—does not do worse and prevent them from doing so entirely. If proof is needed, is there more difference between them and men than among themselves—according to the training they receive, according to whether they are brought up in a city or a village, or according to nationality? Therefore, why should not their training in public matters and in letters, of a kind equal to men's, fill up the gap that commonly appears between their minds and those of men, when we see, likewise, that such training is of such importance that, because just one of its branches—namely, dealing with the world—is common among French and English women and lacking among the Italian, the latter are in general so far exceeded by the former? I say in general because in particular the ladies of Italy sometimes excel, and we have drawn from them queens and princesses who did not lack intellectual ability. Why indeed might not the right sort of upbringing succeed in filling the gap between the understandings of men and theirs, given that in the example I just cited, those of inferior birth surmount their betters purely and simply by dint of this dealing and engagement with the world? For the air breathed by the women of Italy is more subtle and fit for rendering the mind so than that of England or France, as appears by the ability of the men of the Italian climate when compared ordinarily with that of Frenchmen and Englishmen, but I have touched on this idea elsewhere. . . .[47]

---

45. Richard Hillman and Colette Quesnel, in their edition and translation of Marie Le Jars de Gournay, *Apology for the Woman Writing and Other Works* (Chicago: University of Chicago Press, 2002), 76–77; see 77n7.

46. Van Schurman's *Whether a Christian Woman Should Be Educated and Other Writings from Her Intellectual Circle*, ed. and trans. Joyce Irwin (Chicago: University of Chicago Press, 1998).

47. In the above statements, Gournay seems to be noting the engagement of French and English women, compared to Italian, in the larger society, compared to the greater seclusion of the Italian, yet she acknowledges the intellectual merits of two French royal women—the regent Catherine de' Medici and the queen Marie de' Medici and, in general, the preeminence in her day of Italian men in the cultural realm.

Turning to ancient authorities, Gournay argues that Plutarch, Seneca, Plato, and Aristotle among the ancients assumed that women's innate ability was no different than men's. Among moderns, she names among a series of pro-female authors Boccaccio, Erasmus, and Poliziano, all included in this volume, as well as Henry Cornelius Agrippa, one of those who argued the superiority of women.[48] She then turns to a discussion of the French Salic law, which barred women from ascending the throne, and counters it with ancient examples of women who ruled or whose participation in public affairs was welcomed by their kinsmen. If men excel, it is because women have been excluded from the advantages accruing from education and participation in society.

Further, the human animal, taken rightly, is neither man nor woman, the sexes having been made double, not so as to constitute a difference in species, but for the sake of propagation alone.[49] The unique form and distinction of that animal consists only in its rational soul. And if it is permitted to laugh in the course of our journey, the jest would not be out of season that teaches us that there is nothing more like a cat on the windowsill than a female cat. Man and woman are so thoroughly one that if man is more than woman, woman is more than man. Man was created man and female—so says scripture, not reckoning the two except as one;[50] and Jesus Christ is called Son of Man, although he is that only of woman—the whole and consummate perfection of the proof of the unity of the two sexes.[51] I speak thus according to the great Saint Basil in his first homily on the Hexameron;[52] the virtue of man and of woman are the same thing, since God bestowed on them the same creation and the same honor: *masculum et feminam fecit eos.*[53] Now in those whose nature is one and the same, it must be concluded that their actions are so as well, and that the esteem and recompense belonging to these are equal, where the works are equal. There, then, is the declaration of that powerful champion and venerable witness of the Church.

In support of her arguments, Gournay offers examples of female greatness from the Old Testament, and again from classical antiquity, including the Amazon Penthesilea and warrior maiden Camilla. Returning to the evidence of religious texts, she presents, to qualify Saint Paul's seemingly restric-

---

48. Henry Cornelius Agrippa, *Declamation on the Preeminence and Nobility of the Female Sex,* ed. and trans. Albert Rabil, Jr. (Chicago: University of Chicago Press, 1996). Gournay draws many of her arguments from this work, with which she was evidently familiar.

49. As Plato also states in his *Republic;* see Hillman and Quesnel, *Apology,* 86n51.

50. Gournay is alluding to the creation story in Genesis 1.

51. Jesus is born to the Virgin Mary, having been conceived by no human father.

52. For Basil, see Hillman and Quesnel, *Apology,* 87n54.

53. Genesis 1:27: "male and female created he them"; see Hillman and Quesnel, *Apology,* 87n55.

tive injunctions to women, his admiration for his female co-workers, an
admiration shared by his fellow apostles for theirs. Noting the greatness of the
fourteenth-century female saint Catherine of Siena, and pointing out that
women (mainly as midwives) are permitted to perform emergency baptisms,
Gournay proposes that women might be allowed to perform the other sacra-
ments as well, and in effect to become priests, as they are permitted to be in
other world religions. She commends the pro-female views of the saints Jerome
and Gregory.

As for the accomplishment of Judith,[54] I would not deign to mention it,
so particular was it—that is, dependent on the initiative and the will of its
author. No more will I speak of the others of that caliber, though they are
immense in quantity, as they are equally heroic in qualities of every kind as
those that are the crowning glory of the most illustrious men. I do not record
private deeds, for fear that they might seem to be more ebullient manifestations of personal energy rather than of the advantages and endowments
of the female sex. But that of Judith deserves a place here, since it is true
that her plan, coming into the heart of a young woman among so many
feeble-hearted men, in such need, in such a difficult enterprise, and for such
a benefit as the salvation of a people and of a city faithful to God, seems
to be rather an inspired favor and a gift of divine and special grace toward
women than a purely human and voluntary action. So, too, appears that of
the Maid of Orléans,[55] accompanied by much the same circumstances but of
more extensive value, inasmuch as it extended even to the salvation of a great
kingdom and its prince.

> That illustrious Amazon, whom Mars took pains to teach,
> Mows down squadrons, and braves hazards,
> Wearing the hard breastplate upon her round breast
> Whose rosy nipple sparkles with graces:
> To crown her head with glory and laurels.
> She, a mere virgin, dares to confront the most famous warriors.[56]

Let us add that the Magdalene is the only living being to whom the Redeemer
ever spoke these words and promised this august grace: Wherever the gospel

---

54. In the apocryphal book of the Bible, Judith saved the Israelites from a siege by seducing
and slaying the enemy general Holofernes: see Hillman and Quesnel, *Apology*, 92n77.

55. Joan of Arc, martyred in 1431 after helping the French defeat the English and seeing to
the coronation of King Charles VII, was a French national heroine and, in 1920, a canonized
saint.

56. Lines from Virgil praising the Amazon Penthesilea applied by Gournay to Joan of Arc,
the English here translated from Gournay's own French translation of the original Latin: see
Hillman and Quesnel, *Apology*, 93n78.

is preached, you shall be spoken of.[57] What is more, Jesus Christ declared the supreme joy and glory of his resurrection to women first of all.[58] . . . And if men boast that Jesus Christ was born of their sex, we answer that it had to be thus for necessary reasons of decency, since he would have been unable without scandal to mingle as a young person and at all hours of the day and night among the crowds in order to convert, succor, and save the human race, if he had been of the female sex, especially in the face of the malice of the Jews.[59]

But further, if anyone is so dull as to imagine masculine or feminine in God—for although his name may seem to have a masculine sound to it, it does not follow that one sex needs to be chosen above the other to honor or exalt the incarnation of His Son—such a person shows in a plain light that is just as bad a philosopher as he is a theologian. On the other hand, the advantage that men possess by virtue of His incarnation in their sex (if they can draw an advantage from it, given the necessity noted earlier) is counterbalanced by His priceless conception in the body of a woman, by the entire perfection of that woman—the only one to carry that title of perfect among all purely human creatures since the fall of our first parents—and by her Assumption, also unique in a human being. What is more, it may perhaps be said of her humanity that she exceeds that of Jesus Christ in this prerogative—that sex was by no means necessary in him for the Passion and for the Resurrection and the redemption of human beings, his very function, while it was so in her for motherhood, which was likewise her function.

Finally, if Scripture has declared the husband the head of the wife,[60] the greatest folly that men can commit is to take that as a license conferred by their worthiness. For in view of the instances, authorities, and reasons noted in this discourse, by which is proved the equality—let us even say the unity—of graces and favors on the part of God toward the two sexes, and in view of the fact that God declares, "The two shall be but one," and then declares, "The man shall leave mother and father and give himself to his wife,"[61] it appears that this declaration of the gospel is made solely for the express need of fostering peace in marriage. This need would require, undoubtedly, that one of the conjugal partners should yield to the other; for the usual weakness of intellects made it impossible for concord to be born of reason, as should

---

57. Jesus' words, popularly understood to have been spoken to Mary Magdalene; see Hillman and Quesnel, *Apology*, 93n79.

58. To the women who came and found the empty tomb: see Hillman and Quesnel, *Apology*, 93n80.

59. The unavoidable, near-universal premodern anti-Semitism surfaces here.

60. 1 Corinthians 11:3; see Hillman and Quesnel, *Apology*, 95n85.

61. Genesis 2:23–24; Matthew 19:4–5; Mark 10:6–8; Ephesians 5:21–33; Hillman and Quesnel, *Apology*, 95n86.

have been the case in a just balance of mutual authority; nor, because of the imposing presence of the male, could the submission come from his side. And however true it may be, as some maintain, that such submission was imposed on woman in punishment for the sin of eating the apple,[62] that still hardly constitutes a decisive pronouncement in favor of the supposed superior worth of man. If one supposed that scripture commanded her to submit to man, as being unworthy of opposing him, consider the absurdity that would follow: woman would find herself worthy of having been made in the image of the Creator worthy of the holy Eucharist, of the mysteries of the redemption of paradise, and of the sight—indeed the possession—of God, yet not of the advantages and privileges of man. Would this not declare man to be more precious and more exalted than all these things, and hence commit the gravest of blasphemies?

---

62. The argument against which Isotta Nogarola had argued in the dialogue on Adam and Eve; and see also Hillman and Quesnel, *Apology*, 95n87.

Chapter 10: Other Worlds

Introduction

By the sixteenth century, humanism had become the norm in European intellectual circles. The mastery of Latin style, as demonstrated in the humanist genres of the letter, dialogue, oration, and treatise—as well as the composition of lyric and epic verse—was the general prerequisite for the elites who led in political, academic, and even church domains, as for the leisured aristocracy. Religious debates, as seen in Chapter 7, emerged from an intellectual culture infused by humanism, as did the pursuits of philosophy and science, as seen in Chapter 8, and the reevaluation of gender roles, as seen in Chapter 9. In this final chapter, similarly, four individuals emerging from the cultural world that had been formed by humanism, and writing in humanist genres, target matters the first humanists had never envisioned: distant civilizations on other continents, previously unknown, whose very existence challenged the traditional European understandings of the nature of the human being, the structure of the cosmos, and the supremacy of Christian norms. Just as Erasmus and Luther had challenged the Roman church, Copernicus and Galileo the perceived system of the world, and Gournay the subordination of the female sex, those who wrote about the opening up of new worlds shook the stability of the European intellectual synthesis that had just achieved, in humanism, the integration of its ancient pre-Christian and subsequent Christian traditions.

Two of the four figures presented here observed the native cultures of the Western hemisphere: Amerigo Vespucci (1452/1454–1512), who in 1501–1502 sailed along the coastline of South America from Brazil almost as far as the straits later breached by the Portuguese navigator Ferdinand Magellan; and Garcilaso de la Vega (1539–1616), the son of an Inca princess and a Spanish conquistador, was raised in Peru. Two others journeyed east into Asian regions that Portuguese navigators had only recently opened to European consciousness: Saint Francis Xavier (1506–1552), missionary to India, Indonesia, and Japan; and Luís Vas de Camões (c. 1524–1580), the poet who was to Portugal what Cervantes was to Spain and Shakespeare to England, a participant in the Portuguese imperial venture in Asia, and its muse. In sum, from two vantage points on opposite sides of the globe, they offer accounts of the European confrontation with astonishingly new worlds.

Vespucci's enormous discovery is announced in the letter that follows: that the lands Christopher Columbus and his followers had encountered in their journey across the "Ocean Sea," as the Atlantic was then known, were not just a cluster of islands but an entirely "new world"—his words—and a vast and unknown continent. He describes, as well, the natives that he and his companions spoke with and observed, whose customs, featuring total nudity and enthusiastic cannibalism, were also startling to Europeans. Garcilaso's acquaintance with native culture is more profound than Vespucci's, although he, too, mythologizes somewhat in the narration of its past of which a very small excerpt is given here. In his history of the conquest of Peru, his admiration for the ancestral traditions of his people, for he was a *mestizo* as well as a Creole, is elegantly balanced with the boldness and bravery of the conquerors.

Much like Vespucci and Garcilaso, Xavier strives to know and understand the peoples who occupy the regions newly opened to European venturers—those in India and Indonesia as well as in Japan, the subject of the letter of which excerpts are given here. He familiarizes himself with the religious beliefs of these peoples, learns their language, and using it, attempts to persuade them of the superiority of his own Christian worldview. Unlike his counterparts in the Western hemisphere, he must contend with civilizations that are ancient, sustained by documentary and material records of their long past, and staffed by hierarchies of native experts. Camões, finally, expresses little curiosity about those whose lives will be changed by the arrival of the Portuguese and their successors. His goal is to celebrate his nation at a moment of vaunting ambition, when it briefly commanded the lands that touched the Indian Ocean and South China Sea. With Camões, humanism is a triumphalist cultural system married to the politics of empire.

With conscious irony this volume ends with new worlds as described by the cultural tools of humanism, while humanism itself originally gained its energy from its voyage backward in time, to ancient civilizations. Ironic, but appropriate, for the line connecting the humanist journey into the past to the journey into the future of the adventurers represented in this chapter traces the evolution of European culture from the fourteenth to seventeenth centuries.

Amerigo Vespucci

The letter traditionally called *New World* attributed to Amerigo Vespucci (1452/1454–1512)—a humanist text, though one surrounded by a penumbra of scholarly contestation of authorship and veracity—escapes the boundaries of humanism: for it draws not on texts but on observed phenomena as it crowingly describes a world unknown to the ancients. Just as Copernicus would a generation later propose a reconfiguration of the heavens, Vespucci here proposes a reconfiguration of the earth—one that must dislodge, though it does not entirely dispense with, the authority of the classical tradition.

Vespucci was not the first to write about exploratory ventures far from the familiar European core. Columbus wrote four letters describing his successive voyages across the Atlantic (1492–1504); shortly before him, the Portuguese voyagers who sailed along the African coast and on to India and the Moluccas told their own stories; and still earlier, the founder of the genre, the Venetian Marco Polo, told of his twenty-four-year adventure (1271–1295) in Central Asia and China. It is not certain, moreover, how many expeditions there were in which Vespucci participated—he claimed four, possibly in imitation of Columbus—or whether the "public" letters, published in his lifetime, or the "familiar" letters, circulated only in manuscript and discovered and published centuries later, are in fact by him. Further confusion results from the distortions of translation and substandard printing: the letter *New World,* for instance, translated here into English, is based on a Latin text translated, most likely, by the Veronese humanist and architect Fra Giovanni del Giocondo from a lost Italian original most likely by Vespucci. Scholars have tussled over these matters for nearly a century. Vespucci clearly participated in the expedition known as his "third voyage" of 1501–1502, described in the letter *New World,* and probably two more or all three of the others he claimed. And he certainly wrote about his Atlantic ventures in works that are the platform for the published "public" letters, if not those letters precisely as they have reached us. As Luciano Formisano concludes, and his judgment is followed here, the letters attributed to Vespucci are "not pseudo- but rather para-Vespuccian";[1] close enough, for our purposes, to Vespucci himself.

With some confidence, then, we may turn to Vespucci, author and explorer, and the letter addressed to Lorenzo di Pierfrancesco de' Medici that circulated in Vespucci's lifetime under the title *Mundus novus,* or *New World.* The son of a notary, born in Florence at the height of the Renaissance to an old though not especially wealthy family, Vespucci launched his career in 1478–1480 by accompanying his cousin, the Florentine ambassador, on a diplomatic mission to France. On his return, he entered the service of Lorenzo di Pierfrancesco de' Medici, the cousin of the city's ruler, Lorenzo "the Magnificent," acting as secretary, estate manager, and banker. Sent to Seville in 1492, he worked in the office there of the Medici bank, and undertook various commercial ventures. From this platform, his career as explorer was launched, with his first and second voyages (1497–1498 and 1499–

---

1. Luciano Formisano, ed., *Letters from a New World: Amerigo Vespucci's Discovery of America* (New York: Marsilio, 1992), xxxv.

1500) undertaken in Spanish employ; and then, after a move to Lisbon, his third and fourth (1501–1502 and 1503–1504) for the Portuguese. Returning to Seville in 1505, he was appointed "Chief Pilot" by the Spanish king in 1508, tasked to train young navigators in astronomy and cartography. There he died in 1512, his position as royal pilot, for lesser compensation, transferred to his nephew.

The *New World* letter is addressed to Vespucci's old Medici patron, whose death in May 1503 fixes the terminal date for its publication. It was an astonishing success, reprinted within weeks in Venice, Paris, Augsburg, Nuremberg, Cologne, and Strasbourg, among other print centers.[2] It provides in rather flat Latin prose, amid a jumble of other, often exaggerated events, some extraordinary data: the circumstances of the trans-Atlantic voyage; the configurations of the sky of the southern hemisphere; the appearance and habits of the natives, whose perpetual nudity and taste for human flesh were especially noted; and above all, the character of the coastline from Brazil to Patagonia, which extended on a southwesterly line at least as far as 50 degrees south, proving that the landmass it bordered was not an island but a continent—and therefore, a "new world." This last claim was unprecedented; it was surely Vespucci's; and it electrified Europe.

Vespucci—through whatever intermediaries—underscores the novelty of his discovery. The regions he had explored on his journey "can properly be called a 'New World,'" he writes, "since our forebears had absolutely no knowledge of it, nor do any of those who are hearing about it today." After a long and dangerous voyage, God revealed to him "a wholly new continent and an unknown world," which he and his companions determined was a "new land" and "not an island but a continent." Even the heavens were different, studded with stars arrayed in patterns "never seen or described by the ancients." Those who, like himself, had ventured to this new continent knew what it was "to seek a goal which is uncertain and to explore a reality which is totally unknown." He writes this letter so that all Europeans may know "what wonders are are daily to be discovered," for the future is open and undiscovered: "since for all of time since the world began, no one has known the vastness of the earth and all the things contained in it."

Did Vespucci reflect on his countryman Petrarch, who nearly two centuries earlier had longed to commune with the ancients, and who had said in his letter *To Posterity* that he was especially devoted to antiquity "since I always disliked the age in which I lived" (see Chapter 2). For Vespucci, unlike Petrarch, it seems that the past may recede into the distance, for the future beckons with the promise of new worlds.

---

2. Mario Pozzi, *Il mondo nuovo di Amerigo Vespucci: Scritti vespucciani e paravespucciani,* 2nd rev. ed. (Alesandria: Edizioni dell'Orso, 1993), 13–14.

Amerigo Vespucci, *New World,* Letter to Lorenzo
di Pierfrancesco de' Medici (1502/1503)

A few days ago I wrote you at some length about my return from those new regions, which we searched for and found with the fleet, at the expense and by the command of the most serene King of Portugal[3]—and which can properly be called a "New World," since our forebears had absolutely no knowledge of it, nor do any of those who are hearing about it today. Indeed, it surpasses all that the ancients had conceived, since most of them say that there is no continent beyond the equator and towards the south, but only an ocean which they call the Atlantic; and those who believed that there was a continent in that region declared that for many reasons it was uninhabitable. But my recent voyage establishes that their view is false, and entirely contrary to the truth, since in that southern zone I came upon a continent inhabited more fully than Europe or Asia or Africa by an abundant population of humans and animals, and possessed of a climate more temperate and pleasant than can be found in any region known to us. You shall hear of all this below, where I shall give a succinct description of the principal features most worthy of recording and remembering which I saw or heard in this New World.

On 14 May 1501,[4] at the command of the said King, we departed in three ships from Lisbon on our prosperous mission to explore new regions toward the south, and sailed in that direction steadily for twenty months.[5] . . . [After stopping near Cape Verde off the African coast][6] to recover our strength and take on supplies for our journey, we weighed anchor and unfurled our sails to the wind, and setting our path across the vast ocean toward Antarctica, bearing westward for a while before a southeasterly wind.[7] From the day that we left the African coast,[8] we sailed for two months and three days[9] before we sighted land.

---

3. Manuel I, king of Portugal (1495–1521).

4. For alternate but not greatly different dates, see Formisano, *Letters from a New World,* 184n4.

5. Somewhat less; the entire voyage extended from May 1501 to July 1502, or fourteen months.

6. They had sailed past the Grand Canaries to Bezeguiche, present-day Gorée, on the west African coast near the Cape Verde islands; see Formisano, *Letters from a New World,* 184n8.

7. The text reads, "the wind known as Vulturnus," which in classical mythology is a southeasterly one.

8. The text reads "that promontory," i.e., Bezeguiche.

9. But sixty-seven days is written below; see also see Formisano, *Letters from a New World,* 184n10.

What we suffered as we crossed that great expanse of sea, what dangers we faced of shipwreck and bodily harm, and what anxieties tormented us, I leave to the imagination of those who know from long experience what it is to seek a goal which is uncertain and to explore a reality which is totally unknown. To sum it up in a word, know that of the sixty-seven days we sailed, for forty-four days on end we had rain, thunder, and lightening, with a sky so dark that we never saw the sun by day or the stars at night. We were so overcome by fear that we nearly abandoned all hope of survival.

Yet amid these many and mighty terrors of sea and sky, it soon pleased the Almighty to reveal to us a wholly new continent and an unknown world. When we saw it, we were overcome with such joy as you might imagine comes to those who have been rescued from dire calamities and misfortunes. On 7 August 1501,[10] therefore, we dropped our anchor off the shores of that new land, thanking God with solemn prayers and the celebration of the Mass.

Once there, we determined that the new land was not an island but a continent, both because its long coastline did not bend to close a circle and because it abounded with countless inhabitants. For innumerable species of people and tribes, and of wild animals not found in our homeland, as well as many other things which none of us had ever seen, which it would be tedious to enumerate. The great mercy of God shone around us when we landed on those shores: for we were running out of wood and water, and could have survived only a few days more at sea. Honor, glory, and thanks be to God.

We adopted the plan of sailing along the shore of this continent toward the east, never losing sight of it. Soon after we had set out we came to a point where the coastline made a turn to the south. The distance to this point from the place where we had first landed was about 300 leagues.[11] Several times in the course of this journey we landed on shore and conversed amicably with the people who lived there, as you will hear below. I had forgotten to tell you that the distance from the promontory of Cape Verde to the first point we came to on this continent was about 700 leagues; but I estimate that we sailed more than 1800, due partly to our ignorance of the region and the incompetence of the pilot, and partly because of the storms and winds impeding our straight path and forcing us into frequent detours.

Indeed, if my companions had not approached me for assistance, since I knew something of cosmography, no one would have known—as neither the captain nor any pilot did—where we were within 500 leagues. For we wandered about aimlessly, and our instruments—the quadrant and the astrolabe—could only measure the altitude of the heavenly bodies from

---

10. But see Formisano, *Letters from a New World*, 176n3, for a discussion of the timeline.

11. A traditional measure of distance, about 3 miles to a league.

the horizon, as everyone knows.[12] From this point on, they showered much honor upon me. For I showed them that even without a knowledge of marine charts I excelled more at the art of navigation than all the pilots in the world. For these men had no knowledge of it, except for those places which they regularly sailed.[13]

We decided to sail further along the coast beyond the aforesaid point of land where it began to curve southward, and to discover what could be found in these regions. So we sailed along this second stretch of coastline about 600 leagues. We often landed and gathered and spoke with the inhabitants of those regions, who received us cordially, and so we sometimes stayed with them fifteen or twenty days on end, amicably and comfortably, as you will learn below.

No part of that continent is in the torrid zone that extends beyond the equator toward the Antarctic pole, for it begins at the eighth degree beyond the equator. We sailed along the coastline so far that, having crossed the Tropic of Capricorn, we found the Antarctic Pole, 50 degrees above their horizon; and we were 17.5 degrees north of the Antarctic Circle. I shall now proceed to tell what I saw there and learned about the nature of those people and their manner of life and their gentleness, about the fertility of the land, the healthfulness of the air, and the disposition of the heavens and heavenly bodies and especially of the fixed stars of the eighth sphere,[14] never seen or described by the ancients.

First, therefore, as for the people, we found in those regions such a multitude of peoples that no one could ever count them (as one reads in *Revelation*),[15] a gentle people who will be easily led to God. All of them, of both sexes, walk about in the nude, covering no part of the body, and just as they exit from their mother's womb, so they proceed until death. Their bodies are large, sturdy, well-formed and well-proportioned, their skin rather reddish in color, the result, I think, since they go about naked, of being burned by the sun. They have a mass of black hair on their heads, are agile in walking and running, and have open, comely faces, which nonetheless they themselves destroy.

---

12. The quadrant and the astrolabe were the standard instruments of navigation at this time.

13. Vespucci is vaunting his knowledge of cartography and astronomy, which at this time were not standard knowledge for navigators, who relied on maritime charts to guide them to familiar ports. In later life, Vespucci's knowledge in this domain was rewarded by an appointment as royal pilot, as mentioned, with the responsibility to train a new generation of navigators.

14. The eighth sphere was the outermost sphere of the Ptolemaic cosmological system, on which the stars that appeared unmoving, as opposed to the wandering planets, were fixed. Those of the southern hemisphere would appear different than the familiar ones of the northern hemisphere.

15. Perhaps a reference to the biblical book of Revelation 7:4, or 9:16.

For they pierce their cheeks and lips and noses and ears. Do not think that these piercings are small or that they have only one of them: I saw several whose faces each had seven piercings, any one of which could hold a plum. They fill these cavities with exquisite stones of cerulean, marble, crystalline, and alabaster hue, or with bright white bones and other things, artfully worked according to their custom. You would be awestruck if you saw such a sight, really almost monstrous, as a man having a stone in his cheek or jaw, or seven in his lips, of which some are longer than a hands-breadth. I have often wondered at their size and calculated that seven of such stones must weigh 16 ounces, not counting those in their ears, each of which are triply pierced, from which openings there hang rings laden with other stones. And this is the custom only of the men, for women do not pierce their face but only their ears.

They have another custom which is truly horrendous and the height of all human cruelty. For their women, who are libidinous, by a certain artifice cause the genitals of their men to be bitten by certain poisonous creatures, making them swell up so that they appear deformed and loathsome. In consequence, many of the men cut lose their genitals, leaving the untreated wounds to rot, and so they become eunuchs.

They have no textiles—not of wool, nor linen, nor silk—because they do not need them. Nor do they own their own property, but all things are held in common. They live at once without king and without governance, and each person is his own lord. They take as many wives as they want, and the son copulates with his mother, brother with sister, and every man with every woman he encounters. They divorce as often as they wish, following no rules in these matters. For they have no churches and obey no laws, and do not even worship idols. What more shall I say? They live according to nature, and can be called Epicureans rather than Stoics.[16]

There are among them no merchants nor any commerce. The different peoples wage wars among themselves without art or order. The older men convince the youngsters to follow them, and incite them to fight wars in which they cruelly destroy each other. They take captives from the battlefield not to save their lives, but to butcher them for dinner; for those who are victorious eat those who have been vanquished, and along with other kinds of meat, human flesh is commonly consumed. Let me make this quite clear to you: for a father has been known to eat his children and his wife, and I knew a man—one with whom I had conversed—who boasted that he had eaten the flesh of more than 300 human bodies. And again, I stayed twenty-seven

---

16. A witticism; humanists often debated the relative virtues of the Epicurean and Stoic philosophies—both developed during the Hellenistic era—of which, naturally, the natives of South America had never heard.

days in one village, where I saw salted human flesh hanging from the rafters of their huts, in the same way that we are accustomed to hang bacon and salt pork. Still more: they wonder why we do not eat our enemies and eat their flesh for dinner, for they say that it is very tasty.

Their weapons are bow and arrows, and when they head off to war, without any thought of safety, they cover no part of their bodies—behaving in this just like the beasts. We tried as hard as we could to persuade them to give up this unwise practice, and they promised us they would change.

The women, as I have said, who both walk about in the nude and are most libidinous, yet have bodies that are quite lovely and shapely. Nor are they as shameful as one might think, because their shame appears less (although they are fleshy) precisely because their bodies are so beautiful. We noted with wonder that we saw none among them who had sagging breasts, and those who had given birth had wombs as shapely and taut as those of the virgins; and the same could be said for other parts of their bodies, which I shall not mention for the sake of decency. When they could copulate with Christians, impelled by their great lust, they destroyed all chastity. They live for 150 years, rarely get ill, and if they ever experience poor health, they cure themselves with certain roots of herbs.

These are the more notable things that I observed among these people. The air there is certainly temperate and fine, and so far as I could learn from them, they never suffer from any kind of plague or illness which proceeds from foul air, so that, if they do not die a violent death, they live a long life—I believe because southerly winds always blow there, and especially the one we call Eurus, which is for them what Aquilo is for us.[17] They are ardent fishermen, and the waters there are amply supplied with fish of every kind. They are not hunters, most likely because, since there are many species of wild animals and especially lions and bears and countless serpents and other horrid and fearsome beasts, and since also there are huge forests with trees of immense magnitude, they do not dare expose themselves, naked and without clothing or arms, to the great dangers to be found there.

The land in these regions is certainly fertile and pleasant, abounding with many hills, mountains, and numberless valleys, watered with great rivers and wholesome springs, covered with extensive forests, dense and nearly impenetrable, full of all kinds of beasts. Huge trees grow there without cultivation, which produce many fruits delicious to eat and useful for human bodies—while others are quite the opposite—and none of these fruits are like ours at home. Innumerable types of grasses and roots grow there as well,

---

17. Eurus is actually the East wind in Greco-Roman mythology, and Aquilo (Boreas) the North; see also Formisano, *Letters from a New World*, 185nn23, 24.

from which they make bread and excellent salads. They have also many kinds of grains completely unlike our own.

They have no kinds of metals except gold, in which these regions are rich, although we brought back none of it with us on this our first voyage. The inhabitants told us about it, saying that there was a great abundance of gold in the interior, and they seemed to esteem it or prize it not at all. Pearls are found in abundance, as I have already written. If I were to record all the details of what is found there and note all the numerous kinds of animals and their multitude, I would go on endlessly. . . .

A willing interpreter[18] has translated this letter from Italian into Latin, so that all Latins[19] may understand what wonders are daily to be discovered. And may the boldness of those be checked who scrutinize the majesty of the heavens, and who wish to know more than it is fitting to know—since for all of time since the world began, no one has known the vastness of the earth and all the things contained in it.

Praise be to God.

Garcilaso de la Vega, "El Inca"

Garcilaso de la Vega (1539–1616), who always added to his name a further designation, "the Inca," did not discover a New World, but rather, uniquely among European authors of the era, belonged to it—and simultaneously, to the Old World as well. Born in Peru, the illegitimate son of a Spanish conquistador and an Inca princess, he would later write the history of his homeland: the *Royal Commentaries of the Incas, and General History of Peru.* He dedicated the first volume of the work (published 1609) to the Inca heritage—his mother's book, as it were—and the second (published 1616–1617) to the Spanish conquest—his father's. The structure of his masterpiece perfectly mirrored the two aspects of Garcilaso's identity: the scion of a royal Inca lineage, on the one hand, and on the other, a Spanish Christian and humanist.

Until the age of ten, Garcilaso was raised in his mother's household and in the tradition of the Incas. His first language was the native Quechua, and

18. Vespucci writes *iocundus interpres*, which may mean a willing or amiable translator; and it is likely a pun on the translator's name, Fra Giovanni del Giocondo, *giocondo* being the Italian form of *iocundus*.

19. That is to say "all Europeans," or all who share the Latin-based civilization of Western Europe.

his religious beliefs were based on the myths and legends of the Children of the Sun. Each week, the remnant of the Inca community gathered at his mother's table and retold the stories of the glorious Inca civilization. He estimated the number of Incas (members of the royal family, both male and female) he knew as a child at about 200, and the number of lower-caste natives was much greater.

From these colloquies, Garcilaso gathered an unparalleled knowledge of pre-conquest Indian civilization. He would later describe to a European audience the beliefs of the people of Peru; their concept of family; their dress; their knowledge of astronomy, medicine, and mathematics; the flora and fauna of the region; the origins and course of Inca rule; its administrative, architectural, and engineering feats. Although some elements of his account may be mythologized or colored by nostalgia, as the elderly author recalled childhood conversations, nonetheless his access to original information was exceptional, and key points ring true.

The excerpts presented here from the first volume of the *Royal Commentaries* record, first, a conversation of the child Garcilaso with an elder kinsman telling of the origins of Inca civilization, and second, the mature author's first-person statement about purpose and method of writing.

After recalling the regular visits to his mother's table of her Inca kinsfolk, Garcilaso approaches a distinguished elder: "Inca, my uncle, though you have no writings to preserve the memory of past events, what information have you of the origin and beginnings of our kings?" Europeans, he points out, have written histories telling them "when their own kings and their neighbors' kings began to reign and when one empire gave way to another." But the Incas had no books, and must rely on memory and storytelling. "But you, who have no books, what memory have you preserved of your antiquity? Who was the first of our Incas? What was he called? What was the origin of his line? How did he begin to reign? With what men and arms did he conquer this great empire? How did our heroic deeds begin?"

His kinsman responds with a story, the vehicle by which pre-literate peoples record their histories. Long ago, he begins, the Sun lamented that the Quechua people lived "like wild beasts, with no religion or government and no towns or houses, and without tilling or sowing the soil, or clothing or covering their flesh, for they did not know how to weave cotton or wool to make clothes." They ate berries and herbs they found in the wild—as well as human flesh—covered themselves with leaves and bark or not at all, and did not marry or form families. The Sun sent two of his children, a son and a daughter, who were also husband and wife—for sibling marriage was for the Incas, as for the Egyptian pharaohs, a regular practice—to introduce these wild people to civilization. They established a capital city, and taught the natives the tasks they must perform: farming and pasturing for the men, spinning and weaving cloth for the women. These two Children of the Sun thus reigned as "king and lords over all the people" whom they instructed in "reason, government, and good works."

In a second passage, Garcilaso reflects on his childhood experience as preparation for the writing of his book: "I was brought up among these Indians, and . . . I was able to learn during that time something of all the subjects I am writing about, for in my childhood they used to recount their histories, just as stories are told for children." He lived among them until the age of twenty, when he departed for his European career, and so saw, as well, "their idolatry, festivals, and superstitions, which had still not altogether disappeared in my own time." Finally, a tireless ethnographer, from his agemates who were *mestizos* of the first generation like himself, he gathered information about their own villages and families, enriching what he had learned from his own kinsmen.

Thus recovering and preserving his Inca past, Garcilaso wove together the histories of his mother's people and his father's civilization, refusing to write only of the conquerors, memorializing the wisdom of those who had been vanquished, inscribing for posterity the story told to him by an aging kinsman who had wept "to see our Incas no longer ruling and our people bereft of an empire."[20]

Garcilaso de la Vega, "El Inca," *Royal Commentaries of the Incas* (1609–1617)[21]

THE ORIGIN OF THE INCA KINGS OF PERU

. . . After having prepared many schemes and taken many ways to begin to give an account of the origin and establishment of the native Inca kings of Peru, it seemed to me that the best scheme and simplest and easiest way was to recount what I often heard as a child from the lips of my mother and her brothers and uncles and other elders about these beginnings. For everything said about them from other sources comes down to the same story as we shall relate, and it will be better to have it as told in the very words of the Incas than in those of foreign authors. My mother dwelt in Cusco, her native place, and was visited there every week by the few relatives, both male and female, who escaped the cruelty and tyranny of Atahuallpa (which we shall describe in our account of his life). On these visits the ordinary subject of conversation was always the origin of the Inca kings, their greatness, the grandeur of their empire, their deeds and conquests, their government in peace and war, and

20. Quoted by John G. Varner, *El Inca: The Life and Times of Garcilaso de la Vega* (Austin: University of Texas Press, 1968), 144.

21. From Garcilaso de la Vega, "El Inca," *Royal Commentaries of the Incas and General History of Peru* (Austin: University of Texas Press, 1966) , trans. Harold V. Livermore, as edited by Karen Spalding (abridged ed.; Indianapolis, IN: Hackett Publishing Co., 2006), 2–7.

the laws they ordained so greatly to the advantage of their vassals. In short, there was nothing concerning the most flourishing period of their history that they did not bring up in their conversations.

From the greatness and prosperity of the past they turned to the present, mourning their dead kings, their lost empire, and their fallen state, etcetera. These and similar topics were broached by the Incas and Pallas[22] on their visits, and on recalling their departed happiness, they always ended these conversations with tears and mourning, saying: "Our rule is turned to bondage" etcetera. During these talks, I, as a boy, often came in and went out of the place where they were, and I loved to hear them, as boys always do like to hear stories. Days, months, and years went by, until I was sixteen or seventeen. Then it happened that one day when my family was talking in this fashion about their kings and the olden times, I remarked to the senior of them, who usually related these things: "Inca, my uncle, though you have no writings to preserve the memory of past events, what information have you of the origin and beginnings of our kings? For the Spaniards and the other peoples who live on their borders have divine and human histories from which they know when their own kings and their neighbors' kings began to reign and when one empire gave way to another. They even know how many thousand years it is since God created heaven and earth. All this and much more they know through their books. But you, who have no books, what memory have you preserved of your antiquity? Who was the first of our Incas? What was he called? What was the origin of his line? How did he begin to reign? With what men and arms did he conquer this great empire? How did our heroic deeds begin?"

The Inca was delighted to hear these questions, since it gave him great pleasure to reply to them, and turned to me (who had already often heard him tell the tale, but had never paid as much attention as then) saying:

"Nephew, I will tell you these things with pleasure: indeed, it is right that you should hear them and keep them in your heart (this is their phrase for 'in the memory'). You should know that in olden times the whole of this region before you was covered with brush and heath, and people lived in those times like wild beasts, with no religion or government and no towns or houses, and without tilling or sowing the soil, or clothing or covering their flesh, for they did not know how to weave cotton or wool to make clothes. They lived in twos and threes as chance brought them together in caves and crannies in rocks and underground caverns. Like wild beasts they ate the herbs of the field and roots of trees and fruits growing wild and also human flesh. They covered their bodies with leaves and the bark of trees and animals' skins. Others were naked. In short, they lived like deer or other game, and even in

---

22. The Incas were the males of the principal Inca lineages, the Pallas the females; see also Spalding ed. of Garcilaso, *Royal Commentaries*, 2n2.

their intercourse with women they behaved like beasts, for they knew nothing of having separate wives."

I must remark, in order to avoid many repetitions of the words "our father the Sun," that the phrase was used by the Incas to express respect whenever they mentioned the sun, for they boasted of descending from it, and none but Incas were allowed to utter the words: it would have been blasphemy and the speaker would have been stoned. The Inca said:

"Our father the Sun, seeing men in the state I have mentioned, took pity and was sorry for them, and sent from heaven to earth a son and a daughter of his to indoctrinate them in the knowledge of our father the Sun that they might worship him and adopt him as their god, and to give them precepts and laws by which they would live as reasonable and civilized men, and dwell in houses and settled towns, and learn to till the soil, and grow plants and crops, and breed flocks, and use the fruits of the earth like rational beings and not like beasts. . . .

"Finally he told them: 'When you have reduced these people to our service, you shall maintain them in reason and justice, showing mercy, clemency, and mildness, and always treating them as a merciful father treats his beloved and tender children. Imitate my example in this. I do good to all the world. I give them my light and brightness that they may see and go about their business; I warm them when they are cold; and I grow their pastures and crops, and bring fruit to their trees, and multiply their flocks. I bring rain and calm weather in turn, and I take care to go round the world once a day to observe the wants that exist in the world and to fill and supply them as the sustainer and benefactor of men. I wish you as children of mine to follow this example sent down to earth to teach and benefit those men who live like beasts. And henceforward I establish and nominate you as king and lords over all the people you may thus instruct with your reason, government, and good works.'

"When our father the Sun had thus made manifest his will to his two children he bade them farewell. They left Titicaca and travelled northwards, and . . . reached a small inn or resthouse seven or eight leagues south of this city [of Cusco]. Today it is called Pacárac Tampu, 'inn or resthouse of the dawn.' . . . From this place he and his wife, our queen, reached the valley of Cusco, which was then a wilderness.

"The first settlement they made in this valley," said the Inca, "was in the hill called Huanacauri. . . . Then our Inca said to his wife: 'Our father the Sun bids us remain in this valley and make it our dwelling place and home in fulfillment of his will. It is therefore right, queen and sister,[23] that each of us should go out and call together these people so as to instruct them and benefit

---

23. As the Egyptian pharaohs often did, Inca rulers married their sisters; see Spalding ed. of Garcilaso, *Royal Commentaries*, 4n3.

them as our father the Sun has ordained.' Our first rulers set out from the hill of Huanacauri, each in a different direction, to call the people together. . . . The prince went northwards, and the princess south. They spoke to all the men and women they found in that wilderness and said that their father the Sun had sent them from the sky to be teachers and benefactors to the dwellers in all that land, delivering them from the wild lives they led and in obedience to the commands given by the Sun, their father, calling them together and removing them from those heaths and moors, bringing them to dwell in settled valleys and giving them the food of men instead of that of beasts to eat. Our king and queen said these and similar things to the first savages they found in those mountains and heaths, and as the savages beheld two persons clad and adorned with the ornaments our father the Sun had given them—and a very different dress from their own—with their ears pierced and opened in the way we their descendants have, and saw that their words and countenances showed them to be children of the Sun, and that they came to mankind to give them towns to dwell in and food to eat, they wondered at what they saw and were at the same time attracted by the promises that were held out to them. Thus they fully credited all they were told and worshipped and venerated the strangers as children of the Sun and obeyed them as kings. These savages gathered others and repeated the wonders they had seen and heard, and a great number of men and women collected and set out to follow our king and queen wherever they might lead.

"When our princes saw the great crowd that had formed there, they ordered that some should set about supplying open-air meals for them all, so that they should not be driven by hunger to disperse again across the heaths. Others were ordered to work on building huts and houses according to plans made by the Inca. Thus our imperial city began to be settled. . . .

"At the same time, in peopling the city, our Inca showed the male Indians which tasks were proper to men: breaking and tilling the land, sowing crops, seeds, and vegetables which he showed to be good to eat and fruitful, and for which purpose he taught them how to make ploughs and other necessary instruments, and bade them and showed them how to draw irrigation channels from the streams that run through the valley of Cusco, and even showed them how to make the footwear we use. On her side the queen trained the Indian women in all the feminine occupations: spinning and weaving cotton and wool, and making clothes for themselves and their husbands and children. She told them how to do these and other duties of domestic service. In short, there was nothing related to human life that our princes failed to teach their first vassals, the Inca king acting as master for the men and the *Coya,*[24] queen, mistress of the women."

---

24. The *coya* is the Inca queen; see Spalding ed. of Garcilaso, *Royal Commentaries*, 6n4.

GARCILASO'S DECLARATION OF HIS OWN HISTORY

... I was brought up among these Indians, and as I frequented their society until I was twenty I was able to learn during that time something of all the subjects I am writing about, for in my childhood they used to recount their histories, just as stories are told for children. Later, as I grew up, they talked to me at length about their laws and government, and compared the new rule of the Spaniards with that of the Incas, contrasting especially the crimes and punishments and severity the latter were dealt with under the two regimes. They told me how their kings acted in peace and war, in what manner they treated their vassals, and how their vassals served them. Moreover, they told me, as if I were their own son, all about their idolatry, their rites, ceremonies, and sacrifices, the greater and lesser festivals, and how they were celebrated. They told me their superstitions and abuses, good and evil auspices, including those they discerned in sacrifices and others. In short, I would say that they told me about everything they had in their state; and if I had written it down at this time, this history would have been more copious. Apart from what the Indians told me, I experienced and saw with my own eyes a great deal of their idolatry, festivals, and superstitions, which had still not altogether disappeared in my own time, when I was twelve or thirteen. I was born eight years after the Spanish conquered my country, and as I have said, was brought up there till I was twenty: thus I saw many of the things the Indians did in the time of their paganism and shall relate them and say that I saw them.

I have also listened to many accounts of the deeds and conquests of those kings in addition to what my relatives told me and what I myself say, for as soon as I resolved to write this history, I wrote to my old schoolmates at my primary school and grammar school, and urged each of them to help me with accounts they might have of the particular conquests the Incas made in the provinces their mothers came from, for each province has its account and knots[25] to record its annals and traditions, and thus preserves its own history much better than that of its neighbors. My schoolfellows earnestly complied with my request, and each reported my intention to his mother and relatives, and they, on hearing that an Indian, a son of their own country, intended to write its history, brought from their archives the records they had of their histories and sent me them. ...

---

25. The Incan *quipus*, knotted cords used as memory devices; see Spalding ed. of Garcilaso, *Royal Commentaries*, 7n5.

Saint Francis Xavier

Just as Vespucci observed the natives of Brazil and Patagonia, and Garcilaso those of the Inca of Peru, Saint Francis Xavier (1506–1552) studied the peoples of Asia but for a different and single purpose: to bring them into the Christian fold. A Basque-speaking native of the tiny kingdom of Navarre perched between Spain and France, Xavier was one of the close companions of his compatriot Ignatius Loyola and a founder under the latter's leadership of the Jesuit order, committed to the advancement of Catholic Christianity in Europe and abroad. That mission, as he argued the case to King John III of Portugal with regard to the occupation of India, was for Xavier the sole justification for empire.[26]

In 1541, he set sail from Europe, rounded the Cape of Good Hope, and pressed eastward to the regions of India, Indonesia, and Japan then being opened up by the Portuguese; he was on his way to China when he died in 1552 on an island under Portuguese control just off the Chinese mainland. In his twelve years of ceaseless missionary work, he added several Asian languages to his store of Basque, Spanish, French, Italian, Portuguese, and Latin, and acquainted himself with the complex web of indigenous religions that flourished in these civilizations, most of them older than the Christian faith he was determined to spread. Equipped with that knowledge, he confronted the well-rooted religious traditions of the East to win converts to a faith whose center of gravity was in his lifetime European and Western.

Wherever Xavier went, he wrote letters: reporting to his superiors, requesting the support of the Portuguese king, advising and disciplining his lieutenants, to whom he passed responsibility for vast realms when he departed for new horizons. These letters, of which 137 are attested,[27] would have puzzled early generations of humanists: they are in whatever language suited his immediate purpose, but mostly Portuguese or Spanish rather than Latin; rhetorically defective, following no clear line of argument and avoiding any kind of embellishment; and intellectually undistinguished, lacking the usual deference to ancient philosophical authority. They are, however, compelling narratives of Xavier's exploits, their few and simple words vigorous and tense with feeling.

The long letter excerpted here describes Xavier's Japanese venture of August 1549 to November 1551, by which the first Christian communities were established in that distant land whose existence had only recently

---

26. M. Joseph Costelloe, ed. and trans., *The Letters and Instructions of Francis Xavier* (St. Louis, MO: Institute of Jesuit Sources, 1992), xxvii.

27. Costelloe, *Letters and Instructions*, xxv. There is additionally one letter fragment.

become known to Portuguese mariners. Accompanied by three Japanese converts intent on introducing their countrymen to their new faith, he landed at the port of Kagoshima at the southern tip of Japan. He later moved on to, among other destinations, Yamaguchi, on the southwestern coast, and finally Bungo, on the southernmost island of Kyushu.

At Kagoshima, Xavier first encountered the congeries of Buddhist sects that were the principal religious institutions of the region, and the obstacle, as well, that he needed to overcome if his program of Christianization was to be successful. Various groups of professional religious, called "bonzes," managed these sects, and commanded the respect of the natives. Equating some of these figures to European equivalents, Xavier describes them as priests, monks, and nuns, the latter wearing distinctive uniforms or habits. He also recognizes, however, the great differences between Japanese religion and European Christianity: "The teachings of the sects come from a mainland which lies near Japan, called China.[28] . . . There are nine distinct creeds,[29] and both men and women, each according to his preference, holds to the teaching he desires, and no one is compelled to belong to this sect or the other, in such a way that there are households where the husband adheres to one sect, and the wife to another, and the children to another; and this is not considered strange among them, for each one follows his own will."

These sects have in common, as Xavier sees it, a penitential structure: they prescribe certain behaviors, or "commandments," which the people fail to observe, but rely upon the bonzes to fulfill the commandments for them, in exchange for which they support the bonzes with revenues, houses, and respect. The bonzes occupy themselves with performing sacrificial penances for the laity, who acquire a kind of certificate, to be buried with them, that will allow their escape from hell. Hell is not eternal, and heaven does not exist. Nor does there exist any notion of the divine Creation of the universe, or of individual, immortal souls. It is these points of difference that Xavier and his colleagues stress as they address potential converts among the Japanese.

Xavier finds the Japanese to be promising: they are "highly intelligent and clear-thinking," and curious about the message he offers. To reach this audience, he and his associates learn Japanese, which takes about a year, and then laboriously construct a primer of Christian theology in the Japanese language but written in the European alphabet.

> We began with a brief presentation of the Creation of the world, explaining what was essential for them to know, that there was one Creator of all things, about

---

28. Buddhism reached Japan from China by way of Korea around the middle of the sixth century CE.

29. For the nine sects and others, see George Schurhammer and Josef Wicki, eds., *Epistolae S. Francisci Xaverii aliaque eius scripta*, rev. ed., 2 vols. (Rome: Apud Monumenta Historica Soc. Iesu, 1944–1945), 256n12.

which they had absolutely no knowledge. . . . Then we came to the Incarnation of Christ, and told the story of the life of Christ and all its mysteries up through the Ascension, concluding with the Day of Judgment.

This primer then becomes the principal tool of their mission: they read from it aloud, expand upon the concepts contained there, invite questions from the listeners and satisfy their doubts, while challenging the precepts of the bonzes, exposing what they see as the failures of the Japanese sects to respond to profound religious issues.

> We persevered for many days in these sessions of questioning and discussion; and after many days passed, [those in attendance] began to become Christians; and the first to do so were those who had seemed most hostile to our preaching and in our debates.

Outraged, the bonzes call upon local rulers to forbid this Christian instruction. Some do; but some, like the ruler of Yamaguchi, support Xavier and his colleagues, who establish small but loyal communities of converts scattered through the places they visited. At the end of the letter, written on his return to India in early 1552, Xavier exhorts his fellow Jesuits to go to Japan to nurture those communities, and so find a deeper satisfaction than in their routines at home. Christianity did indeed make inroads in Japan, until its brutal suppression by the Tokugawa shogunate in the following century, when Christianity became a prohibited religion.

Striking in the story of Xavier's Japanese mission is the reliance on persuasion: the learning of a native language so as to be able to communicate effectively, the construction of a Christian primer that became the springboard for public reading and debate, and the conviction that sufficient argument, grounded in evidence and calling on the rational faculties, would lead to Christian conversion. In this sense, if not on the rhetorical merit of his nonetheless powerful letters, Xavier, too, is a product of the humanist movement.

Saint Francis Xavier, *Letter to His Companions in Europe* (Cochin, 29 January 1552)

May the grace of the Holy Spirit rest always in our souls. Amen.

On 20 August 1549,[30] in peace and good health, we landed in Japan at the city of Kagoshima,[31] the homeland of the Japanese natives[32] who had come with us. The people of the land received us with kindness, especially the relatives of Paul, the Japanese, to whom our Lord God wished to bring the

---

30. Actually 15 August: see Schurhammer and Wicki ed., 254n1.
31. Port city of southernmost Japan.
32. Paul, Antonio, and Joanne: see Schurhammer and Wicki ed., 254n3.

knowledge of the truth, and so about a hundred of them became Christians during the time we stayed in Kagoshima. These pagans were delighted to hear the Law of God,[33] about which they had never heard or known.

The land of Japan is exceedingly large, and consists of islands. Only one language is spoken throughout the land, and it is not very difficult to understand. The Portuguese discovered these islands eight or nine years ago.[34] The Japanese people have a very high opinion of themselves, believing that none can rival them in arms and chivalry, and they have little regard for foreigners. They delight in arms, which they hold in high esteem, and prize nothing so much as fine weapons studded with gold and silver. They carry swords and daggers constantly, both indoors and out of doors, and when they go to sleep, they keep them by their pillows. . . .

They behave courteously among themselves, but do not extend those courtesies to foreigners, whom they despise. They spend all they have on clothing, weapons, and servants, putting no wealth aside. They are bellicose and always waging wars, and whoever is strongest gets to rule over the others. They have only one king, but it is 150 years since they have shown him any obedience;[35] and this is why they are constantly at war among themselves.

The land has a large number of men and women who make profession of religion, of whom the men are called bonzes.[36] There are many kinds of bonzes: some who wear gray habits and some who wear black habits; and there is little friendship between them, those with black habits despising those with gray habits, saying they are ignorant and immoral. Among the women there are also bonzes with gray habits and others with black, and each shows obedience to the male bonzes who wear the same color habit. Japan has a great number of these male and female bonzes, which has to be seen to be believed. . . .

The teachings of the sects come from a mainland which lies near Japan, called China.[37] . . . There are nine distinct creeds,[38] and both men and women, each according to his preference, holds to the teaching he desires, and no one is compelled to belong to this sect or the other, in such a way that there are households where the husband adheres to one sect, and the wife to another, and the children to another; and this is not considered strange among them,

---

33. The phrase Xavier uses consistently to denote Christianity.

34. The Ryukyu islands in 1542 and Japan in 1543: see Schurhammer and Wicki ed., 254n4.

35. Since 1338, that is, the beginning of the Ashikaga shogunate: see Schurhammer and Wicki ed., 255n6.

36. The bonzes are Buddhist monks of various sects.

37. Buddhism reached Japan from China by way of Korea around the middle of the sixth century CE.

38. For the nine sects and others, see Schurhammer and Wicki ed., 256n12.

for each one follows his own will. Differences and controversies arise among them about which sect is better, and often these lead to wars.

None of these nine sects address the creation of the world or of souls.[39] All say that there is a hell and a heaven, without declaring what heaven is, nor explaining by whose law or decree some souls are sent to hell.[40] These sects only teach that the men who founded them performed great penances—that is, of a thousand or two thousand or three thousand years—and that they performed these penances for the many souls who were damned because they never performed any penance for their sins. . . .

> *Xavier relates what he has learned about the belief systems of the various Japanese sects. He is struck mainly by what he sees as the penitential system: the professional religious keep the commandments given to the many, and do penance for their sins, in exchange for which they are given lands, funds, and honors.*

I shall now tell you what happened to us in Japan. We had first come to Paul's native city of Kagoshima, as I have said, where as a result of the many sermons which Paul preached to his kinsfolk, he won over nearly a hundred Christians; and he would have won over nearly all of them, if the local priests had not stood in the way. Here we stayed for more than a year. Meanwhile the bonzes told the ruler of this land, who had extensive holdings, that if he permitted his vassals to accept the Law of God, he would lose his lands, and his pagodas would be destroyed and sacked by the people, because the Law of God was contrary to the native creeds, and those who accepted the Law of God would lose their earlier faith in the saints who had founded them. In the end these bonzes persuaded the duke of the land to decree that, on pain of death, no one should become a Christian; and so he decreed that no one should accept the Law of God.

During the year we stayed in Paul's city, we busied ourselves in teaching the Christians, learning the language, and translating much of the Law of God into the Japanese language. We began with a brief presentation of the Creation of the world, explaining what was essential for them to know, that there was one Creator of all things, about which they had absolutely no knowledge, and also other necessary things. Then we came to the Incarnation of Christ, and told the story of the life of Christ and all its mysteries up through the Ascension, concluding with the Day of Judgment. This book, then, on which we labored much, we wrote down in the Japanese language

---

39. Buddhism does not posit a personal, immortal soul: see Schurhammer and Wicki ed., 256n14.

40. Buddhism does not posit a supreme deity who ordains the punishments of hell; and the Buddhist hell is not eternal: see Schurhammer and Wicki ed., 256nn15, 17.

but using our alphabet. We read it to those who had become Christians to teach them how they must worship God and Jesus Christ in order to be saved.

The Christians rejoiced greatly to hear these things, and also those who were not Christians, for it seemed to them to be the truth, since the Japanese are highly intelligent and clear-thinking. If they failed to become Christians, it was from fear of the duke, and not because they did not understand that the Law of God was true and their own ways false.

At the end of this year, seeing that the duke of the land was displeased that the Law of God was spreading, we set out for another land. We took leave of those who had become Christian, who wept to see us go since they felt great love for us, and thanked us greatly for all we had done to teach them how to gain salvation. I left Paul with these Christians, a native of the land and a good Christian, to teach and guide them.

From there we went to another land, whose lord received us warmly, and when we had been there a few days about a hundred people became Christians. By this time one of us knew how to speak Japanese, and reading from the book which we had translated into the Japanese language, and by other teaching, many became Christians. In this place I left Father Cosmo de Torres with the new converts. Juan Fernandez and I went to Yamaguchi,[41] a land ruled by a great Japanese lord. It is a city of more than ten million inhabitants, with houses all made of wood. Here there were many nobles and also others who greatly desired to know what creed it was that we preached. So we determined to preach in the streets twice each day for several days, reading from the book that we had brought, and commenting on what we read. Many people listened to our preaching, and we were called to the houses of the great nobles so that they could ask us about the creed that we preached, and they told us that if it was better than their creed, they would accept it. Many showed their delight in hearing the Law of God; others scoffed, and still others pondered it. . . .

Xavier recounts how he and his companions are mocked in the streets of Yamaguchi. Since few converts are made there, they went to the city of Miyako,[42] which also proved unpromising. Returning to Yamaguchi, they are able to obtain the protection of the duke for their missionary efforts, which now meet with success.

We then told him that if he wished to confer a benefit upon us, we sought nothing more than that he permit us to preach the Law of God in his lands, and to allow those who wished to convert to do so. He kindly gave us his permission, and ordered notices to be placed throughout the streets of the

---

41. A city and province of southwestern Japan.
42. Modern Kyôto, Japan.

city in his name saying that he was pleased that the Law of God would be preached in his lands, and that all those who wished to convert could do so. At the same time, he gave us a monastery as a kind of college in which we could stay. While we stayed in this monastery, many persons came to hear us preach the Law of God, which we usually did twice a day. At the end of our sermon there were always discussions which lasted a long a time. We were continually engaged in responding to the questions or in preaching. . . . We persevered for many days in these sessions of questioning and discussion; and after many days passed, [those in attendance] began to become Christians; and the first to do so were those who had seemed most hostile to our preaching and in our debates.

Of those who became Christians, many were nobles, who once they converted became such friends of ours that I could not stop writing about it. They explained to us fully the native creeds, of which, as I said earlier, there were nine, each different from the others. Once supplied with accurate knowledge of what these creeds contained, we presented arguments to prove them false, each day challenging certain of their rules and beliefs, to which they did not know how to respond, neither the bonzes or nuns or sorcerers or anyone else who opposed the Law of God. When the Christians saw that the bonzes could make no response, they rejoiced greatly, and each day their faith in God grew greater, while the other natives present at these sessions lost faith in the erroneous sects in which they believed.

Seeing that many became Christians, the bonzes were greatly troubled, and they reproached the converts for having abandoned their own creeds and accepted the Law of God. The Christians said to them, along with those who were considering conversion, that if they became Christians it was because it seemed that the Law of God accorded more with reason than did their creeds; and because they saw, too, that we answered the questions that they put to us, while the defenders of the native creeds could not respond to the challenges we made to them. The teachings of the Japanese sects have no understanding (as was said earlier) of the creation of the world—the sun, the moon, the stars, the heavens, the earth and the sea, or anything else—which to them seems to have no beginning. What most impressed them was our saying that their souls have a Creator who created them.

Xavier records something of the Christian missionaries' discussions with the natives of Creation, heaven and hell, and the goodness of God, meeting with some incomprehension and much interest.

In this city of Yamaguchi, in the space of two months, after many questions were asked and answered, five hundred persons, more or less, were baptized, and by the grace of God, some were baptized each day. Many revealed to us the schemes of the bonzes and their sects; if it were not for them, we would have learned nothing about the idolatry of the Japanese. Those who became Christians love us with a heartfelt love, and believe me, they are Christians in truth.

> *Xavier describes the hostile reaction of the bonzes to the missionaries and their message, and how they were countered. He is invited to visit the duke of Bungo,[43] an ally of the Portuguese. While Xavier was in Bungo, the duke of Yamaguchi commits suicide amid a local rebellion, and the duke of Bungo dispatches his brother to be the new duke of a pacified Yamaguchi, and a protector of the new Christian community there.*

In all the time that we stayed in Japan, which was more than two and one-half years, we were supported always by the alms ordered to be given us while in this place by the most Christian king of Portugal;[44] for when we left for Japan he ordered to be given us more than 1000 *cruzados*.[45] How much we have been favored by His Highness can scarcely be believed, and how much he has expended in giving us such generous support for colleges, houses, and all other necessities.

Having left Yamaguchi for Bungo, I decided to sail on a Portuguese ship[46] to India to meet with and be consoled by the Brothers in India, and to recruit Jesuit priests suited for Japan, and also to gather in India some necessary supplies that are lacking in Japan.

I arrived in Cochin[47] on 24 January 1552, and was warmly received by the Viceroy. This April, priests will go from India to Japan, and the envoy of the duke of Bungo will return in their company. I hope in the Lord God that they will bear much fruit in those regions; for among a people so prudent and intelligent, eager for knowledge, obedient to reason, and capable in every way, they cannot fail to bear much fruit. May our labors achieve their end, and may they last forever.

> *Xavier describes the efforts now being made by his associates in Yamaguchi to learn more of the Japanese language and culture and to teach the Christian faith. He then speaks of China as a mainland near Japan, a wealthy and peaceful land of strict laws, effective government, and intelligent people, from whence came the sects popular in Japan. Here he will go next to preach*

---

43. A former province of southeastern Japan.

44. John III (r. 1521–1557).

45. A Portuguese coin, stamped with a cross.

46. He did so in mid-November 1551; see Costelloe, "Introduction," xx.

47. Now Kochi, on the southwestern coast of India.

*Christianity. He invites his learned European colleagues to find satisfaction by
going to Japan and continuing the missionary work in progress there.*

Because I landed in Cochin at a time when the ships are preparing to sail, and
I have been occupied by so many visits from my friends, which interrupted
my writing, this letter has been written in much haste, its points not put in
order, and the narrative faulty. Accept it for its good intentions. There is so
much to write about Japan that the task is endless. I fear that what I have
written will annoy you, as there is so much to read. I console myself that those
who find it tedious to read may ease their discomfort by setting it down.

With this I shall close, without being able to do so, since I write to my
loved and cherished fellow priests and brothers, and about such dear friends
as are the Christians of Japan. And so I close by asking our Lord God to
reunite us all in the glory of paradise. Amen.

Luís Vas de Camões

Poetry was one of the five *studia humanitatis,* or "studies of humanity," that
the humanists valued;[48] and of the three major genres of poetry, the most
ancient and the most esteemed was the epic, dignified above all by the *Iliad*
and *Odyssey* of Homer and the *Aeneid* of Virgil. The final section of this
chapter, as of this volume, considers an epic poet, Luís Vas de Camões (c.
1524–1580), author of *The Lusiads* (1572),[49] a celebration of the Portuguese
nation, of the burgeoning Portuguese empire, and of Vasco da Gama, the
preeminent Portuguese navigator whose journeys established Portuguese
footholds in Africa and Asia. As has been seen, where Saint Francis Xavier,
the Portuguese apostle of Christianity in Asia, considers the mission of religious conversion to be the real and indispensable purpose for empire, his
contemporary and compatriot Camões reverses that order of priority. For
him, imperial expansion is inherently worthy; the extension of the Christian
faith, though desirable, ancillary. In his epic *Lusiads,* Camões has found
a perfect vehicle for that ideological assumption, since epics traditionally
heroize political aggression and its agents.[50] His work achieves the culmina-

---

48. See the introduction to Chapter 1 of this volume.

49. The name "Lusiad," or the epic story of Lusitania, was the Latin name of the ancient
Roman province in western Iberia that would one day be Portugal.

50. For the political ramifications of epic in general and of the *Lusiads'* in particular, see the
studies cited in Texts and Studies, 343.

tion of what others examined here attempted: the consummated marriage of humanism and imperialism.

To those for whom the term "imperialism" summons up images of the British empire, it comes as a surprise that the Portuguese empire was the first modern empire, and arguably the most enduring: for it lasted from its first extra-European conquest in 1415—of Ceuta, on the north African coast—until it surrendered its sovereignty over East Timor in 2002. The empire was both maritime, a network of coastal stations and commercial ports, and territorial, extending over expanses of land and exercising rule over diverse native peoples. It stretched from Brazil in the west; to Africa; to South, Southeast, and East Asia as far as Nagasaki; and to the islands of the future Indonesia, from where it dominated Indian Ocean trade. That trade made Portugal wealthy—its kings taking a whopping 20 percent of all profits—at least into the seventeenth century, when it yielded to larger competitors.

In this imperial venture, Camões played an active role. Educated in the classics in his youth by his uncle, chancellor of the University of Coimbra (Portugal), he enlisted in the imperial forces, following in the footsteps of his wandering father, who had sought his fortune in Portuguese India and died in Goa. Camões lived mostly in Asia, his *curriculum vitae* boasting in addition to military campaigns and bureaucratic posts prosecutions for fraud and assault. Throughout these travels and posts, he wrote poems, composing his *Lusiads* largely during a bureaucratic stint in the Portuguese port at Macau (China), although publishing it only after his return to Portugal in 1570. The epic made him a national hero, a fitting honor even for a man with a speckled career who was, nonetheless, the architect of modern Portuguese language and culture.

The *Lusiads* bears the imprint of its author's experiences throughout, but perhaps nowhere more succinctly than in the final canto, of which excerpts are given here. In this culminating section of the epic, the sea goddess Tethys, who with her nymph companions has lured Vasco da Gama and his men to an island paradise, reveals to the hero the full future expanse of the Portuguese empire to which his explorations had vitally contributed. She begins by presenting the framework of the cosmos—as Beatrice had done in Dante's *Paradiso* (c. 1308/1321)—reviewing the main features of the Ptolemaic model that, by the time Camões wrote, had already been challenged by Copernicus. Then focusing on the earth at its center, she guides his gaze to the lands where Portugal would exercise dominion: from the Cape of Good Hope, which da Gama was the first European to traverse; up the east coast of Africa to Egypt; across the Red Sea to Arabia and the Persian Gulf to Iran; on to India, the Indochinese peninsula, China, and Japan; southward again to the islands of Oceania; back, via Sri Lanka, to Madagascar, off the African coast; and finally, looking westward, to Brazil. Having completed her epiphanic tour of the future Portuguese empire, Tethys bids farewell to her guests and sends them on their way to their homeland, to inform their king of the new lands to which he, through their efforts, now holds title.

From his own travels, Camões knew many of the sites Tethys describes from her mountaintop perch. To his personal experience, he added what he had learned from the reports of other Portuguese mariners, and supplied further details drawn from the ancient geographers Strabo and Pomponius Mela, with whose works he was thoroughly familiar. With these materials, the poet wove together his own past with Portugal's, in a grand epic celebration of empire.

Luís Vas de Camões, *The Lusiads (1572)*

Tethys speaks to da Gama: [76] "On you, sir, God, who is Supreme Wisdom, bestows the privilege of seeing with your corporeal eyes things of which ordinary mortals, wretched and wandering, have never before had knowledge. Follow me, you and the others, with bold and forceful step, but cautiously, up this forested path." So she spoke, and led him through a dense wilderness, steep and perilous for mere humans to traverse.

[77] Soon they reached a lofty peak, surrounded by a meadow which sparkled so with emeralds and rubies that it seemed to declare the ground they walked on was divine. Here they beheld a globe, floating in the air, penetrated by a light so brilliantly clear that its center was as visible as its circumference. [78] . . . Every part of it, as contrived by a divine hand, its beginning and its end, [79] it was uniform, perfect, and sufficient to itself, like the Archetype, God himself, who had created it. Struck with marvel and delight, da Gama stood and gazed upon it, deeply moved.

Then the goddess said: "Here before your eyes is an image, in miniature, of the cosmos, in which you may see where you now stand, and where you will go, and what it is that you desire. [80] You see here the great machine of the universe, ethereal and elemental, as it was fashioned by the wisdom of God, high and profound, who is at once the beginning and the final end of all things. God is he who encircles and encloses this round and sparkling globe; but what he is, no one knows, for to such knowledge the human mind cannot extend.

[81] "This outermost sphere which rotates around the others, nestling the other smaller spheres within it, shining with a light so brilliant that it blinds men's eyes and vanquishes their minds, is called the Empyrean. Here dwell the pure souls that attain the Supreme Good, which God alone can understand and encompass, for there is on earth no semblance of it. . . .

Tethys lays out the whole plan of the Ptolemaic cosmos, governed by the Christian God with the aid of his angels. Inside the outermost sphere is another, the Primum Mobile, which rotates rapidly, carrying along at the same time the other spheres contained within it. The first of these is the Crystalline,

followed by the sphere of the fixed stars, on which are embedded the constella-
tions of the Zodiac. Then come the spheres of Saturn, Jupiter, Mars, the Sun,
Venus, Mercury, and the Moon.

[90] "All these spheres, you may observe, have different patterns of movement: some heavy and slow, some light and swift, some flying far from the central axis of the earth, others scarcely departing from it, according to the will of God the omnipotent father, who made fire and air, wind, and snow, all of which lie, as you can see, close to the innermost sphere, adjacent to earth and sea.

[91] "This central sphere is the home of men, who not content to suffer only the perils met on solid ground, boldly venture out on the shifting waters. Those wild seas divide the world into various regions, as you see, inhabited by different peoples and ruled by different kings, with different customs and different laws. [92] This one is Christian Europe, grander and finer than the others for its governance and might. That one is Africa, greedy for the goods of this world, uncivilized and savage, with its promontory, the Cape of Good Hope,[51] looming at its southernmost point, that until now had been denied you. Observe this vast land, nearly infinite, inhabited by a people who know not the Law of God.

[93] "Here is the great empire of Mwenemutapa,[52] with its wild people, naked and black. . . . From this unknown portion of the earth comes gold, the metal most sought-after by men. There is the lake from which the Nile flows, and at the same time, the Zambezi;[53] [94] and there the huts of the Negroes, which have no doors, for they trust as they lie abed in the protection of the king's justice, and their neighbors' good will. . . .

[95] "See there how the Nile originates from lakes unknown to the ancients; teeming with crocodiles, it waters the land of Abyssinia, faithful to Christ,[54] whose inhabitants, uniquely, without fortifications, defend themselves all the better against their enemies. There is the once-famous island of Meroë,[55] now called Noba by the natives. . . . [97] There is the cape once called Aromatic by the natives and now Guardafui,[56] from where begins the passage to the mouth of the famous Red Sea, which takes its color from the bed beneath. This body of water marks the boundary between Africa and Asia. . . .

---

51. The cape so named by da Gama, the first European to navigate around it, in 1497.

52. A southern African Shona state, corresponding roughly to modern Zimbabwe and Mozambique.

53. Camões errs; these two rivers do not originate from the same lake.

54. Ethiopia, Christian since antiquity.

55. A conflation of the city Meroë, capital of the ancient kingdom of Kush, and the nearby island of Meroë, surrounded by branches of the Nile, both in modern Butana, Sudan.

56. At the apex of the Horn of Africa, on the Gulf of Aden.

[100] "Here are the three Arabias,[57] a wide expanse peopled by olive-skinned nomads, where thoroughbred war-horses are raised, fleet-footed and high-spirited. . . . [102] See there Cape Asaborus, which our mariners now call Musandum,[58] the entrance to the Persian Gulf which nourishes Arabia on one coast and Persia[59] on the other. There is the island of Bahrein,[60] where the ocean floor is adorned with rich pearls, the color of the dawn; and there the Tigris and Euphrates rivers together enter the salt water of the Gulf. [103] Beyond is Persia, a great and noble empire, always at war and on horseback. . . .

Pointing out the Strait of Hormuz, which leads from the Persian Gulf to the Gulf of Oman, Tethys' gaze continues eastward toward India, which da Gama had first opened for Portugal.

[105] ". . . See there the lovely Indus, which rises in those mountains, and joined to it, but flowing from another mountaintop, the Ganges.[61] [106] Here is the Sind, a most fertile land, and . . . Cambray, most fruitful, . . . and a thousand other cities, which I shall pass by, now held by you Portuguese. [107] . . . All along this coast, the Portuguese will come in force and, victorious, seize lands and cities, and live there for ages to come. . . .

Tethys describes the Indian kingdoms of Narsinga (with a long digression on the life of Saint Thomas, the supposed apostle of India) and Orissa, as they were known to the Portuguese, and the Burmese kindoms of Arakan and Pegu. She then proceeds southward through the Indochinese peninsula.

[123] "Now behold the city of Tavoy,[62] the portal to the great and sprawling empire of Siam.[63]. . . Further on lies Malacca, that you Portuguese will make the noble emporium for all the wealth and merchandise that flows among the regions bordering these seas. [124] Powerful ocean waves, they say, invaded the mainland and cut off from it this noble island of Sumatra.[64] . . . [125] And there, where the land comes to a point, lies Singapore, where ships must pass

---

57. The "stony," the "desert," and the "blest," as they were then construed.

58. A peninsula jutting into the Persian Gulf, in modern Oman.

59. Modern Iran.

60. There is one main island, but Bahrein is actually an archipelago made up of many.

61. A description of the Indo-Gangetic river system, which spans from Pakistan across northern India.

62. Modern Dawei, once a center for fishing and pearl-gathering, a city on the southern coast of Myanmar (previously Burma).

63. Modern Thailand.

64. The largest island of modern Indonesia.

through waters narrowed to a strait.[65] . . . [126] And here you see an immense land, studded with the diverse names of a thousand nations of which you've never heard. This one is Laos, mighty in extent and in peoples. . . . [127] Here is Cambodia, through which the Mekong River runs, the "prince of rivers." Even in summer, its tributaries feed it so that it overflows and overcomes the expansive fields, flooding them as does the colder Nile. . . .

[129] ". . . Here the proud empire of China, famed for its lands and wealth beyond all measure, holds sway from the burning tropics to the Arctic.[66] [130] Behold the Great Wall, an edifice not to be believed, which marks the boundary between this empire and its neighbor, a demonstration and proof of its sovereign power, wealth, and worth. Its emperors are not born monarchs, nor do fathers make kings of their sons, but the people choose a ruler renowned for his nobility, wisdom, and virtue.

[131] "Many other regions must remain hidden from you until the time comes to reveal it all. But do not ignore these islands in the sea where Nature most displays its bounty. That one, half hidden in the distance, facing China from whence it may be sought, is Japan, with its abundance of fine silver, soon to be renowned for its obedience to the Law of God. . . .[67]

From China and Japan, Tethys looks south past the South China Sea—conspicuously omitting the Philippines, a Spanish possession—to Indonesia, naming the Banda islands (in the Moluccas, or Spice Islands), Borneo, Timor, Java, and Sumatra; then northwest, to Ceylon (modern Sri Lanka), and the Maldives, islands located just south of the Indian subcontinent; and further west, finally, to Madagascar, completing her tour off the African coast not far from where she had begun.

[138] "These are the new parts of the Orient that you Portuguese are now bestowing upon the world, opening a road to the boundless open sea across which, with such bold hearts, you sail. But it is time also to turn to the West, to view the deed done by a different Portuguese who, aggrieved with his own king sailed for another, opening a route never before taken.[68] [139] Behold

---

65. The island city-state of Singapore at the southern tip of the Malay Peninsula, separated from Malaysia by the strait of Johor and from Indonesia by the Singapore strait.

66. Camões exaggerates the northern extent of China here, and below, he misrepresents the process of imperial succession.

67. In the lifetime of Camões, Saint Francis Xavier (see the previous section of this chapter) had reached Japan and succeeded in converting many to Christianity. Although Japan is no longer a major producer of silver, it was such in the sixteenth century.

68. The Portuguese navigator Ferdinand Magellan, who in 1519–1521 sailed for King Charles I of Spain through the Strait of Magellan, so named after him, and across the Pacific Ocean to the Philippines, where he was killed, while his shipmates completed the first circumnavigation of the globe.

this huge territory stretching from the northern to the southern pole, which will be famed for its mines glittering with Apollonian gold. Your neighbor Castile[69] will have the honor of bending its rude neck to the yoke, with its many nations of different peoples, diverse in customs and beliefs.

[140] "But here where the land bellies outward, you too will have your share, to be discovered by the next Portuguese fleet to sail; it will be called Santa Cruz at first, but later Brazil after its native red brazilwood. Along its coast Magellan will sail in search of its furthest point, a Portuguese venture in truth, even if Spanish in name. [141] After journeying more than half the distance from the equator to the southern pole, he will find living in the land of Patagonia men nearly the size of giants. Then further on, he will come to the Strait that now bears his name, and pass through it to another sea and another land, embraced by Antarctica's chill wings.

[142] "Thus far, O men of Portugal, it has been conceded to you to know of the future deeds that will be done by bold explorers on the seas that are because of you no longer unknown. And now . . . [143] you may board your ships, and set off, while the sea is calm and the wind gentle, for your beloved homeland."

So she spoke; and quickly they departed that happy and blessed island. . . . [144] The sea serene, the wind always mild and never astir, they journeyed on until they caught sight of the land of their birth, for which they always longed. They entered the mouth of the lovely Tagus river, and bestowed upon their country and their king, loved and revered, the glorious prize he had sent them to win. . . .

---

69. By the 1494 Treaty of Tordesillas, the lands of the newly discovered American continents to the west of a meridian 370 leagues (a league measured approximately three miles) west of the Cape Verde islands, were allotted to Castile (modern Spain), and those east, including most significantly Brazil, to Portugal.

TEXTS AND STUDIES

Chapter 1: Antiquity Reborn

Petrarch, *Letters to Cicero* and *Homer*: The translation is based on the edition of Umberto Bosco, in vol. 4 (Books XX–XXIV) of *Le familiari*, ed. Vittorio Rossi (Florence: G. C. Sansoni, 1933–1942), XXIV.3 at 225–27 for the first letter to Cicero, and XXIV.12 at 253–63 for the letter to Homer. I have also consulted the translations by Mario Emilio Cosenza, *Petrarch's Letters to Classical Authors* (Chicago: University of Chicago Press, 1910), at 1–4 and 148–71 for the letters given here, with extensive annotations following in each case; and Aldo S. Bernardo: *Letters on Familiar Matters: Rerum familiarium libri XVII–XXIV* (Baltimore, London: Johns Hopkins University Press, 1985), XXIV:317–18 and 343–50 for the letters given here. For Petrarch and humanism, see especially Gur Zak, *Petrarch's Humanism and the Care of the Self* (Cambridge: Cambridge University Press, 2010); and the essays edited by Victoria Kirkham and Armando Maggi, *Petrarch: A Critical Guide to the Complete Works* (Chicago: University of Chicago Press, 2009); also the classic by Charles E. Trinkaus, *The Poet as Philosopher: Petrarch and the Formation of Renaissance Consciousness* (New Haven: Yale University Press, 1979). See also the comprehensive annotated bibliography by Craig Kallendorf, "Petrarch," in *Oxford Bibliographies Online: Renaissance and Reformation*, http://www.oxfordbibliographies.com /view/document/obo-9780195399301/obo-9780195399301-0026.xml (accessed January 17, 2013).

Boccaccio, *Genealogy of the Pagan Gods, Book XIV*: The translation is based on the bilingual Latin and Italian edition of the *Genealogie deorum gentilium* by Pier Giorgio Ricci included in his magnum *Opere in versi, Corbaccio, Trattatello in laude di Dante, Prose latine, Epistole* (Milan: R. Ricciardi, 1965); Book XIV, from which these excerpts are taken, is found at 900–1061. I have also consulted the edition and partial translation of Charles G. Osgood, first published in 1930 (Princeton: Princeton University Press), and reissued in 1956 (New York: Bobbs Merrill/Liberal Arts Press), an edition that was subsequently reprinted: *Boccaccio on Poetry: Being the Preface and the Fourteenth and Fifteenth Books of Boccaccio's Genealogia Deorum Gentilium in an English Version with Introductory Essay and Commentary.* The magisterial edition and translation of the whole of the *Genealogy* by Jon Solomon is in progress: vol. 1, containing Books I to IV, was published in 2011 (Cambridge, MA: Harvard University Press). Its notes and bibliography, when completed, will present an authoritative guide to Boccaccio and his works, especially the *Genealogy*. See also the comprehensive annotated bibliography by Chris Kleinhenz, "Giovanni Boccaccio," in *Oxford Bibliographies Online: Medieval Studies*, http://www.oxfordbibliographies.com/view/document/obo-9780195396584/obo-978019 5396584-0007.xml (accessed January 17, 2013). Also useful is the website *Decameron Web*, a project of the Brown University Italian Studies Department's Virtual Humanities Lab: http:// www.brown.edu/Departments/Italian_Studies/dweb/index.php (accessed December 4, 2012).

Vergerio, *On Liberal Studies*: This translation is based on Pier Paolo Vergerio, from *De ingenuis moribus et liberalibus studiis*, in Craig W. Kallendorf, ed. and trans., *Humanist*

Educational Treatises (Cambridge, MA: Harvard University Press, 2001), pars. 30, 32–33, and 35–40, at 36–48, even pages of bilingual edition. I have consulted the English translations by Kallendorf (facing the Latin text) and William Harrison Woodward in *Vittorino da Feltre and Other Humanist Educators* (Cambridge: Cambridge University Press, 1897), 96–119; as well as the Italian translation of Eugenio Garin in his *L'educazione umanistica in Italia: Testi scelti e illustrati* (Bari: Laterza, 1949), 63–119. No major biography of Vergerio exists, but for his historical writing, see the fine studies (with critical editions of pertinent texts) of Douglas Robey and John Law, "The Venetian Myth and the *De Republica Veneta* of Pier Paolo Vergerio," *Rinascimento* 15 (1975): 3–59, and Benjamin G. Kohl, "Chronicles into Legends and Lives: Two Humanist Accounts of the Carrara Dynasty in Padua," in Sharon Dale, Alison Williams Lewin, and Duane J. Osheim, eds., *Chronicling History: Chroniclers and Historians in Medieval and Renaissance Italy* (University Park, PA: Pennsylvania State University Press, 2007), 223–48.

Poggio Bracciolini and Cencio Romano, Book Hunters: The translation of Cencio's letter is based on the text published by Ludwig Bertalot in "Cincius Romanus und seine Briefe," in Ludwig Bertalot, *Studien zum italienischen und deutschen Humanismus* (Rome: Edizioni di storia e letteratura, 1975), 2:131–80, at 144–47; originally published in *Quellen und Forschungen aus Italienischen Archiven und Bibliotheken*, 21 (1929–1930), 209–55, at 222–25. The translation of Poggio's letter is based on the edition of Thomas de Tonellis, in *Poggii epistolae* (Florence: Typis L. Marchini, 1832), I:25–29, now reprinted and constituting the third volume of Poggio Bracciolini, *Opera omnia* (Turin: Bottega d'Erasmo, 1964–1969). Both Cencio's and Poggio's letters appear in the English translation of Phyllis W. G. Gordan, which I have consulted: *Two Renaissance Book Hunters: The Letters of Poggius Bracciolini to Nicolaus de Niccolis* (New York: Columbia University Press, 1974), 187–96. Bertalot's introduction furnishes details on Cencio's life and career, for which see also Paul Oskar Kristeller, "Un opuscolo sconosciuto di Cencio de' Rustici dedicato a Bornio da Sala: La traduzione del dialogo 'De virtute' attribuito a Platone," in *Studies in Renaissance Thought and Letters*, 4 vols. (Rome: Edizioni di storia e letteratura, 1956–1996), 2:239–58. Cencio appears as one of the interlocutors in Poggio Bracciolini's dialogue *On Avarice* (late 1420s), trans. Benjamin G. Kohl and Elizabeth B. Welles, in Kohl and Ronald G. Witt, eds., *The Earthly Republic: Italian Humanists on Government and Society* (Philadelphia: University of Pennsylvania Press, 1978), 231–89. See also the comprehensive annotated bibliography by Craig Kallendorf of Poggio's life and works, "Poggio Bracciolini," in *Oxford Bibliographies Online: Renaissance and Reformation*, http://www.oxford bibliographies.com/view/document/obo-9780195399301/obo-9780195399301-0095.xml (accessed January 17, 2013).

Chapter 2: Explorations of the Self

Petrarch, *To Posterity*: Excerpts are taken from *To Posterity (Ad posteritatem)*, in *The Essential Petrarch,* ed. and trans. Peter Hainsworth (Indianapolis, IN; Cambridge, MA: Hackett Publishing Co., 2010), 237–44. Hainsworth's notes are partially followed as noted, but not reproduced in full or verbatim. A version of *To Posterity* is also included in the translation of the *Rerum senilium libri* by Aldo S. Bernardo, Saul Levin, and Reta A. Bernardo, *Letters of Old Age*, 2 vols. (Baltimore: Johns Hopkins University Press), XVIII.1 at 672–79; as well as in several anthologies of Renaissance sources. See now the critical edition and translation by Karl Enenkel in Karl Enenkel, Betsy de Jong-Crane, and P. T. M. G. Liebregts, *Modelling the Individual: Biography and Portrait in the Renaissance: with a Critical Edition of Petrarch's*

Letter to Posterity (Amsterdam: Rodopi, 1998), 243–81; and earlier in the same volume, at 11–49, Enenkel's invaluable study of Petrarch's *Posterity* in relation to the models of Suetonius and Boccaccio: "Modelling the Humanist: Petrarch's *Letter to Posterity* and Boccaccio's Biography of the Poet Laureate." For Petrarch and humanism, see especially Gur Zak, *Petrarch's Humanism and the Care of the Self* (Cambridge: Cambridge University Press, 2010); and the essays edited by Victoria Kirkham and Armando Maggi, *Petrarch: A Critical Guide to the Complete Works* (Chicago: University of Chicago Press, 2009); also the classic by Charles E. Trinkaus, *The Poet as Philosopher: Petrarch and the Formation of Renaissance Consciousness* (New Haven: Yale University Press, 1979). See also the comprehensive annotated bibliography by Craig Kallendorf, "Petrarch," in *Oxford Bibliographies Online: Renaissance and Reformation*, http://www.oxfordbibliographies.com/view/document/obo-9780195399301/obo -9780195399301-0026.xml (accessed January 17, 2013).

Manetti, *On the Dignity and Excellence of Man*: The translation is based on the critical edition by Elizabeth R. Leonard: *Ianotii Manetti, De dignitate et excellentia hominis* (Padua: Antenore, 1975), complete text at 1–144; English introduction at ix–xxxv. See also the translation of the whole of Book IV in Bernard Murchland, ed. and trans., *Two Views of Man: Pope Innocent III on the Misery of Man; Gianozzo Manetti on the Dignity of Man* (New York: F. Ungar, 1966), 63–103; the translation of the letter of dedication and Book IV by Arturo B. Fallico and Herman Shapiro, ed. and trans., *Renaissance Philosophy, 1: The Italian Philosophers: Selected Readings from Petrarch to Bruno* (New York: Modern Library, 1967), 66–101; and the German translation by Harmut Leppin, at 1–140, with critical introduction by August Buck at vii–xxxviii (Hamburg: Felix Meiner, 1990). Charles Trinkaus provides an extended analysis of Manetti's work in his *In Our Image and Likeness: Humanity and Divinity in Italian Humanist Thought*, 2 vols. (London: Constable, 1970), 1:230–58, and Eugenio Garin provides a useful brief analysis in his *Italian Humanism: Philosophy and Civic Life in the Renaissance,* trans. Peter Munz (New York: Harper and Row, 1965), 56–60. Martin Schmeisser's comprehensive monograph *"Wie ein sterblicher Gott—": Giannozzo Manettis Konzeption der Würde des Menschen und ihre Rezeption im Zeitalter der Renaissance* (Munich: Wilhelm Fink, 2006) relates Manetti's anthropology with those of medieval predecessors.

Pico della Mirandola, *Oration on the Dignity of Man*: The translation is based on the critical text of the *Oratio de dignitate hominis* by Eugenio Garin (Florence: Vallecchi, 1942), available online at the Latin Library: http://www.thelatinlibrary.com/mirandola/oratio.shtml (accessed June 9, 2013), §§1–10, 45–47. See also the translation of the oration by Charles Glenn Wallis (orig. 1965) in Paul J. W. Miller's edition of Pico's works *On the Dignity of Man: On Being and the One: Heptaplus* (Indianapolis, IN: Hackett Publishing Co., 1998), 3–34; and the bilingual (Latin/English) edition and translation, with extensive commentary and analysis, in Francesco Borghesi, Michael Papio, and Massimo Riva, eds., *Oration on the Dignity of Man: A New Translation and Commentary* (New York: Cambridge University Press, 2012), 107–277. Other useful translations include those by A. Robert Caponigri (South Bend, IN: Regnery/Gateway, 1956); Arturo B. Fallico and Herman Shapiro in their anthology *Renaissance Philosophy*, vol. 1, *The Italian Philosophers: Selected Readings from Petrarch to Bruno* (New York: Modern Library, 1967), 141–71; and Elizabeth L. Forbes in *The Renaissance Philosophy of Man*, ed. Ernst Cassirer, Paul Oskar Kristeller, and John Herman Randall (Chicago: University of Chicago Press, 1947), 223–54. See also the studies included in M. V. Dougherty, ed., *Pico Della Mirandola: New Essays* (Cambridge: Cambridge University Press, 2008), and the biographies by Jader Jacobelli, *Pico della Mirandola,* 2nd ed. (Milan: Longanesi,

1986), and Fernand Roulier, *Jean Pic de la Mirandole (1463–1494): Humaniste, philosophe et théologien* (Geneva: Slatkine, 1989). See also the comprehensive annotated bibliography by M. V. Dougherty, "Giovanni Pico della Mirandola," in Oxford Bibliographies Online: Renaissance and Reformation, http://www.oxfordbibliographies.com/view/document/obo-97 80195399301/obo-9780195399301-0221.xml (accessed November 5, 2013).

Montaigne, *To the Reader* and *Of Experience*. *To the Reader* (1580), prefatory to Book One, and excerpts from *Of Experience* (1587–1588), Book III #13, are translated from the French text of the Bordeaux edition (1588) of the *Essays*, the three volumes of which are published in facsimile with additional volumes of scholarly apparatus in *Les essais de Michel de Montaigne, publiés d'après l'exemplaire de Bordeaux, avec les variantes manuscrites et les leçons des plus anciennes impressions, des notes, des notices et un lexique*, 5 vols. (Bordeaux: Imprimerie nouvelle F. Peach, 1906–1933). The French text of the Bordeaux edition is online at The Montaigne Project: http://www.lib.uchicago.edu/efts/ARTFL/projects/montaigne/ (accessed September 3, 2012). I have consulted the standard translation of the essays by Donald M. Frame, in *The Complete Essays of Montaigne*, originally published 1973 (Stanford: Stanford University Press), with the essay *Of Experience* at 815–57. It was reissued in 2003, incorporated in Donald M. Frame, ed. and trans., *The Complete Works: Essays, Travel Journal, Letters* (New York: Alfred A. Knopf). Denis Bertrand offers a full exposition of the text of *Of Experience*, which is also reproduced, in Michel de Montaigne, *De l'expérience: Chapitre 13 du Livre III des Essais*, ed. Denis Bertrand (Paris: Gallimard, 2002); and Lawrence D. Kritzman includes a final chapter entitled "Romancing the Stone: 'De l'experience' (III, 13)," 154–92, in *The Fabulous Imagination: On Montaigne's Essays* (New York: Columbia University Press, 2009). For Montaigne as a personal essayist who is among the inventors of the "poetics of self," see Carl H. Klaus, "Montaigne on 'Montaigne': Toward a Poetics of Self," in Klaus, *The Made-Up Self: Impersonation in the Personal Essay* (Iowa City: University of Iowa Press, 2010), 7–18. See also for Montaigne's autobiographical explorations Elizabeth de Mijolla, *Autobiographical Quests: Augustine, Montaigne, Rousseau, and Wordsworth* (Charlottesville: University Press of Virginia, 1994); Nicholas D. Paige, *Being Interior: Autobiography and the Contradictions of Modernity in Seventeenth-Century France* (Philadelphia: University of Pennsylvania Press, 2001); and Patrick Riley, *Character and Conversion in Autobiography: Augustine, Montaigne, Descartes, Rousseau, and Sartre* (Charlottesville: University of Virginia Press, 2004); while the ambiguities of Montaigne's persona are highlighted entertainingly in Sarah Bakewell, *How to Live, Or, a Life of Montaigne: In One Question and Twenty Attempts at an Answer* (New York: Other Press, 2010). Biographies include the classic Donald M. Frame, *Montaigne: A Biography* (New York: Harcourt, Brace and World, 1965); and George Hoffmann, *Montaigne's Career* (Oxford: Clarendon Press, 1998). George Hoffmann also provides a comprehensive annotated bibliography of Montaigne in *Oxford Bibliographies Online: Renaissance and Reformation*, http://www.oxfordbibliographies.com/view/document/obo-9780195399301/obo-978019 5399301-0107.xml (accessed January 17, 2013).

Chapter 3: The Civic Experience

Bruni, *In Praise of the City of Florence*. The translation is based on the *Laudatio florentine urbis*, in the meticulous edition of Stefano U. Baldassarri based on forty-two manuscript witnesses (Florence: SISMEL-Edizioni del Galluzzo, 2000), 1–35, with critical introduction at xiii–ci; excerpts taken from 4–7 (##6–12) and 30–35 (##76–79, 88–93). Baldassarri's edition replaces Hans Baron's in *From Petrarch to Leonardo Bruni: Studies in Humanistic and Political Literature* (Chicago: University of Chicago Press, 1968), 232–63. Also consulted: the translations of Benjamin G. Kohl in Kohl and Ronald G. Witt, eds., *The Earthly Republic: Italian Humanists on Government and Society* (Philadelphia: University of Pennsylvania Press, 1978), 135–75; and of Alfred Scheepers, *In Praise of Florence: the Panegyric of the City of Florence and an Introduction to Leonardo Bruni's Civil Humanism* (Amsterdam: Olive Press, 2005), 77–120; and the excerpt in *The Humanism of Leonardo Bruni: Selected Texts*, ed. and trans. Gordon Griffiths, James Hankins, and David Thompson (Binghamton, NY: Medieval and Renaissance Texts and Studies in conjunction with the Renaissance Society of America, 1987), 116–21. For Bruni and civic humanism, see especially *The Humanism of Leonardo Bruni*, and the essays in James Hankins, ed., *Renaissance Civic Humanism* (Cambridge: Cambridge University Press, 2003). See also the comprehensive annotated bibliography by Craig Kallendorf, "Leonardo Bruni," in *Oxford Bibliographies Online: Renaissance and Reformation*, http://www.oxford bibliographies.com/view/document/obo-9780195399301/obo-9780195399301-0069.xml (accessed January 17, 2013).

Barbaro, *On Marriage*. The translation is based on *De re uxoria*, ed. Attilio Gnesotto, *Atti e Memorie, R. Accademia di Scienze, Lettere ed Arti in Padova*, NS 32 (1916), 6–105, at 6, 9–16, 19–23, 25–31. See also the translation of the dedicatory letter and the second book in Benjamin G. Kohl and Ronald G. Witt, *The Earthly Republic: Italian Humanists on Government and Society* (Philadelphia: University of Pennsylvania Press, 1978), 177–228; and the 1677 English translation: *Directions for Love and Marriage, in Two Books, Written Originally by Franciscus Barbarus, a Venetian Senator, and Now Translated into English by a Person of Quality* (London: Printed for John Leigh at the Bell, and Tho. Burrell at the Golden Ball, under St. Dunstan's Church, in Fleet Street, 1677). For Barbaro, see Margaret L. King, *Venetian Humanism in an Age of Patrician Dominance* (Princeton: Princeton University Press, 1986), 322–23 and *passim*, and sources there cited; and King, "Caldiera and the Barbaros on Marriage and the Family: Humanist Reflections of Venetian Studies," *Journal of Medieval and Renaissance Studies* 6 (1976), 19–50, rpt. in King, *Humanism, Venice, and Women: Essays on the Italian Renaissance* (Aldershot, UK: Ashgate, 2005), 19–50 (V); also Carole Collier Frick, "Francesco Barbaro's *De Re Uxoria*: A Silent Dialogue for a Young Medici Bride," in *Printed Voices: The Renaissance Culture of Dialogue*, ed. Dorothea B. Heitsch and Jean-François Vallée (Toronto: University of Toronto Press, 2004), 193–205. See also the edition by Claudio Griggio of the letters of Francesco Barbaro: *Epistolario*, 2 vols. (Florence: L. S. Olschki, 1991, 1999).

Rinuccini, *On Liberty*. The translation is based on Alamanno Rinuccini, *Dialogus de libertate*, ed. Francesco Adorno, *Atti e memorie dell'Accademia Toscana di scienze e lettere La Colombaria*, 22 (1957), 265–303, at 271–73, 280–90. The scribe dates the text at the end 10 April 1479, at 303. The Adorno edition is reprinted in Alamanno Rinuccini, *La libertà perduta*, ed. Francesco Adorno, trans. Giuseppe Civati (Monza: Vittone, 2003), 36–148 (even pages), with Italian translation on facing odd pages. I also consulted: the English translation of Renée Neu Watkins, ed. and trans., *Humanism and Liberty: Writings on Freedom from Fifteenth-Century Florence* (Columbia: University of South Carolina Press, 1978), 186–223. Other works by Rinuccini—letters and orations, most in Latin, a few in Italian—are edited by Vito R. Giustiniani in Alamanno Rinuccini, *Lettere ed orazioni* (Florence: L. S. Olschki, 1953). Giustiniani's biographical study of Rinuccini provides full context: *Alamanno Rinuccini, 1426–1499: Materialien und Forschungen zur Geschichte des florentinischen Humanismus* (Graz: Böhlau Verlag, 1965).

Vives, *On Assistance to the Poor*. The translation is based on Juan Luis Vives, *De subventione pauperis sive de humanis necessitatibus*, bilingual edition (Latin and English), ed. and trans. C. Matheeussen and C. Fantazzi, with the assistance of J. De Landtsheer (Leiden: Brill,

2002), Book Two, selections from Chapters 1–4, 88–110. See also the Spanish edition by
Marcel Bataillon, Joaquín Parellada, and Francisco Pons, *Tratado del socorro de pobres* (Valencia:
Editorial Pre-Textos; Alicante: Biblioteca Valenciana, 2006); and two English translations with
critical discussions by Alice Tobriner, *On Assistance to the Poor* (Toronto: University of Toronto
Press in association with the Renaissance Society of America, 1999); and Paul Spicker, *The
Origins of Modern Welfare: Juan Luis Vives,* De Subventione Pauperum, *and City of Ypres,* Forma
Subventionis Pauperum (Oxford: Peter Lang, 2010). Biographies include Antonio Fontán,
Juan Luis Vives (1492–1540): Humanista, filósofo, politico (Valencia: Ajuntament de València,
1992), and Carlos G. Noreña, *Juan Luis Vives* (Nijhoff: The Hague, 1970); Noreña has pub-
lished also several studies of Vives's work. See also Susanne Zeller's exploration of Vives's biog-
raphy with special emphasis on his Jewish origins: *Juan Luis Vives (1492–1540): (Wieder)
Entdeckung eines Europäers, Humanisten und Sozialreformers jüdischer Herkunft im Schatten
der spanischen Inquisition: ein Beitrag zur Theoriegeschichte der sozialen Arbeit als Wissenschaft*
(Freiburg im Breisgau: Lambertus, 2006); and the essays published by Charles Fantazzi in
A Companion to Juan Luis Vives (Leiden, Boston: Brill, 2008). See also the comprehensive
annotated bibliography by Charles Fantazzi, Enrique González González, and Víctor Gutiérrez
Rodríguez, "Juan Luis Vives," in *Oxford Bibliographies Online: Renaissance and Reformation*,
http://www.oxfordbibliographies.com/view/document/obo-9780195399301/obo
-9780195399301-0113.xml (accessed January 17, 2013).

Chapter 4: A World in Crisis

Quirini, *Letter to Pope Nicholas V, on the Fall of Constantinople*:   The translation is based
on the superb edition of Agostino Pertusi, in *Le epistole storiche di Lauro Quirini sulla caduta di
Constantinopoli e la potenza dei turchi,* in *Lauro Quirini umanista: Studi e testi a cura di Konrad
Krautter, Paul Oskar Kristeller, Agostino Pertusi, Giorgio Ravegnani, Helmut Roob e Carlo Seno,*
edited by Vittore Branca (Florence: Leo S. Olschki, 1977), 223–33, with an important introduction at 165–91. For Quirini and the fall of Constantinople, with heartfelt thanks, I have relied
on the work of my former student, Seth Parry: *Fifty Years of Failed Plans: Venice, Humanism,
and the Turks (1453–1503)* (dissertation, CUNY Graduate Center, 2008), chapters 3 and 4.
For Quirini, see in addition to Krautter et al., *Lauro Quirini umanista,* also Margaret L. King,
Venetian Humanism in an Age of Patrician Dominance (Princeton: Princeton University Press,
1986), 419–21 and *ad indicem,* Rashed Marwan, "Der Averroismus des Lauro Quirini," in
Wissen über Grenzen: Arabisches Wissen und lateinisches Mittelalter, ed. Andreas Speer and Lydia
Wegener (Berlin, New York: Walter de Gruyter, 2006), 700–714. For his works on nobility,
see Krautter et al., *Lauro Quirini umanista,* 19–102; and Albert Rabil, Jr., *Knowledge, Goodness,
and Power: The Debate Over Nobility among Quattrocento Italian Humanists* (Binghamton, NY:
Medieval and Renaissance Texts and Studies, 1991), 143–81. His letter to Isotta Nogarola is
published in Nogarola, *Complete Writings: Letterbook, Dialogue on Adam and Eve, Orations,* ed.
and trans. Margaret L. King and Diana Maury Robin (Chicago: University of Chicago Press,
2004), 107–13. For the Venetian maritime empire and the men, like Quirini, who managed
and profited by it, see Monique O'Connell, *Men of Empire: Power and Negotiation in Venice's
Maritime State* (Baltimore: Johns Hopkins University Press, 2009). For the Venetian presence
specifically on Crete, see Sally McKee, *Uncommon Dominion: Venetian Crete and the Myth of
Ethnic Purity* (Philadelphia: University of Pennsylvania Press, 2000). For the reactions of Italian
humanists to the Turkish advance—which has little to say of the response of Venetian humanists, which was extensive—see Nancy Bisaha, *Creating East and West: Renaissance Humanists
and the Ottoman Turks* (Philadelphia: University of Pennsylvania Press, 2004).

Poliziano, *Account of the Pazzi Conspiracy:* The translation is based on Alessandro Perosa's splendid edition: Angelo Poliziano, *Della congiura dei Pazzi: Coniurationis commentarium* (Padua: Antenore, 1958), 3–65, excerpts from 3–5, 24–37, 41–48, 58, 62–65. I have also consulted the translations by Elizabeth B. Welles in Benjamin G. Kohl and Ronald G. Witt, eds., *The Earthly Republic: Italian Humanists on Government and Society* (Philadelphia: University of Pennsylvania Press, 1978), 305–22; and by Renée Neu Watkins and David Marsh in Watkins, ed. and trans., *Humanism and Liberty: Writings on Freedom from Fifteenth-Century Florence* (Columbia: University of South Carolina Press, 1978), 171–83. A complete account of the Pazzi conspiracy in the framework of Medici power and Italian foreign relations is found in Lauro Martines, *April Blood: Florence and the Plot Against the Medici* (Oxford: Oxford University Press, 2003); and a concise summary of the events in John M. Najemy, *A History of Florence 1200–1575* (Malden, MA: Blackwell, 2006), 352–61. For Poliziano's role in Florentine humanism, see especially Peter Godman, *From Poliziano to Machiavelli: Florentine Humanism in the High Renaissance* (Princeton: Princeton University Press, 1998); and Paolo Orvieto, *Poliziano e l'ambiente Mediceo* (Rome: Salerno, 2009). See also the comprehensive annotated bibliography by Craig Kallendorf, "Angelo Poliziano," in *Oxford Bibliographies Online: Renaissance and Reformation,* http://www.oxfordbibliographies.com/view/document/obo-9780195399301/obo-9780195399301-0140.xml (accessed January 17, 2013).

Guicciardini, *The Sack of Rome:* The translation is based on the edition of Carlo Milanesi: Luigi Guicciardini, *Il Sacco di Roma,* in *Il Sacco di Roma del MDXXVII: Narrazioni di contemporanei* (Florence: G. Barbèra, 1867), 1–244; available online at Google Books: http://books.google.com/books?id=YQBOAAAAcAAJ (accessed September 21, 2012); and digitized at http://bepi1949.altervista.org/biblio2/guicciar/GUICCIAR.htm (accessed September 21, 2012). Also consulted: the Luigi Guicciardini, *The Sack of Rome* (New York: Italica Press, 1993), trans. James H. McGregor. Other witnesses to the sack appear in Kenneth Gouwens, *Remembering the Renaissance: Humanist Narratives of the Sack of Rome* (Leiden, Boston: Brill, 1998). Modern studies of the sack include the older narrative of Judith Hook, *The Sack of Rome, 1527* (London: Macmillan, 1972) and the brilliant study of art historian André Chastel, *The Sack of Rome, 1527* (Princeton: Princeton University Press, 1983); see also Kathleen Christian, *Empire without End: Antiquities Collections in Renaissance Rome, c. 1350–1527* (New Haven: Yale University Press, 2010).

Morata, *Letters:* The translation is by Holt N. Parker in his edition and translation of Olympia Morata, *The Complete Writings of an Italian Heretic* (Chicago: University of Chicago Press, 2003), 114–17, 130, 139–41, 174–77, excerpted; footnotes mine except as noted. Parker's introduction is a splendid study, and the principal one available, of the life and works of Olympia Morata, and subsumes the earlier studies and editions from Curione's in the sixteenth century through Lanfranco Caretti's in the twentieth. Parker publishes additional Latin works, with English translations, in his "Olympia Fulvia Morata (1526/1527–1555): Humanist, Heretic, Heroine," in Laurie J. Churchill, Phyllis R. Brown, and Jane E. Jeffrey, eds., *Women Writing Latin: From Roman Antiquity to Early Modern Europe,* 3 vols. (New York: Routledge, 2002), 3: *Early Modern Women Writing Latin,* 133–65. Parker's work on Morata has sparked recent studies: see especially Susanna Peyronel Rambaldi, "Olimpia Morata e Celio Secondo Curione: Un dialogo dell'umanesimo Cristiano," in *La formazione storica della alterità: Studi di storia della tolleranza nell'età moderna offerti a Antonio Rotondò* (Florence: Olschki, 2001), 93–133; Janet Levarie Smarr, "Olympia Morata: From Classicist to Reformer," in Dennis Looney and Deanna Shemek, *Phaethon's Children: The Este Court and Its Culture in Early Modern Ferrara* (Tempe: Arizona Center for Medieval and Renaissance Studies, 2005),

321–43; and Janet Levarie Smarr, "Dialogue and Spiritual Counsel: Marguerite de Navarre, Olympia Morata, Chiara Matraini," in Smarr, *Joining the Conversation: Dialogues by Renaissance Women* (Ann Arbor: University of Michigan Press, 2005), 31–97.

Chapter 5: Machiavelli, Erasmus, and More: Visions of the State

Machiavelli, *The Prince*: Excerpts are from David Wooton's translation of *The Prince* (Indianapolis, IN: Hackett Publishing Co., 1995), 47–55; abridged. Many other translations and editions exist, equipped with valuable introductory analyses. Two major biographies of Machiavelli, both translated from Italian into English, are offered by Roberto Ridolfi, *The Life of Niccolò Machiavelli*, trans. Cecil Grayson (Chicago: University of Chicago Press, 1963), and Maurizio Viroli, *Niccolò's Smile: A Biography of Machiavelli*, trans. Antony Shugaar (New York: Farrar, Straus and Giroux, 2000). Important studies include the classic Felix Gilbert, *Machiavelli and Guicciardini: Politics and History in Sixteenth-Century Florence* (Princeton: Princeton University Press, 1965), and more recently Sebastian de Grazia, *Machiavelli in Hell* (Princeton: Princeton University Press, 1989), and Mark Hulliung, *Citizen Machiavelli* (Princeton: Princeton University Press, 1983); see also the essays in John M. Najemy, ed., *The Cambridge Companion to Machiavelli* (Cambridge: Cambridge University Press, 2010); and for insight into Machiavelli's character, also John M. Najemy, *Between Friends: Discourses of Power and Desire in the Machiavelli-Vettori Letters of 1513–1515* (Princeton: Princeton University Press, 1993). For Machiavelli and republicanism, see J. G. A. Pocock, *The Machiavellian Moment: Florentine Political Thought and the Atlantic Republican Tradition* (Princeton: Princeton University Press, 1975), and Quentin Skinner, *The Foundations of Modern Political Thought*, 2 vols. (Cambridge: Cambridge University Press, 1978); and see also the essays in Gisela Bock, Quentin Skinner, and Maurizio Viroli, eds., *Machiavelli and Republicanism* (Cambridge: Cambridge University Press, 1990), and the essay of Paul A. Rahe, "Situating Machiavelli," in James Hankins, ed., *Renaissance Civic Humanism* (Cambridge: Cambridge University Press, 2003), 270–308.

Erasmus, *On the Education of a Christian Prince*: The translation is based on O. Herding's edition of Desiderius Erasmus, *Institutio principis christiani*, in *Opera Omnia Desiderii Erasmi Roterodami* (Amsterdam: North-Holland Publishing, 1969–), Ordo IV, Tomus I (1974); excerpts from 188–95, 199, 204–6, 210–17, 217–19. Also consulted: *The Education of the Christian Prince*, trans and ed., Neil M. Cheshire and Michael J. Heath, in *Collected Works of Erasmus*, eds. Beatrice Corrigan and Richard J. Schoeck (Toronto: University of Toronto Press, 1974–), 27 (1986): 199–288. These versions come from two multivolumed scholarly projects, the first making the Erasmian corpus available in the original Latin, the second in English translation. The *Institutio* is also available in several other translations and editions. Of numerous biographies of Erasmus, C. Augustijn, *Erasmus: His Life, Works, and Influence* (Toronto: University of Toronto Press, 1991), and James D. Tracy, *Erasmus of the Low Countries* (Berkeley: University of California Press, 1996), are both recent and judicious. A few of a multitude of topical studies: Peter G. Bietenholz, *Encounters with a Radical Erasmus: Erasmus' Work as a Source of Radical Thought in Early Modern Europe* (Toronto: University of Toronto Press, 2009); Lisa Jardine, *Erasmus, Man of Letters: The Construction of Charisma in Print* (Princeton: Princeton University Press, 1993); and Hanan Yoran, *Between Utopia and Dystopia: Erasmus, Thomas More, and the Humanist Republic of Letters* (Lanham, MD: Lexington Books, 2010). Erasmus' circle of correspondents and friends was so large that it amounts to a lexicon of the learned of Europe in his generation: see Peter G. Bietenholz and Thomas B. Deutscher, eds., *Contemporaries of Erasmus: A Biographical Register of the Renaissance and Reformation* (Toronto: University of Toronto Press, 1985–1987). See also the comprehensive annotated bibliography by Erika Rummel and Mark Wilson, "Erasmus," in *Oxford Bibliographies Online: Renaissance and Reformation,* http://www.oxfordbibliographies.com/view/document/obo-978 0195399301/obo-9780195399301-0027.xml (accessed January 17, 2013).

More, *Utopia*: The translation is based on the edition of George M. Logan, Robert M. Adams, and Clarence H. Miller: *Utopia: Latin Text and an English Translation,* 2nd ed. (Cambridge: Cambridge University Press, 2002). Miller's translation is published separately in another edition entitled *Utopia* (New Haven: Yale University Press, 2001); and George M. Logan's edition and translation also appears in a Norton Critical Edition entitled *Utopia: A Revised Translation, Backgrounds, Criticism,* 3rd ed. (New York: Norton, 2011), based on the earlier edition of a work of the same title (1992) by Robert M. Adams. Also consulted: the translations of Paul Turner: *Utopia* (London, New York: Penguin, 1965), and G. C. Richards (1923, revised), eds. J. H. Hexter and Edward L. Surtz, in Vol. 4 (1965) of *The Complete Works of Thomas More,* 15 vols. in 19 (New Haven: Yale University Press, 1963–1986). Also useful is Alvaro de Silva's edition of *The Last Letters of Thomas More* (Grand Rapids, MI: W. B. Eerdmans, 2000), and *A Thomas More Source Book,* ed. Gerard Wegemer and Stephen W. Smith (Washington, DC: Catholic University of America Press, 2004).

See also Hanan Yoran's study of More's Utopian thought in relation to Erasmian humanism: *Between Utopia and Dystopia: Erasmus, Thomas More, and the Humanist Republic of Letters* (Lanham, MD: Lexington Books, 2010); and the two volumes of essays edited, respectively, by A. D. Cousins and Damian Grace, *A Companion to Thomas More* (Madison, NJ: Fairleigh Dickinson University Press, 2009), and George M. Logan, *The Cambridge Companion to Thomas More* (Cambridge: Cambridge University Press, 2011). Also useful are the biographies of Peter Ackroyd, *The Life of Thomas More* (New York: Nan A. Talese, 1998); J. A. Guy, *Thomas More* (London, New York: Oxford University Press, 2000); and Richard Marius, *Thomas More: A Biography* (New York: Knopf; distr. Random House, 1984).

Chapter 6: Humanism and the Arts

Alberti, *On Painting*: The translation is based on the critical edition of *Della pittura* by Luigi Mallé (Florence: Sansoni, 1950), excerpts from Book One at 55–62, 74–75. Mallé's notes reference variants in the Latin version. The Italian text is also available with the facing edition of the Latin version, entitled *De pictura,* ed. Cecil Grayson (Rome: Laterza, 1975, rpt. from Alberti's *Opere volgari,* ed. Grayson, vol. 3, pt. 1; Bari: Laterza, 1973), as is Grayson's edition of the Latin text alone together with Alberti's Latin *De statua,* both with facing English translation (London: Phaidon, 1972); and also Grayson's translation, without original text, annotated by Martin Kemp (London: Penguin, 1991). I have also consulted the English translations of John R. Spencer (rev. ed.; New Haven: Yale University Press, 1966) and Rocco Sinisgalli (Cambridge: Cambridge University Press, 2011), and the German translation, with extensive critical introduction, by Oskar Bätschmann and Sandra Gianfreda (Darmstadt: Wissenschaftliche Buchgesellschaft, 2002).

For Alberti, see especially Anthony Grafton, *Leon Battista Alberti: Master Builder of the Italian Renaissance* (New York: Hill and Wang, 2000); also Thomas Kuehn, "Reading between the Patrilines: Leon Battista Alberti's *Della Famiglia* in Light of His Illegitimacy," in *I Tatti*

Studies: Essays in the Renaissance, Vol. 1, eds. Salvatore Comporeale, Caronie Elam, and F. W. Kent (Florence: Villa I Tatti, 1985), 161–87. For Alberti's contribution to artistic theory, see especially Alberto Ambrosini, *Immaginazione visiva e conoscenza: Teoria della visione e pratica figurativa nei trattati di Leon Battista Alberti, Lorenzo Ghiberti, Leonardo Da Vinci* (Pisa: PLUS-Pisa University Press, 2008), 17–153; and D. R. Edward Wright, *Il De pictura di Leon Battista Alberti e i suoi Lettori, 1435–1600* (Florence: Leo S. Olschki, 2010). Also pertinent are works on Renaissance theories of vision more generally by Samuel Y. Edgerton, *The Mirror, the Window, and the Telescope: How Renaissance Linear Perspective Changed Our Vision of the Universe* (Ithaca: Cornell University Press, 2009), and the essays in *Renaissance Theories of Vision*, eds. John Shannon Hendrix and Charles H. Carman (Farnham, UK: Ashgate, 2010). See also the comprehensive annotated bibliography by David Marsh, "Leon Battista Alberti," in *Oxford Bibliographies Online: Renaissance and Reformation*, http://www.oxfordbibliog raphies.com/view/document/obo-9780195399301/obo-9780195399301-0115.xml (accessed January 17, 2013).

D'Este, *Letters on Painters and Painting*:   The translation is based on Clifford M. Brown, ed., with Anna Maria Lorenzoni, *Isabella d'Este and Lorenzo da Pavia: Documents for the History of Art and Culture in Renaissance Mantua* (Geneva: Librairie Droz, 1982), ##11, 12, 60, 116 (44, 66, 99), for Mantegna; and ##87–92 (81–84), for Bellini. I have also consulted the letters quoted in Julia Cartwright Ady's biography: *Isabella d'Este, Marchioness of Mantua, 1474–1539: a Study of the Renaissance*, 2 vols. (London: E. P. Dutton, 1903). For the d'Este letters, see also Deanna Shemek, "*Ci Ci* and *Pa Pa:* Script, Mimicry, and Mediation in Isabella d'Este's Letters," *Rinascimento* 43 (2003): 75–93; Shemek, "In Continuous Expectations: Isabella d'Este's Epistolary Desire," in Dennis Looney and Deanna Shemek, eds., *Phaethon's Children: The Este Court and Its Culture in Early Modern Ferrara* (Tempe, AZ: Arizona Center for Medieval and Renaissance Studies, 2005), 269–300; and Shemek, "Isabella d'Este and the Properties of Persuasion," in Jane Couchman and Ann Crabb, eds., *Women's Letters across Europe, 1400–1700: Form and Persuasion* (Aldershot, UK: Ashgate, 2005), 123–40. For d'Este as court lady and patron, see especially Daniela Bini, ed., *Isabella d'Este: La primadonna del Rinascimento* (Modena: Il Bulino, 2001); Clifford M. Brown, "A Ferrarese Lady and Mantuan Marchesa: The Art and Antiquities Collection of Isabella d'Este Gonzaga (1474–1539)," in Cynthia M. Lawrence, ed., *Women and Art in Early Modern Europe: Patrons, Collectors, and Connoisseurs* (University Park, PA: Pennsylvania State University Press, 1997), 53–71; Stephen J. Campbell, *The Cabinet of Eros: Renaissance Mythological Painting and the Studiolo of Isabella d'Este* (New Haven: Yale University Press, 2004); Sylvia Ferino Pagden, Christian Beaufort-Spontin, and Clifford M. Brown, eds., *Isabella d'Este: Fürstin und Mäzenatin der Renaissance: "la prima donna del mondo"* (Vienna: Kunsthistorisches Museum, 1994).

Dürer, *Letters to Willibald Pirckheimer*:   The translation is based on the critical text by Max Steck of Albrecht Dürer's *Schriften, Tagebücher, Briefe* (Stuttgart: W. Kohlhammer, 1961), at 109–17. I have also consulted the 1913 translation by Rudolph Tombo, Jr. in Albrecht Dürer, *Dürer's Record of Journeys to Venice and the Low Countries*, ed. Roger E. Fry (New York: Dover Publications, 1995), 3–14. For Dürer see especially Jeffrey Chipps Smith, *Dürer* (London: Phaidon, 2012), whose splendid Chapter 5 (159–81) is devoted to the artist's second journey to Venice; also the essays in *The Essential Dürer* (Philadelphia: University of Pennsylvania Press, 2010), eds. Larry Silver and Jeffrey Chipps Smith, especially those by Andrew Morrall on the artist's two Venetian journeys (99–114), and by Corine Schleif on the relationship between Dürer, his wife, and Pirckheimer (185–205). For the impact of Venetian and Italian style on Dürer, see Katherine C. Luber, *Albrecht Dürer and the Venetian Renaissance* (Cambridge: Cambridge University Press, 2005); for Dürer and Italy more broadly, Sybille Ebert-Schifferer and Kristina Herrmann-Fiore, eds., *Dürer, l'Italia e l'Europa* (Milan: Silvana Editoriale, 2011); and for Dürer and European cultural movements, David Price, *Albrecht Dürer's Renaissance: Humanism, Reformation, and the Art of Faith* (Ann Arbor: University of Michigan Press, 2003). See finally the comprehensive annotated bibliography of sources and studies by Jeffrey Chipps Smith, "Albrecht Dürer," in *Oxford Bibliographies Online: Renaissance and Reformation,* http://www.oxfordbibliographies.com/view/document/obo-9780195399301/obo -9780195399301-0159.xml (accessed January 17, 2013).

Cellini, *Autobiography,* **Book II:**   The translation is based on the critical edition of Lorenzo Bellotto: *La vita* (Parma: Fondazione Pietro Bembo: U. Guanda, 1996). I have also consulted the classic translation of Victorian connoisseur John Addington Symonds: *The Autobiography of Benvenuto Cellini,* Harvard Classics vol. 31 (New York: P. F. Collier, 1910), available also in several other editions, including the illustrated edition of John Pope-Hennessy, *The Life of Benvenuto Cellini* (London: Phaidon Press, 1949); and the recent translation by Julia Conaway Bondanella and Peter E. Bondanella: *My Life* (Oxford: Oxford University Press, 2002). Dino S. Cervigni provides a useful study of the *Life: The Vita of Benvenuto Cellini: Literary Tradition and Genre* (Ravenna: Longo, 1979); and Derek Parker, an easily-digested biography, *Cellini: Artist, Genius, Fugitive* (Stroud: Sutton, 2003).

Chapter 7: Humanism and Religion

Valla, *On the Donation of Constantine:*   This translation is based on the text of the *De falso credita et ementita Constantini donatione* included in the bilingual edition and translation by G. W. Bowersock, *Valla: On the Donation of Constantine* (Cambridge, MA: Harvard University Press, 2007), 3–11 and 155–61; Bowersock utilizes the critical edition of Wolfram Setz in *Quellen zur Gestesgeschichte des Mittelalters,* vol. 1 of the *Monumenta germania historica* (Weimar, 1976); cf. Bowersock, 185. Also consulted, in addition to Bowersock's translation, is the translation of Christopher B. Coleman, *The Treatise of Lorenzo Valla on the Donation of Constantine* (New Haven: Yale University Press, 1922; rept. Toronto: University of Toronto Press in association with the Renaissance Society of America, 1993). Of numerous studies, those dealing principally with Valla and religion include Salvatore I. Camporeale, *Lorenzo Valla: Umanesimo e teologia* (Florence: nella sede dell'Istituto nazionale di studi sul Rinascimento, 1972); Camporeale, *Lorenzo Valla: Umanesimo, Riforma e Controriforma: studi e testi* (Rome: Edizioni di storia e letteratura, 2002); Giovanni di Napoli, *Lorenzo Valla: Filosofia e religione nell'Umanesimo italiano* (Rome: Edizioni di storia e letteratura, 1971); Mario Fois, *Il pensiero cristiano di Lorenzo Valla nel quadro storico culturale del suo ambiente* (Rome: Libreria editrice dell'Università gregoriana, 1969). See also the recent study of Lodi Nauta, *In Defense of Common Sense: Lorenzo Valla's Humanist Critique of Scholastic Philosophy* (Cambridge, MA: Harvard University Press, 2009); and the essays edited by Ottavio Besomi and Mariangela Regoliosi, *Lorenzo Valla e l'Umanesimo italiano: Atti del convegno internazionale di studi umanistici (Parma, 18–19 Ottobre 1984)* (Padua: Antenore, 1986). See also the comprehensive annotated bibliography by Craig Kallendorf, "Lorenzo Valla," in *Oxford Bibliographies Online: Renaissance and Reformation,* http://www.oxfordbibliographies.com/view/document/obo-978 0195399301/obo-9780195399301-0129.xml (accessed January 17, 2013).

Lefèvre d'Étaples, *Exhortatory Letter on Translating the Gospels into French.* This translation is based on the edition by Eugene F. Rice of *The Prefatory Epistles of Jacques Lefèvre d'Étaples and Related Texts* (New York: Columbia University Press, 1972), 449–56. I have also consulted the translation of Herman Shapiro and Arturo B. Fallico, ed. and trans., *Renaissance Philosophy, 2: The Transalpine Thinkers: Selected Readings from Cusanus to Suarez* (New York: Modern Library, 1967), 169–75. For Lefèvre, see also Guy Bedouelle, *Lefèvre d'Étaples et l'intelligence des ecritures* (Geneva: Droz, 1976), and Philip E. Hughes, *Lefèvre: Pioneer of Ecclesiastical Renewal in France* (Grand Rapids, MI: W. E. Eerdmans, 1984); also the studies published in *Jacques Lefèvre d'Étaples (1450?–1536): Actes du colloque d'Étaples les 7 et 8 Novembre 1992,* ed. Jean-François Pernot (Paris, Geneva: Champion, 1995); the classic studies by Eugene F. Rice, "Jacques Lefèvre d'Étaples and the Medieval Christian Mystics," in *Florilegium Historiale: Essays Presented to Wallace K. Ferguson,* eds. John Gordon Rowe and W. H. Stockdale (Toronto: University of Toronto Press, 1971), 89–124, and "The Humanist Idea of Christian Antiquity: Lefèvre d'Étaples and His Circle," *Studies in the Renaissance* 9 (1962): 126–60; and Augustin Renaudet's essay "Une problème historique: La pensée réligieuse de J. Lefèvre d'Étaples," in his *Humanisme et Renaissance: Dante, Pétrarque, Standonck, Érasme, Lefèvre d'Étaples, Marguerite de Navarre, Rabelais, Guichardin, Giordano Bruno* (Geneva: Droz, 1958), 201–16.

Ochino, *Dialogue about the Thief on the Cross.* This translation of the *Dialogo del ladrone in croce* is based on Ugo Rozzo's edition of Bernardino Ochino, *I dialogi sette e altri scritti del tempo della fuga* (Turin: Claudiana, 1985). I have also consulted the translations of Elisabeth G. Gleason in *Reform Thought in Sixteenth-Century Italy* (Chico, CA: Scholars Press, 1981), 35–44, and Rita Belladona, in Bernardino Ochino, *Seven Dialogues* (Ottawa, Canada: Dovehouse Editions, 1988). Roland H. Bainton includes a biographical sketch of Ochino in *The Travail of Religious Liberty: Nine Biographical Studies* (Philadelphia: Westminster Press, 1951), 149–76. For Ochino's relationship to Cardinal Gasparo Contarini, see Gigliola Fragnito, "Gli 'spirituali' e la fuga di Bernardino Ochino," in *Fragnito, Gasparo Contarini: Un magistrato veneziano al servizio della cristianità* (Florence: Leo S. Olschki, 1988), 251–306. For Ochino's influence on the famous poet Vittoria Colonna, and through her the even more famous artist Michelangelo, see Emidio Campi, *Michelangelo e Vittoria Colonna: Un dialogo artistico-teologico ispirato da Bernardino Ochino, e altri saggi di storia della riforma* (Turin: Claudiana, 1994).

Contarini *et alii, Report on the Reform of the Church.* This translation of the *Consilium de emendanda ecclesia* is based on the Latin version found in *Concilium tridentinum: Diariorum, actorum, epistularum, tractatuum nova collectio,* eds. S. Merkle et al., 13 vols. (Freiburg in Breisgau: Herder, 1901–1938), 12:131–45. I have also consulted the translation of John C. Olin in Olin, ed., *Catholic Reform: From Cardinal Ximenes to the Council of Trent, 1495–1563* (New York: Fordham University Press, 1990), 65–79. Works of Contarini's cited in the notes to this introduction include his *Office of a Bishop,* ed. and trans. John Patrick Donnelly (Milwaukee: Marquette University Press, 2002), and *La republica e i magistrati di Vinegia,* ed. Vittorio Conti (Florence: Centro editoriale toscano, 2003), a facsimile reprint with Conti's useful introduction. Elizabeth G. Gleason offers a substantial biography in her *Gasparo Contarini: Venice, Rome, and Reform* (Berkeley: University of California Press, 1993); and for Contarini's relationship to the circle of religious reformers, Constance M. Furey, *Erasmus, Contarini, and the Religious Republic of Letters* (Cambridge: Cambridge University Press, 2006). Of the many studies of Contarini's career, see especially those by Gigliola Fragnito gathered in her *Gasparo Contarini: Un magistrato veneziano al servizio della cristianità* (Florence: Leo S. Olschki, 1988); and those in *Gaspare Contarini e il suo tempo: Atti del Convegno, Venezia, 1–3 Marzo 1985,* eds. Gigliola Fragnito and Francesca Cavazzana Romanelli (Venice: Edizioni studium catto-lico veneziano, 1988); and published separately, those of Felix Gilbert, "Religion and Politics in the Thought of Gasparo Contarini," in *History: Choice and Commitment* (Cambridge, MA: Belknap Press of Harvard University Press, 1977), 247–67; Gigliola Fragnito, "The Expurgatory Policy of the Church and the Works of Gasparo Contarini," in Ronald K. Delph, Michelle Fontaine, and John Jeffries Martin, eds. *Heresy, Culture, and Religion in Early Modern Italy: Contexts and Contestations* (Kirksville, MO: Truman State University Press, 2006), 193–210; Paul F. Grendler, "Gasparo Contarini and the University of Padua," in Delph et al., *Heresy, Culture, and Religion,* 135–50; J. B. Ross, "Gasparo Contarini and His Friends," *Studies in the Renaissance* 17 (1970): 192–232; and Ross, "The Emergence of Gasparo Contarini: A Bibliographical Essay," *Church History* 41.1 (1972): 22–45.

Chapter 8: Humanism, Science, and Philosophy

Ficino, *Letters*:   The translation is based on Sebastiano Gentile's edition of Ficino's *Lettere,* 2 vols. (Florence: L. S. Olschki, 1990, 2010), Book One, letters ##24–26 and #38, at 1:51–56, 73–76, with invaluable introduction at 1:xiii–lxv. I have also consulted the English transla-tion of *The Letters of Marsilio Ficino,* ed. and trans. the Language Department of the School of Economic Science, University of London, 8 vols. (London: Shepheard-Walwyn Publishers), at 1 (1978): 64–67, 79–82. Studies of Ficino are numerous, many of them quite recent, and many by the leading scholars of Renaissance thought. See the brief introductions to Ficino by Christopher S. Celenza, in James Hankins, ed., *The Cambridge Companion to Renaissance Philosophy* (Cambridge: Cambridge University Press, 2007), 72–96; Celenza's online article "Marsilio Ficino," *The Stanford Encyclopedia of Philosophy (Spring 2012 Edition),* ed. Edward N. Zalta, at http://plato.stanford.edu/archives/spr2012/entries/ficino/ (accessed December 27, 2012; and Brian P. Copenhaver and Charles B. Schmitt, *Renaissance Philosophy* (Oxford: Oxford University Press, 1992), 143–63; also the essays in *Marsilio Ficino: His Theology, His Philosophy, His Legacy,* eds. Michael J. B. Allen and Valery Rees, with Martin Davies (Leiden: Brill, 2002), and Craig Kallendorf's comprehensive annotated bibliography "Marsilio Ficino," in *Oxford Bibliographies Online: Renaissance and Reformation,* http://www.oxfordbibliogra phies.com/view/document/obo-9780195399301/obo-9780195399301-0080.xml (accessed January 17, 2013).

Copernicus, Preface to *On the Revolutions of the Celestial Spheres*:   The translation is based on the 1543 edition of Copernicus' *De revolutionibus orbium coelestium* (Nuremberg: apud Ioh. Petreium), available as downloadable pdf files from the NASA Astrophysics Data System at Harvard University: http://ads.harvard.edu/books/1543droc.book/ (accessed January 5, 2013). I have also consulted Edward Rosen's translation of the Preface to Pope Paul III, with masterful critical apparatus, published in his *Nicholas Copernicus on the Revolutions: Translation and Commentary* (Baltimore: Johns Hopkins University Press, 1992), 3–6. For Copernicus' achievement, Rosen's *Copernicus and the Scientific Revolution* (Malabar, FL: Krieger, 1984), the introduction at 11–134 followed by selected readings is still a superb intro-duction, while André Goddu's *Copernicus and the Aristotelian Tradition: Education, Reading, and Philosophy in Copernicus' Path to Heliocentrism* (Leiden: Brill, 2010) offers a most useful account of Copernicus' intellectual formation. Important recent studies of the construction and reception of the Copernican theory include Owen Gingerich, *The Book Nobody Read: Chasing the Revolutions of Nicolaus Copernicus* (New York: Walker and Company, 2004);

and Robert S. Westman, *The Copernican Question: Prognostication, Skepticism, and Celestial Order* (Berkeley: University of California Press, 2011). More popular overviews include Jack Repcheck, *Copernicus' Secret: How the Scientific Revolution Began* (New York: Simon and Schuster, 2007) and Dava Sobel, *A More Perfect Heaven: How Copernicus Revolutionized the Cosmos* (New York: Walker, 2011). Sheila Rabin provides an excellent concise overview in her "Nicolaus Copernicus," online at *The Stanford Encyclopedia of Philosophy (Fall 2010 Edition)*, ed. Edward N. Zalta, at http://plato.stanford.edu/archives/fall2010/entries/copernicus/ (accessed January 3, 2013).

Galileo, *Letter to the Grand Duchess Christina*: The translation is based on the edition of the letter appearing in Galileo's *Opere* by Fernando Flora (Riccardo Ricciardi Editore, 1953), *Lettere*, XIV, online at: [http://it.wikisource.org/wiki/Lettere_(Galileo)] accessed 10/6/2013. I have excerpted some 2,000 of nearly 13,000 words. I have also consulted the edition Franco Motta, *Lettera a Cristina di Lorena: sull'uso della Bibbia nelle argomentazioni scientifiche* (Genoa: Marietti, 2000), 67–147, with extended analytical introduction by Mauro Pesce at 7–66; the translation by Maurice A. Finocchiaro of the *Lettera a Cristina di Lorena*, from *The Essential Galileo* of which he is editor and translator (Indianapolis-Cambridge MA: Hackett, 2008), 9–145; and the important critical study of Alfredo Damanti, *Libertas philosophandi: teologia e filosofia nella* Lettera alla granduchessa Cristina di Lorena *di Galileo Galilei* (Rome: Edizioni di storia e letteratura, 2010). Important biographies, each illuminating a different aspect of Galileo's elusive character, include Mario Biagioli, *Galileo Courtier* (Chicago: University of Chicago Press, 2006); Stillman Drake, *Galileo at Work: His Scientific Bibliography* (Chicago: University of Chicago Press, 1978; and David Wootton, *Galileo: Watcher of the Skies* (New Haven: Yale University Press, 2010). See also the comprehensive annotated bibliography by Ian Glass, "Galileo Galilei," at Oxford Bibliographies/Renaissance and Reformation: http://www.oxfordbibliographies.com/obo/page/renaissance-and-reformation (forthcoming).

Descartes, *Discourse on Method*: Excerpts here are from the translation by Donald Cress of the *Discours de la méthode*, reprinted in the edition of Roger Ariew of René Descartes, *Philosophical Essays and Correspondence* (Indianapolis, IN; Cambridge, MA: Hackett Publishing Co., 2000), 46–82, excerpts from Parts I through IV at 46–48, 50–51, 54–58, 60–61. See among useful introductions to Descartes' life and works, Desmond M. Clarke, *Descartes: A Biography* (New York: Cambridge University Press, 2006); John Cottingham, *Descartes* (Oxford: Oxford University Press, 1998); Stephen Gaukroger, *Descartes: An Intellectual Biography* (Oxford: Clarendon Press; Oxford University Press, 1995); A. C. Grayling, *Descartes: The Life of René Descartes and Its Place in His Times* (London: Free Press, 2005); and Geneviève Rodis-Lewis, *Descartes: His Life and Thought*, trans. Jane Marie Todd (Ithaca: Cornell University Press, 1998). See also the comprehensive annotated bibliography by Justin Skirry, "René Descartes," In *Oxford Bibliographies Online: Philosophy*, http://www.oxfordbibliographies.com/view/document/obo-9780195396577/obo-9780195396577-0031.xml (accessed January 17, 2013).

Chapter 9: Women and Humanism

Nogarola, *Dialogue on the Equal or Unequal Sin of Adam and Eve*: The translation given here is that of Margaret L. King and Diana M. Robin, in their edition and translation of Isotta Nogarola, *Complete Writings: Letterbook, Dialogue on Adam and Eve, Orations* (Chicago: University of Chicago Press, 2004), 145–58, at 145–51, 156–58. Some changes have been made in punctuation for clarity; the footnotes are reproduced with some abridgement except where noted. For Nogarola, see especially the introduction of King and Robin to the *Complete Writings* at 1–19, and the analysis of Nogarola's dialogue on Adam and Eve by Thelma S. Fenster, "The Defenses of Eve by Isotta Nogarola and Christine de Pizan, Who Found themselves in Simone de Beauvoir's Situation," in Pamela Benson and Victoria Kirkham, eds., *Strong Voices, Weak History: Early Women Writers and Canons in England, France, and Italy* (Ann Arbor, MI: University of Michigan Press, 2005), 58–77; and Katharina Fietze, "Eine gewisse neue Theologie: der Dialog der Isotta Nogarola 'Uber die gleiche oder ungleiche Sünde Evas und Adams' von 1451," in Elisabeth Gössmann, ed., *Kennt der Geist kein Geschlecht?* (Munich: Iudicium, 1994), 76–91, followed by German translation of text at 92–107. See also the study by Janet Levarie Smarr, "Dialogue and Letter-Writing," Chapter 4 of *Joining the Conversation: Dialogues by Renaissance Women* (Ann Arbor, MI: University of Michigan Press, 2005), 130–53; and the discussion of Nogarola's role in Jane Stevenson, *Women Latin Poets: Language, Gender, and Authority, from Antiquity to the Eighteenth Century* (Oxford: Oxford University Press, 2005), 156–76.

Cereta, *Letters to Bibolo Semproni and Lucilia Vernacula*: The translation given here is that of Diana M. Robin in her edition and translation of Laura Cereta, *Collected Letters of a Renaissance Feminist* (Chicago: University of Chicago Press, 1997), 74–82, with footnotes considerably abridged. For Cereta, see especially Robin's introduction at 3–19. See also the studies by R. Natasha Amendola, "Weaving Virtue: Laura Cereta as a New Penelope," in *Virtue Ethics for Women 1250–1500*, eds. Karen Green and Constant Mews (Dordrecht: Springer Science and Business Media, 2011), 133–43; Jennifer Cavalli, "Fashioning Female Humanist Scholarship: Self-Representation in Laura Cereta's Letters," in Elizabeth L'Estrange and Alison More, eds., *Representing Medieval Genders and Sexualities in Europe: Construction, Transformation, and Subversion, 600–1530* (Farnham, UK; Burlington, VT: Ashgate, 2011), 145–59; Amyrose McCueill Gill, "Fraught Relations in the Letters of Laura Cereta: Marriage, Friendship, and Humanist Epistolarity," *Renaissance Quarterly* 62, no. 4 (2009): 1057–97; and Janet Levarie Smarr, "Dialogue and Letter-Writing," in *Joining the Conversation: Dialogues by Renaissance Women* (Ann Arbor: University of Michigan Press, 2005), 130–53.

Fedele, *Oration in Praise of Letters*: The translation given here is by Diana M. Robin, editor of Cassandra Fedele, *Letters and Orations* (Chicago: University of Chicago Press, 2000), with paragraph breaks added and notes abridged. See also the more recent edition of Fedele's works with Italian translation: Cassandra Fedele, *Orazioni ed epistole*, ed. Antonino Fedele (Venice: il Poligrafo, 2010), with the text of the oration in praise of letters at 62–71, and Diana Robin's essay "Cassandra Fedele's *Epistolae* (1488–1521): Biography as Ef-facement," in Thomas F. Mayer and D. R. Woolf, eds., *The Rhetorics of Life-Writing in Early Modern Europe: Forms of Biography from Cassandra Fedele to Louis XIV* (Ann Arbor: University of Michigan Press, 1995), 187–203.

Gournay, *The Equality of Men and Women*: The translation is by Richard Hillman and Colette Quesnel in their edition of Marie Le Jars de Gournay, *Apology for the Woman Writing and Other Works* (Chicago: University of Chicago Press, 2002), 72–95, at 75–77, 81–82, 86–87, 92–95. The notes are mine, with references as needed to the Hillman and Quesnel edition. For Gournay's understanding of gender equality, see also Douglas Lewis, "Marie De Gournay and the Engendering of Equality," *Teaching Philosophy* 22, no. 1 (1999): 53–76. Biographies of Gournay include Michèle Fogel, *Marie de Gournay: Itinéraires d'une femme savant* (Paris: Fayard, 2004), and Marie-Thérèse Noiset, *Marie de Gournay et son œuvre* (Jambes, Belgium:

Éditions Namuroises, 2004). See also the studies by Jean-Claude Arnould, "Y a-t-il une place pour les femmes dans la creation littéraire: Marie de Gournay et la figure de l'autrice," in *Les Femmes dans la critique et l'histoire littéraire,* ed. Martine Reid (Paris: Champion, 2011), 13–29; Leah L. Chang, "The Hand of Gournay," in Chang's *Into Print: The Production of Female Authorship in Early Modern France* (Newark: University of Delaware Press, 2009), 175–209; Dorothea B. Heitsch, "Cats on a Windowsill: An Alchemical Study of Marie De Gournay," in Kathleen P. Long, ed., *Gender and Scientific Discourse in Early Modern Culture* (Farnham, UK: Ashgate, 2010), 218–38; Dorothea B. Heitsch, "From Dialogue to Conversation: the Place of Marie de Gournay," in Heitsch and Jean-François Vallée, eds., *Printed Voices: The Renaissance Culture of Dialogue* (Toronto: University of Toronto Press, 2004), 114–33; and Carol Pal, "Marie de Gournay, Marie du Moulin, and Anna Maria van Schurman: Constructing Intellectual Kinship," in Pal, *Republic of Women: Rethinking the Republic of Letters in the Seventeenth Century* (Cambridge: Cambridge University Press, 2012), 78–109.

Chapter 10: Other Worlds

Vespucci, *New World,* **Letter to Lorenzo di Pierfrancesco de' Medici:** The translation is based on the edition of Mario Pozzi in *Il mondo nuovo di Amerigo Vespucci: Vespucci autentico e apocrifo* (Milan: Serra e Riva, 1984), 88–120, even pages, at 88–106 and 120; 2nd rev. ed. entitled *Il mondo nuovo di Amerigo Vespucci: Scritti vespucciani e paravespucciani* (Alesandria: Edizioni dell'Orso, 1993), where the text appears at 102–32; see also the facsimile reprint of one of the first editions, from 1503–1504, in Luigi Firpo, ed., *Colombo, Vespucci, Verazzano: Prime relazioni di navigatori italiani sulla scoperta dell'America* (Turin: Unione Tipografico Editrice, 1966), 85–93. I have also consulted the translations of David Jacobson in Luciano Formisano, ed., *Letters from a New World: Amerigo Vespucci's Discovery of America* (New York: Marsilio, 1992), Letter V, 45–56, and the older translation of Clements R. Markham in *The Letters of Amerigo Vespucci, and Other Documents Illustrative of his Career* (London: Hakluyt Society, 1894; facs. rpt. Farnham, UK; Burlington, VT: Ashgate, 2010). For Vespucci, see the popularizing biography of Felipe Fernández-Armesto, *Amerigo: The Man Who Gave His Name to America* (New York: Random House, 2007), and, similar in tone, the chapter "Vespucci's Tabloid Journalism, 1497–1504," in David Abulafia's *The Discovery of Mankind: Atlantic Encounters in the Age of Columbus* (New Haven, CT: Yale University Press, 2008), 241–61, and the chapter "A Letter that Changed the World," in Giancarlo Masini with Iacopo Gori, *How Florence Invented America: Vespucci, Verrazzano, and Mazzei and Their Contribution to the Conception of the New World* (New York: Marsilio Publishers, 1998), 3–54. See also the learned essays on Vespucci and the era of exploration more generally in Annalisa d'Ascenzo, ed., *Mundus Novus: Amerigo Vespucci e i metodi della ricerca storico-geografica: atti del convegno internazionale di studi, Roma-Firenze 27–30 Novembre 2002* (Rome: Società geografica italiana, 2004).

Garcilaso, *Royal Commentaries of the Incas***:** Excerpts are given here from the classic translation by Harold V. Livermore of Garcilaso's *Royal Commentaries of the Incas and General History of Peru* (Austin: University of Texas Press, 1966) as edited recently by Karen Spalding (abridged ed.; Indianapolis, IN: Hackett Publishing Co., 2006), 2–7. Spalding's annotations are utilized as noted. From the same era and publisher comes the very readable biography by John Grier Varner: *El Inca: The Life and Times of Garcilaso de la Vega* (Austin: University of Texas Press, 1968). Of recent biographies and studies, see especially Christian Fernández, *Inca*

Garcilaso: Imaginación, memoria e identidad (Lima: Fondo Editorial, Universidad Nacional Mayor de San Marcos, 2004); Elena Romiti, *Los hilos de la tierra: Relaciones interculturales y escritura: El Inca Garcilaso de la Vega* (Montevideo: Biblioteca Nacional, 2009); and José Antonio Mazzotti, *Coros mestizos del Inca Garcilaso: Resonancias andinas* (Lima: Bolsa de Valores de Lima; México, D.F: Otorongo Producciones; Fondo de Cultura Económica, 1996); also the studies in Raquel Chang-Rodríguez, ed., *Entre la espada y la pluma: El Inca Garcilaso de la Vega y sus Comentarios Reales* (Lima: Fondo Editorial de la Pontificia Universidad Católica del Perú, 2010).

Xavier, *Letter to His Companions in Europe*: The translation is based on letter #96, *Sociis in Europa degentibus*, in George Schurhammer and Josef Wicki, eds., *Epistolae S. Francisci Xaverii aliaque eius scripta*, rev. ed., 2 vols. (Rome: apud Monumenta Historica Soc. Iesu, 1944–1945), 2:242–79, at 254–56; 258–61; 263–64; 266; 273–74; and 279. I have also consulted the English translation of M. Joseph Costelloe in *The Letters and Instructions of Francis Xavier* (St. Louis, MO: Institute of Jesuit Sources, 1992), 326–43; see there too Costelloe's excellent introduction at xiii–xxx. See also for Xavier's missionary work, Rita Haub and Julius Oswald, eds., *Franz Xavier, Patron der Missionen: Festschrift zum 450. Todestag* (Regensburg: Schnell and Steiner, 2002), especially Angela Fischer-Brunkow's essay "Franz Xaver als Missionar in Japan: (Inter)kulturelle Aspekte der frühen Japanmission im 16. Jahrhundert," at 81–102; and the still-valuable classic by Charles Ralph Boxer, *The Christian Century in Japan, 1549–1650* (Berkeley: University of California, 1951). See also the authoritative biography of Georg Schurhammer, *Francis Xavier: His Life, His Times*, trans. M. Joseph Costelloe, 4 vols. (Rome: The Jesuit Historical Institute, 1973–1982); as well as the richly-illustrated popular biography of Miguel Corrêa Monteiro, *Saint Francis Xavier: A Man for all Others*, trans. Peter Ingham (Lisbon: CTT Correios de Portugal, 2006), and the essays edited by Ignacio Arellano, Alejandro González Acosta, and Arnulfo Herrera, *San Francisco Javier entre dos continentes* (Madrid: Iberoamericana; Frankfurt am Main: Vervuert, 2007).

Camões, *The Lusiads*: The text, a prose rendering of the author's verse, is taken from Canto X:76–144 in *Os Lusiadas*, original Portuguese text edited by Hernâni Cidade, from Camões' *Obras completes*, vols. 4 and 5 (Lisbon: Sá da Costa, 1946–1947), online at http://www .oslusiadas.com, (accessed February 14, 2013); also available in *Os Lusíadas*, ed. Frank Pierce (Oxford: Clarendon Press, 1973). I have also consulted the prose translations of William C. Atkinson in *The Lusiads* (Harmondsworth, Middlesex, UK: Penguin Books, 1952), as well as the verse translations of Leonard Bacon in *The Lusiads of Luiz de Camões* (New York: The Hispanic Society of America, 1950) and of Landeg White in *The Lusiads* (Oxford: Oxford University Press, 1997). For Camões, see William J. Freitas, *Camoens and His Epic: A Historic, Geographic, and Cultural Survey* (Palo Alto, CA: Institute of Hispanic American and Luso-Brazilian Studies, Stanford University, 1963), and for the Portuguese cultural context, see the essays in Alfred Hower and Richard A. Preto-Rodas, eds., *Empire in Transition: The Portuguese World in the Time of Camões* (Gainesville, FL: University Presses of Florida and the University of Florida Press/Center for Latin American Studies, 1985). For the *Lusiads* and the epic tradition, see James Nicolopulos, *The Poetics of Empire in the Indies: Prophecy and Imitation in La Araucana and Os Lusíadas* (University Park, PA: Pennsylvania State University Press, 2000), and David Quint, *Epic and Empire: Politics and Generic Form from Virgil to Milton* (Princeton: Princeton University Press, 1993), superseding C. M. Bowra's classic *From Virgil to Milton* (London: Macmillan, 1945).

INDEX

abuses, of church power or practice, xvii, 198, 199, 200, 202, 204, 206, 221–29 and 221n55

Africa, 298, 300, 320, 321, 323

Agrippa, Henry Cornelius Agrippa von Nettesheim, 288, 292

Alberti, Leon Battista, xvi, xvii, xviii, 167–76, 183; *On Architecture*, 170; *On Painting*, xvi, 167–76; *On the Statue*, 170

Alexander the Great, 286, 287

Alfonso I, king of Naples, 44, 46, 201

Amalthea, sibyl, 278 and 277–78n31

Americas, European encounter with, 296–311 (*see also* Brazil, Peru)

Arabia, 321, 324

Aristarchus of Samos, 246n25

Aristides, Aelius, 70

Aristophanes, 247n27

Aristotle, xi, 44, 105, 245n23, 251, 270, 272, 286, 287, 292; Aristotelianism, xiii, 52, 55, 207

arithmetic (discipline). *See* Mathematics

artist, social role of, 168, 170, 171, 176, 182, 183, 184, 190–92

Ascham, Roger: *The Scholemaster*, 22

Asia, European encounters with, 296–97, 312–26 (*see also names of individual countries*)

astronomy (discipline), xvii, xviii, 20, 240–55, 299, 301, 302, 306

Athena, goddess, 278 and 277–78n31

Augustine, saint, 18 and n19, 50, 268, 271

autobiography (genre), xvi, 169, 190–97, 288

Bahrain, 324

Bandinelli, Bartolommeo (Baccio), 193 and n36

Bandini, Bernardo, 115, 116, 117

Barbarigo, Agostino, doge of Venice, 284

Barbari, Jacopo de', 187 and nn22 and 23, 189

Barbaro, Francesco, xiv, 29, 69–70, 77–85, 94, 105; *On Marriage*, 69–70, 77–85

Bartolomeo da Montepulciano, 28, 32

Basil of Caesarea, the Great, saint, 292

Bellarmine, Roberto, cardinal, 249

Bellini, Giovanni, xvi, 168, 177–82, 184, 186

Bembo, Bernardo, 233

Bessarion, cardinal, 105

Bible, xviii, 46, 53, 198, 199, 200, 207, 208, 209, 211, 217, 222, 231, 242, 247, 248–55, 270, 278, 288, 292 (*see also* Gospels, New Testament)

biography (genre), 44, 158

bishops, 222 and n57, 224–28

Boccaccio, Giovanni, x, xii, 1, 2, 5, 8n8, 11–19, 20, 21, 28, 29, 44, 167, 199, 240, 265, 275, 277–78n31, 282, 292; *Genealogy of the Pagan Gods*, 11–19, 167, 199; *On Famous Women*, 11, 265, 275, 277–78n31; *On Mountains, Woods, Springs, Lakes, Rivers, Swamps, and on the Names of Seas*, 11; *On the Fates of Famous Men*, 11

Boleyn, Anne, 158

Bologna, University of, 21, 39, 42, 240

Borgia, Cesare, cardinal, 143 and n2

Bracciolini, Jacopo Poggio, 115, 116

Bracciolini, Poggio, xiii, 3, 27–32, 33n34; *Letter to Guarino Veronese*, 30–32

Brazil, xix, 296, 299, 312, 321, 326

Brescia, 274

bronze casting, 191–97

Bruges, 94, 95, 100

Bruni, Leonardo, xiv, 27n30, 29, 32, 69–77, 86, 114; *In Praise of the City of Florence*, 69–77, 114

Buddhism, in Japan, 313

Burckhardt, Jacob, 169–70

Calvin, John, 104, 129, 134 and n44, 214

Cambodia, 325

Camilla, ancient warrior maiden, 292

Camões, Luís Vas de, xix, 296, 297, 320–26; *The Lusiads*, xix, 320–26